Crime and Society in England, 1750–1900

THEMES IN BRITISH SOCIAL HISTORY
edited by John Stevenson

This series covers the most important aspects of British social history from the Renaissance to the present day. Topics include education, poverty, health, religion, leisure, crime and popular protest, some of which are treated in more than one volume. The books are written for undergraduates, postgraduates and the general reader, and each volume combines a general approach to the subject with the primary research of the author.

Currently available

THE ENGLISH FAMILY, 1450–1700
Ralph A. Houlbrooke

POVERTY AND POLICY IN TUDOR AND STUART ENGLAND
Paul Slack

CRIME IN EARLY MODERN ENGLAND, 1550–1750
J. A. Sharpe

GENDER IN ENGLISH SOCIETY, 1650–1850: The Emergence of Separate Spheres?
Robert Shoemaker

LITERATURE AND SOCIETY IN EIGHTEENTH-CENTURY ENGLAND
W. A. Speck

CRIME AND SOCIETY IN ENGLAND, 1750–1900 (Third Edition)
Clive Emsley

THE LABOURING CLASSES IN EARLY INDUSTRIAL ENGLAND, 1750–1850
John Rule

POPULAR DISTURBANCES IN ENGLAND, 1700–1832 (Second Edition)
John Stevenson

SEX, POLITICS AND SOCIETY: The Regulation of Sexuality since 1800 (Second Edition)
Jeffrey Weeks

HEALTH AND SOCIETY IN TWENTIETH-CENTURY BRITAIN
Helen Jones

NEWSPAPERS AND ENGLISH SOCIETY, 1695–1855
Hannah Barker

THE PROFESSIONS IN EARLY MODERN ENGLAND, 1450–1800
Rosemary O'Day

POPULAR CULTURES IN ENGLAND, 1550–1750
Barry Reay

THE ENGLISH TOWN, 1680–1840
Rosemary Sweet

Crime and Society in England, 1750–1900

THIRD EDITION

Clive Emsley

PEARSON
Longman

Harlow, England • London • New York • Boston • San Francisco • Toronto
Sydney • Tokyo • Singapore • Hong Kong • Seoul • Taipei • New Delhi
Cape Town • Madrid • Mexico City • Amsterdam • Munich • Paris • Milan

PEARSON EDUCATION LIMITED

Edinburgh Gate
Harlow CM20 2JE
United Kingdom
Tel: +44 (0)1279 623623
Fax: +44 (0)1279 431059
Website: www.pearsoned.co.uk

First published 1987
Second edition 1996
Third edition published in Great Britain in 2005

© Pearson Education Limited 2005

The right of Clive Emsley to be identified as author of this work has been asserted
by him in accordance with the Copyright, Designs and Patents Act 1988.

ISBN 0 582 78485 9

British Library Cataloguing in Publication Data
A CIP catalogue record for this book can be obtained from the British Library

Library of Congress Cataloging-in-Publication Data
Emsley, Clive.
　　Crime and society in England, 1750–1900 / Clive Emsley.—3rd ed.
　　　p. cm. — (Themes in British social history)
　　Includes bibliographical references and index.
　　ISBN 0–582–78485–9 (pb)
　　1. Crime—England—History—18th century. 2. Crime—England—History—19th century.
　I. Title. II. Series.

HV6949.E5E47 2005
364.942′09′034—dc22

2004048404

All rights reserved; no part of this publication may be reproduced, stored in a retrieval
system, or transmitted in any form or by any means, electronic, mechanical, photocopying,
recording, or otherwise without either the prior written permission of the Publishers or a
licence permitting restricted copying in the United Kingdom issued by the Copyright
Licensing Agency Ltd, 90 Tottenham Court Road, London W1T 4LP. This book may not
be lent, resold, hired out or otherwise disposed of by way of trade in any form of binding or
cover other than that in which it is published, without the prior consent of the Publishers.

10　9　8　7　6　5　4　3　2　1
08　07　06　05　04

Set by 35 in 10/13.5pt Sabon
Printed and bound in Malaysia

The Publisher's policy is to use paper manufactured from sustainable forests.

Contents

List of tables and figures		vi
Preface and acknowledgements to the first edition		vii
Preface to the second edition		viii
Preface and acknowledgements to the third edition		ix
Abbreviations used in notes		x
1	Introduction: crime and the law	1
2	The statistical map	21
3	Class perceptions	56
4	Gender perceptions	92
5	Environmental perceptions	114
6	Fiddles, perks and pilferage	143
7	The criminal class and professional criminals	173
8	Prosecutors and the courts	183
9	Detection and prevention: the old police and the new	221
10	Punishment and reformation	253
11	Concluding remarks	297
	Further reading: further research	304
	Index	307

List of tables and figures

Tables

2.1 The incidence of 'highway robbery' in Liverpool and Manchester, 1866   27

2.2 Homicides in Wiltshire, 1752–96   42

2.3 Assaults in Bedfordshire based on indictments and recognisances every five years, 1750–1840   45

9.1 Watchmen, patrols, superintendents and beadles acting in the jurisdiction of the Police Magistrates, Union Hall, Southwark, 1 January 1812   228

10.1 Principal offences for which persons were executed, 1755–1814   260–1

10.2 Capital convictions and executions for principal offences, 1775–1815   262

10.3 Capital convictions for animal theft   263

10.4 Capital convictions for sexual offences   264

10.5 Capital sentences, number executed and number executed for murder, 1805–54   275

10.6 'Penal servitude' for petty recidivists   286–7

Figures

2.1 Crime patterns in the early nineteenth century   35

2.2 Homicides and attempted homicides, 1850 and 1860   43

10.1 The pattern of capital convictions and actual executions on Assize Circuits, 1749–1819   257–9

Preface and acknowledgements to the first edition

During the eight or nine years that my historical interest has concentrated on questions of crime and policing I have benefited enormously from exchanges with many colleagues at conferences, seminars, and through correspondence. I should single out the regular colloquia of the International Association for the History of Crime and Criminal Justice, which enabled me to air material now in Chapters 4 and 8, and the CESDIP/University of Paris V11e seminar, organised by Michelle Perrot and Philippe Robert, which, with its concentration on France and continental Europe, sharpened my perception of English peculiarities. Among the individuals who have responded to my queries and/or who have generously allowed me to read and make use of their research, I would like to take this opportunity to thank Anne Bryson, Shirley Chase, Jennifer Davis, David Englander, David Foster, Janet Gyford, Joanna Innes, Peter King, Roger Ryan, Simon Stevenson and Steve Wilson. Jim Sharpe and John Styles have always been generous with advice and they both kindly commented on a draft of the book. John Stevenson, the series editor, performed the same chore. My thanks to them for their corrections and suggestions; needless to say, the remaining errors are my own. A variety of archivists and librarians have assisted me, particularly the staff of the Bedfordshire County Record Office and the staff of the Open University Library. I am grateful for permission to consult and to cite manuscript material held in the record office of Bedfordshire, Nottinghamshire, Wiltshire, Leeds City, and in University College London. Crown Copyright material is reproduced with acknowledgement to the Controller of H.M. Stationery Office.

Lastly, my apologies to Mark and Kathryn for their father's disappearances into his study when he could have been helping with homework or driving them to various concerts, sports, music practices, or teenage social gatherings. My thanks to my wife, Jennifer, for running the family taxi service during these disappearances, and my thanks to her for a great deal more – hence the dedication.

Bedford
September 1986

Preface to the second edition

In the decade since I finished the first edition of this book interest in the subject has, if anything, increased. Also, particularly with the development of women's history, perspectives have shifted. I have not, however, thought it necessary to change the basic structure of the book. It seemed to work the first time; I hope it will again. There is a completely new chapter on crime and gender; but elsewhere I have settled for amendments and some restructuring within the old chapter format.

Once again my thanks are due to all of those who helped me with the first edition, and to those whose work has stimulated me since. Many of those whose names appear in the footnotes are friends who have always been generous with their advice, and who deserve rather more thanks than simple footnoting will allow. They have also made studying the history of crime fun for me, not least because of the humour which has accompanied several recent conferences; together, we have laughed through the Putteridge Bury blizzard and the penitential cells of Roehampton. But again, above all my thanks go to Jennifer – no longer the family taxi driver (they drive themselves), but still labouring heroically in coping with me.

Bedford
April 1995

Preface and acknowledgements to the third edition

When I wrote the first edition of this book crime and policing were relatively new areas for academic historians. They seem now to be among the most popular areas of British social history.

I have not thought it necessary to change the basic structure of the first and second editions here. I have, however, significantly revised the short chapter on gender that appeared in the second edition, and given it a more central position. In revising this chapter, moreover, I have become conscious of how much more thinking and research there needs to be in this area. Elsewhere I have sought to update the book and, on the advice of friends, colleagues, general readers and those who use the book for teaching, I have expanded one or two sections in ways that I hope will be helpful.

The first edition thanked a number of individuals who had generously offered me advice and the benefits of sometimes unpublished research. The list grows longer and longer but here I particularly want to single out, and thank Barry Godfrey, Peter King, René Lévy, David Philips, Jim Sharpe, Bob Storch and Martin Wiener. Their advice and their publications have contributed enormously to what follows. Any errors, confusions and infelicities are, of course, mine. I also need to thank, once again, the archivists and librarians who have assisted my work. I am grateful also for permission to consult and to cite manuscript material held in the record offices of Bedfordshire, Nottinghamshire, Wiltshire, Leeds City, and in University College London. Crown Copyright material is reproduced with acknowledgement to the Controller of H.M. Stationery Office.

The acknowledgements to the first edition ended with thanks to my wife, Jenny, for acting as the family taxi driver while I lurked, criminally, in my study. She continues to be a family chauffeur and minder, though generally now with small, boisterous grandsons. She also continues to cope with me; for this, and for everything else, the dedication remains the same.

Bedford
March 2004

Abbreviations used in notes

C.C.C.S.P.	*Central Criminal Court Sessions Papers*
C.J.H.	*Criminal Justice History*
E.H.R.	*English Historical Review*
H.J.	*Historical Journal*
H.O.	Home Office Papers in Public Record Office
M.E.P.O.	Metropolitan Police Papers in Public Record Office
O.B.S.P.	*Old Bailey Sessions Papers*
P and P	*Past and Present*
P.P.	*Parliamentary Papers*
R.O.	Record Office, as in Beds. R.O.
T.R.H.S.	*Transactions of the Royal Historical Society*
U.C.L.	University College London

For Jenny

CHAPTER 1

Introduction: crime and the law

The growth of crime in recent years has been unprecedented;[1] so too, has been the recent growth of academic research and publication particularly in the history of crime. Marx, with his usual intellectual penetration, commented: 'the criminal produces not only crimes, but also criminal law, and with this the professor who gives lectures on criminal law'.[2] Academic historians were slow to recognise these insights. Until relatively recently most history books dealing with crime tended to be 'popular' rather than narrowly 'academic'. They concentrated on particular, notorious events or personalities and many depended largely upon anecdotal or literary sources. More general textbook surveys – political, economic and social – rarely addressed the problem of crime. In the last twenty-five years or so, however, historians have increasingly turned their attention to crime and how former societies understood it, and sought to deal with it. They have begun searching among court and police records seeking to assess changes over time and to relate such changes to different economic, political and social contexts. This research is another aspect of 'history from below'. From exploring crowds and their motives social historians have swung, perhaps inevitably, to other kinds of 'lawbreaker' and have sought to estimate crime and to understand at least some of its causes, within different contexts.

This book is an attempt to synthesise recent work on crime and English society from roughly the middle of the eighteenth until the close of the nineteenth century. There is a reference to crime in Wales where the legal system was indistinguishable from that of England; but Scotland, with a different legal system, and Ireland, with its rural and nationalist rebels together with a paramilitary police, receive little attention. The book addresses itself to four key questions: what did contemporaries understand as crime during the eighteenth and nineteenth centuries? What patterns of crime were detected, and have been detected subsequently by historians? Who committed crime? What remedies were attempted to prevent crime and to handle offenders?

A definition of crime that embraces all of its different perspectives and satisfies every generalisation and nuance is probably impossible. The simplest definition describes crime as behaviour which violates the criminal law, behaviour which 'if detected, would lead to prosecution in a court of law or summarily before an accredited agent of law enforcement'.[3] There are problems with this definition. Some public order legislation gives citizens and law officers, particularly police officers, discretionary powers that can be used if they consider it necessary. Among the most obvious examples are 'threatening, abusive or insulting words or behaviour with intent to provoke a breach of the peace, or whereby a breach of the peace may be occasioned'; and, of course, 'resisting or obstructing a constable in the execution of his duty'.[4] This kind of discretionary power increased with the growth of the new police during the nineteenth century, and it even became possible for men to be arrested by the police and then to be given periods of imprisonment by magistrates for being 'suspicious persons'; the 1869 Habitual Criminals Act, for example, provided for a maximum of twelve months' imprisonment on such a charge. Most people would differentiate between such 'offences' and what they consider to be 'real crime' such as murder, rape and theft; but as far as the accused was concerned the result – arrest, trial, punishment – could be the same. Nevertheless the definition of crime as behaviour violating the criminal law has the advantage for the historian of relating behaviour to laws in force at a particular time; thus 'criminal' behaviour is tied firmly to its historical context. It is this definition that informs this volume.

Some historians have used the term 'social crime' to differentiate between 'real crime' or, perhaps better, 'anti-social crime' and those offences that had a degree of community acceptance or can be linked with social protest. The inhabitants of mid-nineteenth-century Manchester had to get their water from taps or pumps in the street or courtyard. Reporting for the *Morning Chronicle*, Angus Reach noted:

Where standpipes or public taps are erected, the charge by the water company is about 10s. a year for every house the inmates of which use the convenience. Of all the petty thefts which occur in Manchester, however, none – although they do not appear in the police returns – are so common as larcenies from taps and pumps.[5]

Probably very few of the water thieves ever considered their behaviour as criminal: even if the water company provided a facility, was not water a man's right and free in the rain and in the rivers? A very small number of offenders set out to justify their behaviour as actions in a kind of class struggle. At the Norfolk Summer Assizes in 1839 William Watts was sentenced to his second term of transportation after having been found guilty of shooting six horses and cattle. Watts declared from the dock that:

he was perfectly satisfied with his sentence but to such a state had they brought the poor of this country by oppressing them with taxes, poor rates, and other things, that it was impossible for a poor man to live by honest means, and all this was to support big-gutted relieving officers, and other folks connected with them and the [Poor Law] unions.[6]

John Rule has suggested that it is useful to think of two main types of social crime during the late eighteenth and early nineteenth centuries: first, those crimes that drew collective legitimation from their explicit protest nature, and second, crimes that, although actions against the law, were not regarded as criminal by those who committed them. Wary of the limitations he includes poaching, illicit distilling, wrecking and smuggling among social crimes.[7] It is also possible to include rioting – particularly over the high cost of food, over enclosures, recruiting, turnpike tolls and so forth – and the appropriation of some perquisites from the workplace as social crimes; 'perks' seem to have been increasingly the objects of criminal prosecution by employers during the eighteenth and nineteenth centuries. Food riots, or disorders over the appropriation of common land, and perks, in particular, demonstrate that there could be different perceptions of justice from that enshrined in the law. Furthermore, the language of the law can obscure the protest nature of some crimes as where, for example, individuals making an attack on an enclosure were indicted on charges of 'forcible entry'; though, by the same token, it must be noted that some prosecutions in summary courts for the offence of 'trespass' were often prosecutions for the theft of growing crops.[8]

While few serious historians would now dismiss eighteenth- and nineteenth-century riots as the work of the dregs of society lacking in any motives other than the desire for drink, plunder and, perhaps, rape, the concept of social crime has its drawbacks. The poor may not have regarded poaching as a crime; 'they almost universally look upon game, when in a wild state, as not being the property of any individual', declared a Bedfordshire Justice before a Parliamentary Select Committee in 1826.[9] But poaching did not merely involve poor men taking game to eke out their meagre diet. There were plenty of gentlemen poachers who were pro-secuted under the Game Laws; in the spring of 1796, for example, the Reverend Francis Barstow was fined £20 by Lincolnshire justices for shooting game without a proper certificate.[10] Moreover, from the mid-eighteenth century until the legislation of 1831 that greatly reduced its profitability, poaching was increasingly a business carried on by organised gangs. In spite of laws forbidding the sale of game there was a ready and expanding market among poulterers, innkeepers and victuallers to provide for the dietary demands of urban gentlemen and well-to-do tradesmen; while the landed gentry's creation of large new game preserves gave poachers, as well as sportsmen, new opportunities.[11] Whether mem-bers of an organised gang, pursuing a business and satisfying a large market, can be adequately described as social criminals is, to say the least, a moot point.

Along the coasts, wreckers believed that they had a right to whatever was thrown up on their shores as a result of storm or misadventure, though legislation prohibiting such activity went back to Edward I. Local sanction of this offence could stretch to Methodist lay preachers, who appear to have participated, and to local parsons, who might receive wine or brandy liberated from wrecks.[12] But what of that other coastal crime – smuggling? The gangs had support from local communities; but they were not averse to violence and intimidation to ensure support. Excessive viol-ence, however, could be counter-productive, as in the case of the savage murder of a revenue officer and his informant in West Sussex in February 1748, which shocked and appalled the local community.[13] Furthermore, smuggling could be big capitalist business. This was especially the case with tea smuggling in the two decades between the end of the Seven Years' War and the Commutation Act of 1784, which reduced the duty of tea by more than three-quarters. During these years wealthy merchants with far-flung interests replaced many of the small-scale smugglers and encroached massively on the legal tea market. Tea was smuggled in large, well-armed vessels; the illicit cargoes were even insured. In the end the smugglers were too efficient. They provided the public with an inexpensive, widely avail-able beverage; at the same time they generated vigorous counter-action by legal tea merchants, the East India Company, and the government, culmin-ating in the 1784 legislation, which dramatically reduced the rewards to be gained from smuggling. Perhaps these smugglers were social criminals, but their actions also promoted 'the international and domestic trade of the kingdom, which, in turn, contributed to the growth of the British economy in the latter part of the eighteenth century'.[14]

During the 1760s there was widespread coining in the West Riding which received considerable support from all sections of the local community. This support was not grounded in an appeal to customary rights or widespread and long-standing hostility to the monopoly of the Royal Mint. Rather it was the result of the failure of the Mint to produce gold coinage of sufficient quality and quantity that provided the coiners with their opportunity; at the same time the offence 'provided a widely diffused source of income during a period of acute depression in the local staple [textile] industry'. Thus, according to John Styles, rather than emerging as a challenge to a new economic order, popularly condoned money making in the West Riding involved the commercial exploitation of an opportunity that was partly the product of a local economic crisis.[15]

Other offences might be tacitly condoned by social groups or communities. At Greystoke in Cumberland in 1827, Mary Kirkbride died of poisoning. The overdose of laudanum that killed her appeared to have been administered by a group of local women, including the wife of one of the overseers of the poor. A wall of silence descended around the case; Mary Kirkbride came from a family notorious for burdening the parish with illegitimate children and for bringing trouble to the community.[16] Six years later the new Metropolitan Police broke up a political demonstration in Calthorpe Street, London; during the fracas P.C. Robert Culley was mortally wounded by a knife thrust. A significant proportion of artisan London believed that the police had acted in a 'ferocious and brutal' manner quite 'unprovoked by the people'. This attitude was reflected in the verdict of the coroner's jury – 'justifiable homicide' – and the subsequent feting of that jury by the populace.[17] Just over half a century later Captain Thomas Dudley and one of his ship's crew, Edwin Stephens, were tried for murdering cabin boy Richard Parker. Dudley had stabbed Parker in the throat with his penknife and bled him to death over his ship's chronometer case. Dudley, Stephens and another seaman, Ned Brooks, then drank the blood and feasted off the body for five days. The incident is horrific; but so too were the circumstances in which Dudley and his crew found themselves. They had been shipwrecked in the South Atlantic and adrift in an open boat for nineteen days with scarcely any food – two tins of turnips and a small turtle caught on the fourth day. Dudley gave a full statement when he was rescued, and was astonished when he and Stephens were arrested; Brooks was a Crown witness. Dudley's defence was that he had observed a custom of the sea; public opinion appears to have acquiesced, though there was disquiet that Dudley and the others had selected the weakest among their unfortunate group rather than drawing lots. Defence counsel argued that Dudley and his crew were outside the jurisdiction of any court as well as of civilised society. The different courts hearing the case over a seven-month period fudged and hedged over the legal and ethical problems. Dudley and Stephens were found guilty and sentenced to death for murder; but, in the event, they were only required to serve a token period of hard labour.[18]

The killings of Kirkbride, Culley and Parker have not been described as 'social crimes' yet, to the extent that each was condoned or excused by different social groups, the label would not be entirely inappropriate. This underlines some of the problems in using the term: if the armed poacher or armed smuggler was a social criminal, why not the killer of P.C. Culley? and if the killer of P.C. Culley, why not the killers of Kirkbride and Parker, save that the former were well-to-do and, apparently, acting in cold-blooded premeditation while their victim was poor and unfortunate; while Parker was not killed in the context of class struggle. The value of the concept of social crime is that it draws attention to the fact that laws were not universally accepted and that some offences, on some occasions, could be legitimised by social groups and communities. But used as a blanket term for certain offences rather too many lawbreakers are cloaked in the mantle of Robin Hood; as E. P. Thompson warned 'there is not "nice" social crime here and "nasty" antisocial crime there'.[19]

Radical criminologists have fulminated about modern legal systems in the western world which drag hundreds of poor, petty offenders through the courts but allow large-scale corporate offences to go unprosecuted.[20] It is clear that considerable sums were embezzled and otherwise fraudulently appropriated in the late Hanoverian and Victorian periods, and that employers sometimes flouted laws or cut metaphorical corners and real costs which cheated their workforce and endangered life. Herbert Spencer believed that fraud was endemic in railway companies a decade after the beginning of the 'railway mania' of 1844 to 1847. It was not that the company directors were morally lower than the community as a whole but that:

there is the familiar fact that the corporate conscience is ever inferior to the individual conscience – that a body of men will commit as a joint act, that which every individual of them would shrink from did he feel personally responsible.

In addition there was a remoteness from the effects of corruption:

Hence in railway affairs a questionable share transaction, an exorbitant charge, a proceeding which brings great individual advantage without

apparently injuring any one, but which, even if analysed in its ultimate
results, can but very circuitously affect unknown persons living no one
knows where, may be brought home to men who, could the results be
embodied before them, would be shocked at the cruel injustices they
had committed – men who in their private business where the results
can be thus embodied, are sufficiently equitable.[21]

Sixty years later Judge Edward Parry warned how 'knaves' running building societies, investment schemes and similar organisations took money
from the poor, but structured their contracts in such a way that they were
legally immune from prosecution even when the poor man's savings were
squandered or lost. Often it was a matter of class and education:

Fraud is a more complicated offence than larceny, and defrauders
sometimes get the better of the law. Cheating is not always a crime,
and successful cheating is a question of better education.[22]

Nineteenth-century gentlemen were aware of corporate crime and of legal,
but reprehensible, corporate behaviour, yet it was not these kinds of
offence which much vexed either theorists of crime or legislators. The law
was very slow to act against abuses in the commercial world; and while,
for example, the 1844 Company Act required that auditors examine a
company's books before it could function legally, there was no requirement that 'auditors' be accountants. It was not until the twentieth century
that balance sheets and profit and loss accounts had to be published,
and only after the Second World War did investors get any real protection.
Legislation against abuses in factories and mines, and against the truck system for paying wages, was passed in the first half of the nineteenth century;
but the inspectorate established to enforce the factory legislation was few
in number and limited in powers. Furthermore the inspectors were discouraged from prosecuting offenders. In 1876 Alexander Redgrave looked
back over more than thirty years as clerk to the factory inspectorate:

In the inspection of factories it has been my view always that we are
not acting as policemen . . . that in enforcing this Factory Act, we
do not enforce it as a policeman would check an offence which he is
told to detect. We have endeavoured not to enforce the law, if I may use
such an expression, but it has been my endeavours . . . that we should
be the advisors of all classes, that we should explain the law, and that
we should do everything we possibly could do to induce them to observe
the law, and that a prosecution should be the very last thing we should
take up.[23]

Of course it is unlikely that the rulers of a state will legislate against their own interests or supporters; it might, therefore, be argued that the nineteenth-century state, dependent on a new economic order involving a new level of capitalist investment, a burgeoning factory system and a massive exploitation of coal and iron, would not act against the financiers, owners and employers in this new order except when compelled by the most flagrant abuses. This is not an argument that can be either proven or disproved; it depends very much on a predetermined attitude to the state and the society which emerged during the industrial revolution. It might better be argued, and with a greater reference to the evidence, that the policy of state intervention in these areas was complex, fluctuating and often tentative. Tightening up on financial fraud is an exceedingly difficult task for legislators and, subsequently, for the courts. What, for want of a better term, can be called *laissez-faire* ideology also had a role; there was a fear that too much legislation and too much inspection would inhibit Britain's industrial development. Inspectors and inspections cost money, and no nineteenth-century treasury minister, let alone parliament, would have been prepared to sanction the kind of expenditure necessary to check a significant proportion of abuses on the factory floor or at the coal face. There were other restraints also; in the case of some chemical processes, the unchecked side-effects of which destroyed vegetation and harmed the health of the workforce, there was simply insufficient expertise to enable the control of noxious and dangerous vapours until well into the nineteenth century; and the noxious vapours of the Alkali Industry, like the general pall of smoke which hung over industrial cities and also endangered health, were seen as signs of Britain's progress and a mark of full employment. Such feelings were to be found as much among the workers, whose health was threatened, as among the employers, whose factories did the threatening.[24] Furthermore, the illegal use of juvenile labour was connived at by some of the workforce, and safety precautions were resented by workers if they slowed up the work process, especially if this might consequently have an impact on wages rates. It was even suggested, during the 1890s, that female workers discarded the respirators and protective clothing given by more reputable employers 'because they hide the charms of the wearers'.[25]

Given that corrupt, dangerous, fraudulent and otherwise reprehensible activities did not become crimes until the law decreed, this raises another series of questions about who makes the law, who administers it, and what legislators and agents of the law think they are doing. In the middle of the eighteenth century Adam Smith could suggest to students at the University of Glasgow that:

when . . . some have great wealth and others nothing, it is necessary that the arm of authority should be continually stretched forth, and permanent laws or regulations made which may protect the property of the rich from the inroads of the poor . . . Laws and governments may be considered in this and in every case as a combination of the rich to oppress the poor, and preserve to themselves the inequality of the goods which would otherwise be soon destroyed by the attacks of the poor, who if not hindered by the government would soon reduce the others to an equality with themselves by open violence.[26]

Observing England during the early 1830s, Alexis de Tocqueville concluded that the law was, indeed, functioning in such a fashion:

The English have left the poor but two rights; that of obeying the same laws as the rich, and that of standing on an equality with them if they can obtain equal wealth. But those two rights are more apparent than real, since it is the rich who make the laws and who create for their own or their children's profit, the chief means of getting wealth.[27]

Few Victorian gentlemen would have agreed with such assessments. In 1865 *The Times* published a leading article on the case of a Mr Payne, treasurer of the Manchester Relief Fund, who had pocketed £2,400 from the fund. It noted how Payne had avoided prosecution because the law was simply not geared to cope with such an offence. The legislation regarding embezzlement, 'that is, of receiving money and not accounting for it', passed in the reign of George III, applied only to clerks and servants. *The Times* was highly critical of the way in which the law had been framed, but it did not perceive that one class had seen crime as emanating only from another class, rather the problem was that the law did not yet reach the desired national consensus; 'in many respects [it] still lags behind the dictates of true morality and the moral sense of the people'.[28] It was this view that the law derived from consensus, and that, while the process might be long and drawn out, abuses, as they were detected, were reformed, which dominated in the nineteenth century. In 1898 the Attorney General could assure members of parliament that everyone, prisoners included, had confidence in the administration of justice in England.[29] A consequence of this, at least in part, was that criminals could be portrayed as a separate class, outside consensual society and making war upon it.

But, as was noted in the discussion of social crime, laws were not universally accepted during the eighteenth and nineteenth centuries. In a seminal essay Douglas Hay described the eighteenth-century English criminal law as one of the 'chief ideological instruments' of the ruling class:

It was easy to claim equal justice for murderers of all classes, where a universal moral sanction was more likely to be found, or in political cases, the necessary price of a constitution ruled by law. The trick was to extend that communal sanction to a criminal law that was nine-tenths concerned with upholding a radical division of property.

[The law] allowed the rulers of England to make the courts a selective instrument of class justice, yet simultaneously to proclaim the law's incorruptible impartiality and absolute determinacy.[30]

Hay's challenging thesis has not gone uncriticised. John Langbein has insisted that 'the criminal law is simply the wrong place to look for the active hand of the ruling classes' and he emphasises the fact 'that gentlemen prosecutors were few and far between'.[31] This latter point has been developed more fully by Peter King arguing that:

the criminal law may more fruitfully be described as a multi-use right within which the various groups in eighteenth-century society conflicted with, cooperated with and gained concessions from each other.[32]

The simple division which posits a ruling class making and administering the law, and a ruled class on the receiving end, obscures the often marked differences between agents of the law and prosecutors.

It might also be urged, against Hay, that there was no systematic attempt to plug every loophole in the defences of property during the eighteenth century. Some of the legislation was catch all; the Black Act 1723 is the most notorious example.[33] However, a reconstruction of how eighteenth-century parliaments actually made criminal statutes challenges the image of an undifferentiated ruling class legislating in its own interest. The debates were real and heated; the interests represented in these debates were not confined to the landed gentry; and there were positive notions advanced of propriety and public interest. When, in 1751, Henry Bankes introduced a bill to protect the owners of mines from theft and robbery he met considerable opposition; yet here was a supporter of the government and the brother of a gentleman who was a leading member of a consortium running the only graphite mines in Britain, mines that were constantly being invaded by the local population of Borrowdale. What concerned the members of parliament who opposed the bill was a matter of legal principle; was it right to make illegal taking from the ground a felony? A second, much narrower bill was eventually passed in 1752, but its passage was difficult and the offence was not made capital.[34]

No-one has produced an hypothesis for the law in nineteenth-century England that parallels the complexity, power and subtlety of Hay's for the preceding century. The traditional, some might say anodyne, view has it that humanitarian reformers like Sir Samuel Romilly and Sir James Mackintosh, through tireless efforts, brought an awareness both inside and outside parliament that the criminal justice system needed reform and particularly that the two hundred or so capital statutes of England's Bloody Code required drastic surgery. While such men stressed the barbarity of the legal code, other reformers like John Howard paved the way for improvements in the prison system that, it was believed, would give offenders the opportunity and the time to reflect upon their evil ways and, in consequence, reform themselves. Change, or rather reform and improvement, was thus the product of the humanitarianism inherent in the Enlightenment and its perception of man as a rational being. In Britain the picture fitted well with the all-pervading Whig interpretation of history as progress.

The Whig view of progress in the criminal justice system was frontally assaulted by Georg Rusche and Otto Kirchheimer.[35] They linked different systems of punishment with different social structures: thus, under feudalism, there was an increase in corporal punishments since, in most cases, the body was the only property accessible; the mercantile system saw a change to forced labour and the penitentiary; the industrial system required a free market in labour and, in consequence, corrective detention gradually replaced forced labour. Change during the Enlightenment stemmed less from an altruistic desire to make punishment more humane than from the twin desires to protect the rising bourgeoisie from arbitrary punishment from above and from social upheaval from below brought about by brutal and unequal punishment. More recently the French philosopher-historian, Michel Foucault, has described within the Enlightenment a growing desire to establish a disciplined society which he does not see as related specifically to changing economic and social structures. The savage punishments of the old regime often created a bond between the offender and the crowd assembled around the scaffold; punishment might engender feelings of revulsion, but it did not necessarily frighten and consequently it did not deter. What was needed was a new system of punishment that would: '[H]omogenize its application. Reduce its economic and political cost by increasing the effectiveness and by multiplying its circuits'.[36] Foucault's aim was much wider than explaining changes in the criminal justice system. He sought to describe a whole pattern of cultural change involving the relationship between new forms of knowledge and the shifting strategies and institutions through which power was and is exercised. Prisons were a key element here, but so too were asylums, barracks, factories, hospitals and schools. Together with these institutions went new forms of expert knowledge, notably in medicine and psychiatry, which could also be used to enclose and restrict the body.

In the last analysis all of these hypotheses are unproveable; they are also deterministic. The Whig view sees change as rational and progressive; opponents of reform thus become blinkered and reactionary. The idea that alternative developments were possible and might have been equally rational and progressive is implicitly denied. The Rusche and Kirchheimer hypothesis is more apparently deterministic: no matter what men do as individuals the economic and social structure within which they labour would seem to determine all. Foucault's assessment is stimulating in the questions that it poses and it has generated considerable debate, discussion and research.[37] But, ultimately, Foucault's theory of new forms of knowledge seems to deny the possibility of alternative visions within a given period of history. Moreover, while Foucault might describe changes, he does not explain what drove them, why and how.

It is difficult to see how changing ideas about crime and criminals, and changing practices in criminal justice and punishment during the eighteenth and nineteenth centuries could not have been related to changing ideologies and economic and social structures. The question is whether the links were quite as one way as Rusche and Kirchheimer and Foucault suggest; or whether, as Gordon Wright has argued with reference to France:

It is more likely that the relationship between values and socioeconomic base, then as now, was reciprocal – that base and value-system combine to shape society's view of men and the world.[38]

The economic, political and social structure of a society creates a framework in which the criminal justice system functions and men may draw parallels between that system and new modes of production. Michael Ignatieff has shown how the rhetoric which equated men with machines was common to both prison reformers and industrialists in early nineteenth-century England.[39] But the framework created leaves room for a variety of alternatives, and many pressures ranging from perceptions of a nation's traditions to financial stringency can combine to ensure that ideals are not realised by legislators, let alone their agents.

Eighteenth-century parliaments tended to legislate for local problems, even the Black Act addressed a local problem; but gradually, and increasingly, legislators began to see crime in a national context. Peel's reorganisation of the criminal law during the 1820s was itself symptomatic of this change. Yet laws passed in the context of perceiving a national problem still had to be implemented by local agents on the streets and in the courts who may have had a different perception from that of the majority at Westminster. The law may have been deemed impartial and, increasingly, the product of consensual values by members of the judiciary, by legislators, theorists and so on, but the law had to be interpreted and enforced by local agents who had their own assumptions, interests, and prejudices, and who could be, on occasions, at odds with each other.[40]

Offenders were brought before one of three principal kinds of court during the eighteenth and nineteenth centuries: petty sessions, quarter sessions or assizes. The least serious offences could be dealt with summarily by magistrates sitting alone, or in pairs in petty sessions. The petty sessions became increasingly formal and regularised during the period, with the venue often moving from private accommodation, possibly an inn, to a more formal building. The magistrate who presided was, technically, a royal appointment; in practice, in the counties he was selected by the Lord Lieutenant for approval by the Lord Chancellor. He had to be a man of some wealth and social standing to have his name entered on a county's commission of the peace. Then, before he could act, he had to be of sufficient public spirit to take out his *dedimus potestatem*, which involved travelling to the county town, swearing an oath before the clerk of the peace, and paying the appropriate fees. Corporate boroughs also had magisterial benches generally composed of some combination of the mayor and aldermen; borough corporations were usually self-perpetuating oligarchies of the principal inhabitants until the Municipal Corporations Act of 1835 established a common system of election for town councils. This Act also sought to separate the executive arm of town administration (the town council) from the judicial arm (the magistrates), and required that borough magistrates be supervised by a recorder, a barrister appointed by the Crown; but throughout the nineteenth century town councillors continued to be selected as borough magistrates. The number of offences that could be tried summarily increased during the eighteenth century and even more markedly during the nineteenth, particularly with the passage of the Juvenile Offenders Acts 1847 and 1850 and the Criminal Justice Acts 1855 and 1879. In the larger towns and cities, stipendiary magistrates, acting in what were increasingly referred to as 'police courts', took on more and more of the burdens of summary jurisdiction. The first stipendiaries were appointed in London in 1792. But these paid professionals, like their unpaid associates and predecessors, were gentlemen; after 1835, however, they had to have served a minimum of five years at the bar as a barrister.

The courts of quarter sessions heard more serious offences that were prosecuted on indictment. These courts met four times a year, hence their name. They were established in both counties and corporate towns and, in theory though rarely in practice, all serving magistrates in the respective county or town could attend and hear the cases in a body presided over by a chairman. Again, as the nineteenth century wore on, there was a greater degree of formality in the proceedings and in the buildings, which were increasingly part of, or attached to the shire or town hall. At the borough sessions the chairmanship of the magistrates' bench was taken over by the supervisory recorder. The verdicts at quarter sessions were decided by juries but the magistrates decided upon the sentence.

The most serious indictable offences were tried before judges and juries at assizes. The judges were drawn from London's experienced legal elite; they were commonly appointed from barristers with, on average, some two decades practice at the bar. During the eighteenth and early nineteenth centuries there were two assizes each year held in the major county towns of most counties at Lent and during the summer; Northumberland, Cumberland, Westmoreland and Durham were the exceptions, each having only one assize a year. Emergencies, such as serious food riots in Sussex in 1795 and the Luddite troubles, could lead to special assizes being held. The nineteenth century saw experiments with different numbers of assizes in different counties. The metropolitan equivalent of the assizes was the court meeting at the Old Bailey which was holding eight sessions a year during the 1750s; in 1834 the Old Bailey was enlarged and rehoused in the new Central Criminal Court.

During the eighteenth and early nineteenth centuries the Old Bailey had the nearest thing to a judge specialising in the criminal law in its principal presiding judge, the Recorder of London. The two or three judges who assisted at the Old Bailey, and the judges who, in pairs, rode the six assizes circuits in Lent and summer, were all drawn from one of the three principal law courts – King's Bench, Common Pleas or Exchequer – where the work was predominantly civil. Indeed, half of the work at the assizes was civil and at each assize one of the two judges would deal with the civil cases while the other heard criminal matters. Thus, for much of the period, most of the individual judges who dealt with criminal cases had relatively little

contact with the criminal law. Furthermore, the judges were always cos-
seted on circuit, consequently they probably had even less understanding
and knowledge than the magistrates of the lives and situations of the
offenders brought before them.

Edward Parry recognised the possibility of judicial bias:

*In every age your judge will be tinged with the prejudices of his time
and his class, and I cannot see how you can expect to grow middle-class
judges in hot-beds of middle-class prejudices without the natural
formation of a certain amount of middle-class bias in the thickness of
their middle-class wood.*[41]

But Parry did not regard this as a problem for the enforcement of the law
and for attitudes towards offenders. How far magistrates and judges acted
as much because of assumptions and prejudices is an issue that will recur
below. What the working-class accused made of the gentlemen who sat
as magistrates and judges, particularly the latter in their sumptuous and
increasingly archaic garb, will remain an open question. It is clear, however, that 'gentlemen' monopolised the judicial benches, and a brief glance
through any court records will show that, in general, people from another
social class monopolised the dock. But that said, while one class may have
made the law and administered it in the courts, this was by no means the
only class to use the law for redress and it was not unknown for the law to
protect the poor against the well-to-do.[42] It is also clear that, as a group,
the ruling class believed its own rhetoric concerning equality before the
law and the need for impartiality and independence in the judicial process.
Such beliefs dictated behaviour.

Magistrates and judges were not the only agents of the law who were
called upon to interpret the law. The nineteenth century saw the creation
of the new police in Britain. While histories of the police in Britain have
tended to ignore the issue, it is clear that the policeman on his beat had discretion in identifying some behaviour as criminal or not and in deciding
what action to take. He could take the offender into custody occasionally,
if he so wished, using a discretionary charge; he could warn him or
her, ignore him or her, or even administer summary chastisement with fist,
truncheon, cape, or whatever else came to hand.[43] It was largely victimless
offences that were open to such discretion – drunkenness, prostitution,
street gaming and, especially on Sunday, street selling. If a crime, a theft
for example, was reported to a policeman and the offender was identified
or subsequently detected then, probably, an arrest and prosecution would
result. But the reporting of a crime and the identification of an offender by

witnesses in itself required a perception on the part of victim and/or witnesses that a crime had been committed and that legal action should follow. Discretion in matters relating to crime began well before the legislators and the courts; and policemen were not, generally, the initiators of the processes designed to control criminal behaviour.

Teasing out perceptions and the use of discretion are as central to the historian's understanding of crime as studying legislation and enforcement. In the narrowest sense Langbein may be correct in insisting that the criminal law is 'the wrong place' to seek out 'the active hand' of the ruling class; but perceptions of crime and of the criminal, discretion in using the law, new legislation and new systems of enforcement, are all important issues for the historian approaching relationships within a given society and assessing how different societies functioned and evolved.

Rather than attempting a chronological survey of crime and the various developments in the criminal justice system together in short, meaningful chunks, the book is divided thematically. Roughly, the first half explores perceptions and, as far as they are ever ascertainable, the realities of crime from several angles: the statistical evidence, class perceptions, gender perceptions, the perceived differences between urban and rural crime, the extent of crime at the workplace. Chapter 7 is designed as a kind of coda, rounding off the first half with a discussion of the usefulness of the concepts of a 'criminal class' and 'professional criminals'. The second half of the book looks at developments in the pursuit, the prosecution, and the treatment of offenders: the courts, the police, and punishment. The final chapter attempts to pull the whole together with some conclusions.

Notes and references

1 **Sir Leon Radzinowicz** and **Joan King**, *The Growth of Crime: The International Experience*, Penguin, Harmondsworth, 1979, p. 15.

2 Quoted by **Paul Phillips**, *Marx and Engels on Law and Laws*, Martin Robertson, Oxford, 1980, p. 161.

3 **J. A. Sharpe**, *Crime in Early Modern England 1550–1750*, 2nd edn, Longman, London, 1999, p. 6.

4 For modern discretionary offences see **David J. Smith** and **Jeremy Gray**, *Police and People in London*, Gower, Aldershot, 1985, pp. 13–15.

5 **J. Ginswick** (ed.), *Labour and the Poor in England and Wales 1849–51: The letters to the Morning Chronicle*, 8 vols, Cass, London, 1983, i, 25.

6 Quoted by **John E. Archer**, *'By a flash and a scare'. Arson, Animal Maiming, and Poaching in East Anglia 1815–1870*, Clarendon Press, Oxford, 1990, p. 214.

7 **John G. Rule**, 'Social crime in the rural south in the eighteenth and early nineteenth centuries', *Southern History*, **1** (1979), pp. 135–53: see also the 'Conference Report' in *Bulletin of the Society for the Study of Labour History*, **25** (1972), pp. 5–12.

8 **John Bohstedt**, *Riots and Community Politics in England and Wales 1790–1810*, Harvard U.P., Cambridge, Mass., 1983, p. 197; **Janet Gyford**, ' "Men of Bad Character": Property crime in Essex in the 1820s', unpublished M.A., University of Essex, 1982, p. 64.

9 *P.P.* 1826–27 (534) vi, *Select Committee on Criminal Commitments and Convictions*, p. 34.

10 Lincs. R.O. Kesteven Quarter Sessions Minute Books, Epiphany 1796–Easter 1802, f. 19. The Minute Book gives a tantalising glimpse of what may have been some kind of feud developing between Barstow and the two magistrates who fined him for his Game Law Offence – the Reverend John Myers and John Hutchin. The preceding November these same magistrates had fined him £20 for wearing hair powder without a licence (f. 4).

11 **P. B. Munsche**, *Gentlemen and Poachers: The English Game Laws 1671–1831*, Cambridge U.P., New York, 1981, *passim*.

12 **John G. Rule**, 'Wrecking and coastal plunder', in **Douglas Hay, Peter Linebaugh, E. P. Thompson** *et al.*, *Albion's Fatal Tree: Crime and society in eighteenth-century England*, Allen Lane, London, 1975, pp. 184–5.

13 **Cal Winslow**, 'Sussex smugglers', in Hay, Linebaugh, Thompson *et al.*, *Albion's Fatal Tree*, pp. 136–9 and 159, note 1.

14 **Hoh-Cheung** and **Lorna H. Mui**, 'Smuggling and the British tea trade before 1784', *American Historical Review*, lxxiv (1968), pp. 44–73 (at p. 73).

15 **John Styles**, ' "Our traitorous money-makers": The Yorkshire coiners and the law, 1760–83', in **John Brewer** and **John Styles** (eds), *An Ungovernable People: The English and their law in the seventeenth and eighteenth centuries*, Hutchinson, London, 1980, pp. 247–8.

16 **Virginia Berridge** and **Griffith Edwards**, *Opium and the People: Opiate use in nineteenth-century England*, Allen Lane, London, 1981, p. 82.

17 **Charles Reith**, *British Police and the Democratic Ideal*, Oxford U.P., London, 1943, p. 143; **Gavin Thurston**. *The Clerkenwell Riot: The killing of Constable Culley*, Allen and Unwin, London, 1967. (Both Reith and Thurston completely miss the point of the popular hostility to the police on this occasion.)

18 **A. W. Brian Simpson**, *Cannibalism and the Common Law*, Chicago U.P., Chicago, 1984, *passim*.

19 'Conference Report', *Bulletin of the Society for . . . Labour History*, 1972, p. 10.

20 **David M. Gordon**, 'Capitalism, class and crime in America', *Crime and Delinquency*, xix (1973), pp. 163–86 argues that the loss resulting from 'Index Crimes' (i.e. robbery, burglary, larceny etc.) is only a fifth of the loss resulting from unreported commercial theft, embezzlement and fraud, yet the criminal justice system is almost entirely concerned with the former. See also, *inter alia*, **Steven Box**, *Power, Crime and Mystification*, Tavistock, London, 1983.

21 **Herbert Spencer**, 'Railway morals and railway policy', *Edinburgh Review*, C (1854), pp. 420–61 (at pp. 426–7).

22 **Edward Abbot Parry**, *The Law and the Poor*, Smith, Elder & Co., London, 1914, pp. 154–6 and 201.

23 Quoted by **W. G. Carson**, 'The institutionalization of ambiguity: Early British Factory Acts', in **Gilbert Geis** and **Ezra Stotland** (eds), *White-Collar Crime: Theory and research*, Sage, Beverly Hills, 1980, p. 168.

24 **Colin A. Russell, Noel G. Coley** and **Gerrylynn K. Roberts**, *Chemists by Profession: The origins and rise of the Royal Institute of Chemistry*, Open U.P., Milton Keynes, 1977, pp. 42 and 102; **A. E. Dingle**, ' "The monster nuisance of all": Landowners, alkali manufacturers, and air pollution, 1828–64', *Economic History Review*, xxxv (1982), pp. 529–48.

25 Carson, 'The institutionalization of ambiguity', pp. 159–60; **Brian Didsbury**, 'Cheshire Saltworkers', in **Raphael Samuel** (ed.), *Miners, Quarrymen and Saltworkers*, RKP, London, 1977, pp. 156–8; **Anthony S. Wohl**, *Endangered Lives: Public health in Victorian Britain*, Dent, London, 1983, pp. 270–2 and 275 especially.

26 **Adam Smith**, *Lectures on Jurisprudence*, **R. L. Meek, D. D. Raphael** and **P. G. Stein** (eds), Oxford U.P., New York, 1978, p. 208.

27 **Alexis de Tocqueville**, *Journeys to England and Ireland* (ed. J. P. Mayer), Anchor Books, New York, 1968, p. 78.

28 *The Times*, 14 January 1865.

29 **Graham Parker**, 'The prisoner in the box – The making of the Criminal Evidence Act, 1898', in **J. A. Guy** and **H. G. Beale** (eds), *Law and Social Change in British History*, Royal Historical Society, London, 1984, p. 163.

30 **Douglas Hay**, 'Property, authority and the criminal law', in Hay, Linebaugh, Thompson *et al.*, *Albion's Fatal Tree*, pp. 26, 35 and 48.

31 **John H. Langbein**, 'Albion's fatal flaws', *P and P*, 98 (1983), pp. 96–120 (at pp. 102 and 119).

32 **Peter King**, 'Decision makers and decision-making in the English criminal law, 1750–1800', *H.J.*, **27** (1984), pp. 25–58 (at p. 53); see also, **Peter King**, *Crime*

Justice and Discretion in England, 1740–1820, Oxford U.P., Oxford, 2000, especially chapter 11.

33 **Sir Leon Radzinowicz**, *A History of English Criminal Law*, 5 vols, Stevens, London, 1948–86, i, 49–79; **E. P. Thompson**, *Whigs and Hunters: The origins of the Black Act*, Allen Lane, London, 1975, *passim*. Both Radzinowicz and Thompson categorise the Black Act as typical of the eighteenth-century Bloody Code, and Thompson explains the legislation in terms of the ruthless Hanoverian ruling class acting in its own interest against the foresters who were resisting that class's assault on customary rights. However, recent research has identified a crucial and narrowly political motive behind the legislation, namely the Jacobite connection of the foresters, and this does put a very different complexion on the issue. **E. Cruikshanks** and **H. Erskine-Hill**, 'The Waltham Black Act and Jacobitism', *Journal of British Studies*, xxiv (1985), pp. 358–65.

34 While Bankes wanted to make the taking of black lead from mines a felony, it is not clear that he wanted to make the offence capital. The problem is that eighteenth-century bills never included the intended punishment; the punishment was left blank for the committee to fill in after the second reading. Unless ancillary documentation survives, which it does not seem to in this case, the precise intentions of the bill's promoters remain unclear. For the problems in assessing the legislation that went into the Bloody Code see **Joanna Innes** and **John Styles**, 'The crime wave: Recent writing on crime and criminal justice in eighteenth-century England', *Journal of British Studies*, xxv (1986); *idem*, 'The "Bloody Code" in context: Eighteenth-century criminal legislation reconsidered. A report on work in progress', unpublished paper, December 1984. My thanks to the authors for permission to read and to cite the latter.

35 **Georg Rusche** and **Otto Kirchheimer**, *Punishment and Social Structure*, Russell and Russell, New York, 1968, *passim*.

36 **Michel Foucault**, *Discipline and Punish: The origins of the prison*, Penguin, Harmondsworth, 1978, p. 89.

37 See especially **Michelle Perrot** (ed.), *L'Impossible Prison: Recherches sur le systéme au XIXe siècle*, Seuil, Paris, 1980.

38 **Gordon Wright**, *Between the Guillotine and Liberty: Two centuries of the crime problem in France*, Oxford U.P., New York, 1983, p. 22. Wright implies, however, that Foucault sees a precise relationship between the socio-economic base and his changing forms of knowledge which I do not take to be the case; and this lack of relationship is very much the criticism of Jacques Leonard who describes Foucault's theory as 'machinery without the machinist' or 'strategy without generals'. **Jacques Leonard**, 'L'historien et le philosophe', in Perrot, *L'Impossible Prison*, p. 14 especially.

39 Michael Ignatieff, *A Just Measure of Pain: The penitentiary in the Industrial Revolution 1750–1850*, Macmillan, London, 1978, *passim*.

40 For example Norma Landau has described the antagonism of certain eighteenth-century magistrates towards the officers of His Majesty's Customs and Excise which led to them frequently diminishing statutory fines imposed on offenders prosecuted by the officers. **Norma Landau**, *The Justices of the Peace, 1679–1760*, University of California Press, Berkeley and Los Angeles, 1984, pp. 223–6.

41 Parry, *The Law and the Poor*, pp. 100–1.

42 For example David Englander has shown how the wage-earner knew how to use the law to advantage against the landlord. **David Englander**, *Landlord and Tenant in Urban Britain 1838–1918*, Oxford U.P., Oxford, 1983, p. 38 and (for Scotland) pp. 39–44.

43 **Clive Emsley**, ' "The thump of wood on a swede turnip": Police violence in nineteenth-century England', *C.J.H.*, **6** (1985), pp. 125–49.

CHAPTER 2

The statistical map

Many of the key questions, certainly many of the most popular questions about crime, are quantitative. How much was there? Was it increasing or decreasing? Which types of crime were most prevalent at particular periods or in particular places? Even the central question: did economic and social change foster different kinds of criminality requires statistical evidence to hazard an answer. Yet the statistical evidence of crime is fraught with dangers and difficulties.

Criminologists who engage in statistical debates often employ criminal statistics adjusted to take account of population growth or decline, and of changes in age structure. Some historians of crime in the eighteenth and nineteenth centuries have also used this kind of data, though there is the obvious problem of reliable population figures for the period before 1801. The statistics discussed in this chapter are raw figures; nevertheless, as will be explained below, the enormous population changes of the two centuries must always be borne in mind in any assessment of the statistical pattern of crime.

The period of this volume can be divided roughly into three, given the kinds of statistics available to the historian. Before 1805 there are no national crime figures. Historians of the eighteenth century, seeking to tackle the questions that require quantifiable answers, have to do their own counting of indictments, trials and convictions in the judicial records – either in the fragmentary assize records at the Public Record Office, or in the quarter sessions records in County Record Offices. Generally speaking there is little surviving evidence from eighteenth-century petty sessions; even though sentences passed at petty sessions were meant to be filed at quarter sessions, the surviving records suggest that few were. In 1827, when the Home Office requested that county clerks of the peace send returns for Game Laws convictions over the preceding seven years, an active magistrate counselled Peel:

I fear those returns must necessarily be so deficient as to give a most erroneous impression as to the enormous increase of offences of that nature, it being the practice of magistrates out of sessions or at petty sessions to omit returning such convictions so generally that in many cases not a tenth part, perhaps not a twentieth part of the actual number of convictions which have led to imprisonment and its pernicious consequences have been sent to the Clerks of the Peace to be recorded.[1]

In 1810 the government published figures of committals for indictable crime in England and Wales going back to 1805; and from then on these statistics were published annually. It was the controversy over the Bloody Code which appears to have first occasioned the collection and publication of these statistics. The 1830s and 1840s witnessed the flowering of the statistical movement in Britain and from 1834, thanks to Samuel Redgrave, the Criminal Registrar, the published criminal statistics were reorganised under six main types of offence – a classification that has survived, more or less unchanged, to the present:

1   Offences against the person (ranging from homicide to simple assault)

2   Offences against property involving violence (robbery, burglary, etc.)

3   Offences against property not involving violence (larceny, etc.)

4   Malicious offences against property (arson, machine breaking, etc.)

5   Offences against the currency

6   Miscellaneous offences (including riot, sedition, and treason)

From 1836 the statistics of commitments to prison began to be systematised and published in an annual digest. Statistics had a quantitative connotation during these years, but this was generally subsidiary to the main concern of collecting and arranging facts illustrative of the condition and resources of the state; indeed it was not until the twentieth century that statistics came to mean solely numbers and the methods of analysing them. The early statistical movement generally took statistical facts to be pure and uncontroversial; by deploying these facts social investigators sought to stand aside from party but, nevertheless, to push for reforms. Reforming ideals guided the statistical movement, and 'moral statistics' lay at its heart with a concentration, primarily, on education, then on crime and, less frequently still, on religion. These reformers urged greater accuracy and greater sophistication in the collection of criminal statistics and pointed to what they took to be the superiority of the French in this respect.[2] In 1856 an appendage to the County and Borough Police Act established the modern tripartite split in British criminal statistics, and from 1857 these statistics consisted of, first, indictable offences reported to the police that had not necessarily resulted in an arrest or been 'solved'; second, committals for trial, both on indictment and before summary jurisdiction; and third, the number of persons convicted and imprisoned.

While the 'criminal class' is not the concern of this chapter it is worth noting, tangentially, another variety of statistics prepared by policemen and regularised from 1857. These were the figures of 'known thieves and depredators' in a particular police district. The major problem with these statistics is that it was not until the close of the century that any form of guidance was given as to what this category should contain. One stalwart of the Statistical Society lamented in 1860:

What is meant by 'known thieves and depredators', is not, so far as I know, anywhere defined. *Nor do the police in the different parts of England attach the same meaning to the term. In Yorkshire, and generally throughout the North of England, they profess to return no one as a known thief who is ever known to do any 'honest work'. In the South, with the exception of the large towns, every man is entered as a 'known thief', who had ever been known to steal.*

Thus Birmingham had one thief to every 134 honest men, but one committal for every 246 inhabitants, while Liverpool had one thief to every 1,155 honest men and one committal for every 55 persons.[3] An analogous problem exists with the numbers of 'habitual criminals' collected following the Habitual Criminals Act 1869 and the Prevention of Crimes Act 1871. This legislation gave the police considerable supervisory powers over those who had been convicted of more than one offence and could therefore be considered as 'habitual' criminals. Policemen could arrest habituals on suspicion and it was then incumbent on the accused to show that he was not intending mischief when apprehended, or else he could be sentenced to a maximum of twelve months' imprisonment. The difficulty with the statistics of habitual criminals, as recorded by the Criminal Registrar, is that they seem to contradict the evidence of other sources about crime: London appears to have been the scene of most crime, and certainly it was metropolitan crime which created the most scares, but in the lists of habitual criminals London comes a long way down the list. The cause of this discrepancy seems principally to stem from the reluctance of the stipendiary magistrates in the metropolis to accept the way in which the police wished to use the legislation, and they exploited loopholes in the law to this end on the grounds that 'we cannot punish a man merely for being in the streets, although he may be a convicted thief and the well-known associate of bad characters'. In this respect the independent, professional magistrates of London acted very differently from many of their lay brethren in the provinces.[4]

Leaving aside the problem of defining members of the criminal class and known thieves and depredators, the chief difficulty with the principal forms of criminal statistics is the 'dark figure', that is the number of offences committed of which there is no record because no-one bothered to, wished to, or was able to report a particular offence. Committals or indictments leave an even bigger gap between themselves and what might be hypothesised as 'the actual amount of crime' since they necessitate an accusation against a particular, identified individual. Experts were aware of the dark figure at least from the end of the eighteenth century. In his *Treatise on the Police of the Metropolis*, Patrick Colquhoun noted: 'Under the present system there is not above one offence in one hundred that is discovered or prosecuted'.[5] Edwin Chadwick and his colleagues investigating crime and policing during the 1830s:

found that in respect to the crimes against property and other classes of crime, that the number of cases pursued bore little or no relation to the cases of crime actually committed. We found large masses of crime with scarcely any pursuit at all . . .[6]

In 1867, after ten years of the more detailed tripartite criminal statistics, James T. Hammick, a barrister and member of the council of the Statistical Society, declared:

It is certain that the actual amount of crime committed can never at any time be ascertained. Robbery is sometimes carried on for years without detection; and the unwillingness of persons to make known and to prosecute frauds by servants and others will always render the returns on this head [i.e. crimes reported to the police] incomplete.[7]

The numbers of committals and indictments which form the basis of the criminal statistics for some two-thirds of the period covered by this volume are obviously some way from any measurement of actual crime. They are the end-product of a variety of filters and require, at the very least, a victim prepared to prosecute or someone prepared to report an offence, and an individual who has been accused and apprehended. But individual prosecutions were also the product of a social, economic and political context that changed from decade to decade, even from year to year. In some years the context may have provoked a ferocious response to a particular offence, in others the response could have been far more lenient. Over two hundred prosecutions for sedition in England have been counted for the years 1792 to 1801. This was probably two hundred more than in the preceding decade, and is probably an underestimate of the number of charges laid. It reflects the growth of Painite radicalism in England during the decade of the French Revolution; it also reflects the panic of many men of property and their determination to crush Jacobinism at home as well as abroad.[8] A Mancunian who cursed the King, his chief minister and the latter's policies following the severe impact of the 1784 Fustian Tax may have been cautioned or completely ignored. The same man damning the King, his chief minister and the latter's policies a decade later, as the cost of the Revolutionary Wars demanded more and more sacrifices in men and money, was much more likely to find himself before the courts charged with seditious words. Of course, such a narrow 'political' offence as speaking sedition is only likely to occur in public before an audience that can provide a witness or two. Yet similar variations can be suggested with reference to the prosecution of other crimes. A statistical increase in indictments for petty theft during the years of dearth in the eighteenth and early nineteenth centuries may reflect a genuine increase in theft brought about by necessity. It may also reflect some farmers and gentlemen determined to make examples by prosecutions rather than by admonitions, so as to dissuade anyone else who might also be tempted to offend because of the severity of the time; though, conversely, some gentlemen appear to have been inclined to more leniency towards property offenders in times of distress. A rapid growth in the number of prosecutions of juveniles for theft in London in the late eighteenth and early nineteenth centuries may have been, in part, the result of the city's rapid growth, and the decline of apprenticeship and living-in service. These processes were not new, however, and changing attitudes among victims, magistrates, police and prison reformers, together with the declining use of capital punishment and financial incentives for prosecutors, were all, probably, equally important. In particular in London in the early nineteenth century there appears to have been a greater preparedness to draw young people into the criminal justice system, to label them as criminal and to identify them as a significant part of a criminal problem.[9]

In some instances the fear of increased crime, of itself, may have generated an increase in prosecutions. In November 1765 the printer of the *Chelmsford Chronicle* appears consciously to have used one or two robberies and some reports of robberies both to boost his sales and to assert his newspaper's claim to being the key organ of information in Essex. His emphasis on these offences, in turn, generated arrests on flimsy evidence and rewarded him with yet more copy. The stereotypical bandit gangs described in the newspaper were never apprehended.[10] The London garrotting panic of 1862 appears to have provoked an increase in prosecutions for street robbery. Once press, police and private individuals were aware of the offence, they began to see it all around. James Pilkington M.P. was 'garrotted' in Pall Mall on 17 July 1862. There had been only fifteen robberies with violence in the metropolis in the first six months of the year, but as the panic gathered momentum in the aftermath of the attack on Pilkington, and as *The Times* orchestrated a press attack on philanthropists for being too soft on the kind of 'habitual criminals' who became 'garrotters', so the number of reported incidents, and prosecutions, increased: in September there were two alleged garrottings, in October twelve, in November thirty-two.[11]

Changes in policing could also affect the statistics of crime. In 1828 two parliamentary select committees agreed that most of the apparent increase in crime manifested in the committal figures before them was the result of better enforcement and changes in classification.[12] The establishment of the new police forces from the 1830s invariably produced local increases in the numbers of individuals committed for public order offences: drunk and disorderly, drunk and incapable, obstructing the highway, vagrancy. These offences were essentially public and arrests were relatively easy. Directives to individual police forces to clamp down on any one of such offences could produce a sudden peak in local statistics. In October 1869, for example, the Chief Constable of Bedfordshire reported that for the year ending in September his men had apprehended 291 vagrants as opposed to only 105 the preceding year. The increase was 'accounted for by the Police receiving instructions last January to apprehend all Vagrants offending'. The year ending in September 1870 appears to have seen things get back to normal with a mere 117 such arrests.[13] It was less easy to yield such dramatic results following instructions to clamp down on housebreaking, burglary and robbery, yet changes or differences in the way that such offences were recorded affected the figures. A sub-committee of Manchester City Council contrasted the incidence of 'highway robbery' in Liverpool and Manchester for the year 1866. The figures were as follows

TABLE 2.1 *The incidence of 'highway robbery' in Liverpool and Manchester, 1866*

	Highway robberies	Apprehensions	Percentage of apprehensions to offences
Liverpool	56	10	17.7%
Manchester	217	136	62.6%

(Table 2.1). On the surface there appeared to be a major difference in the incidence of the crime and in the police clear-up rate. But the sub-committee went on to note:

In Manchester every robbery from the person, accompanied by violence, in the street or elsewhere . . . is classified as highway robbery; whilst . . . in Liverpool, as well as in other places, those robberies only which are committed in the streets and highways, and accompanied by violence, are thus classed in the return.[14]

It must be recognised further that the perceptions of victim and of police could influence the labelling of an offence. The difference between robbery and larceny from the person was technically that violence was employed in the former; but the two offences overlap and the eventual way in which a crime was recorded could depend on how the victim and/or police wished to conceive of 'violence'. A similar problem existed with burglary and some larceny: the decision to proceed with a summary prosecution under the Criminal Justice Act, or with an indictment at assizes, could rest with the police perception of the accused's character and whether or not he had previous convictions; it would seem that if the accused was 'known' to the police then the police would opt for the more serious charge.[15]

In 1879 the Metropolitan Police found itself under attack in the press because of what appeared to be an increase in offences against property; the statistics showed 735 burglaries and breakings reported in 1877; and 2,429 the following year. In a confidential memorandum prepared for the Home Secretary the police responded that the *Pall Mall Gazette* had taken as its baseline the year 1871 – a year of prosperity, and a year in which, the police insisted, there was less 'crime' than any other during the decade. But in addition there had been a recent change in the way certain serious crimes were recorded, and this, it was argued, exacerbated the distortion:

From the establishment of the Metropolitan Police down to October 1877 it was the practice to classify offences against property according to the practical rather than the exact legal standard. An entry into a dwelling

house by day was not described as a housebreaking, nor by night as a
burglary unless there was a clear breaking by force. Therefore entrances
effected by false keys, by open or unfastened doors and windows were set
down as 'larcenies by this or that method' and not as housebreaking or
burglary . . . That this change [in October 1877] was legally right there
may be little doubt, but the effect of its being suddenly carried out was
disastrous . . . To it a very large – fully three quarters – proportion of the
additional burglaries and housebreakings occurring in 1878 over 1877
may be attributed.[16]

The following decade, within two years, the number of women convicted
of soliciting in London fell by more than fifty per cent: from 3,233 in 1886
to 1,475 in 1888. 'This enormous decrease', commented a leading contemporary criminologist, 'is not due to a diminution of the offence, but to a
change in the attitude of the police'.[17]

Changes in the law also affected criminal statistics. The succession of
acts, beginning in the mid-eighteenth century, which allowed prosecutors'
and witnesses' expenses, probably had some impact on indictment levels.[18]
New laws also meant new crimes. The creation of income tax to help
finance the Revolutionary and Napoleonic Wars led to the new crimes of
income tax evasion and making false declarations of income.[19] Raising the
age of consent to 13 years in 1875 and to 16 years ten years later, brought
men with proclivities for sex with young, teenage girls within the category
of offenders. But sexual assaults were always notoriously under-reported.
During the nineteenth century there appears to have been a reluctance
among women and girls to report sexual offences not least because of the
embarrassment involved in discussing intimate parts of the body. Also
many working-class women were probably discouraged by the reluctance
of male officials to take such charges seriously, especially when a man from
a higher social group was involved; and if a trial did take place the woman's 'virtue' and 'fantasies' were as much at issue as the man's actions. In
some cases middle-class women were able to conceal sexual assaults under
prosecutions for breach of promise.[20] The creation of income tax and
changing the age of consent probably had an imperceptible impact on the
overall crime figures. The Elementary Education Act 1870, however,
resulted in 96,601 parents being brought before the courts in the first year
and, allegedly, half a million were prosecuted in the first twenty years of
the legislation.[21] Of course, many would deny that these offenders were
'criminals' in the sense that thieves, rapists and murderers were 'criminals';
as one contemporary put it:

Few people . . . would say that 'crime' was increasing and civilisation demoralising us because we now compel parents to send their children to school, and hale before the magistrates those who fail to do so, not having yet been accustomed to accept the new law.[22]

Yet theft and assault figures were also affected by legislation particularly when indictable offences were shunted into summary jurisdiction categories. This happened, for example, with a succession of acts passed in the middle years of the nineteenth century: 1847, the Juvenile Offenders Act; 1850, a second Juvenile Offenders Act; 1855, the Criminal Justice Act. The consequent fall in committals on criminal indictments was erroneously taken by one of the pioneers in the use of statistics in the history of crime as a real fall in crime.[23] However, when the statistics of convictions at both quarter sessions and under the summary legislation are considered there appears a marked increase in crime. This seems best understood not as an increase in crime *per se*, but as an increase in prosecutions before summary courts which were greatly facilitated by the legislation.[24]

The succession of problems with criminal statistics led J. J. Tobias to despair of their utility in his *Crime and Industrial Society in the Nineteenth Century*. The only firm relationship that, he believed, existed was 'that changes in chief constable produce changes in one series of figures'. He preferred to rely on literary analyses for assessing the pattern of criminality, and this while noting that it was common for nineteenth-century assertions 'on the topic of crime to be backed up with statistics, either taken from official or other publications or drawn from personal investigations'.[25] In fact some of the nineteenth-century experts did rather more than 'back up' their assertions with statistics; the Reverend William Douglas Morrison 'proved' that there was virtually no link between destitution and crime by a tortuous statistical analysis involving a variety of different figures.[26] Tobias generally accepted Morrison's perception of a 'criminal class' lurking in the big cities. As David Philips has pointed out in his telling criticisms of Tobias, the use of literary evidence, albeit from 'powerful authorities' (Tobias's term) are 'useful and instructive in showing what people thought about these subjects; they do not establish the truth of these questions'.[27]

Tobias's concern was, simply, that crime statistics were just too dangerous and too unreliable for any value to be made of them. Rather different warnings have emanated from others. Some criminologists argue that the further a criminal record is from an original act, the less use it has for any analysis of the pattern of criminality.[28] Thus the figures of crimes reported to the police are more significant than those of cases processed by the courts; for the eighteenth century, when there was no police, the indictments presented in the courts provide the surviving record closest to a criminal act. Yet the police too are bureaucratic agents involved in the control of crime and in consequence some radical criminologists have insisted that since all criminal and judicial statistics are the products of the decisions and purposes of those responsible for the control of crime, they can never be used as a measure of actual criminal activities.[29] Historians who seek to use crime figures have to confront these challenges.

In a study of street violence in Victorian cities, Rob Sindall has insisted that the only way around these problems is to study the statistics 'not as a reflection . . . of a phenomenon but as a phenomenon in themselves', not as a measure of 'what was happening, but of what people believed was happening'.[30] But the same point could be made about much historical evidence. The historian's sources are fragmentary and opaque; they have to be interrogated and interpreted with care. Few sources ever reveal a simple answer and few historians worth their salt would seek to base general conclusions on one set of source material, least of all, perhaps, on the statistical evidence of something whose definition is as elusive as is that of crime. It would be indefensible to accept these statistics as a measure of actual levels of crime. It would be foolish, without considering other evidence and without considering the origins of the statistics, to accept them as precise guides to the pattern of crime; in the same way that the dark figure remains a mystery, so too must be the variation between the dark figure and the number of crimes reported and/or prosecuted. The statistics, used with caution, provide a starting point, a hypothesis, for patterns of both criminal activity and responses to perceptions of that activity.

J. M. Beattie and Douglas Hay, who have produced the most cogent statistical work on eighteenth-century crime, have both urged the value of counting indictments to assess overall patterns. For Beattie:

if the forces governing the selection of cases to be tried worked roughly the same way from year to year, or at least did not change randomly and wildly, then changes in the number of indictments might be expected to derive from changes in the number of offences . . . Some would argue . . . that until we learn what the relationship is between the known and the unknown by a study of pre-trial processes and arrangements it will be impossible to interpret changes in the levels of prosecuted offences. In that case we will wait for ever.[31]

Hay pushes the case one stage further suggesting that the argument for abandoning criminal statistics in favour of assessing the criminal justice system alone is 'logically untenable':

Unless one proves that control is overwhelmingly, irresistibly determinant of indictment levels . . . then officially recorded crime must be the net result of both the behaviour of those subject to the law and those controlling it. In short, if changes in levels of behaviour likely to be prosecuted are said to be unknowable, then the causes of sequential changes in the legal response (or precipitant) are also unknowable.

Moreover, he suggests that the eighteenth-century indictment might give a more accurate picture of the pattern of crime than the statistics amassed by the modern bureaucratic police since eighteenth-century prosecutions were initiated by private individuals and 'there was no equivalent to the effect of police practice and attitudes, usually considered the most serious biasing influence on present statistics'.[32]

Peter King's recent study of Essex relies heavily on the evidence of indictments and contrasts statistics that he has assembled with those collected by others working on different counties. King underlines the difficulties and dangers of these statistics. If, for example, only one in ten of the crimes committed during the century was prosecuted, then a 5 per cent increase in decisions to prosecute because of a particular panic could result in a 50 per cent increase in the indictments available for the historian to count. Over several counties the statistics reveal an increase in the level of indictments in the late eighteenth century, but, as King points out, it is impossible to determine whether this 'was caused by a rise in the proportion of property offenders being indicted or by an increase in actual lawbreaking activity.' However, as he also explains, the number of individuals on a gaol calendar for trial was something that contemporaries used to assess the level of crime. It also had an impact on jury and sentencing decisions.[33]

For almost twenty years V. A. C. Gatrell's analysis of the nineteenth-century judicial statistics for England and Wales held an unchallenged position. Gatrell argued that the national figures, taken over a long term, ironed out regional idiosyncrasies and freak periodic fluctuations to give a general picture of the pattern, though naturally not the level, of crime. While admitting that control reactions to some lesser offences might be 'highly unstable, irregular, and even whimsical' he emphasised that:

in respect of the more serious and traditional thefts and acts of violence, the actions of the controllers will be very much more, even if not absolutely, constrained by a long-standing and traditional consensus as to the heinousness of the criminal act and the unquestionable desirability of as direct an action against it as possible, and also by public expectation that the law be evenly and efficiently enforced and that justice appear to be done.[34]

Furthermore, he pointed out, while working-class suspicion of the new police never died out during the nineteenth century, the working class were ever more inclined to use the processes of the police and the law when they were the victims of crime. This, he suggested, in the long term, served to narrow the gap between actual indictable crime and recorded crime. The statistical decline in theft and violence after the 1840s further supports his argument since this decline occurred at the very time when police and court activity, and public co-operation with this activity, were increasing. However, as Gatrell's arguments appeared to have gained the status of orthodoxy, Howard Taylor forcefully restated a much more critical and sceptical approach to the national figures. Taylor emphasized how changes in policing and prosecution, especially when taken over by public agencies, can affect the statistics. He also stressed how a police agenda might encourage police manipulation of the figures and how government funding of the criminal justice system may itself have limited the pursuit of some prosecutions and hence insertions into the overall statistics. These latter suggestions have, in turn, prompted a strong counterblast with a challenge for less assumption and more hard evidence of police working together as an interest group and of Treasury limitations on costs.[35]

Taking the various forms of raw crime statistics over the whole period from 1750 to 1900 the following pattern emerges: a gradual increase in theft and assault during the second half of the eighteenth century, becoming much steeper in the second decade of the nineteenth century and continuing at a steady rate until the close of the 1840s. For the second half of the nineteenth century the figures show a gradual decline in theft and violence, though housebreaking and burglary remain at a constant and thus at a proportionately greater level. Within this overall pattern there are marked annual fluctuations, as well as peaks and troughs extending over slightly longer periods than one year. Second, the statistics suggest that the most common crime – well over half and often more than three-quarters – throughout the whole period was small-scale theft. Third, the great majority of offenders – generally three in four – were male. There was a strong concentration of young men in their teens and early twenties; and across the eighteenth and nineteenth centuries the number of female

offenders – at least those coming before the principal courts – was proportionately in decline.[36] These latter points fit well with what is known of
crime in contemporary society; while the overall pattern of crime during
these 150 years can readily be accommodated within historical understanding of the development of English society during the period.

The gradual increase in eighteenth-century crime might be accounted
for, at least in part, by the increase in population. It might also partly be
explained with reference to increasing possessions, urbanisation and the
capitalisation of industry. There was more to steal in an expanding town,
but also, given the looser ties between urban and capitalist employers and
their workforce, the desire to settle offences without recourse to the law
may have diminished. Beattie's research on Surrey and Sussex has revealed
more indictments in the urban parishes in, and on the fringe of, the
metropolis. Peter King's study of Essex presents a similar picture, though
it also suggests that the convenience of a local court was, of itself, an
encouragement to prosecution, for those small towns with their own
courts have greater levels of crime recorded in the proceedings of these
courts than those towns whose individuals had to trek to county quarter
sessions to conduct a prosecution. As noted in the introduction, the
eighteenth century saw an increase in the number of capital statues, giving
rise to the descriptive phrase 'the Bloody Code'; but the great majority of
capital prosecutions – ninety-five per cent or more – in the second half of
the century were based on statutes enacted before 1742, many of which
went back to the Tudors.[37] The periodic fluctuations in theft during the
century have been explained with reference to war and dearth, though not
by the simplistic assumptions that dearth automatically led to more theft,
and that massive demobilisation also, automatically, led to more theft as
former soldiers and sailors, thrown onto the labour market, were compelled to steal for want of money and employment.

Analyses of the statistics, and the content of indictments and surviving
depositions, taken together with a variety of other evidence suggest two
things. First, enlistment in time of war removed those persons from the
community who most commonly were indicted for property offences in
times of peace, namely young men in their late teens and early twenties.
Such young men seem to have been particularly vulnerable to the temptation of criminal activity for a variety of reasons. During the eighteenth
century young men in their late teens and early twenties were often living-
in apprentices or servants of different sorts. Some may have been tempted
into crime to acquire money to support their leisure activities and to establish a degree of independence alongside their peers in these difficult waiting

years before full independence as a labourer or artisan; in 1797 John Crow, aged 16, admitted to Constable Joseph Putt of the Borough Police Office that he had taken three bushels of coal from a barge 'to get a few shillings to keep the holidays with'.[38] Some absconded or were thrown out by their masters and were, in consequence, unable to use the local employment market; their existence became, at least for a while, marginal; they were forced to move on looking for work, vagrants were invariably eyed with suspicion and the labelling process of 'vagrant' equals 'thief' could become self-fulfilling. The fact that war removed such young men was not lost on contemporaries. As the American War of Independence closed, George III expressed concern that 'the number of idle persons that this peace will occasion' would increase the number of highwaymen; and in the summer of 1795 the *Leicester Journal* commented: 'At Lincoln there is but one prisoner for trial [at the Assizes]; at Cambridge not any; and at Norwich during the last year, there have been but six persons. This, at least, is one benefit arising from the war [against Revolutionary France]'.[39] Second, it was often only when these young men were removed from the community that the impact of dearth becomes really apparent in the figures for theft; in years of dearth, which coincided with war, figures for indictments for property crime can be seen to go up and married men and women, for whom wheat prices were of vital importance to the family budget, became more evident among the accused.[40] Yet there is a problem, as yet scarcely analysed, which may undermine this war/theft relationship, namely the number of young men who were apprehended in wartime but who, before any indictment was preferred against them, were encouraged or pressurised to enlist. Figures are fragmentary, yet there appear to have been very large numbers recruited in this way, indeed numbers quite possibly sufficient to account for the drop in indictments for theft in wartime.[41] Lastly, while it would be difficult to prove or to quantify, it is possible that the eighteenth-century newspaper press played a role at least in reinforcing concern about crime at the end of wars. When peace came the newspapers found themselves with space to fill because of a decline in exciting, foreign, war news; crime stories were exciting and possibly increased reporting of crime helped to generate increased fears which, in turn, generated decisions to launch prosecutions against offenders as a warning to others. Significantly the Colchester 'crime wave' of 1765, which was certainly reinforced by press reporting, came in the aftermath of war.[42]

The sharp increase in the crime figures for the period following the Napoleonic Wars, and which continued until the middle of the century, is well known, though not thoroughly explained. The committal statistics

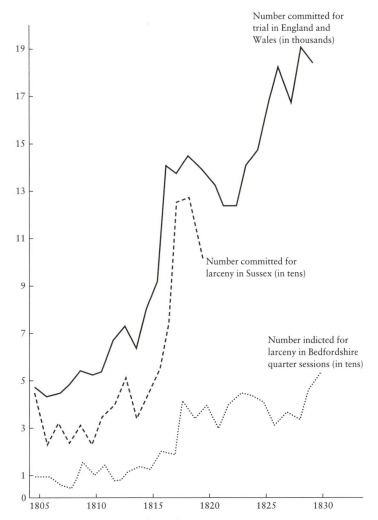

FIGURE 2.1 *Crime patterns in the early nineteenth century*

Source: Based on figures in *Parliamentary Papers*, Sussex gaol calendars (my thanks to Steve Wilson for these) and Bedfordshire indictments. For the increasing trend 1805–18, county by county, see *P.P.* 1819 (585) VIII *Select Committee on Criminal Laws*, Appendix I, vii

published by the government show an increase of nearly seven times between 1805 and 1842 – the latter year seeing the peak of committals for the period, 31,309 of them. The increase in population was enormous during these years but, at about eighty per cent, it was well below the increase measured in the crime statistics.[43] Moreover the crime increase seems to have been as marked in predominantly rural counties, like Bedfordshire and Sussex, as it was overall (Figure 2.1). The statistics show a steady level until 1811, followed by an upward trend especially marked by the post-war peaks in 1817 and 1819. After a brief decline there is a steady upward movement resuming in the mid-1820s to the peak in 1832. Again there is a brief decline followed by another upswing to the all-time peak of 1842, then a further decline followed by an upswing to the lesser peak of 1848. What is especially noticeable about the peaks of committals in the first half of the nineteenth century is how they coincide with years marked by economic depression and political unrest. Several historians and social scientists have commented on the way in which crime appears to increase during times of concern about popular disorder.[44] The correlation suggests, first, that victims might have been more ready to prosecute because of the general feeling of insecurity, second, that offenders were more inclined to steal because of economic hardship, and possibly, third, that the political unrest momentarily weakened some of the usual inhibitors which discouraged theft. None of these hypotheses can be proved, but they warrant some further discussion. A further element also merits some consideration: the end of the eighteenth and the beginning of the nineteenth centuries saw a marked increase in the number of dedimuses obtained annually by magistrates in England and Wales. In part this increase may be accounted for by new commissions of the peace issued to each county following the accession of a new monarch; but from about 150 dedimuses a year from the mid 1760s to the end of the 1780s, the annual average increased generally to over 200 with peaks of about 300 at the accession of George IV and 400 at the accession of William IV. More active justices meant more men available to hear complaints and issue warrants.[45]

A new level of awareness and concern about popular disorder can be detected among the propertied classes in the aftermath of the Gordon Riots of 1780; it continued through the years of war against Revolutionary and Napoleonic France – years punctuated by rioting in response to food shortages, high prices and recruiting demands. The concern among the propertied was aggravated, probably, by lurid reports of street massacres and guillotinings in France as well as by the demands, and less often, the menaces of British Jacobins; this concern did not end with the defeat of France. The thirty years following Waterloo were themselves punctuated by rioting sparked by both economic and political motives; they also witnessed mass demonstrations calling for a variety of reforms, and peaceful or not, these demonstrations provoked fears. Also after the wars Britain's propertied classes peered with fascinated horror at the burgeoning slums of, particularly, the new industrial cities. The late 1830s and the 1840s were the years of the most acute anxiety; it fed on economic depression as well as the radical and industrial agitation which culminated in 1842 with the second Chartist petition and the Plug Plot. H. A. Frégier coined the term 'les classes dangereuses' in 1840; and while the Parisian poor may, in the event, have been far more dangerous to the bourgeoisie than any of their British counterparts, Frégier's term was rapidly anglicised and taken over by British men of property as much to define their fears as any social group lurking in the city slums.[46] Alongside the concern about disorder there were changing attitudes to the poor and irritation among the propertied at having to dig deeper into their pockets to find money to finance, first, the wars against France, and second, the poor rates which were aggravated by the wars. Peace brought an end to income tax, but the rapid demobilisation of the armed forces and the restructuring of major sectors of the economy from war to peace, meant little reduction in the poor rates and often quite the reverse. It was during the wars that the Reverend Thomas Malthus had published his *Essay on the Principle of Population as it affects the Future Improvement of Society*. The *Essay*, running through several editions and an enlargement, presented a pessimistic picture of the poor, implying that it was their own improvidence and immorality that led to problems of over-population, food shortages and, consequently, to high poor rates. While Malthus's arguments did not go unchallenged, they manifestly convinced many.[47] However, any simple equation that prosecutions were greater in times of popular unrest because gentlemen of property were increasingly concerned about such unrest and increasingly suspicious of, and irritated by the poor, falls down on the evidence of the very large number of humble prosecutors. A combined anxiety involving popular disorder and crime in the first half of the nineteenth century does not appear to have stopped at class divides.

The debate on the standard of living of the early nineteenth-century working class is a historical controversy that has run and run; but whether or not the overall standard of living declined or improved, there is no question that there were periods of serious distress for large numbers of the population. Around a quarter of a million men were demobilised on to a contracting labour market at the end of the wars in 1814 and 1815. The wartime boom in agriculture came to an abrupt end while unemployment became acute in industrial districts which, like the coal and iron districts of Shropshire, had been geared up for war production. Matters were compounded by the repeal, in 1814, of the Elizabethan Statute of Artificers and Apprentices. Legislation over the preceding half century had whittled away at the statute; the repeal removed the last protection for artisans against the employment of cheap labour.[48] The years up to the middle of the century witnessed cycles of economic booms and slumps. The slump of the late 1830s and early 1840s was the nadir; 1842 was possibly the worst year for unemployment in the entire century with thousands, especially in the urban areas of the northern industrial districts, compelled to sell or pawn their possessions and to rely on charity, soup kitchens or the New Poor Law. On the land the agricultural worker, increasingly distanced from his employer, was in at least as unfavourable a situation as his urban counterpart in the succession of crises. The decline of protection for, and supervision of, young males which resulted from the repeal of the Statute of Artificers and the continuing decline of living-in conditions for both urban and rural workers, probably strengthened the forces pushing young men into a marginal existence in their early years of adulthood. But the peaks of committals, coinciding with the depths of the economic depressions, suggest that some offenders stole to keep body and soul together. David Philips noted among those committed in the Black Country during the 1830s and 1840s, an increase in the numbers of adults in their late twenties and thirties in the depression years, which suggests people turning to illegal activity when jobs and money were short.[49] A confession that protested hunger and poverty in mitigation quite probably was an attempt to get more lenient treatment, but it might still have been the truth and the incidence of such confessions is striking. At the Old Bailey in December 1816, for example, sixteen-year-old William Dennison admitted stealing a coat: 'I do not wish to add falsehood to fraud, I own I took the coat, but it was from mere distress.' John Waldon, who worked from time to time for a cabinet maker admitted stealing a stool that he had been instructed to deliver: 'The distress of my family caused me to act as I did. I was going along with the stool as my master had desired, and the gentleman asked me if I would sell it, and I did.' Twenty years later Sarah Field admitted pawning some of her widowed landlady's possessions: 'It was through distress – I meant to take them out the next day.'[50] In rural Bedfordshire in the spring of 1819, as the worst of the post-war depression came to an end, Thomas Parkins was indicted for stealing two faggots from the property of the Honourable William Waldergrave of Cardington: 'I was in great distress, my Wife near lying in, I went to get a faggot, to make her a bit of fire.' The following year two men and a boy were indicted for stealing fowls, ten bushels of soot, and a bridle from a farmer. 'I was in distress' protested William King, 'I had neither money nor victuals, and was forced to do something . . . I was going about the country to look for work.' 'I could get no work,' declared fellow offender John Gascoigne, 'nor any victuals and was driven to it . . . we were to have ten pence a bucket for the soot . . . we roasted one of the fowls under a hedge.' In 1822, John Stone of Leicester was prosecuted for stealing a watch:

I am a poor Stocking Weaver in distress. I was travelling into Leicestershire, after having been to London to offer myself for a soldier; but was not tall enough. My parents are in distress, my Father out of employment. I have eight brothers and sisters . . .

The voluntary statements of two of the three men charged in 1830 with stealing two smock frocks from a Dunstable draper put another slant on the motives of such petty offenders – John Morgan: 'I was very much distressed and I done it for the purpose of being taken up'; James Lilburn: 'I was very much distressed and did it to be taken up.'[51]

The incidence of this kind of protest by the accused and the known plight of poor labourers in the early nineteenth century prompted George Rudé to suggest that historians divide crime into three main categories for analysis: '(1) *acquisitive* crime; (2) "social" or "survival" crime; and (3) *protest* crime, or protest made in breach of the law'.[52] There are several problems with this. Rudé himself noted the difficulty of fitting '*some* violent crimes' (my italics) into the scheme. But the squalid nature and apparent petty causes of the overwhelming majority of violent crimes raise the question as to whether the scheme is at all applicable to crime against the person with the exception of poaching affrays and other major disorders that could fit under the 'protest' crime category. But even applied solely to property crime the scheme has problems. It has already been suggested that a plea of poverty may have been true; it may also have been false. Can a historian always determine whether a crime is either 'acquisitive' or 'survival' in origin? Is it not possible for an offence to be both? In January 1766 Sarah Plint, otherwise Anne Price, was prosecuted at the Old Bailey by William Thompson, an engraver, for stealing bed linen and other property from the room where she lodged. A single woman living alone in a single lodging room in eighteenth-century London was likely to be on the margin of existence, but Plint/Price was noted in court for having a string of aliases and for having been twice tried for similar offences; she was found guilty and sentenced to seven years' transportation. In January 1801, John Brand was prosecuted at the Old Bailey by John Gregory, his master a potato merchant, for stealing 63 lbs of potatoes. Brand protested:

I have a large family, and every necessary of life is excessively dear; and it is in the habit of the trade to allow men potatoes for their family's use; I was taking these home for that purpose.

Gregory responded: 'I paid him sixteen shillings a week, besides potatoes for his family's use, whenever he asked for them.' On the occasion of the theft Brand made no such request; the jury accepted Gregory's word. Rudé himself gives several examples of men and women accused of petty thefts – thefts which, at first glance, might appear to have been 'survival crimes' – who, when they were apprehended, had pockets full of pawn tickets; of course 'survival' may have prompted their action but this suggests that for some petty offenders the practice of stealing and pawning was becoming a habit.[53]

If hard times on occasions prompted people to steal, they might also have prompted the poorer victim to lash out with a prosecution when, in better times, he or she might have been prepared to compound the offence or even ignore it. The working man who lost his tools, some clothing, foodstuffs, or money through theft was, like the offender, unquestionably more vulnerable to economic pressure in lean years.

Much crime during the first half of the nineteenth century was, without question, 'acquisitive'; even some of that which might, at first glance, be presumed 'protest' or 'survival'. Some sheep theft, for example, was well organised and involved large numbers of animals over large distances,[54] all of which suggests enterprise and planning rather than simply the promptings of hunger and unemployment or a desire for revenge on a particular farmer. Furthermore, one of the few seasonal studies of crime has shown that while there was a peak in both summary and indictable crime in the dead season of winter when little employment was available for agricultural workers and groups like building workers, there was also an August and autumn peak at precisely the moment when employment was at its peak: the indictable offences for the August and autumn peak were less than those for winter, but summary offences were about equal. Summary offences generally encompassed the theft of growing crops and such crops were, of course, most available in the late summer and autumn; but some indictable offences were also of this type.[55] The mobility of summertime fairs and of harvest time also provided opportunities for petty theft; and the fear of criminality among mobile workers encouraged the possessors of property to be wary of itinerant strangers.

Overall, the larceny statistics for the second half of the nineteenth century also show some correlation between the peaks of offences known to the police and the years of high unemployment and need. But V. A. C. Gatrell has pinpointed a significant structural change between the two halves of the century. After the 'hungry forties' the working class rarely had to contend with the coincidence of high food prices and economic depression which so marked certain years of the late eighteenth and early nineteenth centuries. This was due, in part, to a rise in the export market for industrial goods which enabled firms to offset short-term contractions in the home market. At the same time stable, even declining, food prices helped many sections of the working class to ride out short-term periods of unemployment. Together, Gatrell suggests, these elements help to explain the overall decline in theft and violence in the second half of the nineteenth century: put at its simplest, during this period the poor became less habituated to theft because they were less subjected to periods of severe unemployment coinciding with serious subsistence problems. In addition, the growth and the professionalisation of the new police probably had some deterrent effect; the destruction of the rookeries for urban improvements removed some of the most impenetrable Alsatias; the Vagrancy Acts meant a stricter supervision of the casual poor.[56] It might also be urged here that, if indeed there is a link between people's fear of popular disorder and the fear about crime which, in turn, leads to more prosecutions, then a decrease in such fears might, in turn, lead to less prosecutions for petty crime. While there may have been periodic concerns about the dangerous classes during the second half of the nineteenth century, the anxieties never appear to have been as acute as in the preceding half century.

The statistics discussed so far have generally been those relating to property offences. It was offences against the person, sometimes involving robbery and sometimes not, which provided the most spectacular and terrifying images of criminality during the eighteenth and nineteenth centuries: the Ratcliffe Highway murders, which left two families gashed and bludgeoned to death in the East End of London in December 1811 and which sent ripples of fear throughout the country; the metropolitan garrotting panics of the mid-1850s and 1862, which set a trend for describing a variety of robberies in London and the provinces as 'garrottings' – on one occasion, even an attempted suicide was so described; the butchery of Jack the Ripper in East London in the autumn of 1888, which also reverberated in the provinces.[57]

Homicide is the most dramatic crime of violence, and it is generally acknowledged that, for a variety of reasons, it is probably among the most frequently reported offences. The statistics for homicide are therefore probably closer to the real level of the offence. However, the extent to which homicide levels can be taken as a guide to the overall level of interpersonal violence is anyone's guess. While people were concerned about homicide throughout the eighteenth and nineteenth centuries, it was never a statistically significant offence. Anxiety about murder and a perceived increase in violent robbery in London led to more severe legislation in 1752, but there were only ten convictions for murder during the year and

TABLE 2.2 *Homicides in Wiltshire, 1752–96*

Homicides committed:

(a) by parent(s)	42 (33.3%)	(includes 31 infanticides of illegitimate offspring)
(b) by spouse	4 (3.1%)	(includes 1 wife killing husband)
(c) by other member of family	7 (5.5%)	
(d) by person(s) clearly known to victim	11 (8.7%)	(includes 7 apprentices dying as a result of treatment received from master or mistress)
(e) as a result of fighting	14 (11.1%)	
(f) during robbery	4 (3.1%)	
(g) during riot	3 (2.3%)	
(h) by person unknown	17 (13.4%)	(12 of which appear to involve the murder of unwanted illegitimate babies)
(j) in unspecified situation	24 (19%)	(though fighting or acquaintance between the victim and the perpetrator appears probable in several instances)
Total	126	

Source: Based on the evidence in R. F. Hunnisett (ed.), *Wiltshire Coroners' Bills 1752–1796*, Wiltshire Record Society, xxxvi (1981)

this was exceptional; the annual average for murder convictions in London and Middlesex, between 1749 and 1771 was four.[58] An analysis of the Wiltshire coroners' bills between 1752 and 1796 reveals that murder as part of robbery was very rare in the county, and even when the large number of infanticides are removed from the figures, most homicides can be seen to have been committed within the family or among people known to each other (Table 2.2). In Victorian England the homicide rate reached 2 per 100,000 of the population only once, in 1865; generally it hovered around 1.5 per 100,000 falling to rarely more than 1 per 100,000 at the end of the 1880s and declining still further with the new century. In round figures this means that between 1857 and 1890 there were rarely more than 400 homicides reported to the police each year, and during the 1890s the average was below 350. Moreover, a closer look at Victorian homicides reveals that, while the fear may have centred around being murdered by a burglar or a similarly ferocious member of the 'dangerous classes', in most homicides assailant and victim were known to each other, and often they were related; the very high arrest rate in cases of malicious wounding reported to the police would appear to stem partly from the same cause.[59] Figure 2.2 is a breakdown of all the homicides and attempted homicides

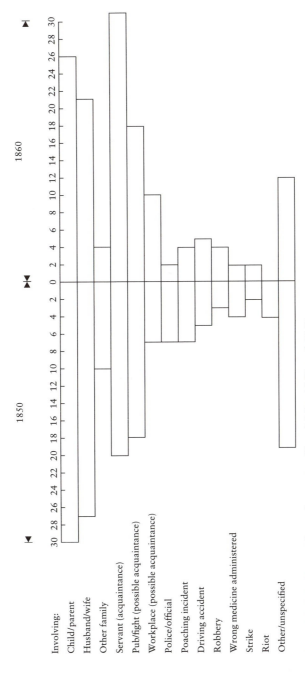

FIGURE 2.2 *Homicides and attempted homicides, 1850 and 1860*

reported in *The Times* for England and Wales during the years 1850 and 1860. The years have a significance to the extent that they both witnessed grisly murders carried out by robbers, murders which prompted many column inches in the press. The Reverend G. E. Hollest was murdered in his house at Frimley, Surrey, by burglars in the autumn of 1850, an incident which prompted considerable concern and which was instrumental in the creation of the Surrey Constabulary. In August 1860 Mary Emsley, a seventy-year-old widow, was murdered by George Mullins, a former policeman, subsequently a plasterer who had done some work for the victim and who robbed her after the murder.[60] Yet such murders, by strangers and by persons out for gain, were exceptional. Far more common were mothers accused of killing or attempting to kill their children (twenty-two in 1850 and eighteen in 1860) and husbands killing or attempting to kill their wives (twenty-two in 1850 and nineteen in 1860). A detailed study of homicide in London over the period 1860 to 1900 has produced similar conclusions: the overwhelming majority of victims were known to their killer, and invariably were related.[61]

Yet few incidents of violence against the person went as far as homicide and a large number were never tried on indictment. Assault is a very broad category ranging from a threatening gesture to a savage attack which all but results in the victim's death. During the eighteenth century many cases of assault were pursued at civil law; in some instances a magistrate arbitrated between the parties negotiating a financial settlement, or he could require the assailant to enter into a recognisance to keep the peace either towards the victim, or the monarch's subjects in general. All of this makes estimating the scale of inter-personal violence extremely problematic.

Table 2.3 gives a breakdown of the assaults taken before the Bedfordshire magistrates every five years between 1750 and 1840 noting where the assailant was indicted and where he or she was simply required to enter into a recognisance to keep the peace; it must be noted that in the latter instances the 'assault' may have been purely verbal. Most striking here is the very high number of assaults on women, only one-third of which were prosecuted on indictment; nineteen of these sixty-one assaults were by husbands on their wives. Understandably perhaps, and in contrast to the attacks on women, about eighty-five per cent of attacks on authority, in the shape of constables or overseers of the poor, were indicted. In all, offences against the person constituted rather more than one-tenth of the statistics of crime available for the nineteenth century: about ten per cent of the committals made on indictments between 1834 and 1856; just over ten per cent of crimes known to the police between 1857 and the end of the

TABLE 2.3 Assaults in Bedfordshire based on indictments and recognisances every five years, 1750–1840

VICTIMS	ASSAILANTS																Total assailants
	Gentry		Professional		Farmer		Tradesman/artisans		Husbandman/gardener		Labourer/servant		Women		Unknown		
	I.	R.*	I.	R.	I.	R.	I.	R.	I.	R.	I.	R.	I.	R.	I.	R.	
Gentry	—	2	—	—	1	—	—	2	—	—	—	5	—	—	—	—	10
Professional	—	1	—	—	—	—	—	—	—	—	—	2	—	—	—	—	3
Farmer	—	—	—	—	—	1	1	1	—	1	—	8	—	—	—	—	12
Tradesman/artisan	—	—	—	—	—	—	1	6	—	1	4	6	—	—	2	2	22
Husbandman/gardener	—	—	—	—	—	—	—	—	—	—	—	—	—	—	—	—	
Labourers/servants (including gamekeepers)	—	1	1	—	—	1	3	2	1	—	11	7	3	—	—	1	31 (19 indictments)
Constables/overseers	—	1	—	—	—	—	3	1	—	1	21	2	2	—	3	—	34 (29 indictments)
Women	—	1	—	—	1	3	3	8	—	1	2	17	1	9	13	2	61† (20 indictments)
Children	—	—	—	—	—	1	—	1	—	2	—	—	—	—	2	—	6
Unknown	—	2	—	—	—	—	—	2	—	—	21	21	5	2	14	8	72
Total indictments/recognisances	—	8	1	—	2	6	11	23	1	6	59	68	11	11	34	13	

* I. indicates indictment, R. indicates recognisance
† 19 of these 61 cases specified husbands assaulting wives; there is one incident recorded in these years of a woman brought to court for assaulting her husband

century; and about fifteen per cent of summary committals in the second half of the century. Assaults on authority, in the shape of policemen, formed a significant percentage of nineteenth-century assaults and declined at a slower rate than common assault; they constituted about fifteen per cent of summary prosecutions for assault in the 1860s and about twenty-one per cent in the 1890s.[62] Probably many of these assaults were simply men – and the typical assailant in all varieties of assault was male – resisting arrest or obstructing the police in their duty; but others were horrific in their scale of viciousness, and it was not unknown for police constables to try to get their retaliation in first.[63]

A degree of physical punishment meted out to dependants seems to have been accepted, or at least tolerated, across social groups during the eighteenth and well into the nineteenth century; thus masters beat their servants, husbands their wives, parents their children. Yet there were limits. In 1786 a Bedfordshire magistrate wrote to the quarter sessions about William White of Westoning who he had committed to gaol for not finding sureties to keep the peace towards his wife, Mary:

the Man seems to have a savage stupid idea that he may beat his wife as much as he pleases provided he does not kill her: perhaps a little confinement may shew him the error and the Justices will do what is proper upon the occasion.

In 1802 William Long, a yeoman of Upper Stondon, was bound over to keep the peace towards one of his labourers, John West, after accusing West of helping himself to too much bread and cheese and then setting about him with a 'knotty stick made from a crab tree'.[64] Moreover the limits of tolerance appear to have been declining. While the statistics are problematic, a study of sentencing policies in Essex suggests that, at the end of the eighteenth and beginning of the nineteenth centuries, assailants were less likely to plead guilty, less likely to be acquitted and, if found guilty, less likely to receive a small, nominal fine and more likely to be imprisoned.[65] But there was still a long way to go; in 1847 an Essex farmer noted in his diary when he took his horse-whip to a servant-boy who had defrauded him of money.[66]

While the beating of servants was increasingly becoming unacceptable, few doubted the beneficial effects of a sound thrashing for naughty boys, but even here the evidence is contradictory. Some working-class parents, not known for gentleness towards their own children, often took strong exception to their children being beaten by teachers; yet others invited the local policeman in to chastise a difficult child.[67] Wife beating began to cause disquiet early in the Victorian period, at least in respectable middle-class circles, yet it appears to have been accepted as a fact of life in many working-class communities. And whatever the disquiet, even on the rare occasions when such treatment resulted in death, it was possible for a court to find mitigating circumstances. In 1850 Frederick Gilbert was acquitted of the manslaughter of his wife after it was noted in court that he was a good, sober workman and his wife had been a drunkard.[68] Nearly forty years later Robert Knowles, a respectable Preston butcher who had killed his wife with a kick from his steel-tipped clog, had the resulting charge of murder reduced to manslaughter, and was then recommended to mercy by the jury since his wife was a drunkard and 'a scandal to her sex'.[69] A study of violence between working-class men and women in London during the third quarter of the nineteenth century charts a decline in its incidence, possibly because of growing respectability and rising living standards which reduced stress on the male as the principal economic provider. Perhaps also the cult of respectability made wives even less likely to complain since such assaults were shameful, a sign of a lack of re-spectability; and in the growing suburbs assaults were less public, less likely to disturb the neighbours, while the bruising was less visible than on the crowded tenement stair.[70] The question remains, of course, as to what extent the pattern of violence between working-class men and women in London can be taken as typical for England and Wales. In Wales the pattern appears to have been similar with a decline from mid-century; however, women in Cardiff, Swansea and Newport were not bashful about the injuries inflicted on them and their children, parading them and embarrassing police-court officials with requests for help and summonses. In Preston, however, where, in the year before the First World War, the chairman of the police court used wife beating as a metaphor for the general level of crime, per-ception of a decline came only at the turn of the century.[71]

The cult of respectability may itself have contributed to one variety of homicide: of those children in Figure 2.2 allegedly killed by their mothers, at least four in 1850 and at least seven in 1860 died immediately after their birth and were illegitimate. These deaths, however, probably constituted only a tiny percentage of the incidence of infanticide during these years. Though, in general, homicide might be one of the best-reported crimes, infanticide was notoriously under-reported and rarely came before the criminal courts. It was difficult to get coroners to hold inquests on dead infants, and even when a coroner did register a verdict of murder the assizes jury was often reluctant to return a verdict indicating culpability on the mother's part.[72] Other cases, involving the deaths of older children, reveal appalling instances of neglect and ill-treatment, as in the case of Maria Hook who, aged four years, allegedly weighed only six pounds when she died following months of dreadful treatment by her step-mother.[73] The cases of family violence that reached the courts were, almost certainly, only the tip of a very nasty iceberg.

Drink was often remarked upon as a cause of violence in the family. In May 1850 Patrick Barry returned home drunk to his rooms in Jennings Buildings, Kensington, and proceeded to kick his wife to death.[74] Drink could be seen as a mitigating circumstance for the violent offender as in the case of Frederick Gilbert noted above. Far more commonly, however, and especially among earnest temperance reformers, drink was seen as a fundamental cause of all crime. The Reverend James Nugent, a chaplain of Liverpool Borough Prison, informed the House of Lords Select Committee on Intemperance in 1877 that nine out of ten of the convicts in that prison were there 'directly or indirectly through drink'. William Hoyle, a Lancashire cotton manufacturer and pillar of the temperance community, had published *Crime in England and Wales in the Nineteenth Century: an Historical and Critical Retrospect* the year before he appeared before the committee. He deployed statistics to demonstrate a direct correlation between the increase in crime and the increases in beer shops and public houses. Other witnesses were less zealous and suggested only a connection between crimes of violence and drink,[75] a connection explored in some detail in the sober historical analysis of Gatrell and Hadden. Placing the figures for assault and drunkenness alongside the business cycle, they have shown slight increases in these during years of prosperity suggesting that high wages and high employment led to a greater consumption of alcohol which, in turn, contributed to more violent crime. However, for the last quarter of the century in particular the overall trend in the statistics of both violent crime and drunkenness has been downwards. This may be explained, in part, by what contemporaries perceived as the civilisation or moralisation of the population; perhaps, indeed, the Victorian virtues of morality and probity, of good works and service to others, actually succeeded in reducing the level of harm to persons and property.[76] Perhaps also there was a decrease in anxiety about small-scale, drink-related vio-lence.[77] Such a decrease would link with the diminishing fears about the dangerous classes from the mid-nineteenth century which, it has been sug-gested above, contributed to a decline in the reporting, and the prosecu-tion, of small-scale theft. There is a further element worth considering. Much of the recent work on women's history has emphasised the notion of separate spheres and new ways of controlling women during the nineteenth century. It may be that the statistical decline in theft and, especially, violence in the second half of the nineteenth century is a reflection of a better socialisation of young, especially working-class males during this period, and that the physically aggressive behaviour regarded and accepted as traditionally masculine was being controlled and stigmatised to a greater extent than before.

While there seems to be an interplay between criminal statistics and periodic fears of crime and disorder, it is also probable that the collection and publication of national crime statistics led to the perception of crime as a national impersonal problem. During the eighteenth century, when there were no such statistics, crime was essentially a personal problem for victims and accused. Statistics made crime national and made the criminal a national bogeyman. Crime could now be shown to be offences perpetrated on a large scale against respectable people by a group which by being measured statistically – whatever the faults of the statistics – could be defined collectively as criminals or the criminal class. This perception of criminals as a group is the subject of the next chapter.

Notes and references

1 Quoted in **Eric Stockdale**, *A Study of Bedford Prison 1660–1877*, Phillimore, London, 1977, p. 130. The Reverend Philip Hunt who sent this warning to Peel might be considered as having been at least an accessory to what some would consider as one of the greatest thefts of the early nineteenth century; as chaplain to Lord Elgin he played a key role in the removal of the Elgin Marbles from the Acropolis.

2 **M. J. Cullen**, *The Statistical Movement in Early Victorian Britain: The foundations of empirical social research*, Harvester, Brighton, 1975, especially pp. 1–16 and 72–4. For a detailed introduction to nineteenth-century criminal statistics see **V. A C. Gatrell** and **T. B. Hadden**, 'Criminal statistics and their interpretation', in **E. A. Wrigley** (ed.), *Nineteenth-Century Society: Essays in the use of quantitative methods for the study of social data*, Cambridge U.P., Cambridge, 1972.

3 T. Barwick Lloyd Baker, 'Abstract and inferences founded upon the official returns of England and Wales for the years 1854–59, with special reference to the results of reformatories', *Journal of the Statistical Society*, xxiii (1860), pp. 427–54 (at pp. 436–7).

4 S. J. Stevenson, 'The "Criminal Class": Legislation, labelling and prosecution in the late nineteenth century'. Paper presented to Urban History Group, Economic History Society Conference, Cheltenham, 4 April 1986. For a more

extended treatment see *idem*, 'The "Criminal Class" in the mid-Victorian city: A study of policy conducted with special reference to those made subject to the provisions of 34 & 35 Vict. c.112 (1871) in Birmingham and East London in the early years of registration and supervision', unpublished D. Phil., Oxford University, 1983.

5 Patrick Colquhoun, *A Treatise on the Police of the Metropolis*, 3rd edn, 1796, p. vii.

6 U.C.L. Chadwick MSS 'Police Memoranda etc., undated (post 1850)', probably referring to the 1836–9 Royal Commission on Constabulary.

7 James T. Hammick, 'On the judicial statistics of England and Wales with special reference to recent returns relating to crime', *Journal of the Statistical Society*, xxx (1867), pp. 375–426 (at p. 392).

8 Clive Emsley, 'An aspect of Pitt's "terror": Prosecutions for sedition during the 1790s', *Social History*, 6 (1981), pp. 155–84; see also *idem*, 'Repression, "terror" and the rule of law in England during the decade of the French Revolution', *E. H. R.*, C (1985), pp. 801–25. Extrapolating from prosecutions in the West Country, Steve Poole estimates that there may have been as many as seven or eight times as many sedition prosecutions: S. R. Poole, 'Popular politics in Bristol, Somerset and Wiltshire, 1791–1801', unpublished Ph.D., University of Bristol, 1993, pp. 173–90.

9 Heather Shore, *Artful Dodgers: Youth and crime in early nineteenth-century London*, Boydell/Royal Historical Society, Woodbridge, 1999.

10 Peter King, 'Newspaper reporting, prosecution practice and perceptions of urban crime: The Colchester crime wave of 1765', *Continuity and Change*, 2 (1987), pp. 423–54.

11 Jennifer Davis, 'The London garrotting panic of 1862: A moral panic and the creation of a criminal class in mid-Victorian England', in V. A. C. Gatrell, Bruce Lenman and Geoffrey Parker (eds), *Crime and the Law: The social history of crime in Western Europe since 1500*, Europa, London, 1980, p. 205.

12 Cullen, *Statistical Movement*, p. 14. The committees were: the Select Committee on Criminal Commitments and Convictions and the Select Committee on the Police of the Metropolis.

13 Beds. R.O. QEV 4.

14 'Discrepant criminal statistics', *Journal of the Statistical Society*, xxxi (1868), pp. 349–53 (at p. 352).

15 See the discussion in Jennifer Davis, 'Law breaking and law enforcement: The creation of a criminal class in mid-Victorian London', unpublished Ph.D., Boston College, 1984, pp. 137–9, 152–8 and 246–51.

16 H.O. 45.9755. A60557.

17 William Douglas Morrison, *Crime and its Causes*, London, 1891, p. 6.

18 For this legislation see below, pp. 191–2.

19 Perhaps the first such offender to be prosecuted was Micah Gibbs, a gentleman of Wellow who was found guilty by the Somerset quarter sessions in October 1800 of producing fraudulent certificates to the tax commissioners at Bath. He was fined £200 and sentenced to four months in Ilchester Gaol where he was to remain until the fine was paid. Somerset R.O. QS Minute Book CQ2 2/4(3).

20 Susan S. M. Edwards, 'Sex crimes in the nineteenth century', *New Society*, 13 September 1979, pp. 562–3. Before 1875 it was a felony to have sexual intercourse with a child aged ten or under, but only a misdemeanour with a child between ten and twelve years.

21 E. G. Du Cane, 'The decrease of crime', *Nineteenth Century*, xxxiii (1893), pp. 480–92 (at p. 485); William Douglas Morrison, 'The increase of crime', *Nineteenth Century*, xxxi (1892), pp. 950–7 (at pp. 951–2).

22 Du Cane, 'The decrease of crime', p. 485.

23 K. K. Macnab, 'Aspects of the history of crime in England and Wales between 1805–60', unpublished Ph.D., University of Sussex, 1965, p. 347. Macnab does remark that the decline is 'rather suspicious'.

24 David Philips, *Crime and Authority in Victorian England*, Croom Helm, London, 1977, pp. 132–5 and 146.

25 J. J. Tobias, *Crime and Industrial Society in the Nineteenth Century*, Penguin edn, Harmondsworth, 1972, ch. 2 and appendix; quotations from pp. 25 and 19 respectively.

26 Morrison, *Crime and its Causes*, ch. 4.

27 Philips, *Crime and Authority*, p. 20.

28 Thorsten Sellin, 'The significance of the records of crime', *Law Quarterly Review*, lvx (1951), pp. 489–504.

29 See, *inter alia*, Jason Ditton, *Contrology: Beyond the new criminology*, Macmillan, London, 1979, especially ch. 2. For the most prolonged and sophisticated argument in favour of using statistics for the study of eighteenth-century crime see J. M. Beattie, *Crime and the Courts in England 1660–1800*, Oxford U.P., Oxford, 1986.

30 Rob Sindall, *Street Violence in the Nineteenth Century: Media panic or real danger*, Leicester U.P., London, 1990, p. 26.

31 J. M. Beattie, 'Judicial records and the measurement of crime in eighteenth-century England', in Louis A. Knafla (ed.), *Crime and Criminal Justice in Europe and Canada*, Wilfred Launier U.P., Waterloo, Ontario, 1981, p. 138.

32 Douglas Hay, 'War, dearth and theft in the eighteenth century: The record of the English courts', *P and P*, 95 (1982), pp. 117–60: quotation at pp. 159 and 151 respectively.

33 Peter King, *Crime, Justice and Discretion in England 1740–1820*, Oxford U.P., Oxford, 2000, ch. 5 especially, quotation at p. 134.

34 V. A. C. Gatrell, 'The decline of theft and violence in Victorian and Edwardian England', in Gatrell, Lenman and Parker (eds), *Crime and the Law*, p. 248.

35 Howard Taylor, 'Rationing crime: The political economy of criminal statistics since the 1850s', *Economic History Review*, li (1998), pp. 569–90; *idem*, 'The politics of the rising crime statistics of England and Wales, 1914–1960', *Crime, histoire & sociétés/Crime, history & societies*, 2 (1998) pp. 5–28; Robert M. Morris, ' "Lies, damned lies, and criminal statistics": Reinterpreting the criminal statistics in England and Wales', *Crime, histoire & sociétés/Crime, history & societies*, 5 (2001) pp. 111–27.

36 J. M. Beattie, 'The criminality of women in eighteenth-century England', *Journal of Social History*, viii (1975), pp. 80–116; *idem, Crime and the Courts*, pp. 243–8; David Jones, *Crime, Protest, Community and the Police in Nineteenth-Century England*, RKP, London, 1982, pp. 132–4; King, *Crime, Justice and Discretion*, especially ch. 8; Macnab, 'Aspects of crime', especially pp. 59 and 341–8; Philips, *Crime and Authority*, pp. 147–50, 151–2.

37 Hay, 'War, dearth and theft', p. 146 and note 78.

38 *O.B.S.P.* 1796–97, no. 335, p. 321.

39 Sir John Fortescue (ed.), *The Correspondence of George III*, 6 vols, London, 1928 vi, p. 387; *Leicester Journal*, 24 July 1795. *The Gentleman's Magazine* commented in November 1772; 'It is worthy of observation, that during the two last years of the last war, viz. 1759, 1760, the number of criminals condemned at the Old Bailey amounted to 29 only, and the days of the Judges' attendance to 46; but that during the two last years of peace, viz. 1770, 1771, the number of criminals condemned have amounted to 151, and the days of the Judges' attendance to 99' (xlii, 541). For similar contemporary concern see Hay, 'War, dearth and theft', pp. 138 and 142.

40 Hay, 'War, dearth and theft', *passim*.

41 King, *Crime, Justice and Discretion*, pp. 156–7.

42 King, 'Newspaper reporting, prosecution practice and perceptions of urban crime'.

43 Macnab, 'Aspects of Crime', especially appendices 1 and 2.

44 T. R. Gurr, *Rogues, Rebels and Reformers: A political history of crime and conflict*, Sage, Beverly Hills, California, 1976, p. 10; Abdul Lodhi and

Charles Tilly, 'Urbanisation, crime and collective violence in nineteenth-century France', *American Journal of Sociology*, 79 (1973), pp. 296–318 (at p. 296); J. A. Sharpe, *Crime in Early Modern England 1550–1750*, 2nd edn, Longman, London, 1999, pp. 263–68.

45   Norma Landau, *The Justices of the Peace, 1679–1760*, University of California Press, Berkeley and Los Angeles, 1984, p. 395.

46   See the discussion in Gertrude Himmelfarb, *The Idea of Poverty: England in the early Industrial Age*, Faber and Faber, London, 1984, pp. 393–7.

47   Clive Emsley, *British Society and the French Wars 1793–1815*, Macmillan, London, 1979; Himmelfarb, *The Idea of Poverty*, especially pp. 100–44; Joseph Lowe, *The Present State of England in Regard to Agriculture, Trade, and Finance*, 2nd edn, London, 1823, pp. 210–24.

48   John Rule, *The Experience of Labour in Eighteenth-Century Industry*, Croom Helm, London, 1981, pp. 95–6 and 114–19.

49   Philips, *Crime and Authority*, pp. 145–6 and 163–4.

50   *O.B.S.P. 1816–17*, no. 20, p. 11 and no. 73, p. 38; in both instances the jury recommended mercy: in Dennison's case judgment was respited; Walden was fined 1 shilling and discharged. *C.C.C.S.P. 1836–37*, no. 64, pp. 80–1; Field, also recommended to mercy, was imprisoned for one month.

51   Beds. R.O. QSR 24/271; QSR 24/229; QSR 25/324; QSR 1830/409.

52   George Rudé, *Criminal and Victim: Crime and society in early nineteenth-century England*, Clarendon Press, Oxford, 1985, p. 78 and ch. 5 *passim*.

53   *O.B.S.P. 1765–66*, no. 84; *O.B.S.P. 1800–1*, no. 105, p. 77; Rudé, *Criminal and Victim*, p. 93.

54   John Rule, 'The manifold causes of rural crime: sheep-stealing in England c. 1740–1840', in John Rule (ed.), *Outside the Law: Studies in crime and order 1650–1850*, Exeter Papers in Economic History no. 15, University of Exeter, 1982; R. A. E. Wells, 'Sheep-rustling in Yorkshire in the age of the Industrial and Agricultural Revolutions', *Northern History*, xx (1984), pp. 127–45.

55   Janet Gyford, ' "Men of Bad Character": Property crime in Essex in the 1820s', unpublished M.A., University of Essex, 1982, pp. 63–5.

56   Gatrell, 'Decline of theft and violence', pp. 305–16; Gatrell expresses scepticism about that area upon which 'the Victorians were prone to congratulate themselves . . . most' when noting a decline in crime, namely the assault on juvenile crime from the 1850s (pp. 305–7).

57   T. A. Critchley and P. D. James, *The Maul and the Pear Tree: The Ratcliffe Highway Murders 1811*, Constable, London, 1971, pp. 79 and 96–7; Davis, 'London garrotting panic', p. 205; Sindall, *Street Violence*, especially ch. 4 which emphasises the metropolitan nature of the garrotting panic and the role

of the press in fostering it. Sindall also notes that the statistics indicate a greater incidence of street violence in the north west than in London.

Sir Robert Anderson publicly blamed 'the sensation-monger of the newspaper press' for the scare created by Jack the Ripper in 'Our absurd system of punishing crime', *Nineteenth Century*, xlix (1901), pp. 268–84 (at p. 269). However, Anderson's own role in the Ripper affair (as head of the C.I.D.) was hardly distinguished.

58 **John H. Langbein**, 'Shaping the eighteenth-century criminal trial: A view from the Ryder sources', *University of Chicago Law Review*, 50 (1983), pp. 1–136 (at pp. 44–6). For a discussion of homicide during the eighteenth century see Beattie, *Crime and the Courts*, pp. 77–124.

59 Gatrell, 'Decline of theft and violence', pp. 286–95 and appendices A1 and A2.

60 See, *inter alia*, *The Times*, 2, 3, 5, 8, 14, 19 October 1850; 18, 20, 22, 23, 25, 27 August 1860; and 24, 26, 27 October 1860; **T. A. Critchley**, *A History of Police in England and Wales*, 2nd edn, Constable, London, 1978, p. 98. Although her murder was shocking, Mary Emsley was manifestly not everyone's favourite old lady. Detective Inspector Thornton, in charge of the murder investigation, reported that she 'was possessed of considerable house property situated in very low neighbourhoods of Bethnal Green, Ratcliffe, Stratford, Barking, Dagenham etc., and she was in the habit of personally collecting the greater portion of her rents on a Monday and in consequence of her frequent litigation with her tenants, her very plain way of dressing and living, she became well known at the East End of London'. According to her solicitor she had been threatened by tenants. Neither was she popular with her own family having told them that she intended to leave all her money to build almshouses. M.E.P.O. 3/62.

61 **Philippe Chassaigne**, 'Le crime de sang à Londres à l'époque victorienne: Essai d'interprétation des modèles de violence', *Histoire, économie, société*, 4 (1993), pp. 507–24; and for more detail see *idem*, 'Le meurtre à Londres à l'époque victorienne: Structures socials et comportements criminels, 1857–1900', Thèse de Doctorat, Université de Paris IV, 1991.

62 Gatrell and Hadden, 'Criminal statistics', pp. 269–71; Gatrell, 'Decline of theft and violence', pp. 284–95 and appendix A5.

63 **Clive Emsley**, *The English police: A political and social history*, 2nd edn, Longman, London, 1996, pp. 75 and 231–2.

64 Beds. R.O. QSR 15/191, and QSR 18/67.

65 **Peter King**, 'Punishing assault: The transformation of attitudes in the English Courts', *Journal of Interdisciplinary History*, xxvii (1996) pp. 43–74.

66 Essex R.O. D/DBs F 38 Bretnall's Diary, entry for 10 November 1847 (quoted in Gyford, 'Men of Bad Character', p. 15).

67 Stephen Humphries, *Hooligans or Rebels? An oral history of working-class childhood and youth 1889–1939*, Basil Blackwell, Oxford, 1981, pp. 82–9; Emsley, *The English Police*, p. 80.

68 *The Times*, 7 April 1850.

69 A. James Hammerton, *Cruelty and Companionship: Conflict in nineteenth-century married life*, Routledge, London, 1992, pp. 34–5.

70 Nancy Tomes, 'A "torrent of abuse": Crimes of violence between working-class men and women in London 1840–1875', *Journal of Social History*, xi (1978), pp. 328–45.

71 David J. V. Jones, *Crime in Nineteenth-Century Wales*, University of Wales Press, Cardiff, 1992, pp. 82–3; Hammerton, *Cruelty and Companionship*, p. 42.

72 See below, pp. 102–4.

73 *The Times*, 14 August 1850.

74 *The Times*, 23 May 1850.

75 *P.P.* 1877 (418) xi, *Select Committee of the House of Lords on Intemperance. Third Report*, qq. 8327 and 8401–11. The Earl of Onslow, for one, was not convinced by Hoyle's use of statistics and asked him: 'Do you not think it would be no very difficult matter to prove almost anything you wished to prove by judiciously manipulating statistics from various parts of the country?' (q. 8411).

76 Gertrude Himmelfarb, *The Demoralization of Society: From Victorian virtues to modern values*, Institute of Economic Affairs, London, 1995.

77 Gatrell and Hadden, 'Criminal statistics', pp. 370–1; Gatrell, 'Decline of theft and violence', pp. 291 and 300.

CHAPTER 3

Class perceptions

When Peel proposed the consolidation and rationalisation of the criminal law to parliament in 1826, he announced that he would begin with laws relating to felony:

because I consider the crime of theft to constitute the most important class of crime. There are acts no doubt of much greater malignity, of a much more atrocious character than the simple act of robbery; but looking at the committals and convictions for crime, it will at once be seen, that those for theft so far exceed the committals and convictions for any other species of offence, that there can be no question of its paramount importance in the catalogue of offences against society.

He explained that, in 1825, 14,437 persons had been charged with various crimes; some 12,500, or six-sevenths of those persons, had been charged with theft.[1] Throughout the eighteenth and nineteenth centuries theft of various sorts was the principal offence that occupied the time of the different courts. Most thefts were petty; only a very few involved large sums of money or objects of great monetary value; only a very few involved violence. It was the quantity rather than the quality of the offences which concerned people and, arguably, this has always been the case. But once the decision had been made, albeit unconsciously, to concentrate on quantity, rather than what might be termed 'quality' crime, other things followed. Most of the offenders brought before the courts for these crimes came from the poorer sections of society and, as a consequence as the discourse of 'class' became more and more central to the analysis and perception of society, so criminality tended to be seen as, essentially, a class problem.

Counterfactual history is fraught with danger, yet, if legislators and commentators on crime had concentrated on the few big thefts or embezzlements as their benchmark for crime, rather than on the very many small thefts and incidents of disorders, then the overall perception of criminality and of the criminal class would have been very different. This is not to say that there was a middle-class conspiracy during the nineteenth century when these perceptions developed. Concern about the poor and their 'immoral' or 'disorderly' behaviour went back a long way; J. A. Sharpe has well chronicled the criminalisation of the poor in the early modern period.[2] But, as has already been argued, fear of the poor reached a new peak in the aftermath of the French Revolution and with the experience of the fast-growing and teeming cities in the early nineteenth century. Crime was often perceived as another problem, like sanitation, within the burgeoning urban sprawls.

Of course it was recognised that men of wealth and social standing also committed offences. Throughout the nineteenth century there was concern about various forms of white-collar crime and corruption. At the close of 1843 the *Illustrated London News* gloomily predicted:

If we progress at the same rate for half a generation longer, commercial dishonesty will become the rule, and integrity the exception. On every side of us we see perpetually – fraud, fraud, fraud.[3]

Half a century later the author of an article on limited companies in the journal *Nineteenth Century* lamented that such organisations placed 'a premium upon dishonesty'.[4] It was common for novelists to portray corrupt bankers and businessmen – Bulstrode in *Middlemarch*, Merdle in *Little Dorrit*, Melmotte in *The Way We Live Now*. But such offenders, however common in fiction and in newspaper and journal literature, were not perceived as members of a criminal class and were categorised as 'criminal' with some difficulty, at least until the close of the nineteenth century when biological discourse began to rival class discourse in the analysis of crime and criminality. The illegal and/or immoral actions of white-collar offenders set a bad example to their social inferiors, but these offenders were 'rotten apples' within their social class.[5] It was a consoling distinction to which the middle and upper classes clung; offenders within their social milieu were exceptions and the criminal class was to be found located elsewhere. Poor clerks caught embezzling their employer's money were similarly not regarded as part of a criminal element with society. Public debate on such offences during the 1860s and 1870s concentrated on examining employer–clerk relations. The employers were criticised for not having a proper sense of business management and ensuring that their books balanced, for not providing a better system of surveillance over the clerks who could so easily be tempted by the large sums with which they often had to deal, and for paying the clerks a 'beggarly pittance' hardly commensurate with the trust and responsibility expected of them. 'We can't for a moment dispute the right of merchant princes paying what salaries they deem fit to their clerks', declared a Manchester journal, 'but we would ask, is the system of paying low salaries likely to conduce a high moral tone in the young men employed?'[6]

But if low wages and poverty were regarded as contributing to crime among clerks, this was rarely the case within lower social groups. Throughout the period 1750 to 1900 most experts and commentators went out of their way to deny any relationship between low wages, poverty and the bulk of crime. The main causes of crime were given as moral weakness, luxury, idleness, corrupting literature, parental neglect, and lack of education; any one, or any permutation of these were discussed and debated at length and given different emphases depending upon the prejudices and aspirations of the individuals concerned, and also upon the changing economic and social climate within which they were being presented.

Henry Fielding, novelist and Bow Street magistrate, believed that trade had changed the face of the nation. The old bonds of society had broken down and produced a dramatic alteration in:

the Manners, Customs, and Habits of the People, more especially of the lower Sort. The Narrowness of their Fortune is changed into Craft; their Frugality into Luxury; their Humility into Pride, and their Subjection into Equality.[7]

The increase in crime which prompted his *Enquiry* in 1751 was simply one manifestation of this. The too frequent and too expensive diversions among the lower sort had led to idleness, which, in turn, led 'the more simple and poor spirited betaking themselves to a State of Starving and Beggary, while those of more Art and Courage became Thieves, Sharpers, and Robbers'.[8] Besides proposing changes in the system of prosecution and punishment, Fielding included among his remedies tougher regulations for the drink trade and for drunkenness, for pawnbrokers, and to control vagabondage. He divided the poor into three categories; 'Such . . . as are able to work. Such as are able and willing to work. Such as are able to work, but not willing'.[9] The last category was the largest and Fielding was all for compelling this group to work. But if the idle and immoral poor committed most crimes, Fielding did not see crime simply in class terms. Crime was the result of immorality, but rich and poor occupied the same moral universe and a glance at any of Fielding's novels reveals that he perceived the wealthy and well-to-do to be as guilty of immorality and vice as the poor. In his novels Fielding could describe model magistrates like the honest and benevolent Squire Allworthy in *Tom Jones*; he also often included central characters whose very unworldliness left their virtue and dignity unassailable. Parson Adams, in *Joseph Andrews*, might be comic and quixotic but his virtues were those which an increasingly luxurious and sophisticated society were leaving further and further behind. Like John Gay in *The Beggar's Opera* before him, Fielding could satirise the King's leading minister by paralleling his career with that of a criminal. Sir Robert Walpole was known as 'The Great Man'; Fielding's Jonathan Wild was also 'Great' and one who, early on in the novel, compares the behaviour of the thief with that of the statesman:

how easy is the reflection of having taken a few shillings or pounds from a stranger, without any breach of confidence, or perhaps great harm to the person who loses it, compared to that of having betrayed a public trust, and ruined the fortunes of thousands, perhaps of a great nation.[10]

Such a comparison was to become possible only for radicals in the following century.[11] For Fielding, most crime was committed by the poor led astray by luxury; but crime, with its contributory drunkenness, idleness and poverty, were only symptoms of a deeper lying problem – a new kind of society with a value system rooted in self-interest and individualism. Not every eighteenth-century magistrate or minister agreed with his assessment of the deeper problems yet, in practical terms, control and supervision of the poor who committed crime seemed a possibility.

Fielding believed that the robber:

being too lazy to get his Bread by Labour, or too voluptuous to content himself with the Produce of that Labour, declares War against the Properties, and often against the Persons of his Fellow Subjects.[12]

Sir John Fielding, who took over as Chief Magistrate of Bow Street on Henry's death, was much concerned with the practicalities of fighting this 'war' – crime was located among a certain section of society and the fight had to be carried to them. In 1772, giving evidence before a House of Commons committee enquiring into burglaries and robberies in London, Sir John stated that the present 'gang' of housebreakers were the sons of 'unfortunate people, and of no trade'. He believed that they had started their criminal careers as child pickpockets and had graduated to housebreaking as they grew older 'in order to procure a greater income to supply their increased expenses'. He urged a strict regulation of ballad singers, 'a greater nuisance than Beggars, because they give opportunity to Pickpockets, by collecting people together'. These singers were capable of real work; their songs, moreover were 'generally immoral and obscene'. Even more important was a tighter control of public houses, some of which were kept by 'the most abandoned characters, such as bawds, thieves, receivers of stolen goods'; and all manner of offences were hatched in these establishments.[13]

In the same year that Sir John Fielding addressed the Commons Committee, Jonas Hanway, an influential London philanthropist, published his *Observations on The Causes of Dissoluteness which reigns among the lower Classes of the People*. Crime was not the chief concern of this pamphlet, nor of its much larger successor, *The Defects of Police, The Cause of Immorality and The Continual Robberies Committed Particularly in and about the Metropolis*, published in 1775. Hanway was alarmed by what he thought was an overall moral decline among all classes in what he termed as an 'age of pleasure'. Crime was one of the ways in which this lack of morality manifested itself among the lower classes. Like Henry Fielding, Hanway saw rich and poor as inhabitants of the same moral universe; if the former set a bad example, what could be expected of the latter? 'Whether in high life, or in low, if the desire for money rages in the breast, it is like a dropsy, increased by the gratification of a thirst'.[14] 'Concubinage' and the '*promiscuous commerce* of the sexes' was spreading downwards from those at the top of society who should have been setting a moral example; so also was a weakening of the bonds of 'filial piety'. People of all classes now disdained frugal fare and gorged themselves; the abuse of the liberty of the press by which newspapers printed 'falsehoods and nonsense', together with drinking and gambling all served to make matters worse. Sadly, also the county gentry were declining as gentlemen brought their families to London and indulged in extravagant expense rather than supervising their local poor. Hanway noted that most of those who were executed were young men; they had been 'either bred [as] thieves, or [had contracted] a habit of idleness, and following the example of men in superior life, [had grown] expensive'.[15] The problem here was that apprentices were being given too much freedom by their masters. '*Reading* and *thinking*, when they are not at work, and the habit of sober discipline, are much out of fashion:'[16]

I have good reason to believe there is scarce an apprentice boy, *turned of fifteen years of age, who, contrary to the practice of our forefathers, is*

not suffered to go abroad almost every night, as soon as the shop is shut.
These boys, and young men, challenge it as a kind of right; and if the
master is as dissipated as his servant, which is often the case, he takes
no thought, till he finds himself robbed; which I believe happens more
oftener than he discovers. You will easily conceive it next to impossible
the apprentice should wander abroad, without learning to drink strong
liquors: some go further, and game: many keep bad company: the society
of each other is dangerous. They neglect their Bible, and have as little
relish for a Common Prayer Book. Numbers become a prey to prostitutes,
and accelerate their ruin. Vice is costly: money must be supplied, let it
come from what quarter it may.[17]

Henry Fielding's *Enquiry* continued to be warmly recommended as the
best analysis of crime, its causes and remedies during the 1780s, particularly as the close of the American War of Independence appeared to result
in an increase in crime; it certainly resulted in an increase in indictments
and capital convictions. 'If robbers continue to increase, as they have done
for some time past', lamented the *St James's Chronicle* in November 1784,
'the number of those who rob will exceed that of the robbed'. Martin
Madan, who quoted the *Chronicle* in his *Thoughts on Executive Justice*,
believed that:

No civilized nation . . . has to lament, as we have, the daily commission
of the most dangerous and atrocious crimes, in so much that we cannot
travel the roads, or sleep in our houses, or turn our cattle into our fields,
without the most imminent danger of thieves and robbers. These are
increased to such a degree in numbers and audaciousness, that the day
is now little less dangerous than the night *to travel in . . .*[18]

It was not to be until more than forty years after Henry Fielding's *Enquiry*
that another major analysis of crime in London was attempted.

Patrick Colquhoun, former Lord Provost of Glasgow and one of the
first stipendiary magistrates to be appointed under the Middlesex Justices
Act of 1792, first published his *Treatise on the Police of the Metropolis*
anonymously in 1795. He shared Fielding's and Hanway's belief that
gaming among the young men of the 'middle and higher stations' set a bad
example to the 'lower ranks', an argument that recurred throughout the
nineteenth century. Colquhoun saw crime rooted in the luxurious living
and the improvidence of the poor. Unlike the more sensible 'middle ranks'
the poor indulged themselves with, for example, exotic seafood even when
prices were high; they had no notions of frugality and care. They spent too

much time in public houses, gaming and generally squandering more than they could afford:

Were we to examine the history of any given number of these our miserable fellow-mortals, it would be discovered that their distresses, almost in every instance, have been occasioned by extravagance, idleness, profligacy, and crimes: – and that their chief support is by gambling, cheating, and thieving in a little way.[19]

But if Colquhoun's image of the poor was, at first glance, reminiscent of Fielding's, his perception of society and the ultimate cause of the poor's behaviour was very different. Colquhoun had trade connections himself and the protection of commerce on the Thames was one of his prime interests; it prompted his other significant study of crime and police, *A Treatise on the Commerce and Police of the River Thames*. He gloried in the wealth and prosperity that trade had brought to the Thames, and thus to London and to the nation as a whole. Admittedly this wealth brought temptation, but the real problem was the breakdown of religion and moral rectitude among the poor. Some of this he attributed to deliberate subversion and, while he named no names, he clearly had the popular radicals and free thinkers among the English Jacobins in mind.[20] The remedy was to be found in better control and supervision of lower orders. He insisted that in parts of Europe there were not the burglars and highwaymen who could be found in England; the reason was to be found in:

a more correct and energetic system of Police, joined to an early and general attention to the employment, education, and morals of the lower orders of the people; a habit of industry and sobriety is thus acquired . . .[21]

Between 1795 and 1807 Colquhoun's Treatise on the *Police of the Metropolis* went through seven English editions and was considerably enlarged.[22] If such a publication history is a mark of success then, indeed, the book was a tremendous success. Colquhoun had his critics, notably over his assertion that moral deterioration and crime were getting worse; and others winced at what one critic termed his 'prudish political puritanism' which would seek to control the poor with an un-English system of police.[23] Yet he struck a chord with the propertied classes of the metropolis and elsewhere. Colquhoun had sympathy for people in dire distress and he organised soup kitchens for the 'industrious' poor of Spitalfields in the famine years of the 1790s, but the poor's problems in his estimation had no connection with a changing society; the poor suffered largely because of their own idleness and improvidence. 'Idleness is a neverfailing road to criminality. It originates generally in the inattention and the bad example of profligate parents.'[24]

During the half-century following the first edition of Colquhoun's *Treatise on the Police*, questions of crime and police became key concerns of successive governments. Select committees of parliament presented reports on different aspects of the policing of London in 1812, 1816, 1817, 1818, 1822, 1828, 1833 and 1834; and between 1836 and 1839 the Royal Commission on the Rural Constabulary held its deliberations and drew up its report and recommendations.

Those select committees meeting before the creation of the Metropolitan Police in 1829 heard some witnesses who challenged Colquhoun's belief that the morals of the poor were deteriorating. But all saw crime as a problem emanating from the poorer sections of society; it was the mass of petty offences which gave cause for concern, since the more 'atrocious offences' like highway robbery were considered to be in decline.[25] The committees of 1816 and 1828 were particularly concerned at what seemed to be an increasing number of juvenile offenders; witnesses blamed first indigent, or vicious and abandoned parents who ignored their offspring, and second, and to a lesser extent, shopkeepers and stall-holders who foolishly exposed their wares unprotected in front of their shops or stalls.[26] Echoing the argument of Sir John Fielding, something of a consensus emerged that juvenile offenders started with petty theft and then progressed to more serious offences; incarcerating them with older, hardened offenders served only to accelerate the process. The 1816 committee was obsessed with drink as a contributory factor to crime and with public houses harbouring prostitutes, thieves and vagabonds; witnesses who appeared unconcerned, or who played down the significance of public houses, were questioned with rigour and persistence.[27] Ten years later two M.P.s suggested in the House of Commons that unemployment and poverty may have been contributing to crime.[28] Several witnesses made a similar link before the 1828 committee; but Sir Richard Birnie, the chief magistrate of the Bow Street police office, insisted that if there was less depravity among them then more of the poor would find employment, and increasingly this kind of assertion became the most popular except among those of a radical persuasion.[29]

John Sayer, a Bow Street police officer, agreed in 1816 that he was acquainted with 'a great number of the dangerous characters or suspect persons who are constantly about London'.[30] Birnie and another stipendiary magistrate, John Rawlinson, told the 1828 committee that the police knew who the thieves infesting London were.[31] In this they followed a tradition among 'professional policemen' going back at least as far as Henry Fielding, that much crime was the work of 'professional', readily identifiable, criminals. Henry Fielding wrote of an organised gang of about a hundred carrying out robberies; they were well practised at using disguises; they rescued colleagues who were caught, bribed prosecutors and used corrupt lawyers and false witnesses.[32] Colquhoun, never a man to conjure with small figures when confronted with a problem, estimated that there were 115,000 persons living in London wholly or partly by different forms of crime. Among these were a hard core of 2,000 'Professed thieves, Burglars, Highway Robbers, Pickpockets, and River Pirates'; and these numbers, he feared, would increase when peace threw back into society the criminals siphoned off by the armed forces in wartime.[33] Such thinking informed the beliefs of the Metropolitan Police from its creation. The Royal Commission on the Rural Constabulary sought information from the divisional commanders of the Metropolitan Police and it received precise figures. The superintendent of P division, for example, was particularly thorough declaring that his jurisdiction contained, '2 burglars. 2 housebreakers. 1 highway robber. 14 pickpockets. 48 common thieves. 4 obtainers of goods by false pretences. 1 receiver of stolen goods. 1 horse stealer. 3 dog stealers and 4 utterers of base coin'.[34] What these figures actually represented is an open question, but the Report of the Royal Commission was able to present statistics of 'Depredators, Offenders and Suspected Persons' for the Metropolitan Police District, for Liverpool, Bristol, Bath, Hull and Newcastle-upon-Tyne. It insisted that the figures were meaningful and were among the benefits of properly organised police systems.[35] As was noted in the preceding chapter, from the late 1850s figures such as these were published in the Judicial Statistics, though without any guidance being given to the individual constabularies as to what they should include. The collection and publication of these statistics, in themselves, helped give a further reality to the perceptions of the existence of a criminal class.

The Report of the Royal Commission on the Rural Constabulary sought to give an explanation for crime across the whole of England and Wales. It was largely drafted by Edwin Chadwick, but he did not dominate the Commission as has sometimes been assumed. Criminality, according to the Report, was rooted in the poorer classes, particularly those who roamed the country: 'the prevalent cause [of vagrancy] was the impatience of steady labour'.[36] Chadwick, and by implication his fellow commissioners, was either unaware of, or simply ignored the seasonal nature of much nineteenth-century employment and the consequent need for many, even urban dwellers, to spend time moving from place to place and from job to job.[37] Poverty and indigence, insisted the Report, did not lead to crime; criminals suffered from two principal vices – 'indolence or the pursuit of easy excitement', and they were drawn to commit crimes by 'the temptation of the profit of a career of depredation, as compared with the profits of honest and even well paid industry'.[38] Criminals then, made a rational decision to live by a life of crime because of its attractions; furthermore they knew that the lack of a preventive police would probably enable them to get away with any offence.

What Chadwick had done, with deliberate emotive language, was to identify a criminal group within the working class, a group that possessed those habits which, to his mind, were the worst habits of the class as a whole. These habits were then given as the causes of crime. Other experts and reformers who investigated and analysed crime in the middle years of the century subconsciously performed much the same sleight of hand: they identified criminals as a group within the working class, ascribed to that group the habits and vices of which they most disapproved, or the disadvantages which they most sought to alleviate. These habits and/or disadvantages then became the prime causes of crime. Such an analysis had been embryonic in Colquhoun, perhaps even in Fielding, but to achieve its full shape the moral fervour of early Victorian reformers was required, coupled with the frightening spread of urbanisation and the perception of a society irrevocably divided into social classes.[39]

Seven of the expert witnesses who were called before the 1828 select committee on Police in the Metropolis had given drink as a contributory factor in crime. In 1834 a select committee enquiring into drunkenness concluded that the 'vice' was declining among the middle and upper classes, but increasing among the labouring classes with a notable impact on crime. 'The spread of Crime' the Committee declared, in a sentence as notable for its purple prose and passion as its length:

in every shape and form, from theft, fraud and prostitution in the young, to burnings, robberies and more hardened offences in the old; by which the gaols and prisons, the hulks and convict transports are filled with inmates; and an enormous mass of human beings, who, under sober habits and moral training, would be sources of wealth and strength to the country, are transformed, chiefly through the remote or immediate influence of Intoxicating Drinks, into excrescences of corruption and weakness, which must be cut off and cast away from the gangrenous contamination of its whole frame, leaving the body itself in a constant state of that inflammatory excitement, which always produces exhaustion and weakness in the end; and thus causing the country to sacrifice every year a larger portion of blood and treasure than the most destructive wars occasion; the innocent population thus made criminal, being, like the grain subjected to distillation, converted from a wholesome source of strength and prosperity into a poisoned issue of weakness and decay.[40]

In the sense that employment and good wages led to greater consumption of liquor, which, on occasions, contributed to a greater incidence of offences against the person, the statistics of crime suggest that the committee in one respect were groping in the right direction, but the thinking behind their equation was far more crude and simplistic and, clearly, offences against property were as much their concern as violence. The problem, as the committee perceived it, was the poor's lack of morality.

The 'lack of moral training' was not a new issue in 1834, but it was taken up and emphasised by a clutch of educational reformers over the next two decades particularly as concern grew about juvenile delinquency and as a new legal definition and discourse developed about the criminal child.[41] Individuals like Mary Carpenter, Joseph Fletcher, James Kay-Shuttleworth, Jelinger Symons and John Wade urged that proper education would lead to a diminution of crime; but it was not secular education merely involving reading, writing and arithmetic which they wanted. Symons explained that:

when the heart is depraved, and the tendencies of the child or the man are unusually vicious, there can be little doubt that instruction per se, *so far from preventing crime, is accessory to it.*[42]

Better education might simply produce better educated criminals; already there were complaints that the reading matter of the working classes was 'decidedly reprehensible in their moral tone, pandering to the worst passions of their readers, and regularly venting forth nauseous details of seduction, crime and horror'.[43] What was needed was essentially Christian and moral education that would explain to the working classes their true station in life. John Glyde, a self-educated artisan who dabbled in Owenism and Chartism and who published extensively on his native Suffolk, urged:

It is to our low neighbourhoods, and to the neglected children roaming the streets, that we must look, if we would check the current of crime . . . It is in the dwelling-place of the poor that the zealous must labour for the

dissemination of Christian principles, and teach men the value of their
relative duties as members of society. This is the fountain head of crime,
and it is here that the evil must be grappled with.[44]

This education had to instil in the young habits of industry, and if bad
parents or the efforts of ragged schools or Sunday Schools failed to do this,
then reformatory schools would have to take over, substituting for the
parents and preparing juvenile offenders for a moral adulthood. Symons
summed the situation up as follows:

[Labour] is the backbone of reformation. No one can attach more
weight than I do to the agencies of religion and kindness. They touch
the heart and soften the asperities of a vicious nature, even if they fail to
Christianise. But there must be a change of habit as well as of mind, and
the change of habit mostly needed is from some kind of idleness to some
kind of industry. We are dealing with a class whose vocation is labour;
and whose vices and virtues are infallibly connected with indolence or
industry. *There is no penitence either in man or lad who shirks hard*
work; nor is there any better evidence of the reality of the conversion
of a criminal than the sweat of his brow. [my emphasis][45]

Of course it was difficult for even the most respectable member of the
working class to work up a sweat by hard physical labour if he was unemployed. Even the most provident of the working class who, for example,
delayed a marriage until they had amassed what they felt to be sufficient
capital to set up home together, could find their nest-egg consumed by
a sudden spell of unemployment.[46] Contemporary gentlemen recognised
that the want of regular employment could contribute to crime, but this
was because the working class lacked moral fibre as a result of their ignorance, idleness, dissoluteness and drunkenness – habits that the young
often picked up from bad parents. Thomas Plint, the Leeds reformer,
explained that the working class had difficulty in withstanding 'the fiery
ordeal of protracted idleness, and its inevitable concomitant, protracted
temptation'. The longer an economic crisis continued, the greater the
temptation:

The occasional act becomes a constant habit; principle is overlaid, and
conscience drugged and stupefied . . . Nor does the return to prosperity
obliterate the evil which a long cycle of distress has produced. Work may
be resumed, and the former comforts gladden the household, but the trail
and slime *of the moral evil which has dwelt in the heart and ruled there,*
remains, and will evidence itself in a thousand forms.

Yet it remained the individuals within 'the operative classes' who were at fault rather than the system.[47] For Plint's contemporaries, like the Reverend John Clay, the Chaplain of Preston Gaol, and Matthew Davenport Hill, the Recorder of Birmingham, it was possible to argue that times of economic prosperity linked with the moral weakness of the working class to tempt them into crime.[48]

The 1830s and, particularly, the 'hungry forties' witnessed apocalyptic visions of society shared by men at opposite ends of the political spectrum. Engels asserted that 'the incidence of crime has increased with the growth of the working-class population and there is more crime in Britain than in any other country in the world'. Crime was an aspect of the new social war which worsened with every passing year. Sir Archibald Alison, the Tory Sheriff of Lanarkshire, perceived:

destitution, profligacy, sensuality and crime [advancing] with unheard-of rapidity in the manufacturing districts, and the dangerous classes there massed together combine every three or four years in some general strike or alarming insurrection, which, while it lasts, excites universal terror.[49]

It was during the 1840s that the Chartist G. W. M. Reynolds began publishing *The Mysteries of London*, which, with its sequel, were 'probably the longest, best-selling fiction of the time'.[50] The former was inspired by Eugene Sue's *Les Mystères de Paris*, the best-selling novel in France during the 1840s, and with scenes of appalling savagery and violence as well as sexual titillation, Reynolds gave his readers a frightening portrait of a brutalised, savage poor – a truly dangerous class.

The middle classes in England readily accepted H. A. Frégier's term 'the dangerous classes' as descriptive of the creatures inhabiting the most squalid districts of the burgeoning cities. The French historian, Louis Chevalier, built on Frégier's perception to describe early nineteenth-century Paris as a pathological city in which the labouring classes merged into the dangerous classes while frightened bourgeois conceived of themselves like pioneers in the frontier-America portrayed by James Fenimore Cooper – men surrounded by savages.[51] While many aspects of Chevalier's analysis are open to criticism, his description of how the middle classes perceived their social inferiors strikes a chord with the English experience: if nothing else the poor looked very different in physique as well as dress.

In 1862 the Reverend H. W. Holland writing on 'professional thieves' in the *Cornhill Magazine* described how any visitor entering a thieves' district would be struck by the inhabitants' strange dress and physiognomy; the adults were 'seedy and sleepy' while the children 'lounge about, looking very suspicious and preternaturally sharp'. He went on to explain that:

Nearly all habitual thieves, male and female, die of consumption, and under or about thirty-five years of age. Drink, debauchery, irregular hours, the sudden transitions from luxuries to a low prison diet – these things soon kill them off.[52]

The question immediately posed by such descriptions is, what was the difference between the lifestyle and life expectancy of these 'professional thieves' and those of the poorer sections of the working class? Whatever the early statisticians may have argued about improvements in life expectancy, the tables published during the middle years of the nineteenth century revealed a significant difference between the life expectancy of the working class and that of their social superiors; and very large numbers of the working class died before the age of thirty-five. Tuberculosis, 'the Captain of the Men of Death', the 'White Plague', was a remorseless killer of the urban poor, and while it declined during the nineteenth century it still accounted for perhaps one-third of all deaths from disease during the Victorian period.[53] Poor nutrition, in the context of long hours and hard physical labour, together with appalling and unchecked industrial diseases, ensured that even if the adjectives 'seedy' and 'sleepy' might be questioned, the physiological differences between the working class, particularly the poorer sections, and the middle class were certainly real.

In another article on thieves in the *Cornhill Magazine*, Holland, who claimed to have lived among them for two years, noted that even 'the worst of them' spoke gloomily of their future, given the efforts of policemen, prisons, ragged schools and reformatories – the metaphor he used was telling and typical – 'just as a Red Indian would complain of the dwindling of his tribe before the strong march of advancing civilization'.[54] During the 1850s to 1870s a succession of intrepid explorers picked up their notebooks, as often as not found trusty guides among the stouthearted, blue-uniformed, helmeted, guardians of law and order, and penetrated the dark and teeming recesses of poor working-class districts. They then wrote up their exploits for the vicarious delight of the reading public as journeys into criminal districts where the inhabitants were best compared with Red Indians or varieties of black 'savages'. Among the first of these explorers was Angus Reach who, reporting on the manufacturing districts for the *Morning Chronicle*, accompanied a sub-inspector of the Manchester Police into the depths of Angel Meadow. They entered a 'low lodging house':

*Hot as the place was, most of the women had shawls about their heads.
They were coarse looking and repulsive – more than one with contused
discoloured faces. The men were of that class you often remark in low
localities – squalid hulking fellows, with no particular mark of any trade
or calling on them. The women were of the worst class of prostitutes,
and the men their bullies and partners in robberies.*

Continuing their journey Reach and the inspector visited a pub, well
known as the haunt of thieves. The inspector challenged a boy pickpocket:
'The light from a lamp fell upon his face and I never saw a worse one –
little, deep-sunk eyes and square bony jaws, with a vile expression'.[55]
Dickens went 'On Duty with Inspector Field' into the depths of the Saint
Giles Rookery:

*We stoop low, and creep down a precipitous flight of steps into a dark
close cellar. There is a fire. There is a long deal table. There are benches.
The cellar is full of company, chiefly very young men in various
conditions of dirt and raggedness. Some are eating supper. There are no
girls or women present. Welcome to Rats' Castle, gentlemen, and to this
company of noted thieves![56]*

When another explorer took a day trip down the Thames to see a bare-
knuckle boxing match his adventure became 'A Day's Pleasure with the
Criminal Classes'.[57] Such literature reached its apogee with Henry
Mayhew.

Mayhew revived, possibly unknowingly, Henry Fielding's differenti-
ations of the poor when in the first of his eighty-two reports for the *Morning
Chronicle*, he divided the London poor into 'they [that] *will* work, they
[that] *can't* work, and they [that] *won't* work'.[58] Mayhew's reports
showed sympathy for the plight of the poor and an awareness of the problems of the casual nature of so much of the labour in the metropolis, but
when it came to crime he insisted that poverty and casual labour were
causes only in so far as they destroyed 'all habits of prudence and where
there is no prudence, the present affluence cannot be made to provide for
the future want'. He visited a lodging house in Dockland reporting the
inmates' description of their hard lives and their problems in getting work;
yet his report finished with his 'experienced guide' emphasising that few of
these men could be made honest. 'I have known a few in my time that have
been reclaimed, but they are the exceptions, and certainly not the rule.'
Mayhew accepted the analysis of the Constabulary Commissioners a
decade before: criminals were 'essentially the idle and the vagabond'.

Young thieves, he explained, 'love idleness', and while pickpockets rarely drank (it would impede their dexterity) they were 'libidinous . . . and spend whatever money they can spare upon the low prostitutes'.[59] Drink was, nevertheless, a powerful contributor to crime: following some dubious statistical reasoning which set figures for drunkenness alongside figures for larceny and assault, Mayhew demonstrated that the labouring classes were more drunken and consequently more criminal.[60]

Just over a third of the letters for the *Morning Chronicle* were incorporated into Mayhew's massive *London Labour and the London Poor: A Cyclopaedia of the Condition and Earning of those that will work, those that cannot work, and those that will not work*, the first volume, and other sections of which, first appeared in 1851. Here Mayhew began by noting the different physical and mental characteristics of the nomadic street people:

there is a greater development of the animal than of the intellectual or moral nature of man . . . they are more or less distinguished for their high cheek-bones and protruding jaws – for their use of a slang language – for their lax ideas of property – for their general improvidence – their repugnance to continuous labour – their disregard of female honour – their love of cruelty – their pugnacity – and their utter want of religion.

In short, these exotic tribes – 'costermongers strongly resemble the North American Indians in their conduct to their wives' – lacked all of the virtues that respectable middle-class Victorian society held dear. Lurking among these tribes was a separate 'class' of thieves. They were mainly young, they were idle and vagrant, they enjoyed the literature that glorified pirates and robbers, notably Dick Turpin and Jack Sheppard, and, of course, many looked different. Mayhew organised a 'meeting of vagrants' in Shadwell to inquire into their way of life; the gathering was given the sub-heading 'Meeting of Thieves':

. . . never was witnessed a more distressing spectacle of squalor, rags and wretchedness . . . Many were not only good-looking, but had a frank, ingenuous expression that seemed in no way connected with innate roguery. Many, on the other hand, had the deep-sunk and half-averted eye which are so characteristic of natural dishonesty and cunning.[61]

The fourth volume, which first appeared in its entirety in the enlarged edition of 1861–2, concentrated on 'the Non-Workers, or in other words, the Dangerous Classes of the Metropolis'. This was a work by several hands; Mayhew himself set out to define crime and the 'criminal class'.

Crime, he argued, was the transgression of social laws in the same way that sin and vice were, respectively, the transgression of religious and moral laws. The crime of theft, however, transgressed all three varieties of laws. There were two different kinds of criminals: 'the professional and the casual'. The latter committed their crimes 'from some accidental cause' such as malice, lust, shame, temptation, cupidity, want or political prejudice. The professional criminals were 'those who object to labour for their living' and who preferred to live by plundering others. The crimes of 'professional criminals' were 'regular crafts, requiring almost the same apprenticeship as any other mode of life'. These crafts consisted of burglary, various forms of robbery from the person, poaching, coining, smuggling, and working illicit stills.[62] Mayhew gave an extensive breakdown of thieves and their dependants: there were five major headings, twenty subheadings and over a hundred categories, most with exotic slang titles. Under the sub-heading of ' "Sneaksmen", or those who plunder by means of stealth', for example were:

iv 'Till Friskers', or those who empty tills of their contents during the absence of the shopmen.
v 'Sawney-Hunters', or those who go purloining bacon from cheese-mongers' shop-doors.
vi 'Noisy-racket Men', or those who steal china and glass from outside of china-shops.
vii 'Area Sneaks', or those who steal from houses by going down the area steps.
viii 'Dead Lurkers', or those who steal coats and umbrellas from passages at dusk, or on Sunday afternoons.
ix 'Snow Gatherers', or those who steal clean clothes off the hedges.[63]

Whether it was conceivable that a 'Sawney-Hunter' was so wedded to his own trade that he would not indulge in a bit of 'Snow Gathering', should the opportunity arise, was not allowed in Mayhew's categorisation. The question might also have been posed: was there really a living to be made in specialising as a 'Noisy-racket Man'? It seems possible that, in some instances at least, he took the slang for a particular offence and then made a criminal trade out of it. Furthermore it was contradictory for Mayhew to list among 'those who will not work': 'embezzlers or those who rob their employers' and dishonest servants who 'make away with the property of their masters'. Did it make sense to argue that the 'accidental causes' of temptation or want did not contribute to these latter offences, or even to some of the professional crimes such as burglary and poaching? Such questions do not appear much to have vexed either Mayhew or his readers, and while some historians have questioned the reliability of his evidence, others continue to use it uncritically.[64]

The Reverend William Tuckniss, who wrote the introduction to Mayhew's fourth volume, refused to commit himself on the overall trend of crime:

although the criminal statistics of some localities exhibit a sensible diminution in certain forms of vice, we must not forget that an increase of education and a growing intelligence bring with them superior facilities for the successful perpetration and concealment of crime.[65]

But from the middle of the century many commentators were confidently asserting that crime was being checked. James Greenwood, a journalist with experience of the poor districts of London and the police courts, believed that in 1869 there were some 20,000 thieves in the metropolis, yet their numbers had decreased in recent years.[66] The advocates of the reformatory system emphasised the important role that their brain-child was playing in reducing juvenile crime. There remained an irredeemable, incorrigible residuum, which, with the cessation of transportation, could no longer be shipped out of the country. This group was increasingly referred to as the criminal class; the backbone of this class were those defined by Mayhew as 'professional' and by the legislators as 'habitual' criminals. Such men, declared *The Times* in a leading article in 1870:

are more alien from the rest of the community than a hostile army, for they have no idea of joining the ranks of industrious labour either here or elsewhere. The civilized world is simply the carcass on which they prey, and London above all, is to them a place to sack.[67]

In spite of the 'progress of the nation' and the apparent advance of civilisation the question had to be posed: why did this residuum remain?

Greenwood noted that many juveniles resorted to crime because of hunger,[68] yet, in general, habitual criminals were rarely perceived as being brought to crime by poverty. Bad, uncaring parents, drink, the corrupt literature which glamorised offenders, and a general lack of moral fibre continued to be wheeled out as causes of crime. Poverty remained the hallmark of most criminals in the literature of the second half of the nineteenth century, but this was not so much because poverty was regarded as a cause of crime, but rather because crime could not be held to pay. 'Thieving is always a losing game', explained Holland. 'The money they get never does them any good; it never stays with them. It all goes in gambling, debauchery and law expenses.'[69] *The Times*, commenting on the conviction of seven thieves in 1865, believed that they had taken property valued at between £11,000 and £12,000 in six months; of course, it went on, they would not have realised anything like this sum when they fenced it, but, more importantly:

None of them were living in other than mean houses, and some tawdry jewelry about the women seems to represent the extent of their luxury. In fact, they dare not spend much, or they would attract the attention of the police, and they are thus condemned to enjoy their spoil with the same stealthy fear with which they seize it.[70]

Greenwood, in turn, emphasised:

There can be no question that that of the professional thief is a bitterly severe and laborious occupation, beset with privations that moral people have no conception of, and involving an amount of mental anxiety and torment that few human beings can withstand through a long lifetime.[71]

Even if for many the incidence of crime appeared to be decreasing, the problem was how to explain its persistence in the face of the advantages and opportunities provided by the advance of civilisation and the expansion of the mid-century panacea of education. In addition to the old stand-bys of corrupting literature, drunkenness, uncaring and criminal parents, and the mixing of first-time offenders with recidivists in prisons, concepts of heredity and ideas drawn from developments in medical science began to be enlisted for explanation. An eighteenth-century Swiss theologian, Johann Kaspar Lavater, launched a debate on the significance of physiognomy in the late 1780s with the publication of *Physiognomische Fragmente zur Beförderung der Menschenkenntnis und Menschenliebe*. His ideas had, perhaps, a more profound impact in continental Europe, but Victorians confidently believed that the face portrayed the character. The fact that the skull was the shell for the brain underscored much of this way of thinking and in the early nineteenth century studies began to appear of British convicts in the belief that detectable inordinate mental faculties led to crime. They detected irredeemables from the shape of their heads, their desperate fixed expressions and their 'mental bravado'.[72] Visitors to the penal colonies in Australia often declared that the convicts had an unmistakable 'peculiarity of the visage [making them look] different from other men'.[73] A schoolmaster with experience of working in Newgate in the early 1830s noted that the features of prisoners were 'strongly marked with animal propensities'; and this seemed particularly so among some of the boys who had 'an approximation to the face of a monkey'.[74] From the middle of the century, British doctors, like James Thompson who worked in Perth Prison, began collating biological analyses of convicts, thus providing an academic underpinning to the perception of 'animal propensities' by the supposedly foolproof means of empirical research. In the majority of the inmates of the juvenile wing of one English prison Dr Forbes Winslow discovered the boys to have 'the cerebrum . . . badly organised, the crown of the head was nearly flat, the posterior region full. In other words, there was little or no intellect, the moral sentiments were small and the propensities large.' Forbes Winslow shared his findings with the readers of the *Morning Chronicle*,[75] thus contributing to a popular Victorian belief that facial features told character and could be deciphered.

Edwin Chadwick considered crime as a moral problem that could be resolved by effort and organisation. The investigations of medical experts, underpinned by the increasing acceptance of Darwinian ideas, began to challenge this as the nineteenth century wore on. The force of heredity implied that notions of blame and responsibility were much more problematic than Chadwick's certainties would allow. As the leading English psychologist, Henry Maudsley, lamented in *Body and Mind* in 1874:

in consequence of evil ancestral influences, individuals are born with such a flaw or warp of nature that all the care in the world will not prevent them from being vicious or criminal, or becoming insane. . . . No one can escape the tyranny of his organisation; no one can elude the destiny that is innate in him, and which unconsciously and irresistably shapes his ends, even when he believes that he is determining them with consumate skill.[76]

Such recognition that the mastery of personal circumstances and constitution could be exceedingly difficult was given even sharper focus in the last quarter of the century by, on the one hand, the housing problem in London and the studies of the great social investigators, and, on the other, the gradual filtering into Britain of the physiological and psychological theories of the European students of the new science of criminology or, to use the more common contemporary term, criminal anthropology.

At the bottom of the social scale in London, Charles Booth found Social Class A: 'occasional labourers, loafers and semi-criminals'. This was a:

savage semi-criminal class of people [which] had its golden age in the days when whole districts of London were in their undisputed possession.

They mainly desire to be left along, to be allowed to make an Alsatia of their own. Improvement in our eyes is destruction in theirs. Their discontent is their measure of our success.[77]

In meticulous detail Booth outlined the squalor and poverty in which this group lived, and the little different surroundings of Social Class B, only marginally above it. Such revelations fuelled the arguments of those critics of the system of outdoor relief who maintained that mistaken humanitarianism and charity were creating, rather than alleviating, the problem of the unpleasant residuum in the slum districts of cities; charity merely fostered idleness and improvidence. At the same time the work of Booth, and others, with its exposure of bad housing and inadequate diet, encouraged a perception of the residuum as the inevitable workings of social Darwinism. Arnold White, who in the aftermath of the Boer War was a central figure in warning the public about the degeneration of the British race, first expressed some of these concerns during the 1880s. He lamented the exodus from the bracing countryside, which produced fit and sturdy men, to the unhealthy cities, where half the poor were so mentally, morally and physically unfit that the best thing for the nation to do was to leave them alone to die out. Unfortunately the 'criminal and pauperised classes with low cerebral development renew their race more rapidly than those of higher nervous natures'.[78] Yet while criminals could still be seen as part of the residuum, lurking in their slums and, by implication, eager and ready to prey on the respectable, the increasingly popular biological explanation of crime meant that it was no longer necessary simply to define criminality largely in class terms.

The mass of petty thefts and the large number of crimes committed by juveniles continued to be the main objects of concern, but it began to be acknowledged that crime was not simply a problem rooted in the poorer sections of the urban working class. Charles Booth noted that 'every social grade has its criminals, if not by conviction, at least by character'.[79] The new criminal anthropology with its 'scientific' physiological and psychological theories enabled the criminal to be studied as an individual rather than simply as part of a class, and provided an understanding of the criminal as an individual. Reduced to the simplest formula, the criminal was someone who was not 'normal'; normal individuals did not assault, murder, rape, or steal from others. Criminals, therefore, became less a class of offenders by choice and rather more pathetic, and sometimes dangerous, social wreckage, produced by largely impersonal forces. L. Gordon Rylands explained:

the active causes of all kinds [of crime] are these: Defective training or
total absence of any; immoral associates and bad example in prison as
well as out of it; drink; idleness, and the hereditary transmission of evil
tendencies. These causes, however, frequently overlap, and one is often
found to be the effect of another, the only perfectly simple and absolutely
final division is into two main heads, Heredity and Environment, which
comprise all others.

Under the heading of environment Rylands meant the lack of good and
caring parents, the lack of a decent home (more the fault of parents
than anything else), and bad company in the slums and in prison. Such
problems might, he believed, be alleviated by the state taking control of
children found on the streets 'without visible means of subsistence, or
who seemed to be neglected by their parents'; the 'inherited tendencies'
of 'embryo criminals' might thus be nipped in the bud. Theft, suicide,
and 'homicidal monomania' were, however, all hereditary failings; the
irredeemable offender, in Rylands perception, would be best killed. He
was not alone in drawing such conclusions.[80]

In 1890, for a series of 'Contemporary Science' books, Havelock Ellis
published a critical survey of the work of the criminal anthropologists of
Europe and the United States; the book went through four editions in
twenty years. Ellis explained that research into the physical characteristics
of criminals revealed that they were individuals incapable of living by the
standards recognised as binding by a community:

By some accident of development, by some defect of heredity or birth
or training, [the criminal] belongs as it were to a lower and older social
state than that in which he is actually living.

Research into the physical characteristics of the criminal, moreover,
demonstrated that:

[I]n the criminal . . . there is an arrest of development. The criminal is an
individual who, to some extent, remains a child his life long – a child of
larger growth and with greater capacity for evil.

But this did not mean that the criminal was 'an idiot' or even 'merely
weak-minded'. The criminal was far more dangerous. 'The idiot and the
feeble-minded, as we know them in asylums, rarely have any criminal or
dangerous instincts.'[81] Ellis's fervent advocacy of 'social hygiene', by which
civilisation 'at a certain stage . . . is compelled to continue its own course,
and to preserve, perhaps to elevate, the race' by the removal of the 'weak-
minded' was a logical development of these ideas.[82]

Like Ellis, the Reverend William Douglas Morrison popularised for a British audience the work of men like Enrico Ferri, Cesare Lombroso and Gabriel Tarde; indeed he wrote the introduction for an English translation of Lombroso's *The Female Offender*. Morrison deployed the Europeans' conclusions alongside his personal experience as chaplain of Wandsworth Prison to formulate a critique of the existing penal system. He accepted many of the old moral perceptions; crime was rarely prompted by poverty or destitution:

the habitual criminal, as he will very soon tell you if you possess his confidence absolutely, declines to work. He has never worked, he does not want to work; he prefers living by his wits.

The habitual beggar and the vagrant were one and the same. But Morrison was emphatic that crime was not simply a problem found in the lowest recesses of the working class. The debtor was sometimes 'a worse criminal . . . than the thief who snatches a purse'. Furthermore, if imprisoned debtors were included in the tally of convicts:

and if all cases of drunkenness and assault were punished with imprisonment instead of a fine, it would be found that the well-to-do showed just as badly in the statistics of crime as their poorer neighbours.

The fundamental problem was not class but 'degeneracy', and heredity and urban environment were the keys to understanding. 'Degeneracy' was inherited 'when the criminal is descended from insane, drunken, epileptic, scrofulous parents'. It could be acquired when an individual 'adopts and deliberately persists in a life of crime'.[83] The problem was augmented by the highly concentrated population of cities, which led to 'the creation of a large degenerate caste'. Morrison believed that there was a separate 'class' of habitual criminals, but it was 'not to be confounded with the working or any other class' since it was separate and quite distinct from 'the rest of the community'.[84]

The European theorists' notions of the born criminal and degeneracy were never totally accepted, however. There were criticisms that the theorists' samples were too small for any valid generalisation, and that the 'degenerates' were simply those who had refused to be deterred by punishment.[85] At the same time the incorporation of medical men into the criminal administration may have diminished an inclination to theoretical radicalism while, at the same time, enabling medical and psychological experts to have a practical influence on penal policy.[86]

There are two implicit assumptions about the perceptions of the criminal class explored so far in this chapter which warrant some explicit emphasis: first, the criminal class was perceived overwhelmingly as male; second, the perceptions discussed were those of middle-class commentators who had in mind, if not a middle-class, then at least a respectable audience. There were occasional references to women committing crimes, even to them being afflicted by criminal 'diseases'. The Reverend H. W. Holland, for example, suggested:

Probably, kleptomania is no imaginary disease . . . The writer has now one particular instance of it in his mind, in which a young lady of good sense and most respectable station could never be trusted in a shop alone. If this disease can happen in the upper classes, why may it not exist in the lower strata of social life?[87]

But, in general, women were not seen as members of the criminal class in their own right, they were the appendages of male thieves; and, of course, as Mayhew emphasised, the exotic tribes of the cities treated their women in different ways from those expected in civilised society. To the extent that, statistically, women appear to have committed less crime, this perception of the 'criminal' was justified. But it is significant that for women transported for theft in the early nineteenth century the descriptions 'hardened offender' and 'abandoned prostitute' were almost synonymous. This stereotype emerged from the gap that existed between the expectations of the middle class and the mores of the poorer sections of the working class for whom cohabitation was cheaper and sometimes more convenient than marriage.[88] Furthermore, there is a parallel between the Victorian perceptions of the male criminal and the female prostitute. Prostitution itself was not a criminal offence, but there was recurrent concern about 'the Great Social Evil' and, at least from the middle of the nineteenth century, there were determined efforts at control. One aspect of the concern was the belief that prostitutes indulged in petty theft between themselves or upon their clients, and that they consorted with thieves. Several of the social investigators who studied prostitution noted economic hardship as a spur to some women to take up the 'profession', yet even among the most sympathetic investigators economic causes – like the economic causes of some criminal actions – were commonly submerged by generalisations about the prostitute's family environment, her impulsive nature, her restlessness, her desire for quick money and love of luxury. The prostitute's gaudy clothing was, perhaps, the most blatant manifestation of 'luxury' among the poorer sections of society. Dr William Acton's *Prostitution, Considered in its*

Moral, Social and Sanitary Aspects, In London and Other Large Cities (1857) has been hailed as among the most humane and sympathetic studies published during the Victorian period. He did not see prostitution as automatically the slippery slope to damnation; he noted that young women often became prostitutes only for a short while, subsequently returning to more acceptable work and motherhood. But Acton's list of the causes of prostitution has significant echoes of what others listed as the causes of crime among the criminal and/or dangerous classes:

Natural desire. Natural sinfulness. The preferment of indolent ease to labour. Vicious inclinations strengthened and ingrained by early neglect, or evil training, bad associates, and an indecent mode of life. Necessity, imbued by the inability to obtain a living by honest means consequent on a fall from virtue. Extreme poverty. To this black list may be added love of drink, love of dress, love of amusement.[89]

A generation after Acton, Havelock Ellis developed the link between prostitutes and criminals in a rather more explicit manner. He considered that vagabonds dwelt on the borders of criminality and that they possessed more abnormalities than most criminals. Their female counterpart, he believed, was the prostitute:

[I]t is a remarkable fact that prostitutes exhibit the physical and psychic signs associated usually with criminality in a more marked degree than criminal women. While criminal women correspond on the whole to the class of occasional criminals, in whom the brand of criminality is but faintly seen, prostitutes correspond much more closely to the class of instinctive criminals.[90]

Of course members of the working class were aware of crime and criminals; they were more commonly the victims of crime and they both prosecuted and persecuted offenders of different types. Probably, as in some contemporary inner-city areas, members of the working class felt more insecure and more likely to be the victims of some form of crime, than members of the middle class.[91] But working-class perceptions of criminality are less easy to grasp than the confident conclusions of experts or the equally confident descriptions of journalists aimed at a predominantly middle-class audience. The terminology of 'class', aside from the public and written pronouncements of the labour movement, does not appear to have figured much in the language of the working class itself. The late Victorian and Edwardian working class generally referred to themselves as 'the likes of us', 'the labouring sort', or 'working people'. Their social superiors were 'collar-and-tie men', 'the gentry', 'the higher ups', 'the likes of they'. Criminals, when spoken of as a group, may also have been 'the likes of they'.[92] The working class had no need to intellectualise criminals either as a class or as a group acquiring or inheriting degenerate characteristics; though this is not to deny the use of such colloquialisms as 'like father, like son', nor is it to deny the possibility of the working class perceiving those that they recognised as 'criminals' in the terms of the stereotypes depicted in literature.

Some offences, as was noted in the introduction, were not perceived as crimes either by the perpetrators or the communities in which they lived. Poaching is an obvious example. But hostility to the Game Laws was not confined to a single class and spread across social groups, particularly when the creatures defined by the law as protected game were regarded by communities as vermin. During the early 1750s, men of all classes combined to dig up Lord Uxbridge's rabbit warrens which were ruining the commons of Cannock Chase.[93] Over a century later when a Sussex court convicted Robert Dickinson of trespass in search of game, he protested: 'I do not call conies game, I call them vermin, according to the Bible.'[94] Nineteenth-century gentlemen feared that poaching was the first step on the road to a life of crime. Possibly a few did follow such a route, but the problem is ascertaining at what point a poacher who gravitated to another form of crime was rejected by his community. In his study of poaching on Cannock Chase, Douglas Hay concluded that cottagers who poached were seldom active thieves; after all, if a man stole from gentlemen and wealthy farmers he was unlikely to be entirely above suspicion among his neighbours. However, evidence from the sixteenth and seventeenth centuries suggests that villagers were prepared to tolerate a degree of petty theft among known members of the community; and the case of William Herring, a 'yeoman' of East Wilton in Yorkshire, who was transported for sheep stealing in 1793, suggests that it was possible for certain tough individuals to terrorise local communities without opposition or public complaint for several years.[95] Yet even with a 'social crime' like poaching attitudes did change, and changes in the law probably contributed to this change. In 1831, new legislation permitted a much greater number of individuals to enjoy hunting rights, though not tenant farmers and labourers. The Poaching Prevention Act 1862, which empowered police to stop and search suspects, together with the Ground Game Act 1880, which, at last, gave tenant farmers inalienable rights over hares and rabbits on their property, seem to have had the side-effects of reducing sympathy for the poacher and making him appear more of a 'criminal'.[96]

At the same time that some crimes were not perceived as such by certain social groups or communities, several nineteenth-century authors, generally liberals or radicals of various hues, did urge, contrary to the overall picture given in this chapter, that poverty could lead to crime. *The Poor Man's Guardian* even went so far as to suggest that the laws of the country were made by rich men to protect the great evil – property.[97] Yet there was never any suggestion that gaoled 'criminals' were, in any sense, political prisoners. There was violent hostility to the political disfranchisement that went with admission to the workhouse or with receipt of poor relief. Admission to the workhouse or the resort to relief was a constant threat hanging over a significant percentage of the poor and one of the chief condemnations of the New Poor Law was, in Disraeli's words, that 'it announces to the world that in England poverty is a crime'.[98] No radical group called for the political enfranchisement of men in gaol, however. Indeed, from the corresponding societies of the 1790s to the Chartists and beyond, conviction and imprisonment for a crime meant the forfeiture of political rights. This may be explained by the notions of morality that pervaded the thought of nineteenth-century working-class activists as well as the Victorian middle class – criminals, unlike paupers, made a conscious, positive and immoral decision when they committed a crime. At the same time it may also have been a recognition by the radical activists that the working class were as much the victims of crime as the perpetrators – political reform, and parliaments chosen by universal manhood suffrage, would remove the vestiges of inequality within the law.

The literature dealing with criminals that was aimed at the working class was both moralistic and titillating as was much of that aimed at their social superiors; indeed as the nineteenth century wore on there was an increasing overlap between the reading matter of the middle class and the respectable working class. The 'last dying words', with cheap woodcuts at the top of a sheet, which were hawked at public executions throughout the eighteenth, and well into the nineteenth centuries, were infused with a moralistic tone as the condemned was made to repent and to warn others against following in his, or her, footsteps. Some ballads took a similar line, like 'A Shining Night, or Dick Daring, the Poacher':

Be advised then ye young be advised too ye old,
To soberness honesty, industry hold,
For stealing and murder may rise it is clear
From a shining night if 'tis our delight in the season of the year.[99]

The criminals portrayed in such ballads were stereotypes of a pedigree that went back at least as far as the Tudors and Stuarts. In Dick Daring's case, poaching led to more serious crimes, but generally speaking it was drinking and whoring that were held to have put the offender on the slippery slope to perdition. There were some ballads, however, that romanticised the 'criminal'. If 'Dick Daring' was a warning, 'Keepers and Poachers' portrayed the poacher William Taylor as a veritable Sydney Carton:

The judge and the jury unto him did say
'If you wil confess, your sweet life shall be saved.'
'Oh no,' then said William, 'that won't do at all,
For now you have got me I'll die for them all'.[100]

Ballads such as this were rooted in an oral tradition and the notion that poaching was no 'real crime'. Other 'corrupting' material was not. John Gay's *The Beggar's Opera* had rapidly acquired a notorious reputation for leading young men astray, and cheap books telling of the adventures of Jack Sheppard, Dick Turpin and others were similarly looked at askance by middle-class gentlemen; though, of course, the original novels *Rookwood* (1834), which both created and immortalised Turpin's ride to York, and *Jack Sheppard* (1839) were written by the son of a respectable lawyer from the neighbourhood of Manchester, William Harrison Ainsworth. Moreover, while Ainsworth is now relegated to the rank of second-class or 'popular' novelist, he was, at the time, a friendly competitor of Dickens and the two even considered collaborating. Physique, physiognomy and geography are all tokens of class in Ainsworth's novels; critics were worried by what they considered as immorality in his novels, yet the popularity of his characters was seized on by others to produce a variety of imitations in the form of ballads, 'memoirs' and plays as well as novels.[101] Increasingly, with the developments in printing and publishing, and with the growth of literacy in the second half of the nineteenth century, the availability and the amount of this literature became greater. Printers and publishers found an appreciative audience for both adventure stories and lurid tales of 'orrible murder; all the better if they had a basis in fact. In 1868 a man could defend his sons' behaviour before a court on the grounds that literature romanticising criminals had corrupted them. While in 1884 it was said of Ernest Castles, a nineteen-year-old who shot a police constable in Oldham, that his 'mind has been corrupted by the reading of trashy literature'.[102] The following year a London magistrate declared that:

there is not a boy or a young lad tried in our Courts of Justice whose position there is not more or less due to the effect of this unwholesome literature upon his mind.

Publishers, naturally, insisted that 'a moral and healthy tone may be maintained in conjunction with the boldest fiction'.[103] But the power of such literature either to improve or corrupt is not really ascertainable. Most probably it was read primarily for fun and escapism. Probably it reinforced stereotype perceptions of criminals. But members of the working class reacted to individual offenders essentially according to the offences that they committed: petty pilferage at work was often not seen as a crime, theft from a friend or neighbour more generally was; a public house argument that led to blows, or striking a policeman interfering with such an argument outside a pub, might not be perceived as crime, but extreme violence and murder, whatever the circumstances, generally was.

The argument here is not to deny the existence of a criminal class, or at least a group of professional criminals. There were individuals and groups who made a significant part of their living from activities that lay outside the law; probably however, as will be argued below in Chapter 7, the word 'class' implies a large number, and a more homogeneous group than actually existed. But while these individuals may have effected most of the very spectacular and large-scale thefts during the eighteenth and nineteenth centuries, the overwhelming majority of offences were not of this variety. Nineteenth-century experts and commentators looked at who were being processed by the police, the courts and the prisons, never seriously questioned the idea that the multitude of petty thefts (sometimes with the addition of assaults and disorderly conduct) should be the benchmark of criminality, and they then set out to find the causes of this criminality. Since the great majority of offenders came from one social class it was logical to locate the causes of crime within what were generally perceived as the vices of this class. There would be many today who would accept some of the Victorian notions of links between vice and crime: strong drink does appear to have contributed to some incidents of disorder and inter-personal violence; a poor man may have yielded to temptation because of his poverty, yet not every poor man stole, and it might be argued that such nebulous concepts as strength of character and morality do come into play here. The problem was that most nineteenth-century analysts of crime ignored the seasonal and uncertain nature of much employment, and the gruelling aspects of the working-class existence; these certainly contributed to physiological differences between the classes and they probably encouraged the 'vices' (drink, cheap crime literature, rowdiness, consorting with prostitutes) when times were good and when the poor had money in their pockets.

Notes and references

1 *Hansard*, new series, xiv (1826), cols 1218–19.

2 **J. A. Sharpe**, *Crime in Early Modern England 1550–1750*, 2nd edn, Longman, London, 1999, pp. 141–50.

3 *Illustrated London News*, 2 December 1843.

4 **S. F. Van Oss**, 'The "limited-company" craze', *Nineteenth Century*, xliii (1898), pp. 731–44 (at p. 736); see also **Alfred Emden**, 'The crying need for reforms in our company law', *Nineteenth Century*, xxxv (1894), pp. 1033–50.

5 It has been argued that the enforcement of the 1833 Factory Act was guided by the 'rotten apple' thesis and that factory inspectors made the consoling distinction between a majority of respectable employers who would never break the law (though they did) and 'rotten apples'. **W. G. Carson**, 'The institutionalization of ambiguity: Early British Factory Acts', in **Gilbert Geis** and **Ezra Stotland** (eds), *White-Collar Crime: Theory and research*, Sage, Beverly Hills, 1980, pp. 166–7. For a useful historical survey of white-collar crime see **George Robb**, *White-Collar Crime in Modern England: Financial fraud and business morality 1845–1929*, Cambridge U. P., Cambridge, 1992.

6 **Gregory Anderson**, *Victorian Clerks*, Manchester U.P., Manchester, 1976, pp. 37–40.

7 **Henry Fielding**, *An Enquiry into the Causes of the late Increase of Robbers*, 2nd edn, London, 1751, p. xxiii.

8 Ibid., p. 7.

9 Ibid., p. 69.

10 **Henry Fielding**, *The History of the Life of the late Mr Jonathan Wild the Great*, Everyman Edition, London, 1973 edn, p. 18.

11 *Punch*, for example, commented: 'It is true that the criminal may have been led by the example of aristocratic sinners to disregard the injunctions of revealed religion against the adulterer, the gamester, and the drunkard; and having imitated the "pleasant follies" of the great without possessing the requisite means for such enjoyments, the man of pleasure has degenerated into the man of crime. It is true that the poor and ignorant may have claims upon the wealth and intelligence of the rich and learned; but are we to pause to inquire whether want may have driven the destitute to theft, or the absence of early instruction have left physical desires of the offender's native superior to its moral restraints. Certainly not, whilst we have the gallows.' *Punch*, vol. 1, 20 November 1841.

12 Fielding, *An Enquiry*, p. 169.

13 *P.P.* 1812 (127), ii, *Select Committee on the Nightly Watch of the Metropolis*, appendix 8, pp. 34–9.

14 Jonas Hanway, *The Defects of Police, The Cause of Immorality and The Continual Robberies Committed, Particularly in and about the Metropolis*, London, 1775, p. 273.

15 Jonas Hanway, *Observations on the Causes of the Dissoluteness which reigns among the lower Classes of the People; the Propensity of some to Petty Larceny: and the Danger of Gaming, Concubinage, and an excessive Fondness for amusement in high life*, London, 1772, p. 38.

16 Ibid., p. 15.

17 Hanway, *The Defects of Police*, p. 241.

18 Martin Madan, *Thoughts on Executive Justice, with respect to our Criminal Laws, particularly on the Circuits*, London, 1785, pp. 4–5 and 123. Madan's recommendations of Fielding's *Enquiry* is on p. 78; there is a similar recommendation in William Blizard, *Desultory Reflections on Police: With an essay on the means of preventing crimes and amending criminals*, London, 1785, p. 76.

19 Patrick Colquhoun, *A Treatise on the Police of the Metropolis*, 3rd edn, London, 1796, p. 33.

20 Patrick Colquhoun, *A Treatise on the Commerce and Police of the River Thames*, London, 1800, pp. 37–8 and 40.

21 Colquhoun, *A Treatise on the Police*, p. 88. Colquhoun's argument here was highly questionable. It was generally accepted that the most 'correct' and 'energetic' police of the eighteenth century were to be found in France, yet the pre-Revolution rural police, the *maréchaussée*, had problems with brigands, the like of which simply did not exist in Britain. Furthermore the Revolutionary Wars, during which Colquhoun was writing, witnessed an increase in brigandage in France, the Low Countries and the Rhineland.

22 For the popularity of the *Treatise on the Police* see Sir Leon Radzinowicz, *A History of English Criminal Law*, 5 vols, Stevens, London, 1948–86, iii, pp. 221, note 2, and 227–8.

23 'Reflections occasioned by the perusal of a recent treatise on Indigence, etc.', *Monthly Magazine*, xxvi (1808), pp. 108–12 (at p. 111).

24 Colquhoun, *A Treatise on the Police*, p. 88.

25 P.P. 1816 (510) v, *Report on the State of the Police of the Metropolis*, pp. 29, 143–4 and 212.

26 Ibid., pp. 29–30 (for comments on shopkeepers) and pp. 42, 56 and 63 (for comments on parents); P.P. 1828 (533) vi, *Select Committee on the Police of the Metropolis*, p. 57 (shopkeepers) and pp. 48, 59, 85 and 145 (parents).

27 P.P. 1816 (510) v, *Report on the State of the Police of the Metropolis*, pp. 18–21, 38–41 and 48–9.

28 *Hansard*, new series, xiii (1825), col. 300; *Hansard*, new series, xiv (1826), col. 1243. Though it probably needs to be emphasised that in each of these instances the discussion was centred on rural rather than urban crime.

29 *P.P.* 1828 (533) vi, *Select Committee on the Police of the Metropolis*, p. 38; for suggestions that unemployment and poverty may have contributed to crime see pp. 56, 84, 134 and 226.

30 *P.P.* 1816 (510) v, *Report on the State of the Police of the Metropolis*, p. 215.

31 *P.P.* 1828 (533) vi, *Select Committee on the Police of the Metropolis*, pp. 40 and 63.

32 Fielding, *An Enquiry*, p. 4.

33 Colquhoun, *A Treatise on the Police*, p. vii.

34 U.C.L. Chadwick MSS 11 f.2.

35 *P.P.* 1839 (169) xix, *Royal Commission on Constabulary*, pp. 7, 10.

36 Ibid., p. 68.

37 **Raphael Samuel**, 'Comers and goers', in **H. J. Dyos** and **M. Wolff** (eds), *The Victorian City*, 2 vols, RKP, London, 1973, ch. 5.
    For similar statements about vagrancy being a cause of crime see *P.P.* 1852–3 (71) xxxvi, *Select Committee on Police*, qq. 844–5, 1416, 1423–4, 1775, 3004–7 and 3722.

38 *P.P.* 1839 (169) xix, *Royal Commission on Constabulary*, pp. 34 and 67.

39 **David Philips**, 'Three "moral entrepreneurs" and the creation of a "criminal class" in England, c.1790s–1840s', *Crime, histoire et sociétés/Crime, history and societies*, **7** (2003) pp. 79–107.

40 *P.P.* 1834 (599) viii, *Select Committee on Inquiry into Drunkenness*, p. vi.

41 **Heather Shore**, *Artful Dodgers: Youth and crime in early nineteenth-century London*, Boydell/Royal Historical Society, Woodbridge, 1999.
    Susan Magarey has written of the 'invention' of juvenile delinquency between 1820 and 1850 ('The invention of juvenile delinquency in early nineteenth-century England', *Labour History*, **34** (1978), pp. 11–27). There may have been a growth in the concern about juvenile offenders during this period but eighteenth-century commentators like Henry Fielding and Jonas Hanway also expressed anxiety about criminal activities committed by boys and young men, while Peter King and Joan Noel have pointed out an increase in prosecutions of juveniles in the generation before Magarey's study. **Peter King** and **Joan Noel**, 'The origins of "the problem of juvenile delinquency": The growth of juvenile prosecutions in the late eighteenth and early nineteenth centuries', *C.J.H.*, **14** (1993), pp. 17–41.

42 Jelinger C. Symons, *Special Report on Reformatories in Gloucestershire, Shropshire, Worcestershire, Herefordshire and Monmouthshire, and in Wales* (printed in the Minutes of the Parliamentary Committee on Education, *P.P.* 1857–8), p. 236.

43 John Glyde, jun., *The Moral, Social and Religious Condition of Ipswich in the Middle of the Nineteenth Century*, Ipswich, 1850, reprinted S. R. Publishers, Wakefield, 1971, p. 66. The same point was made by Lord Brougham: 'Those who had the mere power to read perused only the narratives of banditti, of swindlers, of thieves; they filled their minds with that species of information which only polluted'. *Hansard*, 3rd series, xc (1847), col. 200.

44 Glyde, *The Moral Condition of Ipswich*, p. 111.

45 Symons, *Special Report on Reformatories*, p. 223.

46 David Vincent, *Bread, Knowledge and Freedom: A study of nineteenth-century working class autobiography*, Europa, London, 1981, p. 49.

47 Thomas Plint, *Crime in England: Its relation, character, and extent as developed from 1901 to 1848*, London, 1851, pp. 84–5. For similar explanations about crime in Suffolk see John Glyde, jun., *Suffolk in the Nineteenth Century: Physical, social, moral, religious and industrial*, London, 1856, pp. 132–3 and 156–8.

48 John Clay, 'On the effect of good or bad times on committals to prison', *Journal of the Statistical Society*, xviii (1855), pp. 74–9; M. D. Hill, *Suggestions for the Repression of Crime, Contained in Charges Delivered to Grand Juries of Birmingham*, London, 1857, p. 109.

49 Both quotations are in David Philips, *Crime and Authority in Victorian England*, Croom Helm, London, 1977, pp. 13–14.

50 Gertrude Himmelfarb, *The Idea of Poverty: England in the early Industrial Age*, Faber and Faber, London, 1984, p. 435.

51 Louis Chevalier, *Classes Laborieuses et Classes Dangereuses à Paris pendant la Première Moitié du XIXe Siècle*, Librarie Plon, Paris, 1958 (English translation, RKP, London, 1973). For a critique of Chevalier, see George Rudé, *Debate on Europe 1815–50*, Harper and Row, New York, 1972, pp. 78–87.

52 H. W. Holland, 'Professional thieves', *Cornhill Magazine*, vi (1862), pp. 640–53 (at p. 653).

53 Anthony S. Wohl, *Endangered Lives: Public health in Victorian Britain*, Methuen, London, 1984, pp. 130–1.

54 H. W. Holland, 'Thieves and thieving', *Cornhill Magazine*, ii (1860), pp. 32–44 (at p. 339).

55 J. Ginswick (ed.), *Labour and the Poor in England and Wales*, 8 vols, Frank Cass, London, 1983, i, p. 79.

56 Charles Dickens, 'On duty with Inspector Field', *Household Words*, iii (1851), pp. 265–70.

57 J. Ormsby, 'A day's pleasure with the criminal classes', *Cornhill Magazine*, ix (1864), pp. 627–40.

58 Henry Mayhew, *The Morning Chronicle Surveyor of Labour and the Poor: The metropolitan districts*, Caliban Books, Firle, 1980, i, p. 40. The first letter in the series was published in the *Morning Chronicle*, 19 October 1849, the last 12 December 1850.

59 Ibid., i, pp. 90, 94, 102 and 107.

60 Ibid., ii, pp. 239–40.

61 Henry Mayhew *et al.*, *London Labour and the London Poor*, 4 vols, London, 1861–62, i, pp. 2–3, 43 and 148.

62 Ibid., iv, pp. 29, 30.

63 Ibid., iv, p. 25.

64 For a good critical assessment of Mayhew see David Englander, 'Henry Mayhew and the criminal classes of Victorian England: The case reopened', in Louis A. Knafla (ed.), *Crime Gender and Sexuality in Criminal Prosecutions: Criminal justice history*, 17, Greenwood Press, Westport, Conn., 2002; for an uncritical use, see Donald Thomas, *The Victorian Underworld*, John Murray, London, 1998, chs 1 and 2.

65 Mayhew *et al.*, *London Labour and the London Poor*, iv, p. xii.

66 James Greenwood, *The Seven Curses of London*, London, 1869 (reprinted, Basil Blackwell, Oxford, 1981), p. 57.

67 *The Times*, 29 March 1870.

68 Greenwood, *The Seven Curses*, pp. 42 and 83.

69 Holland, 'Professional thieves', p. 653.

70 *The Times*, 14 April 1865.

71 Greenwood, *The Seven Curses*, p. 59.

72 David de Guistino, *Conquest of Mind: Phrenology and Victorian social thought*, Croom Helm, London, 1975, pp. 145–53.

73 Quoted in Richard White, *Inventing Australia: Images and identity 1788–1980*, Allen and Unwin, Sydney, 1981, p. 66.

74 Quoted in Philip Priestley, *Victorian Prison Lives: English prison biography*, Methuen, London, 1985, p. 78.

75 *Morning Chronicle*, 11 March 1850.

76 Quoted in **Martin J. Wiener**, *Reconstructing the Criminal: Culture, law, and policy in England, 1830–1914*, Cambridge U. P., Cambridge, 1990, p. 169.

77 **Charles Booth**, *Life and Labour of the People in London. 1st series, Poverty*, 4 vols, London, 1902, i, p. 174.

78 **Arnold White**, *Problems of a Great City*, London, 1886, p. 47.

79 Booth, *Life and Labour, Poverty*, i, p. 175.

80 **L. Gordon Rylands**, *Crime: Its causes and its remedy*, London, 1889, pp. 46, 71, 92 and 251–2. For similar conclusions about the need to exterminate irredeemable offenders see **Leon Radzinowicz** and **Roger Hood**, *The Emergence of Penal Policy in Victorian and Edwardian England*, Clarendon Press, Oxford, 1990, pp. 239–40.

81 **Havelock Ellis**, *The Criminal*, London, 1890, pp. 206, 214 and 229.

82 *Idem, The Task of Social Hygiene*, London, 1912, p. 2.

83 **W. D. Morrison**, *Crime and its Causes*, London, 1891, pp. 85, 140 and 199.

84 *Idem*, 'The increase of crime', *Nineteenth Century*, xxxi (1892), pp, 950–7 (at p. 957); *idem, Crime and its Causes*, pp. 141–2.

85 Radzinowicz and Hood, *The Emergence of Penal Policy*, especially pp. 15–17. There is an illuminating comparative study in **Daniel Pick**, *Faces of Degeneration: A European disorder, c.1848–c.1918*, Cambridge U.P., Cambridge, 1989, see especially ch. 7.

86 Wiener, *Reconstructing the Criminal*, p. 235.

87 Holland, 'Thieves and thieving', p. 340.

88 **Michael Sturma**, 'Eye of the beholder: The stereotype of women convicts, 1788–1852', *Labour History*, **34** (1978), pp. 3–10.

89 Quoted in **Frances Finnegan**, *Poverty and Prostitution: A study of Victorian prostitutes in York*, Cambridge U.P., Cambridge, 1979, p. 7. See also **Judith R. Walkowitz**, *Prostitution and Victorian Society: Women, class and the state*, Cambridge U.P., Cambridge, 1980, pp. 25, 38–9 and 41–5. Acton drew much of his inspiration from the pioneering work in Paris a quarter of a century earlier, of A. J. B. Parent-Duchâtelet. For an excellent introduction to the latter see **Jill Harsin**, *Policing Prostitution in Nineteenth-Century Paris*, Princeton U.P., Princeton, N.J., 1983.

90 Ellis, *The Criminal*, p. 221.

91 For the contemporary concerns see **David J. Smith** and **Jeremy Gray**, *Police and People in London*, Gower, London, 1985, p. 32.

92 **Bernard Waites**, 'The effects of the First World War on aspects of the class structure of English society', unpublished Ph.D., The Open University, 1983, pp. 56–7.

93 Douglas Hay, 'Poaching and the Game Laws on Cannock Chase', in **Douglas Hay, Peter Linebaugh, E. P. Thompson** *et al.*, *Albion's Fatal Tree: Crime and society in eighteenth-century England*, Allen Lane, London, 1975.

94 *Sussex Express*, 1 March 1879.

95 Sharpe, *Crime in Early Modern England*, ch. 4, especially pp. 110–11; **R. A. E. Wells**, 'Sheep-rustling in Yorkshire in the age of the Industrial and Agricultural Revolutions', *Northern History*, xx (1984), pp. 127–45 (at p. 139).

96 **David Jones**, *Crime, Protest, Community and Police in Nineteenth-century Britain*, RKP, London, 1982, pp. 78–9 and 83–4.

97 Himmelfarb, *The Idea of Poverty*, p. 234.

98 Quoted in ibid., p. 182.

99 **V. de Sola Pinto** and **A. E. Rodway**, *The Common Muse: Popular British ballad poetry from the fifteenth to the twentieth century*, Chatto and Windus, London, 1957, p. 236.

100 Recorded on *Waterloo-Peterloo: English folksongs and broadsides 1780–1830*, by the Critics Group, Argo Record Company, 1968.

101 Himmelfarb, *The Idea of Poverty*, ch. xvii. It is interesting to note how time gave respectability. The *Athenaeum*'s reviewer of Ainsworth's *Jack Sheppard* condemned it as a 'bad book' because it contained all the 'inherent coarseness and vulgarity of the subject'. He drew a contrast with Fielding's *Jonathan Wild* and Gay's *The Beggar's Opera* whose effect was to 'raise the public in the moral and intellectual scale'. (Quoted in ibid., p. 428.) The reviewer was clearly ignorant of the obloquy heaped on *The Beggar's Opera* at least until the end of the eighteenth century and the accusations that the character of Macheath was so glamorous that many young men were seeking to emulate him as highwaymen. See **Percy A. Scholes**, *The Oxford Companion to Music*, 10th edn, Oxford U.P., Oxford, 1970, pp. 95 and 101, plate 18.6.

102 *Illustrated London News*, 30 May 1868; *The Times*, 23 May 1884. Summing up the case of a soldier in the Rifle Brigade who had attempted to kill his girlfriend as part of a suicide pact, the judge commented: 'He supposed these people had been reading novels'. *The Times*, 18 July 1860.

103 Both quotations in **Patrick Dunae**, 'The penny dreadfuls: Boy's literature and crime, 1870–1900', *Social History Society Newsletter*, **2**(1) (1977), p. 6.

CHAPTER 4

Gender perceptions

The Victorians had clear ideas about the social hierarchy and social class. They also developed clear ideas about gender and the separate spheres of male and female, public and private. Their ideas about class linked with the large numbers of poor processed by the police and the courts to situate their conception of the criminal as someone from the roughest, most disreputable sections of the working class. Their ideas of separate gender spheres and what was acceptable within those spheres fostered different categorisations of offender, different levels of stigmatisation and, at least arguably, generated the criminalisation of some previously tolerated behaviour.

The statistics of crime and statements about criminals and criminality in the eighteenth and nineteenth centuries suggest that crime then, as now, was broadly an activity of young men. It has been suggested that the concentration on male offenders by predominantly male criminologists has led to theories of criminality becoming focussed almost entirely on male criminality.[1] At the same time, various elements that appear central to different forms of criminal behaviour – aggressiveness, acquisitiveness, competitiveness, initiative – were all incorporated as elements of what might be termed 'normal' and largely acceptable masculine behaviour. The legislation of the eighteenth and early nineteenth centuries, moreover, generally used male nouns and pronouns to describe offenders. This may have contributed to the overall perception of crime as masculine behaviour; on at least one occasion magistrates dismissed a case against a female poacher on the grounds that the legislation appeared only to apply to male offenders.[2]

In 1876, L. O. Pike, one of the earliest Victorian historians of crime, employed the certainties of his age to explain that:

women are less criminal than men not only because they are physically
weaker now, but because they were physically weaker generations ago.
The habit of mind has descended with the habit of body, and the
cumulative effect of ages is seen in modern statistics.

Pike went on to combine the contemporary prejudices of his gender with
a Darwinian perspective. He believed that female criminality was on the
increase, and he put this down to independent women, living in towns,
competing in the labour market and, in the process, adopting masculine
attributes. Some became prostitutes, others stole:

and in proportion as they have rendered themselves independent of
men for their subsistence, they have thrown off the protection against
competition and temptation which dependence on men implies. It follows
that, so far as crime is determined by external circumstances, every step
made by woman towards her independence is a step towards that
precipice at the bottom of which lies a prison.[3]

Such ideas fed off and fed into anxieties about bastardy and prostitution,
the growth of female wage labour and the mixing of the sexes at the
workplace. They also slotted neatly alongside the notions of experts in the
new science of psychiatry like Henry Maudsley and T. S. Clouston who
expressed concerns about the future of the nation if women were increasingly to deny their 'nature', a nature that fitted them for the private sphere
of home and family. For Maudsley, childless women were plagued by 'the
dim craving of something wanting to full womanhood'.[4]

  Men and women were not brought before the courts in equal numbers,
nor has the ratio of male to female accused remained constant. Malcolm
Feeley and Deborah Little concluded that, from the late seventeenth to the
early twentieth centuries, the percentage of women among the accused at
the Old Bailey fell from roughly forty-five to twelve. They considered that
this decline was real and that it reflects shifts in the roles expected of
women and the growth of more private forms of social control.[5] Martin
Wiener has cited their work in his own assessment of the criminalisation of
men during the nineteenth century,[6] though Wiener's interest is much more
in attempts to enforce new definitions of masculinity and his focus is on
violent crime rather than on the much more common property offences.
Peter King, however, is suspicious of Feeley and Little's 'vanishing female'
at the Old Bailey and bringing together work on the assizes and quarter
sessions indictments for five counties between the mid-eighteenth and the
mid-nineteenth centuries, he traces a very different pattern. There are

distinct regional variations, but King's figures suggest that the percentages at the terminal points of his study are similar, that there was an increase in the percentage of women offenders during the period of the Revolutionary and Napoleonic Wars, and that this dropped to a lower percentage only in the period from about 1815 to 1840. The greater percentage of women during the wars might be explained by the pressures of war on women seeking to survive without their principal breadwinner. The smaller percentage of women in the post-war years may, he suggests, be the result of concerns about juvenile offenders, generally perceived as male, and a consequent growth in the prosecution of young men in these years.[7] King's statistics are based on indictments and on a much broader range of courts than Feeley and Little. The judicial statistics that began to appear from 1857, however, show women falling from twenty-seven per cent of those proceeded against for indictable offences to only nineteen per cent by 1890. In the summary courts of Victorian England women generally made up only about a fifth of those convicted.

The legal principle of *feme covert* may have kept many women out of the courts. During the eighteenth and nineteenth centuries the precise legal status of women was nebulous. Writing in the 1760s, Sir William Blackstone insisted that, after marriage, a woman had no separate legal identity, though in stating this his main concern was with the law of property. The principle of *feme covert* held that any woman who committed a felony in company with her husband could argue that she acted under his direction and thus gain an acquittal. Serious felonies such as murder could not be so excused, yet many others were. Blackstone stressed that the principle applied only to married women. Most of the women appearing before the courts in this period were single. It seems possible, however, that *feme covert* worked with traditional ideas of patriarchy to give considerable benefit to women especially in magistrates' courts well into the nineteenth century. The principle appears, for example, to have discouraged employers in the Yorkshire worsted factories from prosecuting women for appropriating materials in all but the strongest cases. It is possible also that the principle was interpreted sufficiently broadly to put young women under the age of majority under the 'coverage' of their fathers.[8]

Feme covert might help to explain the low numbers of women appearing before the courts in the eighteenth and early nineteenth centuries. But, in the light of King's figures for women offenders, it was as the principle fell out of use and ceased to appear in the instruction books written for magistrates that the number of female offenders before the courts continued to fall. Moreover, it is particularly striking that, towards the end of the nineteenth century, there was a preponderance of female recidivists. There were more women than men among those 'habitual offenders' convicted twenty times or more, which suggests that the stigma attached to a female offender, and the consequent difficulties of surviving in honest employment after a period of imprisonment, was even greater than that attached to a male. There is another implication here: if some women committed more crimes than men (or at least were arrested and convicted more often), and thus were appearing more often in the criminal statistics, then the overall decline in women offenders in the second half of the nineteenth century was even greater than the bald statistics imply. Lucia Zedner has suggested that the decline in the statistics of female criminality during the Victorian period may be explained by a changing diagnosis of serious female offenders as the nineteenth century wore on. Rather than morally corrupt and depraved, such offenders began to be seen as feeble-minded or prisoners of their 'special bodily functions' (to use Maudsley's term) and were thus moved out of the criminal justice sphere.[9] The use of the terms 'kleptomaniac' for women thieves from the middle class or 'nymphomaniac' for women demonstrating any form of sexual desire was symptomatic of this, linking, as it did, the offence/disease with female sexuality and using this to re-emphasise woman's secondary position in nature.

While notions of patriarchy, reinforced by the principle of *feme covert* may have kept women from the courts, it is unlikely that there was any significant 'dark figure' that would put the number of female offenders on a par with male offenders. Criminal activity, however, was often gendered. Poaching, in the sense of shooting, snaring or trapping game was almost always conducted by men. But women were involved in the black market carrying and selling of poached game and also, more commonly, in collecting eggs. Field girls were ideally situated for informing poachers, and even gamekeepers, of the whereabouts of game birds' nests.[10] Country women stole milk by unlawfully milking cows, but countrymen and women alike were guilty of stealing poultry, growing crops and wood.[11] Breaking and entering and robbery at night tended to be male offences, and overall men appear to have taken a much wider range of goods than women. The evidence from late eighteenth- and early nineteenth-century London suggests that in cases of shoplifting women tended to take gloves, stockings and textiles; but then these were goods sold by mercers and linen drapers where women tended to be the main customers. Women's clothing was useful for theft since petticoats and cloaks offered places for concealment. Shopkeepers and their assistants were often wary of women with cloaks, and in court lawyers and judges might ask if a cloak was worn by the accused as a way of implying intent. Men were more inclined to take goods that were smaller and that could be concealed in a hand, but some male thieves sought to walk out of a shop brazenly with their booty. Men also commonly took goods of greater value than women, such as hardware, jewellry, clocks and watches. Both sexes took food and clothing. More women than men were prosecuted for picking pockets, though the archetypal pickpocket in early nineteenth-century London was commonly described as an assertive, precocious young male. The offence itself appears to have been gendered in time and place. Men tended to be accused of committing the offence in crowds and in daylight; women were more often accused of picking pockets after dark and in less public places. Such female offenders were also commonly accused of being prostitutes.[12]

Contemporary opinion often considered that women brought before the courts were connected in some way with prostitution. As has been suggested above, for the Victorians, 'prostitutes' were the female equivalent, or female half, of the criminal class.[13] The prostitute was the total negation of the ideal of womanhood in the Victorian period but also in the rather less repressive Hanoverian century. Significantly, eighteenth-century criminal biographies often described the offender-hero as being brought to crime by involvement with a prostitute or continuing in his life of crime so as to support his lust for them. Commentators on juvenile delinquency in the early nineteenth century were concerned about young males falling under the influence of corrupting women and girls. This kind of portrayal, arguably, re-emphasised the social mores of the day by offering an awful warning of what happened when the natural order of things was broken and when men became subordinate to independent or masterful, and therefore unnatural, women.[14]

Given his preference for Victorian literary, as opposed to statistical, analyses of criminality, it is not surprising to find J. J. Tobias portraying the women of the criminal class as, primarily, the aiders and abettors of their menfolk, with prostitutes playing a key role here. Prostitutes, he suggests, started trouble in pubs 'to draw the police away from the scene of an intended burglary'; they were also 'in league with pickpockets'.[15] But some prostitutes also robbed their clients, and the dark figure here is probably huge since victims were often reluctant to come forward.[16] Any man who did bring a prosecution or make a report to the police could find himself vilified by the courts, particularly with the increasing presence of lawyers in criminal trials from the late eighteenth century; defence lawyers could have a field day with the morals and sullied respectability of such victims.

Tangentially, at least one pimp in Victorian London sought to discipline his women by means of prosecutions for theft.[17] Equally difficult to assess in numerical terms were the brutal physical assaults inflicted on prostitutes by their clients, often the worse for drink, or by their pimps; very few of these were reported. The isolation and danger of the 'profession' is reflected in the fact that all of Jack the Ripper's victims were prostitutes at some time in their lives, and so too, a few years later, were the London victims of Thomas Neill Cream.[18] Contemporary comments about the prostitute, as with the professional criminal, invariably tell us rather more about Victorian perceptions than about the women themselves. In the mid-nineteenth century, prostitutes were to be catalogued with the detritus of society; they were 'dissolute', 'fallen', 'wretched', the 'Great Social Evil' of a society that was eager to stress its morality and progress. Dickens described the life of Sikes's Nancy as 'squandered in the streets and among the most noisome stews and dens of London'. She was '[t]he miserable companion of thieves and ruffians, the fallen outcast of low haunts, the associate of the scourings of the jails and hulks'.[19] As noted earlier, 'abandoned prostitute' and 'hardened offender' were almost synonymous for women transported for theft; and policemen arresting drunken women commonly catalogued them as 'prostitutes'.[20] Towards the end of the century, however, with the developments of psychiatry and the increasing reluctance to perceive of crime and criminals less as simply immoral and more as not 'normal', prostitutes began to be catalogued as coming from the feeble-minded.[21]

Prostitution was not, in itself, a criminal offence; the prostitution offences were specifically soliciting, living off immoral earnings, and running 'houses of ill fame', but these were enforced selectively. In elegant, nineteenth-century York, for example, the influential groups of Catholics, Evangelicals and Quakers took a much stricter line than the worthies of the fast-growing seaport of Hull, where prostitution, around the docks, was a much greater problem. But then the respectable worthies of Hull rarely had occasion to walk in the dockland streets after dark.[22] The elegant London brothels like the Argyll Rooms, Kate Hamilton's and Mott's were largely ignored by the police. Manifestly neither the proprietors, nor the women who catered for gentlemen in these establishments, were perceived as members of a criminal class or as professional criminals; and at this end of the market the profits were handsome. The less salubrious 'houses of ill fame' were more vulnerable, though even in some of the poorest districts the police did not interfere with them.[23] Furthermore, police action did not necessarily solve the problem. In London towards the end of the century, moves against brothels and their keepers resulted in the entrepreneurs of sex opening massage parlours, or using flats that escaped the legal definition of a brothel.[24]

In general the larcenies committed by women appear to have been very petty. Significantly, the only summary offence during the Victorian period for which the number of women convicted was consistently higher than the number of men, was that of 'unlawfully pledging or disposing' under the Pawnbroker's Act.[25] But small thefts, with the goods being pledged at pawnbrokers, also brought women before the higher courts. 'I took these [three spoons and a fork, valued at four shillings] with the intention to pawn them, and when I got my wages to take them out,' declared Elizabeth McLaren, a 24-year-old cook, to the Central Criminal Court in February 1838. 'I took them to the pawnbrokers, they would not lend me much, and I took them back. The washerwoman, who wanted my place, told my master of it.' Nineteen years later Mary Shellito, a laundress, was before the same court for pawning washing entrusted to her; the woman searcher at Barking Police Station, who searched her on her arrest, found eight pawn tickets in Shellito's possession.[26] It is probable that the growth of department stores towards the end of the nineteenth century tempted some middle-class women to steal, but English shops do not appear to have had the same open display policies as their American and French counterparts, and for England the subject of the middle-class woman 'kleptomaniac', as opposed to the working-class woman 'thief', awaits an historian.[27]

It is tempting to take the incidence of homicide as a measure of the pattern of inter-personal violence in a society, but this can only ever be an assumption that it would be difficult, if not impossible to verify. Violence was most commonly associated with men. Historians have charted new models of masculinity emerging from the late seventeenth century that increasingly rejected any ready recourse to violence by to preserve their honour or reputation. There was a new politeness, a greater concern with the skills of conversation, with new, restrained standards of behaviour, and with ways of acquiring reputation through public activity, church and work. The shift is most clearly detectable in eighteenth-century London and among the elite and the middling sort.[28] It did not mean a quick end to violence between men, and by men against women; and the working-class 'hard man' remained a figure attracting respect well into the twentieth century.[29] The courts of Victorian England, however, appear increasingly to have taken it upon themselves to discipline men for violent behaviour and to seek to impose the new levels of what was considered to be acceptable behaviour. The extent to which provocation was accepted by judges as a defence in cases of homicide – both manslaughter and murder – was increasingly restricted and men who assaulted or killed were treated with much more severity at the end of Victoria's reign than at the beginning.[30]

While they made up the overwhelming majority of violent offenders, men were not alone in being violent. Some women beat, or otherwise ill-treated, servants and apprentices; on occasions such violence caused death or injury and landed the assailants in court.[31] Women fought each other; less commonly they fought with men and a few fought with the police. Jane Smith, for example, fiercely assaulted two police officers in Hull when they tried to arrest her for being drunk and disorderly. A local newspaper turned to classical allusions for its description.

The prisoner was of Amazonian build, and had conducted herself more like a fury than anything else. She was obliged to be hand cuffed and have her legs strapped together to keep her from kicking any one she came near, and it took five men to convey her in a cart to the station house.[32]

Like their menfolk, Irish women had a particular reputation for violence.[33] Among the criminal anthropologists of nineteenth-century Europe the violent female offender was regarded as even more vicious and dangerous than her male counterpart; and it was common, in different theories, for violent female behaviour to be linked to the menstrual cycle.[34]

Although 'unnatural' women used their fists, feet and weapons to commit assaults and murder, it was the female poisoner who, almost by definition, acted secretly and without overt physical aggression, who became a *bête noire* of the nineteenth century.[35] The horror of the female poisoner was probably sharpened by the idea of domesticity and the preparation of food being central elements within the woman's separate sphere of behaviour. Wilkie Collins created the passionate, unscrupulous poisoner, Miss Gwilt, for his labyrinthine *Armadale* (1866), but there was also the occasional 'real' story for the press to latch on to. Eliza Fenning, a servant girl, was executed in 1815 for allegedly attempting to kill the family that employed her with poisoned dumplings.[36] Much later in the century Florence Bravo, Adelaide Bartlett and Florence Maybrick had husbands die in suspicious circumstances; and the cases were further spiced by adultery.[37] The wife who was accused of murdering her husband generated an enormous amount of popular interest. The offence was the ultimate negation of the behaviour expected of the dutiful wife or servant, and it also reached into the ranks of the respectable middle classes. Yet, for all its notoriety, it was a rare occurrence with perhaps one conviction every three or four years.[38] In the early Victorian period women made up forty per cent of all those tried for murder; but when, towards the end of the century, the statistics for the murder of infants under a year old were separated out, the number of women declined to less than a quarter of the total tried for the offence.[39]

New-born child murder, often described as infanticide, was overwhelmingly a female crime. Like the prostitute and the female poisoner, the murdering mother was a negation of the ideal of womanhood, but throughout the period 1750–1900 the all-male juries and judges were often more moderate in their treatment of an accused than a strict implementation of the law would have allowed. Until 1803 the crime of infanticide was supposed to be tried under an act of 1624. This act had been prompted by concerns about bastardy and immorality; it made the offence capital and presumed that a woman who had concealed the death of her illegitimate child had murdered the child. It required proof of concealment, but it put on the accused the onus of proving, with at least one witness, that a dead infant had been born dead. By the middle of the eighteenth century the act was increasingly perceived as cruel and harsh. In addition, there were new attitudes towards the nature of evidence and new requirements in the standard of proof. More and more juries required the prosecution to prove the killing for a guilty verdict and thus, to all intents and purposes, they turned trials under the 1624 act into murder trials. Juries also increasingly accepted that evidence of a woman having made some suitable preparations for her child's birth was sufficient grounds for acquittal. There was an attempt to reform the law in the 1770s, but repeal did not come until 1803.[40]

The act of 1803 was not the work of penal reformers. It was introduced by the conservative Lord Chief Justice, Lord Ellenborough. He was keen to limit the latitude that was increasingly to be found in the courts in such cases. He also drew on concerns about rising levels of illegitimacy; rising poor rates were already aggravated by the French wars and were felt to be worsened by immoral women turning to the parish for assistance. The bill introduced by Ellenborough was the subject of considerable debate and amendment within parliament; another example of the fact that capital statutes were not simply nodded through, even when emanating from a conservative figure in a period of relative conservative ascendancy. The 1803 act made new-born child murder like any other murder, in that the prosecution was required to prove the offence. But where the murder charge failed the jury could return a verdict of 'concealment of birth', which carried a penalty of up to two years in prison. Again however, as the nineteenth century progressed, jury attitudes continued to act as a check on prosecutions. In 1857, for example, Eliza Higgins, a 21-year-old domestic servant lodged in a London workhouse, was tried for the wilful murder of her baby daughter; the Old Bailey jury hearing the case found her guilty of manslaughter, recommended mercy, and commented that 'the bastardy laws had a strong tendency to increase this class of crime'.[41] According to the evidence of several witnesses before the 1866 Royal Commission on Capital Punishment, juries were reluctant to convict as long as the death sentence remained. 'Practically the law of infanticide hardly prevails,' declared J. H. Parry, a barrister with long experience in the criminal courts. 'Almost always now juries find concealment of birth; and . . . I also find that there is a great reluctance to hang women.'[42] Perhaps part of this 'general reluctance' was the result of juries recognising the plight of the accused. Most of the women brought before the courts charged with infanticide during the eighteenth and nineteenth centuries appear to have been young women, commonly servants, desperate to maintain their positions and their respectability.[43]

Desperate attempts to preserve respectability, and also a determination on the part of married working-class women to limit the size of their families could also lead to abortions, or to the use of baby farmers, the least scrupulous of whom might be better described as baby disposers. The law regarding abortion was progressively tightened during the nineteenth century. Before 1803, abortion was punished by a fine or a short term of imprisonment, and there was no penalty at all for abortion before 'quickening' – that is, when the woman could feel the movement of the foetus at about thirteen weeks. In 1837 the concept of quickening was removed; but until the 1861 Offences against the Person Act it was only the abortionist, and not the pregnant woman, who was guilty of an offence. Legislating against abortifacients was virtually impossible since so many of them were sold as purgatives and remedies for other ailments. Throughout the Victorian period much of the press carried advertisements for a great variety of pills to remove 'obstructions' – a euphemism for an unwanted foetus; and those marketing the products sought ways round the law by, for example, requiring purchasers to make a declaration that they were not pregnant, or by insisting that the pills should not be taken during pregnancy. If the pills failed (and invariably they were quite useless), there was always recourse to an abortionist. Middle-class women might be able to call on the services of a practising doctor; in working-class communities unqualified women who acted as midwives and nurses, and who laid out the dead, appear also to have been generally accepted and employed as abortionists. Baby farmers were individuals, generally women, who, for a fee, would keep children in their own homes.[44] In some instances 'keeping' appears to have been tacitly recognised as a synonym for allowing to die through lack of food and care, or even murdering. The revelations of baby farming in South London, which culminated in the execution of Mary Waters in 1870, led to the Infant Life Protection Act of 1872. This required all persons keeping more than one infant in their homes for more than twenty-four hours to register with local authorities; the local authorities themselves had to draw up regulations regarding facilities and numbers. The new act did not solve the problem; but then parliament recognised that there was a need for cheap baby care. So too, it would seem, did the all-male courts, which continued to be lenient with baby farmers accused of negligence as well as mothers accused of infanticide. Finally, there is little evidence to suggest that the criminal justice system was ever greatly concerned with abortion.[45]

During the seventeenth and eighteenth centuries there was an acceptance that a man might physically chastise his wife. The new ideas of masculinity, however, whittled away at the tolerance of such behaviour and, as noted earlier, at least from the late eighteenth century the courts were beginning to take a more critical view of wife beating.[46] Initially Georgian artisans appear to have been largely immune to these trends and they seem also to have been among the most violent towards their women folk. They feared competition from low-paid female labour, but they depended upon their wives to help support the family. They bonded with each other in their workplaces, pubs and clubs, and heavy drinking was central to the artisan culture. Their attitudes and their drinking arguably fostered domestic violence. In the early nineteenth century, however, a change is detectable as radical working-class spokesmen who urged political and economic reform also began to speak out loudly and publicly against wife beating.[47] Moreover, they urged, a properly respectful and submissive wife deserved protection. Such views became increasingly common across all social classes in Victorian Britain, though within the working-class family particularly, economic pressures and tensions contributed to the continuation of domestic violence. Nevertheless, even in the poorer urban working-class districts where such violence continued to have vestiges of acceptance, neighbours might intervene when a husband exceeded the boundaries that a community recognised; and rural communities might still charivari such a husband.

In general the Victorian courts continued to take an increasingly hostile attitude towards the husband who assaulted a dutiful, virtuous wife, and in 1853 an Act for the Better Prevention of Aggravated Assault Upon

Women and Children set out to specify and limit the amount of chastisement that a husband or father could administer. Nevertheless, 'aggravation' on the part of the wife continued to be considered by some as a just cause, or at least a mitigating circumstance for chastisement, even when such chastisement resulted in death.[48] In 1886 a Birmingham surgeon, Furneaux Jordan, explained to his, and probably to others' satisfaction that on the basis of his observations most battered and murdered wives were of distinct physical types. Their skin:

was often clear, delicate, perhaps rosy. Their hair-growth was never heavy nor long, and the eyebrows were spare and refined. Their upper spinal curves were so formed to give a somewhat convex appearance to the back and shoulders and a more or less forward pose to the head.

But most importantly, they 'had sharp tongues in their heads and an unfailing – unfailing by repetition – supply of irritating topics on which to exercise them'.[49] In addition to such suggestions that the wife who was beaten was asking for it, the wife who responded with counter-violence was likely to receive a sentence from a court in excess of that meted out to violent husbands.

The scale of wife beating is impossible to assess. The police were dissuaded from becoming involved in domestic disputes, while many women were reluctant to take their family's principal breadwinner to court or simply failed to give evidence in court, recognising the impact that even a short spell of imprisonment or a small fine could have on the family budget. A study of spousal abuse in late nineteenth-century Northampton deploys evidence suggesting a slight increase in the offence in the last quarter of the century, and argues that this could have been the result of a crisis of self-esteem among the town's shoemakers deprived of traditional sports and leisure under increased supervision by factory foremen and police officers.[50] Others, however, have suggested that there was a decrease in the scale of such violence towards the end of the century as rising living standards reduced stress on the male as economic provider and as new legislation and rulings were enforced. An amendment to the Matrimonial Clauses Act of 1878 enabled magistrates to order separations in cases where husbands had been convicted of aggravated assaults on their wives, and the husband could also be required to pay a set weekly sum for the maintenance of his wife and children if it was deemed necessary for their future well-being. In 1891 the ruling in the case *R. v. Jackson* finally settled the law that it was illegal for a husband to beat or imprison his wife; the Summary Jurisdiction (Married Women) Act of 1895 allowed women to decide for themselves on separation without the need for a magistrate's order. But again as suggested earlier, it is equally possible that growing respectability inhibited wives even more from complaining, while the noise and results of 'domestic disputes' were less apparent behind the net curtains and garden walls of the increasingly working-class streets of suburbia. As James Hammerton has concluded, it is not possible to sustain any conclusions about a decline in domestic violence before 1914 on the evidence available.[51]

The wife beater, increasingly demonised as the nineteenth century wore on, was perceived essentially as a working-class problem. From the middle of the century, however, feminist critics and conservative moralists began to put more and more stress on the standards to be expected from husbands in marriage. In consequence, there appears to have been a growing intolerance of overbearing male behaviour, whatever an individual's class.[52] The shift was a gradual one, reflected in legislation such as the Matrimonial Clauses Act and court decisions. In the courts the judiciary often led the way, sometimes inflicting heavy sentences on violent husbands when the jury was inclined to recommend mercy because of a wife-victim's drunkenness, scolding, or failure to provide the appropriate domestic arrangements for her husband and children. Such situations generated friction between judge and jury and even, as in the case of George Hall, a Birmingham jeweller's stamper who shot his new, but 'adulterous' young wife, a massive petitioning and press campaign for clemency.[53] But still, for many, the problem of family violence was so abhorrent that it could scarcely be discussed and it was submerged under pieties about the ideal harmony of the family in which the father was dominant and masterful while the mother and children were dutiful and submissive.

Violence by men against women was not confined to marriage. The workplace, as well as the home, provided the spatial context for such violence, as well as for male on male and female on female violence. Similarly, the social context of courtship might result in incidents of male assault.[54] While the dominant, masterful male was presumed to have a rational, enlightened mind, it was also recognised that within his body there was located an unruly sexual urge. Again this was contrasted with the ideal female who was regarded as irrational and prey to her emotions yet, at the same time, sexually passive. The double standard was made explicit in 1871 in the report of the Royal Commission on the Contagious Diseases Acts. The Commission rejected the idea of regular examinations of soldiers and sailors for venereal diseases, as was required of prostitutes under these acts, on the grounds that:

there is no comparison to be made between prostitutes and the men who consort with them. With the one sex the offence is committed as a matter of gain; with the other it is an irregular indulgence of a natural impulse.[55]

At the beginning of the twentieth century the Royal Commission on the Metropolitan Police underlined the double standard further when it rejected the idea of sexual equality in the offence of soliciting. It insisted that legislation to criminalise a man for propositioning a woman, at least if she did not 'resent it, or, at any rate, [showed] no resentment or annoyance', would simply not be acceptable 'to the community at large'.[56] Notions of this sort contributed to problems in cases of that most appalling of offences committed by members of one sex on the other – rape.

Embarrassment, fear, and even ignorance ensured that many victims of rape and sexual assault sought no legal redress. In June 1824 parliament discussed the use of summary punishments for men 'lewdly and obscenely exposing the person'. T. G. B. Estcourt reported the opinion of magistrates:

that the offence was so frequent, and it was so difficult to prevail upon females to overcome their natural delicacy, and prosecute the offender in a court of justice, that some summary punishment was almost indispensable.[57]

Ann Spowage, a maidservant in Nottinghamshire, was rescued from rape by a passer-by in September 1857, but it was eleven days before she gave a deposition to the police. 'I complained about it to my mistress on the Thursday after. I was so shy I hardly dare mention it.'[58] The number of prosecutions for rape and attempted rape remained small throughout the period. In some instances, perhaps the majority, the matter appears to have been settled out of court. Magistrates and grand juries commonly dismissed accusations of rape or attempted rape. It seems probable that more offenders were pursued on charges of indecent assault which were heard at quarter sessions rather than assizes. These were less expensive for the prosecutor, less embarrassing for the victim, in as much as she escaped lengthy cross-examination by a defence counsel, and more likely to end with a conviction since, with rape being a capital offence until 1841, juries again appear to have been reluctant to convict.[59] Eighteenth-century evidence suggests that such prosecutions were more common in rural than urban areas, probably because of the support the victim received from family and friends.[60] Most offences in the Black Country between 1835 and 1860 concerned girls under sixteen years, and often under ten;[61] this also suggests the family acting as the prime movers in a prosecution. Not all women in rural districts were as fortunate, however. Female servants in the countryside were as unprotected from, and as vulnerable to, sexual harassment as any of their urban counterparts; and few in the communities, to which these women were usually strangers, appear to have cared.[62]

Rape trials were invariably as much an examination of the character and purity of the accused as they were of the events of the alleged offence. There was concern that the accused could be the victim of a malicious prosecution, or that, with his natural and powerful sexual urges, the man had been unwarrantably encouraged. The victim needed to show evidence of a vigorous resistance to the attack, and of untarnished honour up until the moment it occurred. As Carolyn Conley has concluded, rape victims were suspect on three counts: they were women, they were admitting to have been outside the supervision of their male protectors, and they were declaring their loss of sexual innocence in public. 'Judges and jurors frequently concluded that no man should lose his respectability, let alone his freedom, for the mere seduction of such unworthy creatures.'[63] The point was put most forcibly in a paper by Charles Routh to the British Gynaecological Society in 1886. Routh took as his subject 'Nymphomania'. He considered incest unthinkable, and insisted that in rape cases signs of assault were insufficient in themselves; the doctor should consider whether the complainant 'is . . . addicted to masturbation? Has her mind been deteriorated by prurient ideas?' and he concluded of all women complaining of sexual assault: 'Except upon the strongest corroborating evidence, the presumption is that they are liars, plausible liars, cunning liars.'[64]

While on several occasions the courts insisted that prostitutes had as much right to protection from rape and sexual assault as any other woman, the reality of court proceedings and jury decisions often suggested otherwise. The case of Mary Duggan, though not specifically involving sexual assault, is illustrative of this. One night in February 1850, Duggan, 'a woman of abandoned character', had left a Yorkshire pub in the company of three men; all four had gone into a neighbouring field. The following morning Duggan was found dead 'with her person exposed and much bruised'. The judge directed the jury to acquit the three defendants charged with causing her death since:

these facts did not amount to the crime of manslaughter. The woman, being intoxicated, had voluntarily accompanied the prisoners; and she was not like an infant who, unable to take care of itself, had been left exposed to the cold and died in consequence.[65]

Rape was overwhelmingly a male offence committed against women. Child sexual abuse was also, almost always an offence committed by men. Notions of masculinity were deployed alongside those of class when such cases came to court. The abusers were labelled as 'monsters'; their offences were a negation of the ideal of the Victorian gentleman and the father as moral protector. Almost always the assumption was that this was also a crime committed by the most vicious lurking within the residuum, and these ideas were played out in court as defendants sought to stress that they were respectable fathers, or that they were being traduced by evil women motivated by malice or thwarted in blackmail attempts. The character of the accused and the accuser in such cases was always important, and the evidence suggests that members of the working class were more likely to be convicted of such offences than members of the middle class.[66]

The contemporary interest in the history of crime began as an attempt to find the voice of those who had been largely ignored in history. The initial concern was the working class, but it is becoming increasingly apparent that there is much to be learned here about attitudes to gender and the development of the concept of the separate spheres. The problem, as ever, is in interpreting what is learned. The evidence underscores the picture of a patriarchal society within which it was expected that men and women limit their activities to their respective spheres; though there is also evidence that new ideals of masculinity required the husband-father to have a significant role in the private family sphere and that women might play an important role in the public sphere of philanthropic work. Certain male offenders might be glamorised since their offending reflected the male virtues of courage, daring and initiative. In rough working-class districts the 'hard man' might achieve an appeal precisely because he showed the toughness and independence to which others might aspire. But perhaps the clearest example is the romantic highwaymen whose appeal spanned the spectrum of social class, though the tendency to invest some literary highwaymen with gentility was obviously directed at the more respectable reader. A romantic highwayman like Ainsworth's Dick Turpin was quite different from Dickens's brutal Bill Sikes; but even Sikes had the attributes of daring and shrewdness. In contrast, by her criminal actions the female offender, in the Victorian period particularly, was seen as challenging, even denying the social position designated for women. Furthermore, while the patriarchal society boasted of protecting the weaker sex, and while the legal process increasingly sought to uphold this boast, the female victims of sexual assaults continued to be seen as somehow at fault and subjected to harsh and extremely personal investigation in the witness box.

Elizabeth Cass, a young seamstress from Stockton-on-Tees, was arrested by P. C. Bowen Endacott in London's Regent Street in June 1887 and charged with soliciting. Endacott insisted that he knew her and had seen her soliciting in the past. Cass had only recently moved to London and was able to produce witnesses that she had hardly ever been out on her own. The case was dropped and Endacott was prosecuted at the Old Bailey for wilful and corrupt perjury. Members of the Metropolitan Police were authorised to begin a collection to provide Endacott with a good defence barrister. Almost the entire proceedings of his trial were taken up with a close investigation of Cass's life before she moved to London and especially her relationship with a married man. Endacott was never called into the witness box and, while his superiors described him as a 'diligent and trustworthy officer', no witness gave evidence to the effect that Cass had been soliciting. Nevertheless, the judge stopped the trial on the grounds that, as there was only one eyewitness corroborating Cass's version of her arrest, it would be inadvisable to proceed. Elizabeth Cass disappears from history, conceivably accepting the anonymity and respectability of the woman's sphere. Endacott was restored to his rank and given charge of policing the British Museum, potentially a very public role.[67]

Notes and references

1 Frances Heidensohn, *Crime and Society*, Macmillan, London, 1989, ch. 5; and see also *idem*, *Women and Crime*, Macmillan, London, 1985.

2 Susan E. Grace, 'Female criminality in York and Hull, 1830–1870', unpublished D.Phil., University of York, 1998, pp. 45–9.

3 L. O. Pike, *A History of Crime in England*, 2 vols, London, 1876, ii, p. 527.

4 Elaine Showalter, *The Female Malady: Women, madness and English culture, 1830–1980*, Virago Press, London, 1987, especially pp. 122–6; **Martin J. Wiener**, *Reconstructing the Criminal: Culture, law, and policy in England, 1830–1914*, Cambridge U.P., Cambridge, 1990, pp. 16–17. For the Maudsley quotation see **Daniel Pick**, *Faces of Degeneration: A European disorder, c.1848–1918*, Cambridge U.P., Cambridge, 1989, p. 212.

5 **Malcolm M. Feeley** and **Deborah H. Little**, 'The vanishing female: The decline of women in the criminal process, 1687–1912,' *Law and Society Review*, **25** (1991), pp. 719–57.

6 **Martin J. Wiener**, 'The Victorian criminalization of men', in **Pieter Spierenburg** (ed.), *Men and Violence: Gender, honor and rituals in modern Europe and America*, Ohio State U.P., Columbus, Ohio, 1998.

7 Peter King, 'Gender and recorded crime: the long-term impact of female offenders on prosecution rates across England and Wales, 1750–1850', in Peter King, *Crime and Law in the Age of Reform, 1750–1850: Remaking justice from the margins*, Cambridge U.P. (forthcoming).

8 Peter King, *Crime, Justice and Discretion in England 1740–1820*, Oxford U.P., Oxford, 2000, pp. 201 and 285–6; Barry Godfrey, 'Workplace appropriation and the gendering of factory "law": West Yorkshire, 1840–1880', in Margaret L. Arnot and Cornelie Usborne (eds.), *Gender and Crime in Modern Europe*, U.C.L. Press, London, 1999.

9 Lucia Zedner, *Women, Crime and Custody in Victorian England*, Clarendon Press, Oxford, 1991, *passim*.

10 John E. Archer, *'By a flash and a scare.' Arson, Animal Maiming, and Poaching in East Anglia 1815–1870*, Clarendon Press, Oxford, 1990, p. 233.

11 Timothy Shakesheff, *Rural Conflict, Crime and Protest: Herefordshire, 1800–1860*, Boydell Press, Woodbridge, 2003, ch. 6.

12 Diedre Palk, 'Private crime in public and private places: pickpockets and shoplifters in London 1780 to 1823', in Tim Hitchcock and Heather Shore (eds.), *The Streets of London: From the Great Fire to the Great Stink*, Rivers Oram Press, London, 2003. There are also some useful comparisons between male and female offending in Grace, 'Female criminality'. Heather Shore, *Artful Dodgers: Youth and crime in early nineteenth-century London*, Boydell/Royal Historical Society, Woodbridge, 1999, p. 59, makes the point about the typical pickpocket. Moreover, Shore's dataset from the Middlesex Criminal Registers implies that there was a majority of males among juvenile pickpockets.

13 See above, p. 80.

14 Philip Rawlings, *Drunks, Whores and Idle Apprentices: Criminal biographies of the eighteenth century*, Routledge, London, 1992, pp. 22–3; Shore, *Artful Dodgers*, p. 10.

15 J. J. Tobias, *Crime and Industrial Society in the Nineteenth Century*, Penguin, Harmondsworth, 1972, pp. 103–7.

16 See, for example, Frances Finnegan, *Poverty and Prostitution: A study of Victorian prostitutes in York*, Cambridge U.P., Cambridge, 1979, pp. 117–24.

17 Jennifer Davis, 'Prosecutions and their context: The use of the criminal law in later nineteenth-century London', in Douglas Hay and Francis Snyder (eds.), *Policing and Prosecution in Britain 1750–1850*, Clarendon Press, Oxford, 1989, p. 415.

18 'Ripperology' is never-ending. The most stimulating recent assessment of the episode, which relates the murders to the cultural context, is Judith Walkowitz, *City of Dreadful Delight: Narratives of sexual danger in late*

Victorian London, Virago, London, 1992. For Cream see **Angus McLaren**, *A Prescription for Murder: The Victorian serial killings of Dr. Thomas Neill Cream*, University of Chicago Press, Chicago, 1993.

19 **Charles Dickens**, *Oliver Twist*, ch. xl.

20 See above, p. 80; **Clive Emsley**, *Policing and its Context, 1750–1870*, Macmillan, London, 1983, p. 122.

21 Wiener, *Reconstructing the Criminal*, pp. 238–9; Zedner, *Women, Crime and Custody*, p. 275.

22 Grace, 'Female criminality', pp. 242–9.

23 **Kellow Chesney**, *The Victorian Underworld*, Penguin, Harmondsworth, 1970, pp. 365–7; Emsley, *Policing and its Context*, p. 140.

24 **Stefan Petrow**, *Policing Morals: The Metropolitan Police and the Home Office 1870–1914*, Clarendon Press, Oxford, 1994, pp. 154–7.

25 Zedner, *Women, Crime and Custody*, p. 36.

26 *C.C.C.S.P. 1837–38*, no. 685; *C.C.C.S.P. 1856–57*, no. 630; and for other examples see *O.B.S.P. 1816–17*, no. 50, and *C.C.C.S.P. 1836–37*, nos 95 and 96.

27 **Elaine S. Abelson**, *When Ladies Go A-Thieving: Middle-class shoplifters in the Victorian department store*, Oxford U.P., New York, 1989, explores the phenomenon in the east-coast cities of the United States. For the contrast in American and English displays see p. 277, note 73. For 'kleptomania' in France see, **Michael B. Miller**, *Le Bon Marché: Bourgeois culture and the department store, 1869–1920*, Princeton U.P., Princeton, N.J., 1981, pp. 197–206.

28 **Robert Shoemaker**, 'Reforming male manners: Public insult and the decline of violence in London, 1660–1740', and **Elizabeth Foyster**, 'Boys will be boys? Manhood and aggression, 1660–1800', both in **Tim Hitchcock** and **Michèle Cohen** (eds.), *English Masculinities 1660–1800*, Longman, London, 1999; **Robert Shoemaker**, 'Male honour and the decline of public violence in eighteenth-century London', *Social History*, 26 (2001), pp. 190–208.

29 **John E. Archer**, ' "Men behaving badly"? Masculinity and the uses of violence, 1850–1900', and **Andrew Davis**, 'Youth gangs, gender and violence, 1870–1900', both in **Shani D'Cruze** (ed.), *Everyday Violence in Britain, 1850–1950: Gender and class*, Longman, London, 2000.

30 **Martin J. Wiener**, *Men of Blood: Violence, manliness and criminal justice in Victorian England*, Cambridge U.P., Cambridge, 2004, *passim*.

31 See, for example, **Frank McLynn**, *Crime and Punishment in Eighteenth-Century England*, Routledge, London, 1989, p. 117; *O.B.S.P. 1829*, no. 751, pp. 350–9.

32 *Hull Advertiser*, 26 August 1836.

33 See, for example, **Carolyn A. Conley**, *The Unwritten Law: Criminal justice in Victorian Kent*, Oxford U.P., New York, 1991, pp. 70–2; **Frances Finnegan**, *Poverty and Prejudice: A study of the Irish immigrants in York 1840–75*, Cork U.P., Cork, 1982, pp. 136–7 and 140; **David Philips**, *Crime and Authority in Victorian England: The Black Country 1835–60*, Croom Helm, London, 1977, p. 149; **Barbara Weinberger**, 'Law breakers and law enforcers in the late Victorian city: Birmingham 1867–77', Unpublished Ph.D., University of Warwick, 1981, pp. 205–7.

34 Pick, *Faces of Degeneration*, pp. 92–4.

35 Sir George Grey, when Home Secretary, told a Royal Commission that he believed women were less likely to commit murder than men, but he noted also that there had been some 'bad cases of poisoning', *P.P.* 1866 (3590) xxi, *Royal Commission on Capital Punishment*, q. 420.

36 See, *inter alia*, 'Eliza Fenning (The danger of condemning to death on circumstantial evidence alone)', *All the Year Round*, xviii (1867), pp. 66–72; see also **V. A. C. Gatrell**, *The Hanging Tree: Execution and the English people 1770–1868*, Oxford U.P., Oxford, 1994, pp. 353–67.

37 **Mary S. Hartman**, *Victorian Murderesses: A true history of thirteen respectable French and English women accused of unspeakable crimes*, Robson Books, London, 1977, especially chs 4–6.

38 **Roger Chadwick**, *Bureaucratic Mercy: The Home Office and the treatment of capital cases in Victorian Britain*, Garland Publishing, New York, 1992, p. 301.

39 Zedner, *Women, Crime and Custody*, p. 38.

40 **Mark Jackson**, *New-Born Child Murder: Women, illegitimacy and the courts in eighteenth-century England*, Manchester U.P., Manchester, 1996. Jackson favours 'new-born child murder' over 'infanticide' on the grounds that the latter has a precise contemporary legal usage.

41 *C.C.C.S.P. 1856–57*, no. 597, p. 47.

42 *P.P.* 1866 (3590) xxi, *Royal Commission on Capital Punishment*, q. 2559; and see also qq. 5, 55–57, 135–42, 1047, 1538, 3299.

43 Elaine Showalter notes that the experts in the new science of psychiatry insisted that, following childbirth, a woman's mind became especially weak and she lost much of her control over her behaviour. They appear to have ignored the low social, and precarious economic, position of the majority of those charged with infanticide. Showalter, *The Female Malady*, pp. 58–9.

44 **McLaren**, *A Prescription for Murder*, ch. 7.

45 Lionel Rose, *Massacre of the Innocents: Infanticide in Great Britain 1800–1939*, RKP, London, 1986, especially chs 10–12; Conley, *The Unwritten Law*, pp. 114–17.

46 See above, pp. 46–7.

47 Anna Clark, *The Struggle for the Breeches: Gender and the making of the British working class*, University of California Press, Berkeley, Ca., 1995, ch. 5.

48 Chadwick, *Bureaucratic Mercy*, pp. 313–19.

49 Furneaux Jordan, *Character as seen in Body and Parentage*, London, 1886, p. 3.

50 Mary Beth Emmerichs, 'Five shillings and costs: Petty offenders in late-Victorian Northampton', Unpublished Ph.D., University of Pennsylvania, 1991, ch. 7 *passim*.

51 Conley, *The Unwritten Law*, pp. 71–81; Maeve Doggett, *Marriage, Wife-Beating and the Law in Victorian England*, Weidenfeld and Nicholson, London, 1992; Nancy Tomes, 'A "Torrent of Abuse": Crimes of violence between working-class men and women in London, 1840–1875', *Journal of Social History*, 11 (1977–8), pp. 328–45; A. James Hammerton, *Cruelty and Companionship: Conflict in nineteenth-century married life*, Routledge, London, 1992, p. 42.

52 Hammerton, *Cruelty and Companionship, passim*.

53 Wiener, *Men of Blood*, pp. 224–7.

54 Shani D'Cruze, *Crimes of Outrage: Sex, violence and Victorian working women*, U.C.L. Press, London, 1998, *passim*.

55 P.P. 1871 (C.408–1) xix, *Report from the Royal Commission on the Administration and Operation of the Contagious Diseases Acts 1866–9*, p. 17. In contrast to the Commission's conclusion, however, there were witnesses who recognised the double standard. R. B. Williams, for example, a committee member of the Rescue Society, protested: 'One of the root causes of prostitution is the widely prevalent immoral sentiment that the quality which is so strongly demanded in women is not to be required in our sex – that incontinency on the part of men is comparatively venial, and that men may have access to women who are not wives. These Acts are based on the same vicious principle, and operate to protect and encourage men in their illicit indulgences. As they thus provide for vice, so will their educational effect be to teach men, and especially young men, that they must have a continual supply of fallen women for their sensual gratification.' *Ibid., Minutes of Evidence*, q. 20, 292.

56 P.P. 1908 (C.4156), *Report of the Royal Commission upon the Duties of the Metropolitan Police*, p. 127.

57 *Hansard*, new series, xi (1824), col. 1082.

58 Notts. R.O. Q.S.D. Deposition of Ann Spowage, 15 September 1857.

59 **Anna Clark**, *Women's Silence, Men's Violence: Sexual assault in England 1770–1845*, Pandora, London, 1987; **Antony Simpson**, 'The "blackmail myth" and the prosecution of rape and its attempt in 18th century London: The creation of a legal tradition', *Journal of Criminal Law and Criminology*, 77 (1986), pp. 101–50; and Gatrell, *The Hanging Tree*, ch. 17.

60 Beattie, *Crime and the Courts*, p. 130.

61 Philips, *Crime and Authority*, p. 269.

62 **Jill Barber**, ' "Stolen Goods": The sexual harassment of female servants in West Wales during the nineteenth century', *Rural History*, 4 (1993), pp. 123–36.

63 Conley, *The Unwritten Law*, pp. 81–95; quotation at p. 95.

64 Quoted in McLaren, *A Prescription for Murder*, pp. 84–5. McLaren also quotes Lawson Tait, the eminent Birmingham gynaecologist and surgeon, who was infuriated by the 1885 legislation that raised the age of consent to sixteen and which he believed could lead to the ruin of respectable gentlemen. Tait persuaded the authorities to let him investigate the subsequent complaints made in the Birmingham area, and out of 100 he considered that only six should result in prosecution.

65 *The Times*, 16 March 1850.

66 **Louise A. Jackson**, *Child Sexual Abuse in Victorian England*, Routledge, London, 2000, especially ch. 6.

67 *C.C.C.S.P. 1887*, no. 1058, pp. 612–31; **Mark Clapson** and **Clive Emsley**, 'Street, beat and respectability: The culture and self-image of the late Victorian and Edwardian urban policeman', in **Louis A. Knafla** (ed.) *Police and War in Europe: Criminal justice history*, **15**, Greenwood Press, Westport, Conn., 2002, pp. 107–31 (at p. 124).

CHAPTER 5

Environmental perceptions

Contemporaries who thought and wrote about crime in England between 1750 and 1900 perceived it largely as an urban problem. London, the largest city in Western Europe, was the focus for the concerns of both Henry Fielding and Patrick Colquhoun. The former lamented that:

Whoever . . . considers the Cities of London and Westminster, with the late vast Addition of their Suburbs; the great Irregularity of their Buildings, the immense Number of Lanes, Alleys, Courts and Byeplaces; must think that, had they been intended for the very Purpose of Concealment, they could scarce have been better contrived.

Colquhoun described London as:

not only the grand magazine of the British Empire, but also the general receptacle for the idle and depraved of almost every Country, and certainly from every quarter of the dominions of the Crown; – where the temptations and resources for criminal pleasures – gambling – fraud and depredation, as well as for pursuits of honest industry almost exceed imagination.[1]

Most of the more alarming, and certainly the best publicised of nineteenth-century crimes were committed in London.[2] Yet some contemporaries looked beyond the metropolis and found crime in the burgeoning urban environments with their teeming, anonymous populations and their uneducated, nomadic poor living in insanitary slums. Thomas Plint fused the assessments of Fielding and Colquhoun when he declared that:

The pickpocket and the thief can find no nesting-place amongst the statesmen of Cumberland and Westmoreland, or the miners of Durham

and Cornwall. They fly to Birmingham, London, Manchester, Liverpool,
Leeds. They congregate where there is plenty of plunder, and verge
enough to hide in.

In 1867 James T. Hammick emphasised 'that the criminal classes are, for
the most part, congregated in the towns'. For the Reverend William
Douglas Morrison it could 'easily be ascertained without the aid of any
figures' that cities were 'the nurseries of modern crime'. Implicit in what
Hammick and Morrison had to say, and explicit in Plint, was the notion
that crime in rural society was not as serious. This was an idea shared by
many and articulated by some opponents of the new police in the 1830s
and 1840s. 'In cities', according to the Reverend Charles Brereton:

the majority of thieves exist in gangs, practise fraud by profession, and
live by a constant series of depredations . . . criminals in the country only
occasionally once or twice a year steal a sheep, pig, corn, hay, wood,
turnips, poultry as the case may be.

This was just one of the many reasons why, according to Brereton, the
Metropolitan Police model was inapplicable to rural England. Towards
the end of the century such ideas had been developed by enthusiasts for the
Settlement Movement who urged young gentlemen to spend time doing
'good works' in slum areas like London's East End. What was lacking in
these districts, according to Canon Barnett, the founder of Toynbee Hall, was
'a leisured class . . . who will see that the laws are carried out and generally
keep the social life going'. Canon Henry Scott Holland, an early enthusiast
for Oxford House, summed this perception up with his call to young gentlemen to 'Come and be the squires of East London'.[3] All of this can best be
understood in terms of the vision of a contented rustic England that developed during the nineteenth century, in which the stability and tranquillity
of rural society were emphasised to compensate for the terrors of urbanisation and recurrent concern about the effects of the industrial economy.

   The attempts of various sociologists and social anthropologists to
explain the differences between rural and urban lifestyles have given a
theoretical underpinning to the belief that rural crime and urban crime
are markedly different. Most notable in this respect is the *Gemeinschaft-*
Gesellschaft dichotomy put forward by the German sociologist Ferdinand
Tönnies: in traditional society, generally equated with rural society, people
live in a face to face community where social mobility is low, customs and
actions are legitimated in terms of custom and precedent; modern society,
in contrast, is impersonal and a variety of voluntarily formed associations

regulate different aspects of social life.[4] *Anomie*, or social instability particularly resulting from the disruption, or disappearance of value systems in the teeming new cities of the nineteenth century, has also been popular in explaining a growth of crime during the great period of industrialisation and urbanisation. At the close of the nineteenth century some European criminologists and social investigators, notably Emile Durkheim, were concerned that the city, together with the spread of 'modern civilisation', was destabilising the 'equilibrium' of certain individuals and prompting degeneracy and deviance. In the words of Havelock Ellis: 'Like insanity, criminality flourishes among migrants, and our civilisation is bringing us all, more or less into the position of migrants'.[5] These concepts implicitly, though perhaps not always consciously, inform the comments of a variety of historians. J. J. Tobias, for example, concluded that:

The large towns during much of the nineteenth century failed to provide the support which former country dwellers had known in the smaller communities from which they came. Entry into the criminal class was a means of finding support; it was entry into an association, informal but none the less, members of which could be found almost everywhere.[6]

Obviously environment to some extent dictates the forms and styles of crime. White-collar crime depends on particular forms of economic and social structure generally rooted in a bureaucratic and urbanised society. Street robbery, by definition, could not happen in a corn field or forest; similarly poaching and sheep stealing, common offences in the eighteenth and nineteenth centuries, could only be rural offences, though not necessarily committed by rural dwellers. Nineteenth-century urban areas in the Midlands, East Anglia and Lancashire contained poachers who made regular forays into the neighbouring countryside.[7] Some London gangs were suspected of secretly killing other animals, notably horses, and then offering to buy the carcasses from the owners for dog meat.[8] Sheep stealers and rustlers were drawn similarly from both town and country, as well as from a variety of social groups; and motives were varied. Rural and urban poverty could be a spur, though it seems possible that in some districts there was almost a tradition of periodically improving the family diet with stolen mutton. Sometimes resentment or revenge appears to have motivated the rural sheep stealer; and, on occasions, as in the case of poaching, sheep were taken to provide butchers with illicit meat for the urban market.[9]

Arson, while it was occasionally employed as a weapon during trade disputes,[10] was primarily a rural offence, and environment was a contributory element. The farmer's house was known and it was unlikely to be in a distinct, middle-class district; his barns and ricks, like his sheep and other livestock were vulnerable on dark nights in ways which factories, or work-shops in tolerably lighted streets, subject to increasing police patrols, were not. A casual agricultural labourer, angered or victimised by a farmer act-ing as employer or Poor Law official, could exact prompt revenge and the chances of getting away with it seemed reasonable. At the very end of 1841 the Reverend Henry Owen, a magistrate living at Haveringham in Suffolk, saw £80-worth of his corn go up in flames. The Chief Constable believed that the outrage was committed 'in consequence of the Revd Mr Owen having punished some persons of bad character in the neighbourhood'.[11] In 1845 William Grange set fire to the hay and corn stacks of John Handysides, a farmer of Ackham in the North Riding, when Handysides dismissed him without payment. Grange declared at his trial that he intended to show Handysides 'an example that farmers should treat their labourers with respect and not clandestinely as he had done'. He was found guilty and transported. The Chief Constable of the East Riding reported to the quarter sessions in January 1864 that the 'illiterate rustic' was easily offended and that:

the majority of these evil-doers, of course, are those who have been discharged from their employments, or punished for offences, or refused favours, or warned to be on their good behaviour, or deluded into an idea of wrong or an insult to their families.[12]

Insurance companies rightly recognised that the problem was not one-sided and warned their agents to enquire whether farmers were deemed 'obnoxious' in their locality before undertaking to offer their services; in addi-tion they surcharged unpopular farmers who were already policyholders.[13]

About half of those arrested for arson in the East Riding during the 1860s were agricultural labourers and several of these were itinerants, locally known as Wolds Rangers – defined by a prosecuting counsel as 'a man who travels the Wolds getting work from day to day and con-sequently being fully conversant with the district'.[14] Vagrants were much involved with a wave of arson in North Wales, the border countries and the Midlands during the 1860s and, according to one contemporary, from then until the closing years of the century arson remained 'a favourite method of [vagrants] venting spite'.[15]

Rural arson was not always the work of isolated individuals; nor was it unknown for villagers to give support to the arsonists by impeding, or at best offering no assistance to the fire-fighters.[16] The epidemic of incendiarism in East Anglia in the 1830s and 1840s appears to have been the work of a few, generally young men, single and unemployed, who were beginning to recognise that there was no future for them on the land. Their furious protest struck a chord with others in the labouring community and may have contributed to the gentry's re-examination of its role in the community and to the provision of allotments and better housing.[17] It would be erroneous, however, to seek to understand every instance of rural arson in terms of class war. Henry Clapham set fire to his brother's stack at Burton Pidsea in the East Riding as part of a family feud.[18] George Serle, alias Edwin Serle, alias Walter Tomlinson, alias Cockayne, alias Thompson, born in Belper, Derbyshire, and a horse trimmer by trade, had a long career of starting fires. In 1854 he was sentenced to one year's hard labour for arson in Derbyshire; five years later he was sentenced to five years' penal servitude for setting fire to stacks of wheat and hay at Biggleswade, Bedfordshire. Shortly after the end of this sentence the Nottinghamshire Lent Assizes of 1866 gave him fifteen years' penal servitude for a similar offence.[19] Serle appears to have delighted in lighting fires. More prosaically, some fires were started by property owners in the attempt to defraud their insurance companies, while others were simply the result of children playing with matches.[20]

Animal maiming was also overwhelmingly a rural crime, for obvious reasons; and it had other similarities with arson. Personal feuds between members of the same social class, revenge, and elements of social protest can be detected among the motives. The brutal, grisly, often very bloody and messy injuries inflicted on the sexual organs of a few of the animal victims suggest that some of the perpetrators might also have been seeking other forms of gratification. There were also some instances of horses being killed as a result of attempted 'horse magic', as teamsmen eager to make their masters' horses the best groomed, with the shiniest coats, employed secret remedies that turned out to be lethal.[21]

The availability of shotguns in rural areas, combined with the greater problems of surveillance, meant that pot-shots were sometimes taken at informants and policemen, probably to a far greater degree than in urban areas. This was especially the case in Suffolk during the rural disorders of the 1840s. In March 1844 Charles Grimmer, a farmer of Pakefield near Lowestoft, heard two shots outside his house and on going to a window he received a shotgun blast in the shoulder. 'Mr Grimmer', noted the Chief Constable:

has on several occasions taken an active part with Police to detect a gang of thieves that reside near him which is the cause assigned for the attempt upon his life.[22]

Rural communities, however, as explained below,[23] were not the only ones in which informers and certain types of offender could find themselves set upon or ostracised.

The level of sophistication might also contribute to both types of crime and responses to crime. The rural poor often did not see Christianity and paganism as mutually exclusive. They combined the two in their own distinctive world view, though paganism became less significant as the nineteenth century wore on.[24] Girls in rural districts, anxious to discover future husbands or to attract particular young men, sometimes butchered and mistreated animals in ways that sickened rational and sensitive Victorians. In February 1848 Mary Brice, Jane Matthews and Sarah Page were brought before Bletsoe Petty Sessions by the Bedfordshire Constabulary under 5 and 6 William IV cap. 59 for torturing a cat. They were fined and sentenced to short periods of hard labour in the house of correction. The prison chaplain was appalled by their offence:

The three females . . . had the barbarous cruelty – a cruelty that sickens the very heart, to open up with a pair of scissors the body of a living cat, and take out her heart . . . the motive was most ignorant and superstitious. It was the belief that, by sticking pins in the poor animal's heart, and then burying it in the earth, they would bring back their lovers. This happened in a village in Bedfordshire in the year 1848![25]

When crimes were committed against them, at least up until the middle of the nineteenth century, the rural poor seem to have been as inclined to go to 'cunning' or 'wise' men as to constables or policemen. It was even alleged that an escaped thief in Norfolk consulted a 'cunning' woman for a 'safe conduct'. These 'cunning' men and women were professionals who charged fees and whose expertise could be purchased to thwart witches and tell fortunes in addition to identifying thieves and finding stolen, or lost, property.[26] There were other ways of dealing with witches, but in the eyes of the law these could constitute assault. The Reverend R. M. Healey was asked by a wheelwright to say a few words over a sow that, the wheelwright believed, was being 'overlooked' by a witch. The traditional way of dealing with a witch who 'overlooked' a victim or an animal, was to stick pins in her chair, or otherwise draw her blood and thus render her powerless. The wheelwright confessed that he had not done this as the witch would take him before the Spilsby magistrates, and Victorian magistrates were 'that iggnerant' that they would have fined him. At Cromer in 1847 a group of boys were brought before the magistrates for stoning the poor woman who carried the local letter bag; they wanted to draw the blood 'of the old witch'.[27]

Some historians, though not specifically with reference to Britain, have detected more significant differences between rural and urban crime. Rural society, it has been argued, being more primitive, had a higher incidence of inter-personal crime than urban areas. In the latter the disorganisation created by urban growth, or simply the greater opportunity for theft provided by the urban environment, led to a greater incidence of property crime.[28] Such conclusions fit comfortably with both Marxian and Modernization theories of social and economic development, though they have received a severe battering directed primarily at the databases upon which they were constructed. Furthermore it has been emphasised by J. A. Sharpe, that property crime, as measured by indictments and executions for such offences, fell markedly between the early seventeenth and early eighteenth centuries, namely during the period generally portrayed as so significant for the rise of English capitalism.[29]

Towns and cities appeared to both eighteenth- and nineteenth-century social commentators as anonymous, dangerous and dirty, particularly those areas where the poorer sections of the community lived. When the poor had only one room for the family then the courtyard, the street and the pub became centres for leisure and recreation, for meeting and arguing; the courtyard and the street became sites for displaying wares, selling hot food and dumping rubbish. Many streets, in consequence, appeared to be owned by the poor; and the elite could never know these teeming, jostling masses in the way that they knew retainers on their estates or supposed that their predecessors had known whole communities. The poor became exotic 'wandering tribes' to be described by a Mayhew; they also became objects of social policy to enable the respectable among them to prosper, and to make the residuum among them respectable. At the same time there emerged a romantic view of a passed Golden Age: for Fielding this was before the corruption of society, and especially of the poor, by the luxury and wealth created by trade; for William Cobbett it was before the development of 'the thing' and 'the infernal wen' of London. The Golden Age was to be found in a romantic Merrie England, and even before Joseph Strutt had published his *Glig Gamena Angel-Deod, or the Sports and Pastimes of the People of England* (1801) or William Thomas had coined the word 'folklore',[30] gentlemen were in pursuit of the popular recreations of rural England so as to preserve them in 'Calendars' or 'Everyday Books'. Historians critical of the shape of the industrial revolution and what it meant for the working class, once implied that it saw the destruction of a reasonably contented rural society. More recently, historians of the customs and rituals of the old rural community have followed a similar tack; the new economic order of industrialising Britain, in its attempt to establish a rational and compliant workforce, battered away remorselessly at the old popular culture with its undeniable brutality, horseplay and lack of deference. The reconstruction of custom and ritual in rural, or 'pre-industrial' communities, has been invaluable; yet some of the conclusions drawn about the criminalisation of aspects of traditional behaviour might tend to mislead.

Largesse was a customary rural practice at harvest time. It was, according to Bob Bushaway, a way 'in which harvest wages were supplemented'. In some areas the chosen chief of a gang of labourers would request money from any person passing a field wherein harvesting was in progress. Elsewhere labourers solicited largesse by going from door to door in a neighbourhood. The behaviour had an implicit element of threat, but it was also a levy 'made on the whole community, as a recognition of and reward for the labourer's work during harvest'.[31] The key questions here are where, if at all, can a line be drawn between largesse and extortion and what the precise difference was between largesse, which folklorists could find acceptable in a rural community of the past, and extortion, which was repugnant? The notion of largesse manifestly did not enter into Lord Fortescue's condemnation of 'sturdy beggars' infesting parts of Devonshire in the 1850s:

Numbers of sturdy beggars, particularly in summer, invade our
farmhouses and cottages and in the absence of the men extort money
or provisions from the women who they find at home. Indeed in this
house I have for some years kept at my own expense an assistant
constable in the shape of a trusty labourer to repel the above class
of visitors, some of whom when they have been saucy I have committed
to Bridewell where they have almost invariably been recognised as old
offenders.

Fielder King, a substantial landholder in Hampshire and Sussex spoke similarly of 'vagrants . . . alarming the females in the house and obtaining alms from fear rather than charity'.[32]

To switch momentarily from a problematic concept taken from the study of rural life to a vicious assault that occurred in the urban world and that created a major stir in newspaper columns: on 3 August 1874 Richard Morgan, a 25-year-old warehouse porter in Liverpool, was on his way home from a day out with his wife and brother, when he was accosted on the corner of Tithebarn Street and Lower Milk Street. John McCrave, alias Quinn, Michael Mullen and Peter Campbell asked him for sixpence;

when he refused they set about him. Samuel Morgan sought to defend his brother. A crowd gathered and urged on the assailants; the crowd cried out a warning when the police appeared, and impeded Samuel Morgan's pursuit of the attackers. Richard Morgan died as a result of his beating; the doctors called it 'nervous shock', finding his heart 'to a slight extent fatty and large, though scarcely to the extent of disease'. Morgan's death brought the phenomenon of the Liverpool 'Cornermen' dramatically to public notice. The Recorder of Liverpool called for more police; his colleagues elsewhere, and a succession of newspapers, expressed outrage at the level of violence. McCrave and his fellows were arrested, tried and executed. They were not harvesters demanding recognition and reward for their work, they came from a community of casual labourers who eked out their existence on Liverpool's docks. That community backed them against both the victim and the police; it would appear to have considered outsiders at least as fair game for the urban equivalent of largesse. The attack on Morgan was not an isolated event.[33]

Mumming was another way of extracting money or goods in the rural community. The mummers performed their plays for all ranks of people and thus, according to Bushaway, emphasised the social cohesion of the old society. Mumming became increasingly obsolete as the nineteenth century progressed.[34] At New Year in Bradford during the 1860s, however, mummers – men and boys with blackened faces – crossed into middle-class districts and even forced their way into middle-class homes demanding money and drink.[35] In 1887 a correspondent of *The Times* expressed alarm about 'the increasingly aggressive character of the roughs' who were to be found in London's suburbs:

> *At Essex Villas, Kensington, yesterday, upon my wife reaching home with a box outside her brougham, a rough who had followed, waiting until the coachman drove off, forced his way into the hall, and refused to leave until he was given something. While the police were being sent for he, during 10 minutes, indulged in the most loathsome abuse, evidently hoping to terrify the lady into acceding to his demands. He only left when the policeman appeared in the street, and then he only strolled away, for, as he stated, he did not care for all the police in London. The policeman would take no action, merely seeing him down the street in a leisurely fashion. At the police station I am informed my only remedy is by summons.*[36]

The Kensington rough described above appears to have made no attempt to act as a mummer or to offer any service, other than his departure, for his payment. But several questions are posed by each variety of urban extortion described here, especially, when money was demanded in the form of largesse or to reward mumming. Obviously Liverpool Cornermen and Bradford Mummers, and London 'roughs', did not see themselves as reinforcing community cohesion; they wanted something, and were prepared to use coercion, intimidation and physical violence to get it. But what did the rural practitioners of largesse and mumming think that they were doing? Their behaviour may, at one time, have reinforced community solidarity. Yet recent historical research has pushed unified village communities further and further back in time; there are doubts about their existence in the mid-sixteenth century;[37] and whether the average, typical mummer or harvest gang leader (whatever such a being was) ever consciously thought in such terms is highly debatable. Furthermore, even in the second half of the eighteenth century, much harvesting was being done by itinerant labouring gangs, and any demands for largesse on their part would hardly have been reinforcing local communities. Unquestionably during the eighteenth and nineteenth centuries there was an assault on such forms of popular culture as largesse and mumming; the question remains as to when such institutions were ever accepted by all participants in the ritual in the ideal form that was allegedly destroyed by the assault on popular culture. Richard Cobb once queried whether research into rioters and their behaviour was not tending to make them rather too respectable.[38] The same question might be posed with reference to the custom and rituals of rural plebeians. It is surely not just cynicism or class prejudice to suggest that some of the men who sought alms and/or largesse in the late eighteenth and early nineteenth centuries were just as nasty and unscrupulous as Fortescue and King implied.

Urbanisation did not destroy the ability of groups bound by work, ethnic, religious or other ties, from existing as communities; nor did it leave the new urban dweller as an isolated individual among a society of strangers. Irish immigrants, and their descendants, remained in readily identifiable enclaves. New migrants sometimes came with recommendations to those from their villages who had gone before. These immigrants brought practices from their rural backgrounds with them, which, like keeping pigs and faction fights were often ill-suited to their cramped urban dwellings. Such behaviour, while it concerned and alienated the native population, may have served to reinforce the communities' Irishness. The smaller levels of immigration by Jews from Holland and Germany in the eighteenth century and from Eastern Europe at the end of the nineteenth century reveals similar communal solidarity. But a comparison of Irish and Jewish immigrants in nineteenth-century British cities also provided an object lesson against the simple equating of immigrant ghetto areas with criminal areas. The Irish were notorious for alleged criminality, though their offences were primarily of the public order variety as is evidenced by a cursory glance at the headlines of any nineteenth-century urban news-paper produced in a town with a significant Irish population, as well as by court records.[39] Jews were singled out as criminal in late eighteenth- and early nineteenth-century London. There was particular outrage in the 1770s following the murder of a servant who tried to resist a gang of Jewish burglars in Chelsea in 1771. Jews appear to have played prominent roles as coiners and receivers in Georgian London; Dickens's Fagin had at least one well-known original in Ikey Solomons. The Jewish community had its share of pickpockets and petty thieves, and the poorer members were known to fight and riot in the same kinds of ways as the poorer classes of London; they were never as closely identified with drink as the Irish, however. The reputation of Jewish criminals prompted a reforming campaign by respectable, well-to-do Anglo-Jewry. Partly because of this reforming campaign and also the strict regulations imposed on tenants in the tenements built for immigrants by Jewish philanthropists, the East European Jews who entered the country towards the end of the nineteenth century acquired a reputation (generally, and not always deserved) for keeping out of trouble. This was even the case when the tenements were sited in what were formerly notorious districts.[40] Turning away from the special case of immigrants, Robert Roberts who was brought up in 'the classic slum' in Salford at the beginning of the twentieth century, recalled how his community was a village with his parents' corner shop one of the focal points. The 'village' had man-made boundaries: railway tracks to the north and south, a different slum village to the east and, to the west, 'lay the middle classes, bay-windowed and begardened'.[41]

The principal problem with the urban–rural division in seeking to understand crime is that it is simply too crude. Urban and rural are oppos-ite ends of a spectrum and however the extremes are defined, there is a vast area between them. Indeed for much of the eighteenth and nineteenth centuries most Englishmen lived in neither big industrial cities nor on the land, but in small towns, some of which, like Exeter and York, boasted the title of city. These small towns were centres for rural society, and had been for centuries: they had markets and fairs; some were the meeting places for quarter sessions and assizes; and some, as boroughs, had their own courts. The focus of these towns remained essentially rural. But, at the same time, there were areas that, while rural in setting, were focused on burgeoning economic and industrial development. The industrial villages of the West Riding provide one example; the pit villages in the coalfields of Durham and Northumberland provide another.

Urban and rural also break down significantly at the extremes. No two cities are entirely similar and different economic structures and different functions provide opportunities for different types of crime. Seaports and garrison towns offered wider opportunities for the 'victimless crime' of prostitution. Ipswich was a garrison town and, with a population of nearly 33,000 in the mid-nineteenth century, it was alleged to have fifty-two brothels.[42] Seaports also generated other forms of crime. In 1811 the magistrates of the Thames Police Office reported:

In our District and Experience . . . we find Riots and dangerous affrays among foreign seamen (many of whom continue on shore until they are destitute and then seek a support by plunder) the most prevalent offences and most difficult to be prevented.[43]

Discharged merchant seamen, their pockets bulging with pay, encouraged other forms of offences. 'Street robberies and particularly larceny from the person (chiefly committed on seafaring people)' appeared the most prevalent forms of crime in the Whitechapel district of Regency London; the perpetrators, according to the magistrates, were 'pickpockets and prostitutes'.[44] The docks and warehouses of major ports provided greater opportunities, if not greater rewards than the much smaller canal wharfs of, for example, Manchester and Birmingham. The prevalence of small metal trades, together with the employment of boys to take unfinished goods from one small workshop to another, was considered a key element contributing to the scale of juvenile offences in mid-nineteenth-century Birmingham.[45]

But if different towns and cities provide different opportunities for crime, the Chicago 'School' of Human Ecology urged, half a century ago, that it is possible to generalise about urban social structure particularly with reference to the zonal arrangements of land-use, physical conditions and demographic structure. Drawing on such conclusions R. N. Davidson has suggested an 'eclectic typology of the urban environment' for portraying urban neighbourhoods in terms of their crime characteristics; 'eclectic because of the stubborn refusal of the ecological dimensions to provide a neat framework to the classification'.[46] While it is not possible for the historian to amass the data of the modern criminologist and thus parallel all of Davidson's nuances, a rough division of the city into centre, commercial and industrial zones, inner-city residential districts and suburbs is of immense value in helping to comprehend the criminal characteristics of urban neighbourhoods in the past.

The city centre attracts crowds to its shops and its entertainments. These crowds provide opportunities for the pickpocket and the prostitute. Shops provide opportunities for shoplifting and, together with offices, for burglary. Entertainments provide the possibilities for affrays and minor assaults. The commercial and industrial zones, often near the centre, provide opportunities for theft and embezzlement though, because the number of people permitted legitimate access is fewer, the level of personal victimisation is also less. However much they structured their perceptions of criminality within contemporary ideology both Fielding and Colquhoun saw the wealth of the metropolis as fostering crime. Colquhoun was particularly concerned about thefts from warehouses and ships on the Thames. Court records, and Arthur Harding's recollections of East End dockers bringing home tea and selling it to corner shopkeepers, reveal such depredations continuing throughout the nineteenth century.[47] In mid-nineteenth-century Manchester, the Chief Constable denied that the factory system had encouraged theft, but 'the warehousing system, from the value and the portable nature of the property left lying about in great ranges of rooms, was to a certain degree prolific of theft'.[48] John Rawlinson, a London Police Magistrate, told the Select Committee on the Police of the Metropolis in 1828, that the increasing exposure of goods in shop doors encouraged theft. A decade later the Superintendent of D Division of the Metropolitan Police noted:

the too frequent practice of shopkeepers exposing their goods for sale outside of their shops [which] affords an easy facility to plunder, together with the ready mode of disposing of such plunder at Marine store shops, old clothes shops etc.

In 1865, echoing the comments of Colonel James Fraser, the Commissioner of the City of London Police, *The Times* expressed amazement at 'the unsuspecting confidence of the commercial, or, at least, the shopkeeping world'. As for pilfering from industrial areas, the Superintendent of K Division of the Metropolitan Police informed the Constabulary Force Commissioners that:

Robberies to an immense extent are daily occurring by workmen at large Factories, but I am informed by the Principals, that the men would not submit to be searched indiscriminately and continually, and that the combination amongst them is so strong that a strike would be the result.[49]

It is apparent that there was a vast amount of theft from the workplace in mid-nineteenth-century London, but it is impossible to put a figure on how much was taken, where from, or by whom.

In contemporary society there is a high concentration of crime and of offenders in certain inner-city residential areas. Davidson divides these areas into two basic sub-types: residual areas, in which there is an element of social cohesion and a degree of balance in the demographic structure; and transitional areas with high turnovers of population and few family units. There was tremendous mobility in the nineteenth-century city, even among the respectable working class; indeed moving could be a mark of respectability, with a move being the only way in that a family could get into lodgings that did not require immediate repairs.[50] But, that said, movement was often not very far within the city and it remains possible to detect both residual and transitional districts.

Not every residual district appeared prone to crime, but some were notorious. Irish districts were singled out as particularly criminal: the Bedern in York, and Caribee Island and Stafford Street in Wolverhampton offer good examples during the thirty or forty years following potato famine. But criminality here was, primarily, a problem of public order.[51] Some, and not simply Irish districts, became virtual 'no-go areas' for the police and, more particularly, for the rent collector and landlord.[52] It may be that there was a high level of theft within such districts that, because of the inhabitants' antipathy to the police, was never reported. Victims might also be intimidated into not bringing charges and this, David Jones has suggested, could be one reason why the statistics might belie the undoubted criminality of the 'China' district of mid-nineteenth-century Merthyr Tydfil, a 'frontier town of the industrial revolution'. While respectable society rejected the population of 'China', that population itself reveals bonds of family, self-respect, independence, and a unity of self-interest.[53] The bonds uniting the community of 'China' would seem similar to those which brought the Liverpudlians of Tithe Barn Street and Lower Milk Street to the defence of McCrave and his fellow Cornermen, and which united the population of the Jago, or Nicol, in Arthur Harding's childhood. The police, and others, stigmatised such areas as the aphorism 'guarding St James by watching St Giles' testifies of itself. Until its destruction in the mid-nineteenth century, notably by the cutting of New Oxford Street, the St Giles 'rookery' was regarded with horror by respectable Londoners, and the Reverend Thomas Beames explicitly compared it with the Faubourg St Antoine of Paris, notorious for its plebeian revolutionaries. Other residential areas stigmatised as criminal were to be found elsewhere in London and in provincial towns and cities at the end of the nineteenth century; as one area was cleared, so the mantle of most criminal district or street was passed to another.[54]

In some respects certain residual areas, especially those where the landlords and rent collectors dare not go and repairs were never made, may have been worse in respect of poverty and squalor than transitional districts with their lodging houses – at least after the creation of the system of lodging house supervision in the mid-nineteenth century. Transitional areas were probably the worst centres of anomie, though there are problems in employing this concept to explain crime; there is no justification for seeing crime as the result of an ill-defined 'social disorganisation' when crime might just as well be considered as a fundamental component of such disorganisation.

Lodging houses with their rootless, generally single, populations were suspect at least from the 1750s when Fielding quoted his friend and colleague, Saunders Welch, High Constable of Holborn, at length on the subject. Welch considered that some of the worst of such houses were to be found in St Giles and in St George, Bloomsbury:

> *with miserable Beds from the Cellar to the Garret, for . . . Twopenny Lodgers . . . in these Beds, several of which are in the same Room, Men and Women, often Strangers to each other, lie promiscuously, the Price of a double Bed being no more than Threepence, as an Encouragement to them to lie together . . . as these Places are thus adapted to Whoredom, so are they no less provided for Drunkenness, Gin being sold in them all at a Penny a Quartern . . . in the Execution of Search Warrants. Mr Welch rarely finds less than Twenty of these Houses open for the Receipt of all Comers at the latest Hours . . . in one of these Houses, and that not a large one, he bath numbered 68 Persons of both Sexes, the Stench of whom was so intolerable, that it compelled him in a very short time to quit the Place.[55]*

Such images recur throughout the nineteenth century and further illustrate the concerns about itinerants and those with no permanent employment, as well as the determination to equate criminality with physical ugliness. Angus Reach, whose description of a 'low lodging house' in Angel Meadow, Manchester, was quoted earlier, reported the city's chief constable as speaking warily of 'a considerable floating population, and a smaller number of persons who are known both to work and steal'.[56]

It is clear that the police stigmatised certain lodging house districts as criminal and, while these were generally the cheapest and poorest, the labelling may have become to some extent self-fulfilling, with those who could avoid lodgings in a stigmatised area making every effort so to do. At the same time, given that the 'crime' problem was understood as centring on the mass of petty thefts, a majority of the offenders responsible for these activities probably were to be found in these districts.

Low lodging houses in St Giles and other poor districts of London, in Angel Meadow and Deansgate, Manchester, and those in Thomas Street, Birmingham, had notorious reputations. The inhabitants of all such districts were doubly vulnerable: on the one hand, having been defined as what a modern sociologist has called 'police property',[57] they suffered regular police searches; on the other, unlike the Irish or the people of Merthyr's 'China', their lack of community cohesion militated against any resistance or unity of self interest. The property of anyone staying in such a lodging house, which obviously would not have been much, was also at risk for most things could be pawned; any property too meagre for the pawnbroker could be taken to the dolly shop, and there was always the second-hand clothes dealer and the rag-and-bone man. Again, estimates of crime within the transitional neighbourhood, and especially one stigmatised as criminal, are impossible given the relationship between the inhabitants and the police.

Many of the poorer inner-city residential areas became even less salubrious as cities expanded and new transport systems fostered the spread of suburban residential districts. The better districts have much lower offender and offence rates in contemporary society; during the nineteenth century, in comparison with residual and transitory areas of the inner city, public order offences in the suburbs appear to have been tiny. Thefts from gardens and burglaries seem to have been the typical offences. The spread of suburbs may have contributed to the fact that the statistics of burglary and housebreaking resisted the general overall decline in crime from the middle of the nineteenth century. Indicative that suburban districts were the more likely target of the professional, calculating house burglar is the fact that it was in these districts of metropolitan London where, from the mid-1880s, policemen on night beats were authorised to carry revolvers. This authorisation came in the wake of two particular burglaries by armed men in Islington and Wimbledon in the summer of 1883 and because of concern over the availability of cheap revolvers manufactured in Germany. It was, however, also the case that from early on police patrolling some fringe districts of London had been issued with edged weapons: cutlasses for the men on foot and sabres for those who were mounted. These weapons were countenanced because of the large size and lonely nature of the beats in these districts, often in the countryside, and the consequent inability of a man to get speedy assistance from the constable on a neighbouring beat should he be attacked.[58]

Suburban residential districts, like the elegant and fashionable areas that were still to be found in the centre of some cities, had their own kinds of offenders. The different kinds of white-collar offenders were often to be found living here, and these districts contained a high proportion of domestic servants among whose numbers lurked some who filched from their employers and, occasionally, even illicitly pawned pieces of their employer's property.

The smaller towns and cities also had their mixture of respectable housing and narrow squalid courts harbouring different kinds of offender and providing the opportunities for different kinds of offence. The respectable inhabitants of mid-nineteenth-century Horncastle, Lincolnshire, for example, with a population just reaching 4,500 in 1841, were concerned about their 'lawless and immoral' inhabitants. Dog Kennel Yard in particular was notorious for its brothels and prostitution. During the 1840s the town was plagued by two gangs: Frank Kent led a group of adolescents who specialised in aggressively harassing country people and vagrants; Jack Sharpe, a labourer, and Maskell Spencer, a blacksmith, led a different group known as 'The Gang', whose offences included poaching and robbery.[59]

Similar gangs, or at least groups of young men in persistent and varied trouble with the authorities, were to be found in what were, more obviously, rural villages. In the summer of 1825 two young men, James Redman, aged 20 and James Grummet, aged 23, were charged with stealing pistols from troopers of the Bedfordshire Yeomanry Cavalry; the troopers had stopped at the Royal Oak public house in the village of Houghton Conquest on their way home from a training exercise and, foolishly, they had left their pistols in the holsters on their saddles. The local constable had considerable difficulty in hanging on to his prisoners; villagers assaulted him and there were attempts to break the prisoners out of the village cage. At the Midsummer Quarter Sessions Grummet alone was convicted. He was positively identified as taking a pistol; Redman was not. Grummet was sentenced to three months' hard labour, but he was no stranger to Bedford Gaol: in May 1818 he had been sentenced to three months for game law offences, and he had received a similar sentence for similar offences in December 1819. On each occasion the gaoler described his behaviour as 'indifferent'. Redman had also been in trouble before. At the Epiphany Sessions in 1822 the Grand Jury had thrown out a bill of indictment for theft brought against him; eighteen months later he was sentenced to one month's hard labour for stealing a duck. In 1824, with two others, he was bound over to keep the peace towards Thomas Sharp of Wilstead. While visiting Houghton Conquest, Sharp had gone into the Royal Oak; showing rather more valour than discretion he suggested to Redman that he moderate his language, upon which Redman ferociously assaulted Sharp aided by the two others. When William and James Page were arrested in 1823 for stealing stockings from a draper's stall at Silsoe Fair, William Page bemoaned that there were seven or eight in Houghton Conquest far worse than him and that 'it was the first time that he had ever got into the Gang'. James Page protested: 'I am not the worst', and named seven who, he believed, were worse, including James Redman and James Grummet. A few weeks after his acquittal for the theft of the yeomanry pistol, Redman was committed for trial on a charge of housebreaking, together with John Hosler, aged 19, and Joseph Redman, aged 26. Hosler was also on James Page's list and had received a sentence of two months' hard labour for wood theft in 1825. At the Bedfordshire Lent Assizes in 1826 all three were found guilty and sentenced to death. All were reprieved: Joseph Redman's apparent previous good behaviour told in his favour since he was given only one year's hard labour; James Redman and John Hosler were transported for life.[60]

Houghton Conquest, where the Redmans, Grummet and Hosler resided, was notorious. During the late sixteenth and early seventeenth centuries it had been a thriving and important country village; over the following century it had declined but in the second and third decades of the nineteenth century its population soared from 507 and 505 recorded respectively in the censuses of 1801 and 1811, to 651 in 1821 and 796 in 1831. The sudden growth of the parish, far above that for Bedfordshire as a whole, possibly led contemporary gentlemen to view it with suspicion; though it should be emphasised that the Parish Register of Houghton Conquest records Grummets and Redmans from the end of the sixteenth and beginning of the seventeenth centuries respectively.[61] According to the Reverend J. W. Burgon, vicar of St Mary's Oxford and subsequently Dean of Chichester, who wrote a brief history of the village during the 1870s, there was a popular saying that 'Bedford gaol would fall when it did not contain a Houghton man'. The streets were said to be unsafe after dark; the roads were impassable in winter. Burgon maintained that the reason for the village's unsavoury nature was the lack of any stable and responsible gentry. The gentry families in the village during its heyday had died out in the seventeenth and early eighteenth centuries. Houghton Park had repeatedly changed hands. The church living became increasingly undesirable; Dr William Pearce, the Master of Jesus College, Cambridge, who held the living between 1786 and 1820, was non-resident. Burgon dated the beginning of a slow improvement from the appointment of the Reverend Thomas Barber as rector in 1821. Barber enforced order in church 'by the power of his lungs' and on the streets 'by the weight of his arm'. He carried a stick, and sometimes used it; and, as a magistrate, Burgon declared, he succeeded in getting some of the worst offenders transported.[62] Of course Barber could not have sentenced men to transportation alone, but he was the magistrate who committed the Redmans, Grummet and Hosler.

Burgon's analysis of why Houghton Conquest became so notorious says as much about his, and his contemporaries' perception of rural life, as it does about the village itself. John Glyde came to what he believed was a startling conclusion after analysing the residences of criminals in mid-nineteenth-century Suffolk: about one-third of the county population were urban dwellers, yet they committed only about one-fifth of the crime. 'The simplicity and innocence of peasant life exists only in imagination.' The poor criminal villagers, he concluded, had been left 'morally and physically a prey to their passions' by land owners, clergy and employers.[63]

Both Burgon's and Glyde's conclusions fit with the nineteenth-century image of two kinds of village – 'open' and 'closed'; a perception that emerged with the Poor Law investigations conducted at the first half of the century. In the closed village, control was firmly in the hands of a single landowner, or a small group of like-minded gentlemen. Their aims were to keep poor rates to a minimum and to preserve their personal amenities such as the views over their country houses or parks. To these ends they bought up land and enclosed commons to make larger agricultural units, game reserves and parks; they also limited settlement and building. Their control meant that they exercised a powerful influence over the local population; only hard-working, deferential, and moral labourers were allowed settlement and the consequent relief in hard times. Open villages had no such controls. They were usually very much larger and sprawling; shopkeepers and independent artisans built cottages for rent which often turned into rural slums. The occupants of these slums provided labour for local farmers in both open and closed villages.[64] Some open villages might be squatter settlements providing labour for a nearby town. Headington Quarry, formerly a waste area on the edge of Shotover Common on the outskirts of Oxford, provides a good example. Many of the men here worked as quarrymen or brickmakers. Physical toughness was regarded as a virtue in the village. Disputes were settled without recourse to the police who patrolled Headington in pairs. Outsiders gave the village a wide birth.[65] Other open villages were viewed with similar horror and were accused of being centres of rural immorality and vice and, in consequence, the havens of burglars and other dangerous criminals. In 1848, Francis Howells was one of the investigators sent by the Poor Law Commissioners to study how the law of settlement and removal was functioning. In his report Howells explained how, about 1840, Lord Manvers had pulled down several cottages at Laxton in Nottinghamshire so as to be rid of the occupants. The evicted families found temporary shelter in the workhouse:

I think it is right to say . . . that these people had become troublesome as poachers and as idle dissolute characters; and I believe that Lord Manvers was considered to have done a good thing when he broke up this gang of bad characters. They did not remain long in the [work]house, but went out and took up their abode in the neighbouring village of Egmanton, where Mr Barrow told me he thought they were the foundation of a gang of burglars. Mr Barrow adds 'We have broken up two different gangs of burglars in Egmanton', an open parish. And this perhaps, is one of the worst evils that the open parishes suffer from the close parishes, that they receive into them the bad characters to whom the owners of close parishes are naturally unwilling to give shelter, and whom they wish to get rid of if they can.[66]

The open–closed village dichotomy was not as clear cut as the poor law literature, and nineteenth-century commentators who worried about idle, disorderly and criminal rural labourers, implied.[67] Detailed analysis of closed villages with resident gentry reveals that these could also contain frequent offenders. Westfirle is a case in point: the Gage family owned ninety-eight per cent of the available acreage in the village and were the largest single employer, yet over one-third of those prosecuted for criminal offences between 1820 and 1850 were prosecuted on more than one occasion and some of the offenders had criminal careers not unlike the men from Houghton Conquest described above.[68] At the same time, research into rural protest suggests, not surprisingly perhaps, that it was the larger villages – the 'open' villages – with their greater proportion of agricultural labourers to employing farmers, and their distinctly higher percentage of independent artisans, which were more likely to participate in such behaviour.[69] Though, occasionally, a few magistrates and gentlemen might sympathise, the machine smashing, the incendiarism, the destruction of game and of property, and the riotous assemblies that popular protest involved, were all criminal actions by law. Moralising contemporaries had little difficulty in making an intellectual leap at this point: if the idle and immoral poor participated in these crimes, then they would also particip-ate in others; poaching thus became the first step on the road to a life of crime. To the extent that they probably contained proportionally more poachers, open villages were more criminal; few permanent labourers seem to have been convicted of poaching on the land of their employer.[70] Also poaching gangs could benefit from the services that certain independent villagers could offer; butchers, for example, were useful to a variety of poachers and sheep stealers; innkeepers might purchase game themselves, or be able to pass it on to, or via, their clientele.

Some industrial villages were 'closed' inasmuch as they were built and run by the employer and his immediate subordinates. While the employer might look to his workforce's moral and intellectual improvement by restricting strong drink and providing schools for children and a mech-anics' institute for his men, he could also enforce discipline through evictions and dependence by establishing his own store; given that the vil-lage could be remote such stores could be a boon, it was the requirements and restrictions that went with it that made the truck system so hated by workers. When the employer was also the local magistrate, his power was complete. 'If the men took any measures against the masters they would not be employed,' commented Thomas Jones Phillips, clerk of the peace at Bedwellty, while explaining to a parliamentary committee in 1842 that there had been no prosecutions in Monmouth under the Truck Act since the iron masters were also the magistrates.[71] But not all industrial villages functioned in this way. In some instances building development was left to independent tradesmen within the village. Furthermore, mining, which was probably the most common reason for the creation of new industrial villages during the late eighteenth and nineteenth centuries, was an indus-try that was far less susceptible to rigorous regulations and supervision of the labour force than factory work. Miners were feared as violent and unruly during the eighteenth century; the image stayed with many mining communities well into the nineteenth century. In 1847 Jelinger Symons told a parliamentary committee that the mining district of Monmouthshire contained 'a larger proportion of escaped criminals and dissolute people of both sexes than almost any other populace'.[72] Thousands poured into County Durham in the second quarter of the nineteenth century to meet the requirements of industry, especially the demand for miners. The pit strike of 1831–2 was noted for its ferocity. After the creation of the county constabulary, policemen were commonly assaulted in pit villages; in 1842 it was argued that the relatively crime-free agricultural districts of the county were financing the police presence in the colliery districts. Yet for all that contemporaries branded the Durham miners as dangerous and criminal, theft does not appear to have been much of a problem in pit villages. In his reports to the *Morning Chronicle*, Angus Reach found that the mining districts of Northumberland and Durham contradicted 'the theories generally entertained upon the connection of ignorance with crime by presenting the least criminal section of the population of England'. Statistically, Reach found that there was a smaller proportion of offenders in the mining districts of Cornwall, Cumberland and Staffordshire. He concluded that the small amount of theft in the north east was probably due to the power of Methodism:

aided by the comparatively isolated condition in which the mining population lives – seldom or never coming in contact with the members of any industrial class except their own, and little exposed to the influences and excitements of great towns.[73]

It might also have been the case that, in the event of a theft, the mining communities were reluctant to involve the authorities, especially the police who guarded blacklegs and assisted at evictions during strikes. Justice for theft in a pit village, at least during the first half of the nineteenth century, may have been rougher and speedier than that sanctioned by the state, but responses probably varied with the nature of the incident.[74]

Environment did have an inter-relationship with crime, but not simply along the lines that the urban–rural division might suggest. During the eighteenth and nineteenth centuries industrialisation and urbanisation changed communities, but the experience was not so shattering that people, especially poor immigrants spreading to cities or sprawling open villages, ceased to live in, and to perceive themselves as part of, communities. Some communities tended to be more law abiding than others, but theorists of crime, policemen and the respectable classes in general tended to perceive any areas where the poor teemed and where there was no visible form of elite control and surveillance, as haven for the dangerous classes. Popular disorder, even when it had recognisable and even modest aims – food at a fair price, the traditional right to use common land – was increasingly perceived as dangerous and criminal. Popular exuberance at fairs and wakes, the noise and 'disorder' that spilled over from pubs, crowded courts, tenements and streets, was perceived similarly, even though it was condoned by the immediate community in which it occurred and, occasionally, might have involved the meting out of popular justice. Some of this disorder and exuberance was criminal in a narrow sense of the word, even if tolerated by both the rural and urban communities in which it occurred. But it seems to have been difficult for those contemporaries fired by 'respectability' and ideas of progress, fortified by Malthusian theory, and recognising that they lived in a society that was changing at a frighteningly rapid rate under the twin impact of urbanisation and industrialisation, to perceive continuities in community behaviour and the difference between different forms of offence.

Notes and references

1 **Henry Fielding**, *An Enquiry into the Causes of the Late Increase of Robbers*, 2nd edn, London, 1751, p. 116; **Patrick Colquhoun**, *A Treatise on the Police of the Metropolis*, 3rd edn, revised and enlarged, London, 1796, pp. xi–xii.

2 See above, p. 41. Among the exceptions to the predominance of London crimes in creating fear was the grisly murder of four-year-old Francis Saville Kent at Road, Wilts, in January 1860. The fascination with the case was partly due, however, to the difficulties experienced by the authorities in identifying the murderer – Francis's sister, Constance. The case generated columns of newspaper comment throughout the year, and see also the comments in **J. F. Stephen**, 'The criminal law and the detection of crime', *Cornhill Magazine*, ii (1860), pp. 697–708. For the report of the Metropolitan Police officer sent to investigate the murder see M.E.P.O. 3/61.

3 **Thomas Plint**, *Crime in England: Its relation, character, and extent as developed from 1801 to 1848*, London, 1851, p. 19; **James T. Hammick**, 'On the judicial statistics of England and Wales with special reference to recent returns relating to crime', *Journal of the Statistical Society*, xxx (1867), pp. 375–426 (at p. 391); **William Douglas Morrison**, 'The increase of crime', *Nineteenth Century*, xxxi (1892), pp. 950–7 (at p. 956); **C. D. Brereton**, *A Refutation of the First Report of the Constabulary Force Commissioners*, 3 parts, London, n.d., Part 1, p. 73; Barnett and Scott Holland are quoted in **Mandy Ashworth**, *The Oxford House in Bethnal Green*, Oxford House, London, 1984, p. 7.
   Angus Reach was something of an exception. In his mid-century reports for the *Morning Chronicle* he noted that 'where great bodies of people, the vast proportion of them labouring poor, are crammed together, crime must abound'. But he also emphasised that there was far more rural crime than many people imagined, indeed the amount was 'of startling magnitude to the many who naturally connect rustic beauties with rural innocence, and take but little account of the fact that the agricultural labourer endures more habitual and more pinched hunger and cold amid his fair fields and woods, than the factory operative amid the dust and smoke of his alley and his mill'.

J. Ginswick (ed.), *Labour and the Poor in England and Wales*, 8 vols, Frank Cass, London, 1983, i, 6.

4 Ferdinand Tönnies, *Community and Society*, trans. and supplemented by Charles P. Loomis, RKP, London, 1955. *Gemeinschaft* is generally translated as 'community'; *Gesellschaft* as 'association', 'organisation' or even 'society'.

5 Havelock Ellis, *The Criminal*, London, 1890, p. 297. For a useful introductory critique see **Howard Zehr**, *Crime and the Development of Modern Society*, Croom Helm, London, 1976, pp. 20–9; see also **Robert A. Nye**, *Crime, Madness and Politics in Modern France: The medical concept of national decline*, Princeton U.P., Princeton, N.J., 1984, especially pp. 149 and 171.

6 **J. J. Tobias**, *Crime and Industrial Society in the Nineteenth Century*, Penguin, Harmondsworth, 1972, p. 108.

7 **David Jones**, *Crime, Protest, Community and Police in Nineteenth-Century Britain*, RKP, London, 1982, p. 66; **John E. Archer**, 'Poaching gangs and violence: The urban-rural divide in nineteenth-century Lancashire', *British Journal of Criminology*, **39** (1999) pp. 25–38.

8 **John E. Archer**, *'By a flash and a scare.' Arson, Animal Maiming and Poaching in East Anglia 1815–1870*, Clarendon Press, Oxford, 1990, p. 211, n. 43.

9 **John G. Rule**, 'The manifold causes of rural crime: Sheep-stealing in England c. 1740–1840', in John Rule (ed.), *Outside the Law: Studies in crime and order 1650–1850*, Exeter Papers in Economic History, no. 15, University of Exeter, 1982; **R. A. E. Wells**, 'Sheep-rustling in Yorkshire in the age of the industrial and agricultural revolutions', *Northern History*, xx (1984), pp. 127–45. See also **K. P. Baun**, 'Social protest, popular disturbances and public order in Dorset, 1790–1838', unpublished Ph.D., University of Reading, 1984, pp. 136–8.

10 **E. J. Hobsbawm**, 'The machine breakers', *P and P*, **1** (1952), pp. 57–70; for an example of arson apparently linked with a trade dispute in early nineteenth-century Liverpool see H.O. 40.18.53–6, Messrs. Gregson and Bury to Peel, and Charles Lawrence to Peel, both 22 March 1824. In July 1842 the board of the Norwich Union resolved to discontinue cotton mill insurance as renewals fell due because of incendiarism in the north west, though it must be remembered that the Norwich Union's strength lay in the insurance of farm stock. Norwich Union Fire Insurance Society Board Minutes, 18 July 1842. My thanks to Dr Roger Ryan for this reference and for general information on this point.

11 Suffolk R.O. (Ipswich Branch) 2577/1, Chief Constable to Home Secretary, 2 January 1842; See also **R. P. Hastings**, *Essays in North Riding History 1780–1850*, North Yorkshire County Record Office Publications, no. 28

(1981), p. 101; **Janet Gyford**, *Men of Bad Character: The Witham fires of 1820*, Studies in Essex History, No. 1, Essex Record Office (1991).

12 Humberside R.O., Chief Constable to quarter sessions, 5 January 1864. I am grateful to David Foster for his quotation and for permission to use and cite his unpublished material on arson in East Yorkshire.

13 Norwich Union Fire Insurance Society, Board Minutes, 31 August 1835, 12 July 1841, 4 December 1843, 4 January 1847. Once again I am indebted to Dr Ryan for references and information on this point.

14 *York Herald*, 26 March 1864. Dr Foster has information on the occupation of eighteen of the forty-two persons arrested for arson between 1863 and 1870; the largest group – eight – were agricultural labourers and/or Wolds Rangers.

15 C. J. Ribton-Turner, *A History of Vagrants and Vagrancy*, London, 1887, p. 313. For this, and the arson outbreak in North Wales, the border counties and the Midlands see Jones, *Crime, Protest, Community*, pp. 202–3.

16 Jones, *Crime, Protest, Community*, p. 48; **Michael J. Carter**, *Peasants and Poachers: A study in rural disorder in Norfolk*, Boydell Press, Woodbridge, 1980, pp. 28–9; **Timothy Shakeseff**, *Rural Conflict, Crime and Protest: Herefordshire 1800–1860*, Boydell Press, Woodbridge, 2003, p. 191.

17 Archer, 'By a flash and a scare', p. 256; Shakesheff, *Rural Conflict*, pp. 195–200.

18 *Beverley Guardian*, 22 October 1864.

19 Beds. R.O. QGV 10/4/13.

20 **A. J. Peacock**, 'Village radicalism in East Anglia 1800–50', in **J. P. D. Dunbabin**, *Rural Discontent in Nineteenth-Century Britain*, Faber and Faber, London, 1974, pp. 32–3. Beds. R.O. QEV 4, Chief Constable's letter 15 October 1844 reports eight accidental fires, 'two of which occurred by children playing with Lucifer matches'. Four of the eighteen arrested in East Yorks for whom occupations are given, were children.

21 Archer, 'By a flash and a scare', ch. 8.

22 Suffolk R.O. (Ipswich Branch) 2577/1, Chief Constable to Home Secretary, 16 March 1844.

23 See below, pp. 183–4.

24 **James Obelkevich**, *Religion and Rural Society: South Lindsey 1825–75*, Clarendon Press, Oxford, 1976, ch. 6 *passim*; **J. F. C. Harrison**, *The Second Coming: Popular millenarianism 1780–1850*, RKP, London, 1978, ch. 3 *passim*, esp. pp. 41–2.

25 Beds. R.O. QGR 1/23, Prison Chaplain's report 4 April 1848; *Bedford Times*, 11 March 1848; for similar behaviour in South Lincolnshire see Obelkevich, *Religion and Rural Society*, p. 292.

26 John Glyde, *The Norfolk Garland*, London, 1872, pp. 58–9; Beds. R.O. QSR
    1824/384 and 1827/368; Obelkevich, *Religion and Rural Society*, pp. 287–91;
    John Rule, 'Methodism, popular beliefs and village culture in Cornwall
    1800–50', in Robert D. Storch (ed.), *Popular Culture and Custom in
    Nineteenth-Century England*, Croom Helm, London, 1982, p. 63.

27 Obelkevich, *Religion and Rural Society*, pp. 275 and 286; Glyde, *Norfolk
    Garland*, pp. 50–1.

28 The idea of rural society being more prone to violent crime and urban
    society more likely to experience property crime was developed particularly by
    French historians as a theory to describe the shifts in criminality as a result of
    a modernising process. It is commonly referred to as 'violence/vol (theft)'. For
    an introduction to the idea, see Iain A. Cameron, *Crime and Repression in the
    Auvergne and the Guyenne, 1720–90*, Cambridge U.P., New York, 1981,
    ch. 6 *passim*. For the nineteenth-century, again with reference to France, see
    A. Q. Lodhi and Charles Tilly, 'Urbanization, crime and collective violence in
    nineteenth-century France', *American Journal of Sociology*, 79 (1973), pp.
    296–318; and see Zehr, *Crime and the Development of Modern Society*.

29 David Cohen and Eric Johnson, 'French criminality: Urban-rural differences
    in the nineteenth century', *Journal of Interdisciplinary History*, xii (1982),
    pp. 477–501; Herbert Reinke, 'Violence in the age of criminal statistics:
    Nineteenth-century Germany', paper presented at the Second International
    Conference on the History of Crime and Criminal Justice, Maastricht, 17–19
    May 1984; J. A. Sharpe, *Crime in Early Modern England 1550–1750*, 2nd
    edn, Longman, London, 1984, ch. 3 *passim* and pp. 252–53.

30 In a letter printed in *Athenaeum*, 22 August 1846.

31 Bob Bushaway, *By Rite: Custom, ceremony and community in England
    1700–1880*, Junction Books, London, 1982, pp. 131–2.

32 H.O. 45.4609, Fortescue to Palmerston, 17 January 1853; *P.P.* 1852–53 (71)
    xxxvi, *Report of the Select Committee on Police*, q. 415.

33 *The Times*, 16 and 18 December 1874, 8 January 1875; and for reports of
    similar cases 8 and 12 January 1875. See also, Rob Sindall, *Street Violence
    in the Nineteenth Century: Media panic or real danger*, Leicester U.P.,
    London, 1990, pp. 60–2.

34 Bushaway, *By Rite*, p. 158.

35 Storch, *Popular Culture*, pp. 1–2.

36 *The Times*, 21 October 1887.

37 Sharpe, *Crime in Early Modern England*, pp. 103–4.

38 Richard Cobb, *The Police and the People: French popular protest 1789–1820*,
    Oxford U.P., 1970, p. 89.

39 Frances Finnegan, *Poverty and Prejudice: A study of Irish immigrants in York 1840–75*, Cork U.P., 1982, ch. 9 *passim*; R. E. Swift, ' "Another Stafford Street Row": Law, order and the Irish presence in mid-Victorian Wolverhampton', *Immigrants and Minorities*, 3 (1984), pp. 5–29.

40 Todd M. Endelman, *The Jews of Georgian England 1714–1830: Tradition and change in a liberal society*, Jewish Publication Society of America, Philadelphia, 1979, especially ch. 8: Jerry White, *Rothschild Buildings: Life in an East End tenement block 1887–1920*, RKP, London, 1980; V. D. Lipman, 'Jewish settlement in the East End of London 1840–1940: The topographical and statistical background', in Aubrey Newman (ed.), *The Jewish East End 1840–1939*, The Jewish Historical Society of England, London, 1981, pp. 25–6 and 32.

41 Robert Roberts, *The Classic Slum: Salford life in the first quarter of the century*, Penguin, Harmondsworth, 1973, p. 16.

42 John Glyde, jun., *The Moral, Social and Religious Condition of Ipswich in the Middle of the Nineteenth Century*, Ipswich, 1850, reprinted S.R. Publishers, Wakefield, 1971, p. 57.

43 H.O. 42.114.147–8.

44 H.O. 42.114.178–80.

45 Tobias, *Crime and Industrial Society*, p. 173; *P.P. 1847, vii, Select Committee on Juvenile Offenders*, q. 227; Barbara Weinberger, 'Law breakers and law enforcers in the late Victorian city: Birmingham 1867–77', unpublished Ph.D., University of Warwick, 1981, pp. 136–40, notes an apparent decline in theft from employers by the 1870s.

46 R. N. Davidson, *Crime and Environment*, Croom Helm, London, 1981, p. 89; for the whole 'typology' see pp. 89–93.

47 See below, pp. 154–5.

48 Ginswick (ed.), *Labour and the Poor*, i, 39.

49 *P.P. 1828 (533) vi, Select Committee on the Police of the Metropolis*, p. 57; U.C.L. Chadwick MSS 11 f. 2; see also ff. 4–5, response of the Superintendent of K Division; *The Times*, 25 March and 14 April 1865; U.C.L. Chadwick MSS 11 f. 27.

50 David Englander, *Landlord and Tenant in Urban Britain 1838–1918*, Oxford U.P., Oxford, 1983, pp. 7–9.

51 See above, note 39. Violent criminality has been noted as high among the foreign born in eastern Germany and in France during the nineteenth century, see Cohen and Johnson, 'French criminality', pp. 486–9 and Vincent E. McHale and Eric A. Johnson 'Urbanization, industrialization and crime in Imperial Germany', *Social Science History*, 1 (1976), pp. 45–78 and 210–47 (at pp. 326–37).

52 Englander, *Landlord and Tenant*, pp. 34–6; **Timothy Cavanagh**, *Scotland Yard Past and Present: Experiences of thirty-seven years*, London, 1893, pp. 24–7. See also Charles Dickens's fulminations in 'New uncommercial samples: an amateur beat', *All Year Round*, i (new series, 1868–69), pp. 414–18.

53 Jones, *Crime, Protest, Community*, pp. 108–9.

54 **Thomas Beames**, *The Rookeries of London, Past, Present and Prospective*, 2nd edn, London, 1852, pp. 65–8 and see also pp. 25, 26. White, *Rothschild Buildings*, pp. 131–2; Lipman, 'Jewish settlement', pp. 25–6; Weinberger, 'Law breakers and law enforcers', pp. 243–4.

55 Fielding, *An Enquiry*, pp. 141–2. Thirty years later William Blizard described similar dwellings constituting 'a sort of distinct town, or district [of London], calculated for the reception of the darkest and most dangerous enemies to society . . . the owners of these houses make no secret of their being for the entertainment of THIEVES!': **William Blizard**, *Desultory Reflections on Police*, London, 1785, pp. 30–1.

56 Ginswick (ed.), *Labour and the Poor*, i, 39.

57 'A category becomes police property, when the dominant powers of society (in the economy, polity, etc.) leave the problems of social control of that category to the police.' **J. A. Lee**, 'Some structural aspects of police deviance in relations with minority groups', in **C. Shearing** (ed.), *Organisational Police Deviance*, Butterworth, Toronto, 1981, pp. 53–4.

58 **Clive Emsley**, ' "The thump of wood on a swede turnip": Police violence in nineteenth-century England', *C.J.H.*, 6 (1985), pp. 125–49 (at pp. 136–8).

59 **B. J. Davey**, *Lawless and Immoral: Policing a county town 1838–57*, Leicester U.P., London, 1983.

60 *Cambridge and Hertford Independent Press*, 16 July 1825; Beds. R.O. QGC 10/1; QSR 25/1823/330; QSR 25/1824/248; QSR/1825/309–16 and 367–72.

61 The population of Bedfordshire increased as follows: 1801–63,393; 1811–70,213; 1821–83,716; 1831–95,400. Thus between 1811 and 1831 the county population increased by some 36 per cent; the increase in the population of Houghton Conquest for the same period was 57.6 per cent.

62 Beds. R.O. P11/28/2/139–65. The parish register of Houghton Conquest suggests a marked decline of gentry families after 1700. **F. G. Emmison**, *Bedfordshire Parish Registers*, xliv MS vols (1931–53), xli (1950).

63 **John Glyde**, jun., *Suffolk in the Nineteenth Century: Physical, social, moral, religious and industrial*, London, 1856, pp. 146–7; **John Glyde**, 'Localities of crime in Suffolk', *Journal of the Statistical Society*, xix (1856), pp. 102–6.

64 **Dennis R. Mills**, *Lord and Peasant in Nineteenth-Century Britain*, Croom Helm, London, 1980, p. 24. But note that not all agricultural proletarians

lived in open villages; some lived in towns and might have a twenty-mile round trip walking to and from work. Finnegan, *Poverty and Prejudice*, p. 64.

65 Raphael Samuel, ' "Quarry Roughs": Life and labour in Headington Quarry, 1860–1920', in Raphael Samuel (ed.), *Village Life and Labour*, RKP, London, 1975.

66 Dennis R. Mills, 'Francis Howell's report on the operation of the Laws of Settlement in Nottinghamshire 1848', *Transactions of the Thoroton Society of Nottinghamshire*, 76 (1972), pp. 46–52 (at p. 51).

67 Mills, *Lord and Peasant, passim*.

68 Shirley Chase, 'Crime and policing in a nineteenth-century "closed" village: Westfirle, East Sussex 1820–50', unpublished research paper. My thanks to Ms Chase for permission to read and make reference to this paper. Similar patterns of frequent offenders can be found in other Sussex villages both 'closed' and 'open'.

69 E. J. Hobsbawm and George Rudé, *Captain Swing*, Lawrence and Wishart, London, 1969, pp. 172–89; B. Reney, *The Class Struggle in Nineteenth-Century Oxfordshire: The social and communal background to the Otmoor Disturbances of 1830 to 1935*, Ruskin College, Oxford, History Workshop Pamphlet, 3, 1970.

70 Jones, *Crime, Protest, Community*, p. 74.

71 P.P. 1842, ix, *Select Committee on the Payment of Wages*, q. 1584; there were similar comments passed with reference to Batley [qq. 280–84], Bradford [qq. 181–83], Chorley [qq. 1771 and 1774] and Pentwyn Works, Pontypool [qq. 2352–58].

72 P.P. 1847, xxvii, part 11, *Select Committee on Education in Wales*, p. 290.

73 Ginswick (ed.), *Labour and the Poor*, ii, 60–1.

74 James C. Burke, 'Crime and criminality in County Durham 1840–55', unpublished M.A., University of Durham, 1980, pp. 123–33. David Philips, *Crime and Authority in Victorian England*, Croom Helm, London, 1977, p. 213, shows that Staffordshire miners were prepared to prosecute if workmates stole from each other.

CHAPTER 6

Fiddles, perks and pilferage

The focus on crime as something committed by 'criminals' belonging to a particular social group, together with the notion that burgeoning nineteenth-century cities were the refuge of this group, helped to lead contemporaries away from a serious consideration and appreciation of one major centre of criminal activity – the workplace. Yet the reorganisation of manufacturing processes during the eighteenth and nineteenth centuries has led some historians to conclude that there was a criminalisation of traditional work practices and of some 'rights' claimed by workers during the period. At the same time, the development of sophisticated financial institutions and the growth of, for example, bureaucratised systems of welfare provided opportunities for appropriation by employees drawn from respectable, and often high-status social groups.

A study of modern workplace crime has concluded that the phenomenon is widespread and that 'in many jobs . . . it [is] often abnormal *not* to fiddle'. The word 'fiddle' is preferred since:

morally it is relatively neutral. It is . . . a 'weasel word'. It allows us to look at part-time crime not so much with complaisance as with empathy. Using the word 'fiddle', we can more readily appreciate the world-view or cosmology of the fiddler.[1]

Contemporary workplace crime, in Gerald Mars's analysis, is determined not by class or social group, but by occupational structure. Every transaction involving commodities has the potential for dishonesty, but the expropriation of a commodity is not always perceived of as 'theft' either by the offender or by the victim. There is an assumption that 'theft', in the form of burglary from a warehouse, is different from 'theft', in the form of pilferage by a warehouseman. At the same time, should the owner of the warehouse send underweight goods from that warehouse to another businessman, then his appropriation is very often termed 'breach of contract' and not a criminal offence. Perhaps fiddling between businessmen is currently the most common form of fraud, and was the most common form of fraud during the eighteenth and nineteenth centuries; unfortunately the topic has been little explored by historians, and the evidence to prove the scale of such fraud would be very difficult to find. While white-collar offenders are not ignored in this chapter, the focus, following the pattern of historical research to date, remains on their social inferiors.

Workplace crime or 'fiddles' come under a variety of alternative headings, most of which are not neutral words but are those employed by employers or, more commonly, agents of the law concerned with repression. Perquisites or 'perks' can be tolerated by an employer; they can also be the objects of periodic clamp-downs. Generally a 'perk' is regarded by the workforce as an entitlement, though it can sometimes be abused to an extent that few employees could, or would seek to, justify. It is a hazy line that separates perks from pilferage or small-scale theft from the workplace. Pilferage can be practised by virtually an entire workforce at a particular workplace or in a particular job; in a few instances it might shade into more organised and more large-scale theft. A third kind of workplace crime can come under the heading of fraud: this can involve deception on the part of both an employer and his employees to profit at the expense of a third party; it can involve deception on the part of an individual selling goods to, or performing a service for, another. Examples of all of these crimes, or 'fiddles', abound throughout the eighteenth and nineteenth centuries.

The largest single employment sector in Britain during the eighteenth, and for much of the nineteenth century, was agriculture. Various labourers and agricultural communities claimed a whole series of allowances or perks that were gradually whittled down or subjected to greater control and supervision. Gleaning was the best known allowance whereby, after the harvest had been gathered, women and children entered the fields and collected the scattered grain that the harvesters had missed.[2] Corn or beans collected in this way could form a significant percentage of the poor rural family's diet or wage. The custom had biblical authority, though it was clearly practised differently from place to place. During the eighteenth century it was known for individuals to object violently to anyone from outside the community seeking to glean in local fields; and farmers who tried to prevent gleaning, or who turned hogs and cattle out to graze on stubble and thus denied access to the poor, were the objects of popular odium and even assault. In *The Farmer's Kalendar* (1771) Arthur Young criticised farmers who denied gleaning to the poor in this way; but Young was also concerned about abuses by the gleaners and, while acknowledging that the custom was generally accepted, he was at pains to point out that the poor had no imprescriptable right to it. A case of theft brought before Bedfordshire Quarter Sessions in 1785 reveals that there were also those among the poor who recognised abuses in gleaning. Ann Smith, a pauper widow of Blunham, deposed that:

whilst she and the rest of the . . . poor people were gleaning after the cart of Mr Matthew West of the said Parish, Farmer, upon the lands of the said Mr West . . . she . . . with . . . Mary Emery and the other gleaners on account of a heavy shower of rain which then and there fell, were obliged to sit down and leave off gleaning. That during this period as they were lamenting to one another that they must go home without their usual quantity of grain or gleaning . . . the said Mary Emery openly declared that she would not go home without her bundle, and that there was Barley enough in the Fields lieing [sic] upon the lands near to them, and that she would have some before she went home, and not come so far for nothing, or words to this effect, and that she did in consequence of this resolution go upon the land of John Wilcher (another farmer in the Parish) adjoining to them, and thereof took about the quantity of a couple of lapfuls in her apron of loose or mowed Barley and put it into an open sack (used occasionally for that purpose of carrying home their grain) which she had with her . . . she appeared to this informant to do it in a felonious audacious manner in defiance of justice and with a wicked heart purposely and designedly to defraud the said John Wilcher of his said property, and not in a wanton jocon [sic] manner or what is commonly called playing the rogue or in fun.[3]

In 1788 the Court of Common Pleas gave judgment in the case of *Steel* v. *Houghton* declaring that there was no specific right in common law permitting anyone to glean without the authority of the farmer who owned the land. 'Though [the farmer's] conscience may direct him to leave something for the poor,' added one judge, 'the law does not oblige him to leave anything'.[4] The soil, the seed, the cultivation and, in consequence, the profits belonged to the farmer to do with as he thought fit. Here was a vigorous defence of property against what many considered as custom: such a defence appears typical of the eighteenth century. Yet it was not necessarily acted upon in such a way in the courts. Magistrates often refused to convict at summary level, and in the majority of cases that have been explored in north-east Essex, it was the farmer who was more likely to be the accused in cases related to gleaning and the landless labourers who were prosecuting him for assault.[5] Perhaps it was partly because of such difficulties that many farmers continued to permit gleaning; at the same time some gleaners continued to abuse what men of property could now term a privilege rather than a customary right. Matthew Munn was a wheelwright who held land next to his house in Potton, Bedfordshire. On 31 July 1790 some five and a half acres of rye lay reaped in his field; it was market day and Munn feared that some of his grain might be stolen so he hid in a ditch behind a hedge. From this vantage point he saw Frances Finding and Jane Jinn, the wives of local labourers, enter his field, but they:

did not confine themselves altogether to gleaning or picking up the loose eares which lay scattered about distinct from the shocks, but every now and then would steal a handful or so out of the shocks.[6]

Magistrates appear commonly to have concluded that a prosecution for larceny could not be supported in a case of gleaning; a larceny charge, they reasoned, was only permissible when the offender took the property of another recognising that he, or more likely in the case of gleaning, she, had no right to it. Farmers did not use the 1788 judgment as the opportunity for a blanket assault on gleaning; the gleaners' case continued to be underpinned by humanitarian and scriptural arguments, and such prosecutions as there were seem to have depended rather more on local farming practice than on a new determination to preserve property rights. Scarcely anyone was prosecuted for gleaning in a wheat field since, in a four- or five-crop rotation, gleaning was one way of ensuring that the field was cleared for winter ploughing. Barley and beans were different: these would be used for livestock feed and farmers feared that if labourers kept livestock then, when the gleanings ran out, they might be tempted to pilfer. Additionally, barley could be undersown with grass to permit grazing between harvest and autumn frosts, but cattle and sheep could not be turned into fields when gleaners were present. Most nineteenth-century prosecutions for gleaning appear to have involved barley or beans. But prosecution was not the only means of discouraging gleaners; farmers could always employ other sanctions given their power as employers or as vestrymen with influence over poor relief and settlement.[7]

As the nineteenth century wore on communities regulated gleaning themselves with the use of gleaning bells that rang to start and finish daily operations. At Rempstone in Leicestershire a Queen of the Gleaners was appointed to supervise. She proclaimed three 'laws':

1st. My attendant shall ring a bell each morning when there are fields to be gleaned.
2nd. Half-past 8 o'clock shall be the hour of meeting, at the end of the village, and I will then accompany you to the field.
3rdly. Should any of my subjects enter an ungleaned field, without being led by me, their corn will be forfeited and bestrewed.[8]

Similar monarchs were appointed elsewhere and their appearance in the nineteenth century might best be comprehended within James Obelkevich's concept of 'pseudo-Gemeinschaft' by which farmers and the village elites sought to re-establish rural customs, but in a manner that underlined the elite's separateness from, and paternalism towards, the labourers.[9] Gleaning gradually disappeared partly as a result of technological change in the shape of mechanical binders and reapers, which were introduced towards the end of the nineteenth century and which transformed harvesting, but probably rather more because a rise in real wages reduced the incentives.

Long after the 1788 ruling by the Court of Common Pleas gleaning continued to be justified in terms of customary rights; the taking of other produce from the land was not open to such justification, though some may have considered that their labour in the fields entitled them to some such 'perks'. Some farmers probably tolerated such behaviour, providing it was only occasional and limited; but such 'perks' or pilferage were difficult to prove unless a man was caught in the act, or with the produce on him. The evidence from eighteenth-century Essex suggests that summary courts dealt with far more cases of vegetable theft than game offences, though historians and, because of their symbolic importance, contemporaries, tended to concentrate on the latter.[10] George Edwards, an organiser of agricultural trade unionism and subsequently Labour M.P. for South Norfolk, recalled that his 'first experience of real distress' came in the year 1855:

On my father's return home from work one night he was stopped by a policeman who searched his bag and took from it five turnips, which he was taking home to make his children an evening meal. There was no bread in the house. His wife and children were waiting for him to come home, but he was not allowed to do so.

Edwards's father was sentenced to fourteen days' hard labour; on his release no farmer would employ him and the family spent the winter in the workhouse.[11] It would, of course, be folly to suppose that every incidence of the appropriation of growing produce was prompted by a labourer's need to feed a starving family or by a belief that his sweat and effort justified a 'perk'. Growing crops could only be taken at certain times of the year; there was a peak of summary indictments in the late summer and autumn when such crops were plentiful but also when there was a peak of agricultural employment. Furthermore, on occasions growing crops were taken by organised gangs. In 1822 eight bushels of apples were stolen from farmer John Burr's land on the outskirts of Bedford. Five men armed with bludgeons cowed his night watchmen and took the apples away in a cart.[12]

Wood gathering for fuel, for building, even for a maypole, like gleaning, was perceived as customary right. There was ambiguity here; picking up fallen wood was one thing, cutting down green branches or living trees was another; and when a cart was brought to carry away the timber it suggests that the offenders were as likely to be involved in selling wood for profit as collecting for their own families' use. Legislation was passed during the seventeenth and eighteenth centuries relating to wood theft – the law, of course, spoke in terms of theft and timber was a valuable commodity for fuel, for building, and to meet the demands of the Royal Navy. Like the ruling on gleaning this legislation can be interpreted as a further, deliberate move to emasculate rural popular culture and to strengthen the defences of private property. But legislation does not act on its own; the laws on wood theft, like the extensions to the Game Laws, gave prosecutors a choice in how they dealt with offenders. Winchester College considered itself plagued by wood stealers during the 1790s: 'near 3,000 trees' were damaged in six or seven years. The Warden and Scholars responded with the full force of the law against five men at the Hampshire Quarter Sessions in 1798; all five were sentenced to seven years' transportation.[13] Yet most offenders still seem to have been brought before magistrates for summary jurisdiction and, if found guilty, sentenced to a small fine or a short term of imprisonment. Prosecutors appear to have considered the nature and frequency of the offence and the character of the accused. The historian cannot consider every single offence and every single offender, but must bear in mind that there were a variety of motives for wood theft. Some undoubtedly did consider that taking wood was a right particularly when pressed by bitter cold or penury. At the other extreme a percentage of wood theft was probably the result of pure vandalism. In 1795 Lord Petre gave troops quartered on Warley Common the authority to cut timber for their needs from his land. The timber was carefully marked out, but during their stay the soldiers ripped up several hundred young trees from an unmarked area.[14]

Agricultural work itself provided opportunities for less ambiguous offences. Thomas Pedder and James Walduck were employed by Christopher Prior in 1818 to thresh wheat 'and to draw straws for platting [sic] and to sell it for our master to women and others applying'. They confessed that, when they sold the straw, they did not give Prior all the money that they received. Five years later farmer Thomas Wiles employed James Smith to thresh his barley; he observed Smith put some of the barley into his own sack. John Palmer, a miller of Luton, was indicted in 1817 for defrauding William Williams. Palmer had received four bushels of wheat for grinding, but had only returned three and one half bushels of wheat and flour mixed. Agricultural instruments were pilfered from the workplace; occasionally perhaps because they could be used at home:

I Never Intended Keeping the Spade . . . I took the Spade to dig Potatoes again . . . I Placed the Spade where any one might See It and It Remained there three hours as the Moon Shone Bright If I Intended Keeping the Spade I should of hid It . . .[15]

But some of the implements taken were most likely acquired for what they would fetch when sold.

'Chips' claimed by the workers in the Royal Dockyards constitute the best known example of an eighteenth-century industrial workplace fiddle. The government was involved directly; its attempts to save money in the yards prompted a succession of investigations that, among other things, drew attention to the workforce's perquisites and, subsequently, provided historians with such a wealth of detail. Other evidence has been left by the steady trickle of offenders dealt with by the disciplinary procedures of the yards themselves or prosecuted in the courts.[16] Originally chips constituted scrap wood that men were permitted to take home from the yards to use as firewood. By the early seventeenth century the authorities considered that perquisite was being abused, not the least when in 1634 a boat-load of 3,500 one-foot long wooden tree-nails was seized at Deptford; the tree-nails had been made by two men out of the chips that they had collected in six years' work in the royal yards. A succession of attempts were made to end or at least to limit the size of chips; a regulation of 1753 stated that they should consist of no more than could be carried, untied, under one arm. But the ambiguity continued until, in 1801, the government succeeded in commuting them to a cash payment. Ambiguity existed also over what constituted a chip and who was permitted to take them from the yards. It was alleged that men spent the last half hour of the working day sawing up new and useful wood to take out as chips. Technically only men working in the yards were allowed to take chips out, yet many others did so such as wives and children who brought in lunch for their menfolk, and even individuals who visited the yards when, for example, the launching of a ship was celebrated. Chips were also stretched in some minds to include nails, paint, ropes, sail-cloth and, indeed, anything which could not be nailed down. During the American War of Independence it was alleged that receivers in Portsmouth were paying 1s.3d. for five pounds of used copper nails; this was more than the average daily wage for the unskilled yard labourer. When, in 1801, the skilled men were asked to state how much they would be prepared to accept to forgo their daily bundle, they estimated the value at 8d.; the basic daily rate for a skilled shipwright or caulker then stood at 2s.1d., though, because of the exigencies of war, they were probably earning three times that amount. But pay in the royal yards was always in arrears: at the close of the Seven Years War wages were fifteen months late and throughout the war against Revolutionary France they were at least three months late. For this reason, if for no other, chips were essential to the workman's existence and were preserved with tenacity. Yard officials, themselves taking unofficial earnings in the form of fees and indulging in a variety of fiddles, were aware of the financial problems of their workforce and this may have fostered a degree of laxity and toleration. Juries in dockyard areas were reluctant to convict the smaller offenders, partly, it would appear, because they accepted chips as a man's right and partly also, perhaps, because they were aware of the essential nature of the chips to the family economy of the workman. Informers were unpopular and sometimes were subjected to counter-charges. The commutation of chips was accompanied by a more regular system of wage payment, though it was not until July 1813 that the men began to be paid on a regular weekly basis. This, together with stricter supervision and police provision, probably succeeded in reducing the amount of material taken from the yards, but pilferage was by no means completely eradicated.[17]

Not only was the Admiralty interested in reducing expenditure by controlling the perks of its manual labourers in the dockyards. It also sought to rationalise the salary system for its clerical establishment and to abolish their unofficial emoluments. Clerks took fees for making out bills, certificates, contracts, warrants and so forth, tasks which produced between two- and three-fifths of their annual income. In the Navy Office clerks also performed 'agency business' by which they settled the accounts of contractors, officers and seamen, and used Navy Office stationery and postage in so doing. The commutation of these perks and the new salary scales were ill-considered and prompted much unrest; in 1800 the clerks in the Navy Office embarked on a go-slow so as to obtain overtime payments.[18]

The Royal Dockyards were exceptional during the eighteenth century for the large number of workers employed on a single site. Industrial production was dominated by the putting-out system whereby men and women worked in their own accommodation using materials received from, and which remained the property of, a master manufacturer. The putting-out system provided opportunities for a variety of fiddles on the part of both masters and outworkers. Clothiers were reported to be using false weights so as to give their weavers greater or smaller quantities for weaving a standard piece at a fixed financial rate; in the former instance they obliged the weaver to weave extra cloth for no extra payment; in the second instance they could reduce the weaver's pay by claiming that the cloth he had returned was of insufficient weight. As in the dockyards employers sometimes paid wages in arrears and this could bind the weaver to an employer and force him to live on credit. Pay might also come in tokens, notes of hand or even counterfeit coppers negotiable at a discount or only with specific retailers in a form of truck. Payments of this kind, however, were not always the result of deliberate fiddles since the English coinage was in a poor state during the eighteenth century. When the war with Revolutionary France compelled the Bank of England to withhold payment in specie in 1798, the problem of finding coinage to pay workers' wages became acute.[19] Outworkers in the textile trades responded to the clothiers' fiddles with a variety of their own by which the employers received back short-length yarn or short-weight cloth; the outworker could then sell off the surplus, or put it to his or her own use. (Most likely *her* own use since short reeling appears in quarter sessions records as predominantly an offence committed by women.) Weavers also insisted on their 'thrums' – the weft ends that were left on a loom after the finished cloth had been removed. Since legally the outworker's materials remained the property of the employer, the retention of thrums constituted an offence: in law this offence was not larceny but embezzlement. Yet employers' attempts to collect thrums as well as finished cloth could lead to trouble. There was a bitter weavers' strike in Essex in the winter of 1757 to 1758 when the Colchester clothiers demanded the return of waste. The intervention of a local M.P., which led to the clothiers' offering 3d. for a thrum, reveals the extent to which the custom was acknowledged both within and outside the industry. The Essex weavers initially considered the commutation payment too small but, in the end, they were compelled to accept it.

Eighty years later Yorkshire worsted manufacturers were still purchasing thrums from their outworkers.[20]

Perks in eighteenth and early nineteenth-century outwork were not confined to the textile industries. Journeymen tailors took 'cabbage' – the pieces of cloth left over after cutting out and, on occasions, rather more than simply the waste shreds were acquired. The practice long outlived the heyday of outwork and was commented on by James Greenwood in 1869:

As with the tailor, so it is with the upholsterer, and the dressmaker, and the paperhanger, and the plumber, and all the rest of them. I don't say that every time they take a shred of this, or a pound of that, that they have before their eyes the enormity of the offence they are about to commit. What they do they see no great harm in. Indeed, point out to them and make it clear that their offence has but to be brought fairly before the criminal authorities to ensure them a month on the treadmill, and they would as a rule be shocked past repeating the delinquency. And well would it be if they were shocked past it, ere misfortune overtake them. It is when 'hard up' times set in, and it is difficult indeed to earn an honest penny, that these rudimentary exercises in the art of pillage tell against a man.[21]

In some trades fiddles did not apply simply to left-overs. Journeymen hatters indulged in 'bugging' by which they substituted cheaper materials for those that master hatters had put out to them. Shoemakers acted similarly buying cheap leather from carriers and substituting it for the more valuable material received from the master; the more valuable leather was then converted to their own use.[22]

Nail-making involved both outwork and production by individual nailers for direct sale. An individual nailer could use up to a ton of iron in a year; the work required little equipment or training, but it was laborious and poorly paid. Nailers not only embezzled the iron that was put out, they also provided a ready market for iron pilfered or embezzled by others. By the late eighteenth century there were said to be 40,000 men, women and children working as nailers in the Black Country as well as thousands of others engaged in the different metal trades. Almost any piece of metal, including gate hinges and latches and bits of agricultural machinery, could be reworked in small family forges or by bigger manufacturers who asked no questions of individuals with metal to sell. These practices continued into the nineteenth century, and other metal working centres appear to have had similar problems to the Black Country. In 1854 a Sheffield grand jury complained that one-fifth of the indictments brought before them were for the theft of scrap metal. The decline of outwork did not mean that industrial workers no longer expropriated raw materials or finished goods; far from it. But the definition of the offence did change. An employer's ownership and possession of goods coincided in a factory or workshop, and consequently any expropriation by an employee who had not been given the goods to work on in his or her own home, came under the legal definition of larceny. Embezzlement increasingly was used to refer simply to fraudulent conversion of money.[23]

Nor was it only in the outwork trades that journeymen claimed perks. At the close of the eighteenth century London's journeymen printers claimed the right to a copy of each book that they printed. In January 1797 George Cawthorne, a printer and bookseller, prosecuted one of his workmen for stealing a book. Reluctantly Cawthorne and two other printers admitted in court that their employees were claiming this 'right'. One printer protested that, if the 'right' was admitted, it would destroy all profits and he personally would stand to lose £20 a week by it. Interestingly, according to the printers, it was the King's printer who was breaking ranks and allowing workmen to take books from the workshop. Sir John Heath, the judge hearing the case, finally stopped the proceedings:

I think, Gentlemen of the Jury, there can be no occasion to go any further; at the same time, the acquittal of this man must not be understood to decide the right.[24]

Nearly eighty years later, in January 1875, a somewhat similar case was brought before the stipendiary magistrates of the Worship Street Police Court. A workman was prosecuted for taking six copies of a lithographic print from his place of work; unlike Cawthorne, the printer accepted his workmen's right to one proof copy if they wished – but one proof copy was sufficient.[25]

Generally speaking throughout the period coal miners were allowed coal for their own use. In eighteenth-century Staffordshire, however, they appear to have taken much larger amounts, which were sold at a profit. There were other fiddles in mining also. If paid by a filled 'corve' miners were known to put large coals at the bottom of a corve leaving plenty of hollow spaces; the top was then filled with smaller coals so that the container merely looked full. In the tin and copper mines of Cornwall tutworkers who sank shafts and drove levels and who were paid by the fathom, allegedly bribed mine captains to over-measure their work. Tributers, who negotiated separate contracts for raising ore in different parts of a mine, were paid according to the value of the ore that they raised; the gangs were known to come to agreements between themselves so that those on a poor pitch, who were earning at a high rate, and those on a good pitch, who were paid at a lower rate, exchanged a little ore and split the resulting profits between them.[26]

Any movement of goods not directly supervised by an employer offered employees an opportunity for fraud or appropriation. In 1800 Richard Pybus was employed by Edward Brumfitt who ran a transport business in Leeds. When goods arrived in Leeds it was one of Pybus's tasks to deliver them using Brumfitt's waggon. On one occasion he was instructed to deliver a package to a merchant, Richard Sissons, and to collect a fee of 9s.11d. Pybus decided to augment the fee to 13s.6d. and, upon discovery, was prosecuted for fraud. Jane Hartwell was 'the letter carrier from Harrold [Bedfordshire] to Bozeat [Northants]'. In 1816 she was prosecuted for taking a £10 banknote from a letter given to her by a Harrold shopkeeper to post in Bozeat. Twenty years later the Metropolitan Police gave the Constabulary Commissioners several examples of individuals absconding when entrusted with money by their employers.[27] Probably Pybus, Hartwell and others were only prosecuted when the scale of the offence was regarded as sufficiently large to merit anything other than a warning or a dismissal. But continual small pilferage could eventually mount up to a significant theft: Frederick Huggins was employed as a porter by Richard Hellaby; one of his tasks was to load the trap of Hellaby's commercial traveller and he regularly took a neck-tie while engaged in this task until, in November 1856, Hellaby prosecuted him for the theft of forty-eight such ties.[28] In large-scale movements of goods the opportunities for fiddling were much greater and could be developed by teams of men into something reminiscent of a perk. The building of and the growth of railways provided wide opportunities for railway staff, generally respectable and skilled men, to appropriate goods in transit,[29] but probably the most notorious examples of this behaviour were to be found on the docks.

Both Patrick Colquhoun and John Binney, one of Mayhew's collaborators, reported dock workers pilfering from cargoes as they unloaded them and taking ships' equipment. The pilfered goods were smuggled out of the docks in bags or strings worn under clothing, or simply in hats and pockets. They could be used by the dockers themselves, or sold to small grocers, publicans, dealers in old iron and anyone else who was in the market.[30] Arthur Harding described a similar pattern existing in the 1890s; Harding's Aunt Liza, who ran a corner shop, bought tea, sugar and whisky taken by dockers, repackaged and then resold it. Everyone involved could profit from such an arrangement: the dockers, Aunt Liza, and Aunt Liza's customers who were able to buy the repackaged goods at less than the usual market price.[31] Colquhoun was appalled that the dockers 'consider it as a kind of right which attaches to their situation, to plunder wherever opportunity offers'. Moreover, he insisted that:

above sixty of these plunderers meet regularly, and subscribed a certain sum for establishing a general fund; out of which the penalty of 40s. adjudged under the Bum-boat Act, to be paid by every person convicted of conveying goods pilfered from vessels, is regularly discharged; by which means the delinquents, instead of going to gaol, are enabled to return to their former criminal pursuits. Some of the members of this club, although apparently common labourers, are said to have their houses furnished in a very superior style and to be possessed of property in the funds to the extent of from £1,500 to £3,000.[32]

It seems unlikely that these extremely wealthy dockers existed outside Colquhoun's fertile imagination, yet clubbing together to pay the fine of a workmate unlucky enough to be caught, prosecuted and convicted, was practised at least much later in the century.[33]

The Constabulary Force Commissioners received evidence of continuous pilferage on the canals. The boatmen removed cloth, ironmongery, liquor, sugar, tea, indeed anything that could be turned to their own use or sold off to a receiver. Some receivers were grocers like Harding's Aunt Liza; others were master manufacturers who took the goods from the boatmen and subsequently sold them as if their own. A variety of dodges were employed to ensure that the loss of goods was not discovered until the boatmen were well clear.[34] The replacement of canal transport by the railway did not abolish such pilferage, it simply changed its location, changed the problems of the fiddlers and of those whose task it was to prevent them. The Constabulary Commissioners noted that carrying firms were 'immediately interested only in the prevention of those depredations in which the losses admit of distinct specification, and for which they can be made accountable'.[35] The firms whose goods were carried were, as their evidence to the Commissioners testifies, well aware of the potential for loss through pilferage and probably made allowance. During the eighteenth century coal-mine owners often loaded more coal into canal boats than was listed on manifests; this was partly because of the difficulties involved in gauging a boat's weight but also because they were well aware that the boatmen sold coal on route and paid off lock-keepers and other officials for an easy, unimpeded journey.[36] Other employers tolerated fiddles that did not hit them personally, but that could be passed on to the purchaser. At the end of the nineteenth century dairy owners admitted that they took the dishonesty of their milkmen into account when calculating wages. The most common fiddle was 'bobbing', or watering the milk and selling the surplus at a profit; such adulteration of milk by milkmen, however, was probably the least of the causes for the atrocious quality of cheap milk in the cities.[37] James Greenwood maintained that the London General Omnibus Company was able to keep their conductors' pay at 4s. for a seventeen-hour day because of an understanding by the employers and their employees that the latter were pocketing a percentage of the daily takings. It was, according to Charles Booth, 'almost as though the omnibus had been hired from the company, and was run by the men on their own account'.[38] An increase in wages and the introduction, not without opposition, of the bell punch finally put an end to this or at least limited the conductor's opportunities for perks.

In general the workplace offences discussed so far were those committed by employees. Several historians have sought to slot their perception of such offences into changes in the economic structure. It has, for example, been urged that the shift to centralised, factory-based manufacture was less the result of this system's proven technical superiority and more because of concern about embezzlement and labour discipline under the out-work system.[39] It has also been argued that a criminalisation of perks took place in the eighteenth century and that this was another aspect of the destruction of a vital artisan culture and of the alienation of the worker from the product of his labour. This was mirrored in rural areas where farmers increasingly distanced themselves socially from their labourers and where notions of property were strengthened by enclosure with the poor rural dweller being reduced to a wage labourer denied the right to graze animals, to pick up fallen wood, or to glean from the fields that he had sown and reaped with his labour – the land was property: using it, or taking things from it when not sanctioned by the owner, was an offence against that property:

Since property was a thing, it became possible to define offences as crimes against things, rather than as injuries to men. This enabled the law to assume, with its robes, the postures of impartiality: it was neutral as between every degree of man, and defended only the inviolability of the ownership of things. In the seventeenth century labour had been only partly free, but the labourer still asserted large claims (sometimes as perquisites) to his own labour's product. As, in the eighteenth century,

labour became more and more free, so labour's product came to be seen
as something totally distinct, the property of landowner or employer, and
to be defended by the threat of the gallows.[40]

Such analyses have considerable attractions in that they draw together and
relate changes in society and the economy and concurrent changes in the
law, in its interpretation and enforcement. There is evidence of a close link
between industrial development and prosecution for industrial theft
in some areas. In early nineteenth-century Wigan, for example, the law
appears to have been administered humanely and impartially by the local
magistracy, except when it was involved with industry. Employers were
rarely prosecuted, and if convicted were only moderately fined for operat-
ing the truck system; on the other hand, heavy sentences were imposed
even for first offences of industrial theft. Workers, including children, were
commonly prosecuted for breach of contract in leaving work without
proper notice, and the sentence in this case was also a heavy fine:[41] the
Master and Servant Act 1823 worked explicitly in the employer's favour
in that he could only be prosecuted in civil law for breach of contract,
the employee was liable to criminal prosecution for the same offence.
Prosecutions for industrial theft rose markedly in the Black Country
between 1835 and 1860: from about fifteen per cent of all larcenies prosecuted to about forty per cent or from about ten per cent of all prosecutions
in one year to about one-third. The increase coincided with a change in the
composition of the local magistracy from a majority of landed aristocracy
and gentry to one of coal owners and industrialists – the principal local
employers. Furthermore, the Criminal Justice Act 1855 authorised summary trial for these petty offences; prosecution thus became cheaper and
quicker, and there was a qualitative leap in the number of prosecutions
during the years immediately following the act.[42] An analysis of prosecutions under this act at eight police courts in mid-nineteenth-century
London reveals employee theft to have been the most common offence, but
equally it reveals that most of these prosecutions were undertaken by small
tradesmen and masters, not by the larger firms and the bigger employers.[43]
At the same time, however, it is apparent that employers did not always
resort to the law to control their workforce; even in the late nineteenth century employers tolerated some fiddles, especially when their profits were
untouched. They might choose to make an example of a single individual
as a warning to others, and only then if his offences were in excess of
the generally accepted and tolerated level; such appears to have been the
situation in the London Omnibus Company, and even here the employers

preferred dismissal to prosecution. Alternatively, as the Superintendent of K Division of the Metropolitan Police informed the Constabulary Commissioners, some employers did not take action because of the solidarity among their workforce, fearing a strike if they did so.[44]

The eighteenth century witnessed a growth in the concept of the monetary wage and, at the same time, a considerable amount of legislation was passed with the intent of controlling the perks of the outworker. This is a central consideration in Peter Linebaugh's study of those executed on London's Tyburn tree: 'Just as the "rights of man" presupposed doctrines of legal "wrongs", so the monetary abstraction of human labour as wages presupposed criminalizing customary appropriation.'[45] Yet it is difficult to sustain the argument that this legislation criminalised what had been legal or at most tolerated before, and passionate as Linebaugh's book is, there are times when it refuses to engage with some of the parallel studies which challenge his assertions. J. A. Sharpe has emphasised that, in the half-century before 1640, it was probably easier to regulate industrial production by patent of monopoly rather than by parliamentary statute.[46] During this period parliamentary government was in decline; the events of the 1640s reversed this process and if there appears something of a flood of legislation relating to outwork during the eighteenth century, it must be remembered that, partly owing to the availability of parliament after 1688 (it now had to meet annually), there was simply very much more legislation of all kinds passed in the eighteenth century. From Tudor times, even before, outworkers could be prosecuted for detaining waste; what the acts of 1749 and 1777 did was to put a time limit on this return – twenty-one days in the first instance, and eight in the second. The Act of 1749 gave magistrates acting summarily the power to punish embezzling outworkers with sentences of prison or corporal punishment from the outset, rather than with the financial penalties for first offences and prison or corporal punishment if the offenders could not pay, as established under earlier legislation. Evidence is fragmentary, yet it appears that a very high proportion of offenders convicted before 1749 could not, or would not pay fines and consequently received corporal punishment. The 1749 Act appears thus to have codified the practice of the courts rather than changed the law both in this respect, and also in as much as the receivers of embezzled goods, who were generally from a more well-to-do social background than the outworkers, continued to be subjected to financial penalties; the receivers had generally paid their fines before 1749, and besides it was against legislative practice to subject men who could be of some substance to immediate corporal punishment. But not all legislation relating to embezzlement during the eighteenth century made offenders liable to immediate custodial or corporal punishment. The most common outwork offence was short reeling and this was the subject of separate legislation in 1774 which led to a small fine, only five shillings for a first offence, rather than prison or whipping, being the most common punishment. There had been modifications in the doctrine that larceny could not be committed by persons to whom goods were temporarily transferred by the owner,[47] yet, during the eighteenth century, no-one appears to have contemplated plugging the loophole in the security of property provided by outwork; there was no attempt to change the legal situation which rendered outworkers only liable to summary prosecution for embezzlement rather than to indictments for larceny before quarter sessions or assizes.

The view that the period of massive industrialisation and capitalisation witnessed a deliberate and corresponding criminalisation of certain work practices and that workplace theft is best understood as a defence of customary rights against attempts to impose a new system of wage discipline is open to two further objections. First, it tends to limit workplace crime to one social group and to put a blanket legitimation on their activities. Second, there is precious little evidence that the bulk of workplace crime was ever conceived as a protest against a new wage discipline; there is similarly little evidence that customary rights were preferred to the new wages. Thrums, chips and cabbage may have been defended as a legitimate right for the workman, yet not necessarily in preference to a regular wage, workplace offences were not always directed against the employer, and the taking of a man's half-finished work, subsequently finished and sold by another as his own – a common offence in the late eighteenth-century metal trades – can hardly be construed as a legitimate perk.[48] When dockers or boatmen or railwaymen 'knocked off' cargo, their actions may have been sanctioned by tradition and protected by communal solidarity, yet they could never have been defended in court as was attempted, not without success or a sympathetic hearing, by weavers who had taken thrums, colliers who had taken coals and rural labourers who had taken wood or gleanings without authority. Furthermore, there were other offences committed by employees at their place of work for which the word perk is in no sense applicable: the shopman who took money from the till, or who took anything else that caught his eye; the domestic servant who appropriated his or, more commonly, her employer's property. The number of such cases that came before the courts almost certainly constitute only a tiny fraction of the number of offences that were discovered. On occasions an employer might mark his money or his goods to check up on such petty pilfering:

John Fewkes of Basford in the County of Nottingham, cordwainer, maketh oaths and saith the prisoner William Parnell has worked for me for about 6 months last and during that period I have missed different articles belonging to me. I also keep a Beer Shop which the prisoner frequented and I have lately missed tobacco therefrom . . . on the morning of Thursday the 9 August I marked 16 papers of tobacco by putting my name in the inside of them and I put them in the draw where they were usually kept in the Bar.[49]

Domestic servants, and possibly some other employees, might also be 'tested' for honesty with coinage or paper money left where they were likely to see it.[50] The dismissal of a dishonest servant was far easier, far cheaper and, perhaps, less demeaning or embarrassing than a prosecution. Lastly, the question might be posed: if fiddling is to be condoned by one social group, why not by another that also took advantage of a lack of workplace supervision? White-collar offences, almost by definition workplace offences, and fiddles by different kinds of tradesmen, were also subjects of controlling legislation, though, admittedly this was often less well structured and, for a variety of reasons less well enforced.

James Greenwood reserved some of his most savage denunciations for the shopkeeper who used false weights and measures or who adulterated food and drink. Such an offender was:

by far a greater villain than the half-starved wretch who snatches a leg of mutton from a butcher's hook, or some article of drapery temptingly flaunting outside the shop of the clothier, because in the one case the crime is perpetrated that a soul and a woefully lean body may be saved from severance, and in the other case the iniquity is made to pander to the wrongdoer's covetous desire to grow fat, to wear magnificent jewellery, and to air his unwieldly carcase annually at Margate.[51]

But such frauds long pre-dated the tradition of an annual seaside holiday. In the mid-eighteenth century they were compounded by regional variations in weights and measures; localities cherished their variations and this impeded the proposals of a parliamentary committee in 1758 that national standards be adopted and that all weights below one pound should be made of gold, silver, brass, copper or bell metal, and all those above a pound should be made of brass, copper, bell metal or cast iron.[52] There was also the problem of laxity among local authorities and/or their officials. A miller who returned short weight of flour could be indicted for fraud, but most traders guilty of market-place offences were dealt with under the common law. Market juries, local magistrates and part-time inspectors of weights and measures were responsible for acting against corrupt practices. This area has been little studied, but it is conceivable that external events, such as a bad harvest leading to a food shortage and high prices, on the one hand, tempted unscrupulous market traders and bakers to maximise their profits by defrauding their customers and, on the other, encouraged men to be on the look-out for such frauds and to prosecute. In April of the famine year of 1795, for example, three men were hailed before Richard Colt Hoare in petty sessions, accused of selling underweight bread.[53] In 1802, following hard on the heels of another subsistence crisis, Bedfordshire magistrates meeting in petty sessions at Biggleswade reported that, until a recent inspection by the current inspector of weights and measures, there had never been any such thing in the district. The result of the inspection was that eighty-seven persons were summonsed, but the magistrates 'presuming ignorance in all Persons against whom such Informations were exhibited fined each in the lowest Penalties allowable by Law and took away the defective Balances, Weights and Measures'. The role of inspector, like that of constable, did not suit many. The widow of John Kilpin, one of the inspectors in Bedfordshire, explained that her husband had 'dreaded and disliked' his tasks and kept putting them off, hating to leave his family 'to be exposed to the Abusive Insulting language and rough treatment of the People to whom he was sent'.[54] Significantly when the new police were established during the 1830s–1850s, many senior officers were given the tasks of inspectors of weights and measures.

The adulteration of food and drink was an even more difficult offence to police. John Bright, while President of the Board of Trade, maintained that 'adulteration . . . arises from the very great and, perhaps, inevitable competition in business; and that to a large extent it is prompted by the ignorance of customers'. He went on to say that it would be quite impossible, as well as intolerable, to have inspectors continually checking goods in shops. These comments made James Greenwood furious; he pointed out that France and Germany had both a better system of inspection and much stiffer penalties.[55] To the extent that an investigation of adulteration required the taking of samples and then analysis, however, Bright had some justification in arguing that inspection was impossible: qualified and competent chemists were not plentiful, while the cost of sufficient inspectors would have been looked at askance by the Treasury, by parliament and by taxpayers. Change came gradually, beginning with the Food and Drugs Act of 1860; but the number of inspectors remained small and the fines inflicted on offenders were trifling – in 1899 4,319 prosecutions were brought for adulterating food and the average fine was £1.16s.8d.[56] The offenders in such instances were labelled not so much as 'criminals' but as 'rotten apples'; among some of their fellows they might simply have been perceived as 'unlucky'.

Some shopkeepers did well out of systems of truck, even after early nineteenth-century legislation sought to put an end to the practice. The problem with truck legislation was that the magistrates who were to enforce it were often the employers who practised it, especially as industrialists became more prominent on magisterial benches. Employer magistrates would not have heard cases brought against themselves for infringing the Truck Acts: the Victorian elite was not so hypocritical as to have tolerated such behaviour, after all the law was just and impartial and had to be seen as just and impartial.[57] Yet it is difficult to expect that employer magistrates would not have had sympathy for their fellows as victims, or acting as prosecutors, in cases of industrial theft, or as defendants in cases brought under the Truck or Factory Acts.

The expansion of capitalism provided opportunities for more extensive and more profitable workplace fiddles by a variety of company directors, bankers, managers and clerks. The self-regulating money market of the City of London run by financial 'experts', coupled with a general public largely ignorant of the jargon of business documents and legal contracts, provided tempting opportunities for the fraudster. The excesses of the railway mania of the 1840s demonstrated the possibilities in a particularly stark fashion, but it has been estimated that as many as one in six of all company promotions during the nineteenth century was fraudulent.[58] Some of the banking frauds and cases of embezzlement involved enormous sums of money. In 1857 it was revealed that Colonel W. Petri Waugh was indebted to the London and Eastern Banking Company for £244,000, which was just £6,000 less than the entire subscribed capital of the bank. The Colonel was a director of the bank and he had acted with the connivance of J. E. Stephens, the manager. Petri Waugh fled to Spain, where he started a mining company; but his only criminal offence was holding funds while he was a bankrupt. Stephens had committed no criminal offence.[59] In 1882 Charles Magniac, Liberal M.P. for Bedford, received an urgent summons to London by telegraph. He met one of his partners in Matheson and Jardine on the railway station platform:

we both agreed that some fraud must have been committed implicating the firm. This I found on my arrival proved to be the case, but the amount is so gigantic and incredible . . . Over a million in sterling.

The offence had been so simple for the perpetrator:

[S]ubject to the general control of one of the managing partners it was the duty of a young man in the office, a nephew of the Mathesons, to withdraw from delivery to replace in the strong room the securities belonging to the firm and partners. He became so entangled with a scoundrel in speculations on the Stock Exchange and from small beginnings has finally abstracted and made away with securities to such an amount that I am positively frightened to think of it.

It was subsequently learned, though never revealed in any court case, that there was more than one 'scoundrel' involved and that they had participated 'in two similar affairs one [of] which occurred about a year ago – and the other rather more'.[60] Fifteen years later a partner in Baring Brothers' Liverpool house was compelled to resign when it was discovered that he was embezzling large sums. 'William Smith', his real name was never revealed, was suspected by some of his clerks but, fearing for their own jobs, they had never reported their suspicions. Hoping to avoid a scandal, or possibly sympathetic to their partner, Baring Brothers did not prosecute; indeed they gave 'Smith' £150 to pay off some of his debts and paid his salary for three months after his resignation.[61] During the 1850s respected merchants were prosecuted for using fraudulent dock warrants. Robert Ferdinand Preis used such warrants to prove transactions in the grain trade involving amounts large enough to cause fluctuations in London grain prices. J. W. Cole used a similar, sophisticated system of fraudulent warrants with imported metals. Cole's fraud was suspected by the City bankers, Overend and Gurney, but they feared for their own capital if Cole was exposed and bankrupted, consequently they said nothing. In the 1890s there was an outcry over the exposure of a member of parliament, J. S. Balfour, following his development of the pyramid building of multi-company business. Balfour used the share capital of one company to pay the premiums of others in what one clergyman branded 'the biggest crime of the nineteenth century'. He escaped to Argentina on exposure in 1892, and it took three years to arrange his extradition.[62]

Legislation was slow in keeping pace with the opportunities for fraud and fiddling in the business and financial world; there were concerns that such measures might alienate the business community and hinder trade. In some respects this might all be interpreted as middle-class Victorian society looking after its own, yet the victims of the fraudster were themselves middle class. More probably, and more practically, business and financial fraud was often very sophisticated and complex, and its perpetrators often trod a very narrow line between legality and illegality. Most nineteenth-century legislators, policemen and jurymen could easily understand the 'science' of garrotting or housebreaking; the 'science' of business and financial fraud was infinitely more difficult.

Fraud and embezzlement did not occur only at the top of the business and financial world. Clerks were caught taking significant sums from their employers. Of course this was never defended as a perk, but possibly a significant number of these offenders saw themselves as merely 'borrowing' money to tide them over a difficult period. In the second half of the nineteenth century the confidence and security of the position of clerk was seriously eroded by the expansion of the clerical labour force and an influx of women and young men. At the same time the small businessman and other traditional employers of clerks were hit by the great depression and by the growing concentration of capital. Fewer and fewer clerks were able to rise to a partnership with their employers or to establish a business on their own account. Embezzlement, in the modern sense of the word, may have been the only way that some could see to keep up appearances and to maintain themselves at the levels of comfort and respectability expected of the Victorian middle class even at its lower end.[63]

In the same way that legislation did not keep pace with the opportunities for offences in the business and financial world, so too, it did not keep pace with the opportunities for corruption and misconduct in public life, which expanded with the growth of bureaucratic organisation and regulation. 'Old corruption', the patronage system by which the Crown and its ministers oiled the cogs of administrative and parliamentary machinery was under attack at least from the early years of George III's reign. Reformers emphasised the importance of public well-being over the profit of the individual holding office and, increasingly, their arguments won the day in public. The system of patronage, which reached its apogee under the Whig oligarchy, was in retreat in the early nineteenth century, yet revelations of misconduct by men in public life, of corrupt practices at elections and elsewhere, continued throughout the Victorian period. No nineteenth-century parliament contemplated drafting principles of conduct for men in public life, however, nor posing questions about possible procedural or structural weaknesses in administrative and regulatory systems which provided the opportunities for corruption and misconduct. Paradoxically it was probably partly because of the outward dominance of morality that such questions were not posed. Victorian society was confident, proud of its industrial development, of its commerce and of its constitutional system, each of which, it boasted, were models for the world. Such a society was hardly likely to turn it upon itself to contemplate immorality within the structures of which it was so proud. Great store was put by the personal integrity of men in public life and, as in the case of white-collar crime, those who were exposed for transgressing the bounds of the expected, moral conduct were viewed as the exceptional 'rotten apples'. Perhaps they were exceptional; but then corrupt dealings are secretive and are hard to prove. Anti-corruption legislation, such as the Public Bodies Corrupt Practices Act 1889, arrived on the statute book, it has been argued, 'almost as an aside to the mainstream of legislative activity'.[64] This particular act followed the revelations in the interim report of the Royal Commission enquiring into the Metropolitan Board of Works; several architects holding official positions in London were shown to have been feathering their nests with a variety of practices bordering on blackmail and extortion, as well as profiteering by the secretive acquisition of land scheduled for major development. The Royal Commission put the blame on a weak departmental head and the lack of expert supervision in several key areas. No criminal charges were brought on the grounds of insufficient evidence and because of the immunity offered to witnesses. Ten years later revelations of secret commission payments in many trades and professions prompted the Lord Chief Justice, Lord Killowen, to introduce the Illicit Secret Commissions Bill, which foundered for a variety of reasons, not the least of which was the problem of how to cope with corruption in private activities. A brief, four-clause bill was eventually passed in August 1906.[65]

While some M.P.s, some senior public servants, and some businessmen seeking or fulfilling government contracts were involved in corruption and misconduct, functionaries lower down the bureaucratic ladder, particularly those with discretionary authority, also found opportunities for personal profit and not always by breaking the law. The old police collected fees, shared fines and rewards, and might also take a cut from the compounding of an offence. The new police were paid regular wages to prevent such abuses and were forbidden to accept gratuities. But, as one mid-nineteenth-century commentator put it:

Policemen are but men, their pay but scanty, their situations precarious, and it would be too much to expect that all are so pure as to decline to make a little money when favourable opportunities present themselves.[66]

Some gratuities did find their way into policemen's pockets, and 'knocking-up' members of the working class early in the morning to enable them to get to work could add a few unofficial pence to the weekly wage. Some detectives picked up extra money by unofficial enquiries or by putting pressure on debtors. Section 16 of the Licensing Act 1872 threatened a fine for any licencee who supplied, either as a gift or for sale, any liquor or refreshment to a police constable on duty, or who offered a bribe to a constable. In April 1897 the Manchester Watch Committee thought it necessary to send a copy of section 16 to all licence holders in the city. Constables collecting 'Christmas boxes' from shopkeepers and 'rents' from market traders slipped closer towards illegality. Some of the new police slipped even further by finding opportunities to profit from close co-operation with thieves – like Constables Jesse 'Juicy Lips' Jeaps and Charles King of London in the 1850s – or with swindlers, like the four London detectives prosecuted in 1877 for assisting betting fraud. Some simply acted on their own like the Chief Constable of Coventry who absconded in 1861 with £56 from the police fund.[67] Both the Old and the New Poor Law provided different officials with opportunities for petty profiteering, fraud and embezzlement. Local tradesmen had lucrative contracts for supplying food and clothing to workhouses, and the workhouse master had considerable discretion in these purchases; it can only be guessed to what extent some tradesmen won or maintained such contracts by gifts freely given, solicited or extorted. At the same time unscrupulous contractors could, and did, supply shoddy goods and adulterated food to maximise their profits; the paupers themselves were rarely in a situation to complain. Senior officials of the poor law administration were also concerned about profiteering by their medical officers.[68] In 1818 two parish constables were indicted at the Bedfordshire Quarter Sessions after claiming expenses respectively of £2.2s and £3.2s.6d. for moving vagrants who had never existed. Nearly half a century later, in 1866, Daniel Harford Cox, an Assistant Overseer, was sentenced to four months in gaol by Bedfordshire magistrates for two separate offences involving Poor Law money amounting to £452.0s.3d.[69] This was small beer compared with some of the amounts that had gone missing in London. During the 1850s there were thirty-three embezzlement and default cases reported in fourteen of the thirty-nine Poor Law Unions and Parishes in the metropolis. Ten of these offences involved the Assistant Clerk of the City of London Union who, during 1855–6, misappropriated £5,821.13s.8d., of which a mere £500 was recovered. Between 1853 and 1856 the collectors of the poor rates in the City Union embezzled £14,342.13s.9d., of which only £674.14s.3d. was recovered.[70]

In cases of fiddling or pilferage at the workplace it was, as ever, working-class offenders who appeared in court most often. The prosecution of such offenders was less likely to provoke a crisis of confidence in the institution for which they worked than the prosecution of directors, managers or clerks. But, more importantly when it came to prosecution, the workplace crimes of working-class offenders, generally, were more easy to detect and, in legal terms, their offences were easier to comprehend and to prove. Even so it would seem that only a tiny percentage of such offences were prosecuted, and only then when other sanctions, such as dismissal, seemed inappropriate, when it was felt that an example must be made to limit such offences, or when a particular offender had chanced his arm beyond the norms regarded as acceptable.[71] Eighteenth- and nineteenth-century workplace crime was manifestly not simply the product of industrialisation, the desire of workers to strike back at an employer or at the developing capitalist system, or to preserve their traditional rights and a vibrant popular culture. An understanding of such crime is severely restricted when explained solely as an element of the developing struggle between capital and labour. It was not the new workplace alone that provided opportunities for fiddles; it was not new attempts to control the workforce that alone criminalised practices of long standing. The milkman 'bobbing' the milk, the petty official of the New Poor Law embezzling from the sums in his care, the government official demanding, or the contractor offering, a secret commission, all fall outside the simple class analysis. Most work, from casual labour to professional, provided opportunities for crime or, if legislation had not yet caught up with it, for what might be termed immoral profiteering.

Notes and references

1   Gerald Mars, *Cheats at Work: An anthropology of workplace crime*, Unwin Paperbacks, London, 1983, pp. 18 and 164. The concept of a 'weasel word' is drawn from **Jason Ditton**, 'Perks, pilferage and the fiddle: The historical structure of an invisible wage', *Theory and Society*, **4** (1977), pp. 39–71.

2   **Bob Bushaway**, *By Rite: Custom, ceremony and community in England 1700–1880*, Junction Books, London, 1982, pp. 138–48; **David H. Morgan**, 'The place of harvesters in nineteenth-century village life', in **Raphael Samuel** (ed.), *Village Life and Labour*, RKP, London, 1975, pp. 53–61.

3   Beds. R.O. QSR 15/1785/81.

4   Quoted in Bushaway, *By Rite*, p. 141.

5   **Peter King**, 'Gleaners, farmers and the failure of legal sanctions in England 1750–1850', *P and P*, **125** (1989), pp. 116–50 (at p. 124).

6   Beds. R.O. QSR 16/1790/46.

7   King, 'Gleaners, farmers and the failure of legal sanctions'; Morgan, 'The place of harvesters', p. 57.

8   Quoted in **Alasdair Clayre** (ed.), *Nature and Industrialization*, Oxford U.P., Oxford, 1977, p. 23.

9   **James Obelkevich**, *Religion and Rural Society: South Lindsey 1825–75*, Clarendon Press, Oxford, 1976, p. 60.

10 **Peter King**, *Crime, Justice and Discretion in England 1740–1820*, Oxford U.P., Oxford, 2000, p. 100.

11 Quoted in Clayre, *Nature and Industrialization*, pp. 19–20.

12 Beds. R.O. QSR 25/1825/345. For the August and autumn peak of summary convictions see above, p. 40.

13 Bushaway, *By Rite*, pp. 222–3.

14 *The Times*, 23 October 1795.

15 Beds. R.O. QSR 23/1817/423; QSR 23/1818/245 and 249; QSR 25/1823/304; QSR 1827/321.

16 **R. J. B. Knight**, 'Pilfering and theft from the dockyards at the time of the American War of Independence', *Mariner's Mirror*, **61** (1975), pp. 215–25; **Roger Morriss**, *The Royal Dockyards during the Revolutionary and Napoleonic Wars*, Leicester U.P., London, 1983, especially pp. 93–6; **John Rule**, *The Experience of Labour in Eighteenth-Century Industry*, Croom Helm, London, 1981, pp. 128–30.

17 A former colleague at the Open University recalls that during his boyhood in Plymouth in the Second World War, his next-door neighbour, who worked in the Royal Dockyards, successfully removed from the yard, piece by piece, a lathe. The lathe was then reassembled at his home.

18 Morriss, *The Royal Dockyards*, pp. 129–35.

19 **John Styles**, 'Embezzlement, industry and the law in England, 1500–1800', in **Maxine Berg, Pat Hudson** and **Michael Sonenscher** (eds), *Manufacture in Town and Country before the Factory*, Cambridge U.P., Cambridge, 1983, pp. 183–4; **Clive Emsley**, *British Society and the French Wars 1793–1815*, Macmillan, London, 1979, pp. 57–8, 120–1 and 151.

20 Rule, *Experience of Labour*, pp. 126–7 and 130–3; Styles, 'Embezzlement, industry and the law', p. 204.

21 **James Greenwood**, *The Seven Curses of London*, London, 1869 (reprinted, Basil Blackwell, Oxford, 1981), p. 109.

22 Rule, *Experience of Labour*, pp. 125–6 and 130; see also 'Conference Report', *Bulletin of the Society for the Study of Labour History*, **25** (1972), p. 13.

23 **Douglas Hay**, 'Manufacturers and the criminal law in the later eighteenth century: Crime and "Police" in South Staffordshire', *Past and Present Society Colloquium: Police and policing*, 1983, pp. 13–15; **David Philips**, *Crime and Authority in Victorian England*, Croom Helm, London, 1977, p. 182; 'Conference Report', *Bulletin of the Society for the study of Labour History*, p. 7. As for the continuance of pilferage by industrial workers after the decline of outwork see the quotation from the Superintendent of K Division of the Metropolitan Police, p. 126 above, and **David Jones**, *Crime, Community, and Police in Nineteenth-Century Britain*, RKP, London, 1982, p. 157.

24 *O.B.S.P. 1796–97*, no. 108, pp. 155–6.

25 **Jennifer Davis**, 'Law breaking and law enforcement: The creation of a criminal class in mid-Victorian London', unpublished Ph.D., Boston College, 1984, p. 279.

26 Rule, *Experience of Labour*, pp. 127–8; see also Philips, *Crime and Authority*, pp. 182–4.

27 Leeds City Archives LC/QS 1/2 f. 117; Beds. R.O. QSR 22/1816/160 and 228–9; U.C.L. Chadwick MSS 11, answers to q. 10.

28 *C.C.C.S.P. 1856–57*, no. 13, pp. l4–l5.

29 Davis, 'Law breaking and law enforcement', pp. 99–103.

30 **Patrick Colquhoun**, *A Treatise on the Police of the Metropolis*, 3rd edn, London, 1796, ch. 3 *passim*; *idem*, *A Treatise on the Commerce and Police of the River Thames*, London, 1800, ch. 2 *passim*; **Henry Mayhew**, *London Labour and the London Poor*, 4 vols, London, 1861–62, iv, pp. 366–70.

31 **Raphael Samuel** (ed.), *East End Underworld: Chapters in the life of Arthur Harding*, RKP, London, 1981, pp. 16–17.

32 Colquhoun, *A Treatise on the Police*, p. 64.

33 Davis, 'Law breaking and law enforcement', pp. 84–99.

34 *P.P. 1877 (418) xi, Select Committee on the House of Lords on Intemperance, Third Report*, qq. 8256–8.

35 *P.P. 1839 (168) xix, Royal Commission on Constabulary*, pp. 48–54.

36 **Harry Hanson**, *The Canal Boatmen 1760–1914*, Manchester U.P., Manchester, 1975, p. 37.

37 **Jennifer Davis**, 'Criminal Prosecutions and their context in late Victorian London', paper presented to the Conference on the History of Law, Labour and Crime, at the University of Warwick, 15–18 September 1983, p. 7; **Anthony S. Wohl**, *Endangered Lives: Public health in Victorian Britain*, Dent, London, 1983, pp. 20–1.

38 Greenwood, *Seven Curses*, pp. 94–107; **Charles Booth**, *Life and Labour of the People of London, 2nd series, Industry*, 5 vols, 1903, iii, p. 311.

39 S. A. Marglin, 'What do bosses do? The origins and functions of hierarchy in capitalist production', *Review of Radical Political Economies*, **6** (1974), pp. 46–55.

40 E. P. Thompson, *Whigs and Hunters: The origin of the Black Act*, Allen Lane, London, 1975, p. 207; see also the paper by Peter Linebaugh in 'Conference Report', *Bulletin of the Society for Labour History*, pp. 11–15.

41 P. C. Barrett, 'Crime and punishment in a Lancashire industrial town: Law and social change in the borough of Wigan, 1800–50', unpublished M.Phil., Liverpool Polytechnic, 1980, pp. 84–6 and 191–5.

42 Philips, *Crime and Authority*, pp. 190–1.

43 Davis, 'Law breaking and law enforcement', pp. 267–70 and 283–4.

44 Davis, 'Criminal prosecutions', pp. 5–6; and see note 24 above.

45 Peter Linebaugh, *The London Hanged. Crime and civil society in the eighteenth century*, Allen Lane, London, 1991, p. 440.

46 J. A. Sharpe, *Crime in Early Modern England 1550–1750*, 2nd edn, Longman, London, 1999, p. 213. For the statutes that sought to control the outwork see Styles, 'Embezzlement, industry and the law', pp. 209–10.

47 Styles, 'Embezzlement, industry and the law', p. 188, and *passim*.

48 Hay, 'Manufacturers and the criminal law', p. 15. At the Labour History Society Conference on Industrial Crime one contributor noted from 'his own experience in the mining industry, [that] the most politically and industrially conscious workers were not sympathetic to pilfering, whereas the less conscious would steal a fellow worker's tools if they would filch something from an employer'. 'Conference report', *Bulletin of the Society for Labour History*, pp. 7–8.

49 Notts. R.O. QSD/1836; for a similar example, on this occasion of a confectioner marking money in his till and catching his shopman see *O.B.S.P. 1796–97*, no. 87.

50 Stephen Humphries, *Hooligans or Rebels? An oral history of working-class childhood and youth 1889–1939*, Basil Blackwell, Oxford, 1981, pp. 170–2.

51 Greenwood, *Seven Curses*, p. 97.

52 Avril D. Leadley, 'Some villains of the eighteenth-century market place', in John Rule (ed.), *Outside the Law: Studies in crime and order 1650–1850*, Exeter Papers in Economic History, no. 15, University of Exeter, 1982, p. 24.

53 Wilts. R.O. Stourhead Archive 383/955, Justice Book of R. C. Hoare 1785–1815.

54 Beds. R.O. QSR 18/1802/13; QSR 20/1808/170.

55 Greenwood, *Seven Curses*, pp. 101–2.

56 Wohl, *Endangered Lives*, p. 54.

57 **D. C. Woods**, 'The operations of the Master and Servants Act in the Black Country 1858–75', *Midland History*, vii (1982), pp. 93–115 (at p. 94); and see below p. 205.

58 **George Robb**, *White-Collar Crime in Modern England: Financial fraud and business morality 1845–1929*, Cambridge U.P., Cambridge, 1992; for the estimate of fraudulent promotions see **H. A. Shannon**, 'The Limited Companies of 1866–83'. *Economic History Review*, 4 (1933), pp. 290–316.

59 **Rob Sindall**, 'Middle-class crime in nineteenth-century England', *C.J.H.*, 4 (1983), pp. 23–40 (at p. 32); for more detail see **R. S. Sindall**, 'Aspects of middle-class crime in the nineteenth century', unpublished M. Phil., University of Leicester, 1974.

60 Beds. R.O. Whitbread MSS (uncatalogued), Magniac to Whitbread, 15 September and 12 October 1882.

61 **Gregory Anderson**, *Victorian Clerks*, Manchester U.P., Manchester, 1976, pp. 35–6.

62 Robb, *White-Collar Crime*, pp. 138–42; **Rev. J. Stockwell Watts**, *The Biggest Crime of the Nineteenth Century and what the Churches say to it*, London, 1893.

63 Sindall, 'Middle-class crime', p. 34; see also in general Anderson, *Victorian Clerks*, and **Geoffrey Crossick**, 'The emergence of the lower-middle class in Britain: A discussion', in Geoffrey Crossick (ed.), *The Lower Middle Class in Britain*, Croom Helm, London, 1977.

64 **Alan Doig**, *Corruption and Misconduct in Contemporary British Politics*, Penguin, Harmondsworth, 1984, p. 69.

65 **Phil Fennell** and **Philip A. Thomas**, 'Corruption in England and Wales: An historical analysis', *International Journal of the Sociology of Law*, 11 (1983), pp. 167–89; **David Owen**, *The Government of Victorian London 1855–89*, Belknap Press, Cambridge, Mass., 1982, chs. 8 and 9.

66 **W. H. Watts**, 'Records of an old police court', *St. James's Magazine*, xii (1865), pp. 499–506 (at p. 506). On occasion, however, members of the new police were permitted to take gratuities and rewards. At the Nottinghamshire Epiphany Sessions in 1856, for example, three police constables from the county force were commended for apprehending a sheep stealer and were rewarded out of county funds; one man received £3, the others £1 each, 'which appears to this court to be a reasonable compensation for their expenses, exertions and loss of time'. Notts. R.O. QSM 1856–60, adjournment sessions 7 March 1856.

67 Clive Emsley, *Policing and its Context 1750–1870*, Macmillan, London, 1973, pp. 128 and 159; **Phillip Thurmond Smith**, *Policing Victorian London: Political policing, public order, and the London Metropolitan Police*, Greenwood Press, Westport, Conn., 1985, pp. 53–4, 69 and 71; Manchester Police Museum, Watch Committee Minutes 1895 onwards, vol. 3, f. 83; **Barbara Weinberger**, 'Crime and police in the late nineteenth century: A case study from the Coventry area', unpublished M.A., University of Warwick, 1976, p. 34.

68 **M. A. Crowther**, *The Workhouse System 1834–1929: The history of an English social institution*, Methuen, London, 1983, pp. 118, 159–60, 216 and 241.

69 Beds. R.O. QSR 23/1818/528 and 529; QGV 10/4/128.

70 U.C.L. Chadwick MSS 16, Police Memoranda etc. (1855–69). Printed return of cases of embezzlement and default by Poor Law administrators in the Metropolis 1853–59.

71 Davis, 'Law breaking and law enforcement', chs 3 and 5.

CHAPTER 7

The criminal class and professional criminals

The use of the term the 'criminal class' was probably at its most common during the 1860s,[1] but the idea of a criminal class and of professional criminals living, at least partly, by the proceeds of criminal behaviour was popular throughout the period. It has also informed the work of several historians of nineteenth-century criminality. 'Entry into the criminal class was a means of finding support,' wrote J. J. Tobias:

it was entry into an association, informal but none the less real, members of which could be found almost everywhere. In gaol or lodging-house or on the road, criminals could find companions in like situation, could exchange experiences and discover common acquaintanceships.[2]

While dubious about Engels's romantic notion that the most courageous members of the very poor became 'thieves and murderers' and waged 'open war against the middle classes', Kellow Chesney drew heavily on the work of investigators like Mayhew and revelled in the underworld slang of Victorian England to give his readers a glimpse of 'gonolphs, footpads and the swell mob' and 'magsmen, macers and shofulmen'.[3]

A few men did get a lot of money from criminal behaviour, but those who made the greatest financial hauls were white-collar offenders who were never considered to be part of a criminal class; and while 'William Smith' of Baring Brothers' Liverpool house, or the embezzling nephew of the Mathesons, may have been considered as professional gentlemen, they were never considered as professional thieves. Similarly, fraudsters like the Bidwell brothers who, in January and February 1873, tricked the Bank of England out of £100,405 7s. 3d., and who attracted enormous crowds on their arrest and removal to London, were rarely considered in the same breath as Bill Sikes.[4]

Others who enjoyed the larger profits from criminal activity were receivers: men like Ikey Solomons, Jonathan Wild, or Jonathan Field. The latter was alleged to have had a headquarters in Barbican and branches in Bermondsey and Whitechapel.[5] But it is doubtful whether any receivers achieved the financial success of the Bidwells or 'Smith'; it is also doubtful whether many large-scale receivers existed. Policemen were always concerned about pawnbrokers acting as receivers.[6] Some unquestionably did, though many more, probably, simply preferred not to ask questions, and others must have received stolen goods unknowingly. Pawnbrokers and, lower down the social scale, the proprietors of 'dolly shops' or 'leaving shops' were important figures to the urban working-class communities of the eighteenth and nineteenth centuries. They provided a vital financial service within these communities, and not simply to the casual labourers. Sometimes certain kinds of goods were left with the pawnbroker on a regular weekly basis – good clothes could be pawned during the week and redeemed for weekends after pay day. Many of the articles of clothing, bed linen, table linen and cutlery taken in a petty theft were hastened to a pawnbroker; but as several divisions of the Metropolitan Police reported to Chadwick and the Constabulary Commissioners, some petty thieves were caught precisely because of the vigilance of pawnbrokers.[7]

A variety of other kinds of dealer and retailer made profits from receiving. There were butchers and poulterers who received game from poachers and who sometimes organised the poaching gangs. Old clothes dealers were suspect in the same way that pawnbrokers were; so too were the owners of chandler's shops who might receive and resell whatever was purloined from ships by dockers, ships crews or ship builders. There were scrap-metal dealers who asked no questions about small quantities offered to them for sale; and there were the grocers, like Harding's Aunt Liza, who received, repackaged and resold. It is, of course, most unlikely that many of these receivers made significant profits from such activities or that many of them could, in any meaningful way, be considered as professional criminals.

From Elizabethan times at least there was concern that children were being taught to be professional criminals. Fagin's school for pickpockets appears to have had some basis in fact and it was confidently asserted that a child starting out as a 'gonolph' street thief, if adept and well-trained, could rise to be a member of the exclusive group of professional pickpockets known as the 'swell mob'.[8] But several points need to be made about pickpockets and their trade. First, rather than the offenders being in thrall to Fagins, it seems probable that a considerable amount of pocket picking, especially by juveniles, was the result of opportunism.[9] Second, different styles of nineteenth-century fashion aided such offenders: a handkerchief poking from the back-pocket of a fashionable mid-century tailed coat was easy pickings. Arthur Harding noted how the bustle, which came in and out of women's fashion in the second half of the century, could have been designed with the thief's requirements in mind. Third, pickpockets worked best in crowds. Harding and his mates worked fairs, markets and races and moved round the country where their work took them.[10] What appears to have been a gang of travelling pickpockets was apprehended in Bedfordshire in October 1860 after Mary Mayne was robbed of one promissory note, value £5, two sovereigns and one half sovereign. The gang consisted of George Brown, a 21-year-old hairbrush stainer born in Leicester, Henry James Green, alias James Middleton, aged 23, a stocking weaver born in Dublin whose last residence was in Nottingham, his wife Jane Green, alias Elizabeth Lockery, aged 20, also a stocking weaver born in Coventry, and William Jones, alias William Johnson, alias David Dunn, a 24-year-old labourer from London. Both Henry Green and William Jones had previous convictions for picking pockets; Jones had been sentenced to seven years' transportation for such an offence at the Old Bailey in 1851 and had been released on licence in 1854.[11] The haul from Mary Mayne, split four ways, assuming it could be matched with similar hauls from the same crowd, may have provided the gang with a modest living. But it was estimated earlier in the century that a pocket-handkerchief thief would have to steal between twenty and thirty handkerchiefs in a week to be able to live off the booty.[12]

Burglary was another crime that most Hanoverian and Victorian commentators considered as a skill, the perpetrators of which were regarded as professional criminals. The fact was generally ignored that some individuals, especially children, who were charged with burglary had merely taken what they could reach through a broken window.[13] Burglars, it was alleged, set out armed with jemmies and false keys; at least as early as 1783 it was being described in parliament as a 'science' with specially made instruments available for the practitioners. Detailed sketches of such instruments made their way into the pages of Victorian magazines, though whether certain tools were indeed 'house-breaking implements' or simply a carpenter's brace and bit may have been purely within the perception of an arresting constable.[14] One or two burglars, however, equipped themselves with weapons that had only one use; press outrage and panic about armed burglars in the 1880s led to a revolver issue to metropolitan policemen on their beats.[15]

Interestingly, during the 1860s when reviewing the working of the old Marlborough Street Police Office, W. H. Watts could write:

There are now no professional highwaymen; there are no professional burglars; there are no localities given over absolutely to the outcasts of society; there are now no colonies of thieves who only live by thieving; no burglars or highwaymen who support existence solely by following out their penal trade. The old haunts of vice are broken up, and the old gangs of offenders have either died off or been utterly dispersed. If you see in the papers that 'burglars' have been captured, you will find, on enquiry, the culprits have mostly trades of their own; if a batch of pickpockets is taken, the chances are that you will discover they have a 'calling' besides that of picking pockets, at which they are able to, and do, maintain themselves when the 'honest fit' is upon them.[16]

Whether Watts was correct in his assessment of the end of an old kind of full-time criminal is difficult to assess. Probably the new police had cleared some petty offenders from the streets, though these would not appear to have been the variety of criminals to whom he was referring. Moreover, it is worth noting that he was writing in the immediate aftermath of the publications of Mayhew and others who wrote in terms of a 'criminal class'. Of course it is most unlikely that anyone who went before the Fieldings, or before Colquhoun or any of his contemporaries who served at the Marlborough Street Police Office, ever gave their trade or calling as burglar, highwayman or pickpocket. But Watts's comments point to the key questions that have to be posed about the eighteenth- and nineteenth-century professional criminal and criminal classes: for how much crime were these 'professionals' or this 'class' responsible? How many professionals were there? How big was the criminal class?

The statistics and the court records suggest that the overwhelming majority of thefts reported and prosecuted were opportunist and petty; most incidents of violence against the person involved people who were either related or who were known to each other. Professional criminals, in the sense of men who went out armed with tools for housebreaking and weapons and who committed more than one offence, might well have carried out the bigger robberies. Probably they committed these robberies as 'professionals' taking precautions and planning carefully, rather than yielding to momentary temptations; possibly fewer of them were arrested and prosecuted. Perhaps, as the new police grew in numbers and gained more experience petty street thieves and opportunist thieves were at greater risk; this may have contributed to the proportionate increase in burglaries during the second half of the nineteenth century as those who were determined to profit from criminal behaviour recognised a need for better planning and organisation, though the problem here is that 'burglary' itself is an elastic term that could be stretched or slackened according to the discretion of prosecutor or police. In short, it would be impossible to prove that most thefts and violence were the work of persons who indulged in criminal behaviour as a way of life.

The notion of a criminal class poses a rather different problem. As was argued earlier the criminal class described by Victorian commentators was largely synonymous with the poorer working class, particularly those who existed by casual labour. Tobias followed this definition, and Chesney's Victorian underworld embraced the same groups, as well as travelling showmen, the organisers of prize fights and so forth. Certainly some people in these social groups committed crimes: families, peer-group gangs – usually of young men – sometimes whole streets or villages had negative attitudes towards some aspects of the law, and towards the police in particular. James Waring, a 16-year-old sweep convicted, with two younger boys, of burglary at the Old Bailey in January 1797, used to pass his booty on to his mother who then took it to the pawn shop.[17] Listing the cases heard at the local Summer Assize in 1843 the *Bedford Mercury* singled out for comment the family of Thomas Smith, a 17-year-old stocking maker from Biggleswade who pleaded guilty to stealing a parcel from a coach:

The father of the prisoner has just completed his term of transportation; his mother has been in prison for a considerable time; his brother is transported; and three years ago the prisoner was also ordered to be transported, but was respited on account of his youth.[18]

Gwenda Morgan and Peter Rushton have suggested that three types of criminal organisation were to be found in eighteenth-century England. There were 'networks' containing individuals who linked with each other periodically and played different roles such as thief or receiver. 'Groups' came together to undertake particular crimes but did not operate together regularly. Finally, there were a few 'gangs', which had a more permanent organisation and which sometimes operated over long distances and over lengthy periods of time; again they had members who played distinct roles. Convicted gang members, both male and female, were among the most successful of the eighteenth-century transportees to avoid surveillance and servitude in America and to escape back to Britain. They may have had their own resources to purchase their freedom from ship's captains or else drew on the assistance of friends in the colonies. But Morgan and Rushton also warn that the term 'gang' was used loosely during the eighteenth century and, generally speaking, whatever the notoriety of some such groups and the fears about them, none of them were responsible for a great deal of criminality.[19] Similar criminal groups, based on families, friendships or community appear to have existed throughout the nineteenth century. At the end of the nineteenth and beginning of the twentieth centuries, Arthur Harding's East End gang picked pockets around the country and then began passing counterfeit money; subsequently they were available for hire as a gang of toughs and were, on one occasion, recruited to terrorise 'blackleg' printers.[20] Merthyr Tydfil's 'China' seems to have remained a criminal Alsatia for many years; and within the transient districts of other towns and cities could be found isolated individuals – wandering labourers, sometimes genuine vagrants who moved from cheap lodging house to cheap lodging house, and if the worst came to the worst to street or hedgerow, or if apprehended, to workhouse or prison. Sometimes these individuals acquired exotic names like the 'Wolds Rangers' of the East Riding or the 'Rodneys' of South Staffordshire 'who go about without any settled residence, and who never work, but live by robbery, and sleep by the coke and engine fires which are numerous in this mining district'.[21] These people were looked upon with suspicion by the respectable inhabitants whose streets or villages they dared to enter. The management of such people was increasingly taken over by the police; they were, in the modern sociological sense, 'police property'. Sometimes the wanderers and vagrants could be dangerous, sometimes they might steal, but it is not particularly helpful to lump them together with the Hardings, the Redmans of Houghton Conquest, the population of 'China', and the few criminal families, and to conclude that, together, they constitute a criminal class, since the only common denominator is the breaking of, often very different, laws.

The notion of a criminal class was, indeed remains, a convenient one for insisting that most crime is something committed on law-abiding citizens by an alien group. The more historians probe the reality of such a class, the more it is revealed to be spurious. Among the main findings of both David Philips's detailed study of crime in the Black Country and Jennifer Davis's work on mid-Victorian London, is the conclusion that no clear distinction can be made between a dishonest criminal class and a poor but honest working class.[22] Simon Stevenson's analysis of those subject to the 'habitual criminals' legislation of 1869 and 1871 reveals how small the number of 'habituals' was; perhaps no more than 4,000 a year throughout the 1870s. Furthermore, he suggests that it is very difficult to conceive of these individuals as either a class or a group of professionals readily and continually identifiable by their behaviour and integrating within some deviant familial lore. A few offenders adopted romantic names and posturings, but there does not appear to have been any specifically 'criminal' argot or practice of tattooing; most of the larcenies committed by these individuals involved goods of paltry value and criminal 'tools' were rarely used in the execution of their crimes. If the 'habitual criminal' did have unsavoury friends and acquaintances, often drawn from his peer group, he was also equally likely to have family support of a rather different kind with parents and sometimes wives urging him to more law-abiding and 'moral' behaviour.[23]

A criminal record led some men to be targeted by the police and, in many instances, men with criminal records had difficulty in finding work. The formal creation of the category of 'habitual criminals' by the Act of 1869 and the Prevention of Crimes Act 1871 probably contributed to such difficulties. Colquhoun highlighted the problem of the newly released prisoner when he asked: 'Without friends, without character, and without the means of subsistence, what are these unhappy mortals to do?'[24] The Victorians also recognised the problem. In January 1857 the Earl of Carnarvon and Henry Mayhew organised a meeting of eighty ticket-of-leave men in Holborn. They heard of their difficulties in finding employment and of harassment by the police.[25] A decade later James Greenwood expressed his doubts about the police supervision of ticket-of-leave men:

There are hundreds and thousands of men in London, and indeed in all great cities, who 'pick-up' a living somehow – anyhow, and who, though they are honest fellows, would find it difficult to account for, and bring evidence forward to show, how they were engaged last Monday, and again on Wednesday, and what they earned, and whom they earned it of. Such men 'job about', very often in localities that, in the case of a man under police supervision, to be seen there would be to rouse suspicions as to his intentions. For instance, many a shilling or sixpence is 'picked up' by men who have nothing better to do, by hanging round in railway stations and steamboat wharves, and looking out for passengers who have luggage they wish carried. But supposing that a man, a 'ticket-of-leave', was to resort to such a means of obtaining a livelihood, and that he was seen 'hanging about' such places day after day by a watchful detective who knew who and what he was, – with what amount of credibility would the authorities receive his statement that he was 'looking out for a chance to carry somebody's trunk or carpet-bag'!'[26]

The attempts of London's stipendiary magistrates to frustrate the supervision of habitual criminals by the Metropolitan Police may have stemmed partly from such a recognition; but the Convict Supervision Office organised within the Metropolitan Police in 1880 claimed, within a few years, to have solved many of the problems.[27] Voluntary attempts at a solution, such as the Discharged Prisoners' Aid Society established in 1857, were also attempted, with varying degrees of success.[28] Yet here again it must be emphasised that the largest number of offenders arrested and imprisoned were always drawn from the ranks of young men; and not all young men arrested for offences in their teens and twenties carried on with a criminal career into their thirties and forties. Parent-Duchâtelet and William Acton both noted that prostitution was a transitory stage for most women who followed the 'profession' during the nineteenth century; women became prostitutes because of temporary economic hardship. Probably the same was true for those who committed the bulk of petty thefts brought before the courts during the eighteenth and nineteenth centuries; criminality, in the form of thefts committed by men from the poorer sections of the working class, was transitory behaviour, possibly fostered by economic hardship, probably encouraged by opportunity. Most thefts, and most crimes of violence, cannot be attributed to professional criminals; nor is it helpful to think of these offences as committed by a group that can, in any sense, be described as a separate class.

But if the 'reality' of a significant criminal class can be questioned, the texts that described the phenomenon, especially in the mid-Victorian years, are significant. These descriptions contributed to the construction of a reality for their readers. They revealed an organised, hierarchical social group that lacked any understanding of religious principles, social duty and virtue – in short a group that was ignorant of the key elements that Victorians liked to think underpinned their society. This gave the reader a sense of superiority over criminals, and a sense too that society was not responsible for the idle and vagrant who belonged to that class. Knowledge of the criminal class alleviated at least some of the uncertainty and fear about crime; and mid-Victorian commentators invariably stressed the watchfulness of the police whose particular expertise enabled them to identify criminals and check their depredations. At the same time, knowledge of the criminal class generated an urgency in the need to prevent juvenile offenders from becoming habitual criminals, and it contributed to a hardening of attitudes towards those defined as the latter.[29]

Notes and references

1 S. J. Stevenson, 'The "criminal class" in the mid-Victorian city: A study of policy conducted with special reference to the provisions of 34 and 35 Vict., c.112 (1871) in Birmingham and East London in the early years of registration and supervision', unpublished D.Phil., Oxford University, 1983, p. 32 note 4.

2 J. J. Tobias, *Crime and Industrial Society in the Nineteenth Century*, Harmondsworth, Penguin, 1972, p. 108.

3 Kellow Chesney, *The Victorian Underworld*, Harmondsworth, Penguin, 1970; the quotation from Engels', *The Condition of the Working Class in England in 1844*, is on p. 99. Donald Thomas, *The Victorian Underworld*, London, John Murray, 1998, relies heavily and uncritically on Mayhew.

4 For the Bidwells see their autobiographies, Austin Bidwell, *From Wall Street to Newgate*, Hartford, Conn., 1895 and George Bidwell, *Forging His Chains: The autobiography of George Bidwell*, Hartford, Conn., 1888. Both are discussed in Philip Priestley, *Victorian Prison Lives: English prison biography 1830–1914*, Methuen, London, 1985.

5 W. H. Watts, 'Records of an old police court', *St. James's Magazine*, x (1864), pp. 458–65 (at p. 460). I am tempted to believe that the 'Field' in Watt's account is a printing error and should read 'Wild'.

6 Patrick Colquhoun, *A Treatise on the Police of the Metropolis*, 3rd edn, London, 1796, p. 13 and ch. 8 *passim*. Colquhoun even proposed an act of parliament to control and supervise pawnbrokers and dealers in second-hand goods, see Sir Leon Radzinowicz, *A History of English Criminal Law*, 5 vols, Stevens, London, 1948–68, iii, appendix 5.

7 U.C.L. Chadwick MSS 11 f. 23: E division response to qu. 11; f. 25: R. division response to qu. 11. For the importance of the nineteenth-century pawnbroker in working-class communities see Melanie Tebbutt, *Making Ends Meet: Pawnbroking and working-class credit*, Leicester U.P., London, 1983; for pawnbrokers as receivers and police informants see especially pp. 70 and 95–9. The fullest discussion of 'receiving' by pawnbrokers, 'dolly shops' and second-hand dealers as well as ordinary, legitimate tradesmen (like butchers or fishmongers buying pilfered paper to wrap their wares) is to be found in Jennifer Davis, 'Law breaking and law enforcement: The creation of a criminal class in mid-Victorian London', unpublished Ph.D., Boston College, 1984, ch. 2.

8 Chesney, *Victorian Underworld*, ch. 5 *passim*. For reference to a similar 'school' in Elizabethan London see J. A. Sharpe, *Crime in Early Modern England 1550–1750*, 2nd edn, Longman, London, 1999, p. 164.

9   Heather Shore, *Artful Dodgers: Youth and crime in early Victorian London*, Woodbridge, Boydell/Royal Historical Society, 1999, pp. 58–61.

10 Raphael Samuel (ed.), *East-End Underworld: Chapters in the life of Arthur Harding*, RKP, London, 1981, p. 78.

11 Beds. R.O. QGV 10/4/23–26.

12 Shore, *Artful Dodgers*, p. 62.

13 Charles M. De Motte, 'The dark side of town: Crime in Manchester and Salford 1815–75', unpublished Ph.D., University of Kansas, 1977, p. 247.

14 *Gentleman's Magazine*, liii (1783), pp. 740–1; Davis, 'Law breaking and law enforcement', p. 146. Several of the Victorian illustrations of housebreaking equipment are reproduced in Chesney, *Victorian Underworld*.

15 Clive Emsley, ' "The thump of wood on a swede turnip": Police violence in nineteenth-century England', *C.J.H.*, 6 (1985), pp. l25–49 (at pp. 136–41).

16 Watts, 'Records of an old police court', xi (1864), pp. 444–52 (at p. 448).

17 *O.B.S.P. 1796–97*, nos 70–1.

18 *Bedford Mercury*, 22 July 1843.

19 Gwenda Morgan and Peter Rushton, *Rogues, Thieves and the Rule of Law: The problem of crime in north-east England, 1718–1800*, U.C.L. Press, London, 1998, pp. 85–95; *idem*, 'Running away and returning home: the fate of English convicts in the American colonies', *Crime, histoire et sociétés/Crime, history and societies*, 7 (2003) pp. 61–80.

20 Samuel (ed.), *East End Underworld*, pp. 78–80 and 121.

21 *The Times*, 16 November 1850, quoting the *Derby Mercury*.

22 David Philips, *Crime and Authority in Victorian England*, Croom Helm, London, 1977; Davis, 'Law breaking and law enforcement.'

23 Stevenson, 'The "Criminal Class" in the mid-Victorian city,' especially pp. 280, 284, 309, 311–31 and 355–61.

24 Colquhoun, *Treatise on the Police*, p. 91.

25 Sean McConville, *English Local Prisons, 1860–1900: Next only to death*, Routledge, London, 1995, pp. 36–7.

26 James Greenwood, *The Seven Curses of London*, London, 1869, p. 125.

27 Stefan Petrow, *Policing Morals: The Metropolitan Police and the Home Office, 1870–1914*, Clarendon Press, Oxford, 1994, p. 79.

28 Priestley, *Victorian Prison Lives*, pp. 283 and 286, for prisoners' attitudes to the Prisoners' Aid Society.

29 Randall McGowen, 'Getting to know the criminal class in nineteenth-century England', *Nineteenth-Century Contexts*, 14 (1990), pp. 33–54.

CHAPTER 8

Prosecutors and the courts

There were significant changes in prosecution and court practice during the period 1750 to 1900. There were also significant changes in the kind of court environments in which criminal cases were heard. On occasions it was an act of parliament that heralded a change; sometimes, however, legislation simply formalised and sanctioned what had come to be existing practice; and many changes were gradual, almost imperceptible except over a long period.

The English legal system provides for any private citizen to initiate a prosecution. During the eighteenth century a few prosecutions were directed by the Treasury Solicitor, notably in coining offences. Some were conducted by the Attorney General, principally cases of treason or sedition; but again the numbers remained small and during the 1790s, the period of the English 'reign of terror', the Crown Law Officers regularly refused to finance prosecutions for sedition and urged magistrates – not always successfully – to organise these locally. The overwhelming majority of criminal prosecutions, more than eighty per cent, were conducted by the victims of crimes or, rather less frequently, by private individuals acting on the victim's behalf; and, reflecting the dominance of the male in eighteenth- and nineteenth-century society, most prosecutors were men.[1]

Victims of a criminal offence had a variety of choices. They could, for example, let the matter drop regarding it as too insignificant or unimportant for a criminal prosecution. Sometimes, and especially in the earlier part of the period under consideration, an offender was dealt with by community action rather than by recourse to the law: a Jewish hawker, caught attempting to steal a ring from a young woman at Huntingdon races in 1753, was seized by a crowd and ducked in a horse pond.[2] However, crowds, and individuals, could not be relied upon always to help a victim.

Stories were reported in the courts of victims, in hot pursuit of thieves, being deliberately impeded either by individuals or by crowds.[3] Probably what happened in these instances was that the activist individuals or crowds took the part of the person who appeared to be the underdog. Arthur Harding recalled crowds taking the part of children at the end of the nineteenth century who, well aware of what they were doing and certain of getting popular support because of their tender years, openly stole from traders' carts and barrows or from shops and stalls.[4]

The occasional attack on, or 'rough musicing' of, a prosecutor is suggestive of communities that felt that certain offenders should not have been prosecuted, or at least should have been proceeded against on a lesser charge. In the summer of 1763 Mrs White, a Spitalfields victualler, prosecuted her servant, Cornelius Saunders, for theft after he had stumbled across her savings in her basement and decked himself out in new clothes. Saunders was found guilty and executed. Many inhabitants of Spitalfields were incensed; Saunders was well known in the neighbourhood primarily, perhaps, because he had been blind from birth. Mrs White's house was attacked by large crowds; her furniture and possessions were thrown out into the street and burned.[5] A rather more complex affair occurred in Bedfordshire half a century later. At the 1817 Summer Assizes, Thomas Flemings was prosecuted for raping fifteen-year-old Sarah Gardener. The latter had been visiting her sister at Tingrith village feast; on the way home she was frightened by a group of Irishmen and, in consequence, her sister asked Flemings to accompany her. It was during the two-mile walk to her parents' house in Ampthill that Flemings raped her. Flemings was found guilty and executed. He went to his death, according to the local newspaper, a true penitent:

he said he had never been guilty of any crime before, nor even summoned before a Magistrate on any occasion whatever; but he had neglected a place of worship and his Maker, which had brought him to that untimely end.

Sarah Gardener's parents then found themselves the objects of popular abuse; crowds of up to 200 gathered outside their house throwing stones, exhibiting effigies: 'one dressed as a man another as a woman and another as a child [and] hallowing and charging the family with having hung the man and that they ought to be hung themselves'.[6]

There is nothing in the surviving details of the Flemings–Gardener case to suggest why the prosecutors were so unpopular, but possibly there was a feeling that the charge of rape was being used rather too freely in Bedfordshire on flimsy evidence. Three rape cases had been brought before the Summer Assizes in 1815; one was thrown out by the Grand Jury, the other two resulted in acquittal. One of these acquittals led to a prosecution for conspiracy at the 1817 Lent Assizes, just five months before the Flemings–Gardener case: the Reverend Robert Woodward and his daughters Sarah and Susannah were indicted for conspiring to prosecute James Harris on a charge of rape and making Susannah pregnant. The Woodwards were found guilty; the daughters were each sentenced to one year's imprisonment and the Reverend Woodward was compelled by the bishop to resign his living – 'a degree of punishment' that, he believed, to be 'beyond what was in the contemplation of the Judge who passed sentence on him'.[7]

Violent hostility towards prosecutors and their witnesses in unpopular cases was not confined to the Georgian period. In Blackburn in November 1862, after the prosecution of four men for night poaching on the land of J. Butler Bowden, crowds turned on the gamekeepers who had given evidence as they left the town hall escorted by eight men from the Lancashire Constabulary. An estimated 400 people then marched on Bowden's house, Pleasington Hall, which they proceeded to stone until driven off by Bowden and his servants firing two or three shots over their heads. A troop of the 16th Lancers and squads of the county constabulary were rushed into Blackburn to maintain order.[8] Traditional rough musicing, with all of its folkloric paraphernalia, tended to fade away during the nineteenth century, though its Welsh variant, *ceffyl pren*, has been noted as late as the 1880s, and manifestations were not unknown in the great cities of mid-nineteenth-century England.[9]

If the offender was known to, or instantly apprehended by, the victim, some personal retribution or private settlement could be sought, or offered, to avoid recourse to the law. Though it must be noted that this was not always the case, no matter how close the bonds between individuals. There are, for example, court records of children stealing from their parents, and being prosecuted for it. There are also examples of parents urging the prosecution of their offspring by those who had been their victims; thus the law could be brought into play as a means of discipline within the family.[10] An agreement to come to some private settlement over a theft was compounding a felony and was itself against the law. In October 1794 Richard Wadeson, a tallow chandler of Worksop, was indicted before the Nottinghamshire quarter sessions for a misdemeanour 'in compounding a felony with Marmaduke Littleover for feloniously stealing, taking and carrying away two pounds weight of candles the goods and chattels of the said Richard Wadeson'. The following January Wadeson appeared before the Court, submitted to the charge and was fined twenty shillings.[11] Offenders brought to court sometimes protested that the prosecutor had agreed to let matters be after a financial settlement. There are similarly occasional statements recorded in court proceedings or depositions that the offender offered money to avoid prosecution. Thomas Richardson, a publican of Carnaby Street, prosecuted John Wilson at the Old Bailey in 1796 for the theft of two quart pewter pots and three pint pewter pots. Richardson testified in court that, when he confronted Wilson at the local watch-house after his arrest:

he made towards me, and said, I will give you ten or twenty pounds if you will not appear against me; I told him to offer me no money for I have suffered so much by pot stealers.[12]

George Burridge told the Bedfordshire quarter sessions in 1832:

I left my watch . . . hanging on the nail over the mantelpiece in my father's house at Steppingly between 7 and 8 in the morning. When I went home at 10 o'clock my watch was gone I have not seen it again. D[efendan]t when he was taken up said he would pay me for the watch and all expenses if I would settle it. I said I would if the magistrate would allow it.[13]

Other alternatives to prosecution continued to be exploited throughout the nineteenth century. Employers could, and often did, simply dismiss pilfering workmen; this, together with the threat that the offender would never be employed again, was a tougher sanction than many courts could impose. Many victims were often satisfied with the return of their stolen property and/or with the scare that they gave the accused by the very fact of involving the police; once property had been restored and the offender had been warned by police involvement, some victims declined to press ahead with prosecutions, or else simply did not turn up for the trials.[14]

Legally assaults were different from thefts in that they were not necessarily felonious. During the eighteenth century many cases of assault were settled with a financial payment being made by the assailant to the victim. Magistrates could be involved in such settlements at petty sessions. At quarter sessions, if it was noted that agreement had been reached between the parties, the punishment imposed by the court could be nominal. In January 1766, for example, William Wesson prosecuted Thomas Turner, a grocer of Derby at the Nottinghamshire Sessions for assault; 'it appearing to the court that [the] prosecutor was satisfied', Turner was fined one penny and discharged.[15] But alleged agreements to make amends with a money payment could be as fraught with difficulties in assault cases as in larceny cases. At the Easter Sessions for Bedfordshire in 1833 Emily Crossley prosecuted Robert Wells for an assault after which she had suffered a miscarriage. Wells complained that 'the woman offered to make it up and did for 5/-'.[16] Again alternative settlements to prosecution continued to be sought and found in cases of assault throughout the nineteenth century. Moreover, it would seem that many working-class prosecutions for assault were part of continuing feuds between families or groups, with the law being employed as one way of the complainant achieving a measure of what he or she considered to be justice, but certainly not bringing the affair to an end.[17]

Some victims of theft who reported their loss to constables or thief-takers were prepared to pay a reward for the return of their property and to ignore the prosecution of the offender; corrupt and unscrupulous constables and thief-takers, working in league with thieves, were happy to fall in with these wishes, splitting the rewards with the offender.[18] Newspaper advertisements or handbills describing the stolen property and offering a reward were regularly employed by victims and not without success in both the recovery of goods and the identification of the offender, and thus in his or her prosecution and conviction; the circulation of information about offences became central to the Fieldings' proposals for improving the system of policing.[19] Some victims went to considerable personal lengths to pursue offenders and regain their property. In the summer of 1769 Richard Wallis, a baker, and William Thornton, a tallow chandler, spent several days chasing the men who had stolen their horses around the southern environs of London. After the theft of ten ferrets, a box, a spud, a dog and a gun, John Jeffries and Thomas Asplen of Thurleigh pursued Samuel Colgrave for two days through the villages surrounding Bedford; subsequently they continued their pursuit into Huntingdonshire and Cambridgeshire, eventually running their quarry to earth in a Cambridge pub.[20] It was also possible for the victim to apply to a magistrate for a warrant to search a suspect's house or lodgings.[21] When an individual had gone to the effort and, like as not, the expense of an advertisement, of finding a constable or thief-taker, or of a personal pursuit, he or she was less likely to balk at the effort and expense of a prosecution. Once judicial agents, particularly magistrates, were involved there was more likelihood of the crime being heard in court; and a warrant for an arrest, generally entrusted to a constable meant, at least, a hearing before a magistrate once the suspect was apprehended.[22]

The number of offences that could be heard and resolved summarily before a single magistrate sitting informally in his parlour or in a local tavern, or before one or two magistrates sitting with rather more formality in petty sessions, increased during the eighteenth century as legislation altered penalties and consolidated existing laws. Summary offences included specific minor thefts such as embezzlement by textile workers, stealing wood or vegetables, as well as, most notoriously, certain poaching offences and, by the Combination Acts, trade union activity. The prosecutor had the opportunity to decide whether he wished to have the accused tried summarily or before a higher court; summary justice was prompt, but the penalties were less severe, involving only a fine or a short period of imprisonment. If the prosecutor was determined to make an example he probably would opt for a higher court and it was also possible for magistrates to advise victims to prosecute in a higher court so as to make an example. In 1792 a Bedfordshire magistrate urged a draper of Biggleswade to prosecute the draper's servant at quarter sessions rather than letting the matter be resolved summarily; he explained to the clerk of the peace that it would have been possible to send the offending youth to the Bridewell for ten or fourteen days 'but as the practice of infidelity in servants is become so General and ought to be discountenanced as much as possible' he had recommended the draper 'to prosecute him as a Thief and if convicted to have him well flogged at Biggleswade Market with leave of the Court'.[23]

The legal guides for magistrates, like Richard Burn's *The Justice of the Peace and Parish Officer*, which went through thirty editions between 1755 and 1845, stated that, unless the offence brought before him was one that could be tried summarily in cases of felony, the magistrate had no alternative to committing the offender for trial in a higher court. In practice, however, often in consultation with the prosecutor, the magistrates employed wide discretion. Sometimes the accused was discharged for lack of evidence. Occasionally some prosecutions, particularly some assault charges, seem to have been brought out of spite, in which case magistrates rejected the complaints. Richard Wyatt threw out Richard Wells's accusation that James Britton had threatened him with violence on the grounds that it was 'litigious, vexatious and frivolous'.[24] But even if there did seem a felony case to answer, magistrates often encouraged reconciliation and interpreted some theft accusations as disputes over ownership. During the 1740s William Hunt studiously avoided the word 'theft' when noting certain cases in his justice book.[25] Samuel Whitbread's notebooks, kept seventy years later, reveal him occasionally seeking to settle matters by correspondence, threats, and bringing parties together, rather than simply committing an offender to trial.[26] In those instances where magistrates persuaded the accuser to drop a charge they were not, at least in their own eyes, compounding the offence, rather they were effectively establishing that there had not been a criminal offence in the first place. Some cases, especially assault cases, might be settled with a monetary payment from the accused to the victim; in poaching cases the accused could have proceedings against him dropped if he entered into a bond not to poach on the victim's land again; in other instances an apology inserted in a newspaper might suffice.[27] In wartime the accused could be recruited into the army or navy without the case going beyond the magistrate; this saved the accused from a possibly lengthy pre-trial imprisonment, and it saved the accuser the expense of a prosecution. In eighteenth-century Essex, at least, such a policy was also pursued in peacetime with the accused being encouraged to enlist in the East India Company's service.[28] Finally, it is apparent that magistrates used their wide powers over vagrants, servants, or those who could be described as 'idle and disorderly', to imprison, or otherwise punish offenders guilty of petty crimes, particularly petty theft.

If it was resolved to take the accused to a higher court the magistrate committed him, or her, for trial; bail was very rarely given in larceny cases and committal generally meant the accused being put in gaol, often for several months before appearing in court – after all, with the exception of London and its environs, there were only four quarter sessions and only two assizes each year for the eighteenth and much of the nineteenth centuries. The magistrate also bound over the prosecutor and any witnesses to attend at the higher court. Still the prosecutor's discretion was not at an end. An indictment had to be prepared for the court; this was then submitted to the grand jury, together with any depositions, for a decision on whether or not there was sufficient cause for the case to proceed to a hearing before magistrates and a petty jury at quarter sessions, or judge and jury at assizes. The bill of indictment was generally prepared by the clerk of the peace, for quarter sessions, or the clerk of assizes. These clerks were solicitors, but very often in cases of theft their task was no more than taking a printed bill and filling in the names of the accused, the victim, and the details of the offence; these details sometimes simply involved writing the word 'larceny' or 'felony'. A particularly determined, or particularly wealthy, prosecutor might employ his own, independent, solicitor to prepare the bill of indictment, in which case the bill could incorporate several separate counts to ensure that, if the accused escaped on one charge, he could be caught by another. Following an attempted robbery of his Soho Works in 1800 Matthew Boulton was determined to have the four accused executed on a charge of burglary. Boulton's son was most impressed with the eight-count indictment prepared by his father's solicitors: 'it appears to be formed like a swivel gun and may be directed to all points as circumstances require'.[29] Yet, during the eighteenth and early nineteenth centuries, prosecutorial discretion in the bill of indictment could also lead to an offence being downgraded so as to ensure that the accused did not face the most serious, generally capital, charge available. Joseph Stenson, a hatter, was prosecuted for theft at the Borough Sessions in Leeds in January 1801: he was accused of taking one canvas bag value two pence, 500 shilling pieces value three pence, 500 sixpenny pieces value two pence and one gold half guinea value one penny.[30] The total value of the money that Stenson was accused of stealing was £38.0s.6d., but by downgrading its value to a mere six pence he could be tried before the borough magistrates on a non-capital charge.

Several of the procedures outlined above could be bypassed. A prosecutor could decide to proceed with a voluntary bill whereby a hearing before a magistrate and the entering into recognisances to appear and prosecute were avoided. In such a case the prosecutor went directly to the grand jury, and it was possible for all of the initial steps to be taken without the accused being aware of what was going on. The accused was even more disadvantaged by *ex-officio* information, which was filed by the Attorney General in the Court of King's Bench. This avoided both an initial hearing before a magistrate and the hearing before a grand jury. *Ex-officio* information gave the Attorney General the opportunity of having the case heard before a carefully selected special jury, and even if the defendant was acquitted he could still be saddled with costs. Both voluntary bills and *ex-officio* informations were the exception rather than the rule; the latter, in particular, were rarely used and were confined to serious misdemeanours, often involving some form of sedition.[31]

The pursuit of offenders, going before magistrates and subsequent court appearances were time-consuming – there was no indication given beforehand of the point at which a trial would be heard at either quarter sessions or assizes and, in consequence, the prosecutor and his witnesses, after having travelled to the county town where a particular court was sitting, could have to wait for several days before their case was heard;[32] for members of the lower classes time was money. Henry Fielding believed that the poor were often discouraged from prosecuting because of the expense. Besides the loss of a day or two's pay, there were also the fees:

it cost two shillings for an indictment to be drawn up by the clerk of the court in Fielding's London,[33] and there was, in addition, the recognizance bond to appear in court. Local prosecution associations had been formed from the late seventeenth century. There were, perhaps, as many as a thousand of these societies at any one time; the greatest numbers appear to have been in the years immediately following 1780. Membership of the associations was generally in the region of twenty to fifty, with gentlemen and farmers predominating in rural areas, and tradesmen and small businesses in urban districts. The members paid a subscription to finance the pursuit and prosecution of anyone offending against one of their number; but they rarely assisted anyone who was not a paid-up member of the association and the poor man thus continued to remain largely dependent on his own resources.[34] Legislation of 1752 authorised the courts to pay expenses in felony cases if the prosecutor was poor and if the accused was convicted. An act of 1778 extended this provision to all prosecutors. Some courts, however, were prepared to pay expenses even if there was no conviction. In October 1785 the Nottinghamshire quarter sessions expressed concern that 'many felonies' were being compounded:

and others not prosecuted for fear that the expenses of the prosecution should not be paid by the county, to prevent the like in future and for encouraging prosecutions against felons . . . it was ordered by the Court that an advertisement be inserted in the Nottingham paper signifying that in all future prosecutions for felonies the reasonable charges of the prosecutors and their witnesses should be paid by the county.[35]

The Leeds Borough Sessions commonly paid expenses at the turn of the century when an accused was acquitted but when the court considered that 'there was reasonable ground of prosecution'. In Essex it was even known for the quarter sessions to award expenses after a bill of indictment had been rejected by the Grand Jury.[36] Unquestionably it was the less well-to-do prosecutors who profited most from this legislation and court practice. The knowledge that expenses were likely to be paid even if a good case failed before a petty jury may have encouraged more poor men to prosecute, though the surviving evidence shows that the poor were not unwilling to seek redress for theft through the law. 'Labourers', servants, gardeners and husbandmen made up something like one-fifth of the prosecutors in larceny cases in the second half of the eighteenth century, with tradesmen and artisans accounting for about two-fifths.[37] Further legislation, culminating in Peel's Criminal Justice Act 1826, extended the provision of expenses to witnesses as well as prosecutors, and to certain misdemeanours (notably the more serious forms of assault) as well as felonies. Peel justified this extension on the grounds that, when expenses were not available 'you frequently close the avenues of justice in instances in which the poorest classes are the sufferers, and in which the public interest loudly demands reparation from the offender'.[38]

Besides the expense of, and time taken up by, a prosecution, Henry Fielding believed that some victims did not prosecute because of a misplaced humanitarianism in not wanting to be the cause of someone being executed.[39] Sir Samuel Romilly, Sir James Mackintosh and other reformers urged this as a principal reason for bringing about a drastic reduction in the number of capital statutes that existed under the eighteenth-century Bloody Code. 'Numerous and respectable witnesses' testified to the 1819 Select Committee on Criminal Laws 'that a great reluctance prevail[ed] to prosecute' in some capital crimes and, unfortunately, this reluctance had 'had the effect of producing immunity to such a degree, that it may be considered as among the temptations to the commission of crimes'.[40] The influence of Mackintosh over this committee (he chaired most of its sessions) certainly coloured its conclusions, and unquestionably influenced the choice of witnesses and the way in which they were prodded for the kind of answers favourable to the reformers' agenda. There is other evidence, such as reducing the value of stolen property so as to reduce the charge, that some prosecutors thought very seriously about the likely outcome if they proceeded with a capital indictment.[41] Yet when, in 1811, the metropolitan stipendiary magistrates were asked a series of questions about the impact of Romilly's act removing capital punishment from the offence of stealing privately from a person (pocket picking), the opinion was overwhelmingly that cost and inconvenience were much greater deterrents to the prosecutor than capital punishment. The Shadwell magistrates had noted a reluctance to prosecute but believed that this was because their jurisdiction bordered the Thames and victims in the area were 'seafaring people who cannot attend properly to the prosecution but are obliged to go to sea'. The Hatton Garden magistrates doubted whether there had been reluctance to prosecute on account of capital punishment 'but a great deal . . . on account of the expense and trouble of prosecuting especially where the property to be recovered is of little value'. One of the stipendiaries from the Queen's Square office elaborated:

The considerable sacrifice of time, the additional cost, nay the heavy *load of expense, the tiresomeness of attendance, and keeping witnesses together, the too frequent petulancies etc etc in the many stages of*

Judicature, and the many painful mortifications frequently endured from examination, and the asperities of cross examination. But that the parties are often deterred from the consideration of a higher description [?] of punishment is not true . . . .[42]

These deterrents to prosecution continued well after the extension of expenses for prosecutors and witnesses and well after the reduction of capital statutes during the 1820s and 1830s. The Constabulary Commissioners were informed by the Metropolitan Police that 'the fear of ultimately having to prosecute deters many from giving information'.[43] Sometimes there was the problem of personal embarrassment, as when clergymen or other gentlemen had their watches stolen while consorting with prostitutes;[44] and such embarrassment, particularly in the moral atmosphere of Victorian society, probably dissuaded women from prosecuting in cases of indecent assault, rape, or attempted rape.[45] A few individuals refused to prosecute from religious scruples,[46] or when they discovered that the offender was one of their own family, or a servant willing to make restitution.[47] Some victims were too frightened,[48] and in East Anglia, and probably elsewhere, incendiarism, or the threat, was used to dissuade prosecutors and magistrates.[49] Other victims, together with their witnesses, were allegedly bribed:

[N]o doubt it often happens that between the committal and the day of trial, the witness on whom the case rests is tampered with or for some pecuniary gain (and in some cases not a small amount) his testimony before the Grand Jury is quite different to what it was before the Magistrate. This is a common practice with old Thieves who say 'Smother it before the Grand Jury' as they know they would stand but little chance should it come into court. Hence the number of Bills ignored without any one knowing the cause, the Grand Jury excepted.[50]

On some occasions the reasons why victims refused to give information and to prosecute remained a mystery to the police, but when the police felt that they could identify deterrents these were, overwhelmingly, loss of time, general inconvenience, and even expense:

Mr Lawrence, New Cut, Lambeth prosecuted a person for felony and a short time afterwards another person robbed him. Mr L declined giving him in charge stating that it was such an annoyance to be detained for so long from business at the Police Office and again at the Sessions. Many instances might be given.[51]

Many instances have occurred where parties have wished to decline prosecuting in consequence of loss of time. Many tradesmen preferring the infliction of a summary punishment rather than attend the sessions. Even after parties have been committed they have again been brought up and summarily convicted at the instance of the party robbed.[52]

In the neighbourhood of Wandsworth, Battersea and Barnes, the market gardeners have declined prosecuting parties for robbing their grounds from the expense attending conviction before a magistrate at Wandsworth. Parties stealing fruit and vegetables are convicted in a small sum and the other expenses . . . amounting sometimes altogether to 7s. or 8s. the party convicted is frequently sent to prison in default and the expense falls upon the prosecutor besides his loss of time etc.[53]

Some nineteenth-century law reformers concluded from the reluctance to prosecute on the part of some victims that England needed some system of public prosecution similar to that in use in Scotland as well as elsewhere in Europe. In 1826 Peel expressed sympathy for the idea believing that it would ensure a prosecution when necessary and prevent frivolous or vexatious prosecutions; he suggested that much could be learned from Scottish practice.[54] During the following decade, and again in the 1850s and the 1870s, proposals were brought forward for such a system even to the extent of bills being introduced in the House of Commons. Each time, for a variety of reasons, the proposals were rejected. There was opposition from a powerful vested interest in the shape of the growing profession of solicitors; they feared a significant loss of income should the state take over prosecutions. There was more general concern about the expense of a system of public prosecution and also of the growth of patronage that would accompanying it. Finally, there was that uniquely English concern of an encroachment on personal and political liberty should the state become involved in prosecutions. A public prosecutor, declared the Clerk of the Peace of Wigan, in the mid-1840s:

would have the power of refusing to proceed in cases where parties thought there ought to be a prosecution, and this power might (and particularly in cases of political excitement) cause a denial of justice. I think that in all cases any man who has sustained injury, ought to be at liberty to put the law in force, and not be deprived of his remedy through the malice or caprice of a public prosecutor refusing to proceed, and therefore leaving him without remedy. If this power is entrusted to a public prosecutor, it will be a greater encroachment upon the right of a trial by jury than any encroachment there has been, and these are not a few.[55]

As a result of such sentiments nineteenth-century legislation only marginally infringed on the rights of the private prosecutor. The Vexatious Indictments Act 1859 limited the opportunities for bringing voluntary bills for certain misdemeanours. A dozen or so other acts authorised only specific inspectors or local authorities to prosecute for certain infringements, and limited the independent civilian prosecutor's discretion in cases concerning excise offences, sedition, or other matters involving sensitive international or domestic affairs. A Director of Public Prosecutions was first appointed in 1879, but for nearly thirty years the function of the post was almost entirely advisory.[56]

Yet, while no nineteenth-century legislation had any dramatic impact on the system of prosecution by private individuals, there was a very significant, if gradual, change brought about with the development of the new police. In certain circumstances, before the establishment of police forces, it could be difficult to find a prosecutor. Joseph Radcliffe, a magistrate of the West Riding, was not prepared to finance the prosecution of Joseph Jubson for seditious words in 1803; after all, he protested to the Home Secretary, the offence was not personal to him. In 1824 Essex magistrates were unwilling to organise and finance the prosecution of people who had attacked an informer; they remembered an earlier prosecution that had resulted in them being saddled with a solicitor's bill for £200.[57] The new police could take on such prosecutions yet, gradually, they extended this role far beyond these instances. The increasing role of the police as prosecutors from the middle of the nineteenth century has been largely ignored by historians and there has been no detailed study, even on a regional basis, of precisely how, when and why the police came to predominate as prosecutors.[58] Constables and local law officers had always had a role in prosecuting misdemeanours such as vagrancy and petty street offences. When the new police forces were established the incidence of arrests for these kinds of offences generally increased; at the same time acts of parliament relating to the police and local government byelaws consolidated and extended the policeman's role in this area. Private individuals could bring prosecutions under police acts, and Charles Dickens expressed satisfaction in having prosecuted a young woman for bad language in the street under a Metropolitan Police Act;[59] but overwhelmingly the police dominated the prosecution of offenders against public order, public decency and public safety. Such offenders were usually processed by the police courts or petty sessions. Probably the step from prosecuting these petty offenders to prosecuting petty thieves was not seen as a particularly great one by the new police as they grew in confidence and professionalism.

In 1855 an experienced attorney, William Foote, informed the Select Committee on Public Prosecutors that he considered the prosecution of offenders as

part of the policeman's duty; it certainly is part of his duty to trace out and detect crime, and if his duty is to trace out and detect crime, it is his duty to trace out the evidence to support the charge.[60]

If, as was repeatedly stated, the key role of the new police was the prevention of crime,[61] what better way to prevent crime than to arrest and ensure the conviction of its perpetrators? Policemen, like their contemporaries, tended to think of crime as something committed by a criminal class; a perception encouraged by the requirement that they submit annual statistics of 'known criminals' in their district along with the figures of crimes reported and arrests made. At the same time it seems probable that the new police were sucked into acting as prosecutors from their early years because of the poverty of some of the victims of theft. The Superintendent of B Division of the Metropolitan Police explained to the Constabulary Commissioners that on one occasion arresting police constables had been obliged to pay for a bill of indictment since the two prosecutors in the case were too poor.[62] It may be significant that in several cases in mid-nineteenth-century Bedfordshire in which the police acted as prosecutor, or joint prosecutor, the victim, or other joint prosecutor, was a woman. Once the police began to step in as prosecutors in cases where the victim was poor or a 'weaker vessel', it was logical that they should step in on other occasions when the victim was simply reluctant. But it is not simply the case that the new police were drawn in as prosecutors because of the poverty or 'weakness' of the victims. Evidence from Lancashire suggests that, from the creation of its constabulary in 1840, senior police officers were considered as akin to public prosecutors, while the clerk of the peace conducted all prosecutions. The Home Office was doubtful as to the legality of this, and the Crown Law Officers advised that neither police officers nor anyone else should be bound over to prosecute when the injured party was unwilling to act;[63] but it is unclear whether the practice was terminated. In 1846 the Nottinghamshire Constabulary preferred three out of 118 indictments at the quarter sessions; another one was preferred by an old-style parish constable. Ten years later the police preferred twenty-two out of 166, with two other indictments preferred by parish constables. In 1866 there were ninety-five indictments at the quarter sessions, of which forty-seven were preferred by the police. These Nottinghamshire cases do not readily reveal much in the way of common characteristics suggesting why some, rather than others, were taken on by the police. Nor was the increase in the number of cases prosecuted by the Nottinghamshire Police either a steady linear progression or precisely parallel with the pattern elsewhere; in London, at least until 1880s, the private prosecutor seems to have dominated.[64]

For victims it probably seemed logical and preferable to hand over prosecutions to the police who increasingly claimed to be the experts in the 'war' against crime. It was particularly preferable since, even though the prosecutor's expenses might be reimbursed, he could still be out of pocket with some costs, or at least feared as much.[65] It was noted above that the market gardeners of south London were reluctant to prosecute for petty thefts of their produce in case they were saddled with costs when the convicted offender was too poor to pay these and a fine. In 1844 a poor man was charged before Oxfordshire magistrates with stealing turnips. He was found guilty and sentenced to pay a fine of two shillings, a further two shillings, being the value of the turnips, and eleven shillings, being the costs of the magistrates' clerk. The man, who confessed that want had driven him to commit the theft in the first place, could not pay and was committed to prison. The magistrates then instructed the prosecutor to pay the clerk's costs. Naturally the man protested:

[he] said he did not understand why he should be saddled with such expenses for merely discharging his duty towards himself and the public, and added something about its being much cheaper letting the thief off with his booty, than seek for punishment for the offence.

The newspaper reporting the case declared such instances to be commonplace.[66] There was some hostility from the legal profession to policemen acting as prosecutors; the police, it was claimed, were not properly trained for such a task, moreover it was protested that they might seek to put over evidence in a partial manner to ensure conviction. There were also stories reported to the mid-century Select Committee on Public Prosecutors of policemen supplementing their low wages by engineering malicious or trivial prosecutions to win the costs that the courts awarded, and sometimes sharing these with disreputable solicitors.[67] In the long term, however, the police assumption of the role of prosecutor may have brought them closer to the working class – as much, if not more, the victims of petty crime as any other group – and helped to foster that police legitimacy which appeared unique to England from roughly the middle of the nineteenth century to the middle of the twentieth.

Between 1750 and 1850 most of the cases brought before assizes and quarter sessions were characterised by a face-to-face confrontation between the prosecutor and the accused. Occasionally the accused said nothing, or made very little response to the charge.[68] They had, after all, had little time or opportunity to prepare a defence while incarcerated in the squalid gaols of the period. They were denied access to depositions and to the names of prosecution witnesses; and even the charges against them could be changed at the last minute.[69] Sometimes the accused attempted to blacken the prosecutor's name: 'I hope your Lordships will examine this woman well', protested eighteen-year-old James Angas when he faced his principal accuser at the Old Bailey in April 1797, 'for she has transported several, and wants to make a property of me; she transported her own son'. Sixty years later Mary Ann Harriet Forbes, aged 16, was prosecuted by her master for stealing his property, after which, without notice, she had left his employ; in court she protested that she had left after he had seized her round the waist, kissed her, and told her to 'pull the bed down'; unfortunately she had made no similar complaint to the arresting police constable, and the court did not believe her.[70] More often than not, however, the defence consisted simply of a denial of the charge and a succession of character witnesses.

The confrontation between prosecutor and accused gradually disappeared during the nineteenth century as, increasingly, it was replaced by a confrontation between lawyers acting for both the prosecution and the defence. Like other professions, the legal profession increased significantly in numbers during the nineteenth century, and while its standards of training remained minimal, legal practitioners of all types jealously preserved and advanced their boasted expertise. Part of this preservation of expertise involved a rigorous demarcation of their sphere of influence. The courts, with their ritual and tradition, were one such sphere; and as the century progressed the non-initiated public were required, more and more, to depend upon, and to pay for, the expert barrister and solicitor when they entered the courts.[71]

During the seventeenth century prosecuting counsel rarely appeared in the criminal courts, and only then in cases such as treason; defence counsel were even more rare, appearing only in complex misdemeanour cases, notably those involving civil or regulatory matters such as liability for the upkeep of roads. The theory was that the accused had no need of counsel since the burden of proof was on the prosecution and the accused was a greater expert on the truth, or otherwise, of what was alleged against him or her, than any lawyer. The trial judge was expected to assist the accused with legal advice when necessary, though the speed of trials and the apparent indifference of many judges suggest that the expectation was rarely met in practice. Concern for the weakness of the accused's position began to be expressed with reference to treason prosecutions towards the end of the century and defence counsel were permitted by the Treason Act of 1696. The *Old Bailey Sessions Papers* began recording the rare appearances by prosecution counsel in other criminal cases during the second decade of the eighteenth century, most notably in murder cases. By the end of the century such appearances were more common, but were by no means the rule; generally speaking prosecuting counsel appear to have been employed primarily in cases where the victims were particularly aggrieved, where the case was difficult, or where the defence was employing counsel and it was feared that this might lead to acquittal. The prosecutors who employed counsel were clearly going out of their way to ensure that the case was conducted correctly and that the verdict was satisfactory; associations for the prosecution of felons appear, perhaps understandably, to have been significant among the employers of counsel. By the 1840s the employment of such counsel seems to have been widespread, particularly at assizes, and was also to be found at quarter sessions. Indeed it was the lack of prosecution counsel at the Bedfordshire Lent Assizes for 1844 that prompted two outbursts from Sir John Pattison, the presiding judge. He interrupted one case to enquire:

why there were no counsel for the prosecution, and observed that it was a disgrace to the county to impose upon the Judge the necessity of acting as a counsel against the prisoner ('an unseemly position' added his Lordship, with emphasis) besides the additional trouble which it entails upon the judge.

Then, when the case against a tramp for stealing a shawl was called, 'his lordship said "There is no counsel I suppose?" and upon the clerk of the arraigns replying in the negative, added, "Ah! Bedford's so poor it can't afford them".'[72]

Defence counsel, according to the evidence of the *Old Bailey Sessions Papers*, began to make very rare appearances in ordinary criminal trials during the 1730s, but for the eighteenth and the early part of the nineteenth centuries their role was not strictly defined and the extent of their participation seems to have varied from one assize circuit to another. Both the accused and his or her counsel could cross-examine witnesses; what defence counsel could not do, until legislation in 1836, was sum up the defence for the benefit of the jury. Judges may have begun to allow counsel to appear for the accused because of the concern about the weakness of the accused's position; this concern also led to a greater querying of hearsay and circumstantial evidence as the eighteenth century wore on, and confessions were often rejected, especially if there was the slightest hint of them being extracted under duress. At the same time, even during the reforming years of the 1830s, a Solicitor General could voice concern that 'improper acquittal' could result from a barrister's eloquence, while another M.P. feared:

that if Counsel were allowed to both prisoner and prosecutor, it would have no better result than giving rise to trials of professional skill. The prosecutor in most cases being the richer, would have the advantage, since it might naturally be supposed that he could obtain the best professional aid.[73]

Some contemporaries suggested that the Prisoner's Counsel Act 1836 favoured professional thieves who could afford counsel, at the expense of poor prosecutors who could not; J. J. Tobias has viewed this suggestion sympathetically.[74] Yet a limited analysis of the employment of counsel suggests that, overwhelmingly, it was prosecutors who hired counsel rather than defendants[75] and throughout the nineteenth century the accused probably remained at a disadvantage.

It was not until the end of the nineteenth century that the accused in criminal proceedings was allowed to give evidence on oath. Two decades of heated debate preceded the Criminal Evidence Act 1898: on one side it was insisted that the accused's ability to give sworn evidence on his own behalf would reduce the number of innocent persons convicted as well as abolish anomalies and bring criminal law in line with civil law; on the other side it was alleged that such a change would disadvantage the nervous, foster perjury and, perhaps most serious, transform the judge from an impartial observer to a bullying French-style inquisitor.[76] It is, of course, impossible to assess how far the accused was disadvantaged by being unable to give sworn evidence, but financial considerations unquestionably limited his options. There were no expenses allowed for the accused; travelling to court as a witness for a defendant could cost an individual expenses for the journey; time spent in court, or waiting to be called, also cost money. Defence counsel cost money. Except in cases of murder there was no provision for legal aid for a defendant, otherwise the cheapest counsel available was through the system known as 'dock briefs' by which the defendant could pay one guinea, plus a clerk's fee, and obtain the service of a barrister without the mediation, and expense, of a solicitor. Barristers were obliged to accept 'dock briefs' but the overall standard of those who undertook criminal work was regarded as inferior. Money was one key incentive for the more able barristers to concentrate on civil business; in the 1840s it was estimated that earnings from the latter were ten times greater than earnings from criminal business. In 1851 it was argued in the *Law Times* that the state had a duty to allow or assign counsel to prisoners who could not afford them, but it was not until the Poor Prisoner's Defence Act 1903 that any significant move was made in this direction.[77]

As trials at assizes and quarter sessions increasingly became contests between lawyers, so judges and juries played less of a central role and, in addition, trials became much longer and much more formal. According to John Langbein there were some negative results from these changes. The increasing appearance of defence counsel meant increasing silence on the part of the accused and new burdens of proof being required from the prosecution, the focus, in turn, became the contest between legal adversaries rather than a system designed to seek the truth.[78] The increasing length and formality of trials, however, had its positive side. During the eighteenth and early nineteenth centuries most criminal trials were over in a matter of minutes; they rarely seem to have taken as long as an hour. Often the jurors did not leave the courtroom to deliberate, but simply went into a huddle, and not a particularly refined huddle. Towards the end of the eighteenth century Martin Madan condemned the practice of courts meeting during the afternoon following a lengthy break for food and drink. It was the drink that created the problems according to Madan; sometimes the judge had to spend an hour bringing the court to order:

and when this is done, drunkenness is too frequently apparent, where it ought of all things to be avoided, I mean, in jurymen *and* witnesses. *The heat of the court, joined to the fumes of the liquor, has laid many an* honest juryman *into a calm and profound sleep, and sometimes it has been no small trouble for his* fellows to jog *him into the verdict – even where the wretch's* life *has depended on the event!*

Madan claimed to have witnessed such incidents personally. A press report of an 1844 assize graphically describes a jury huddling in the court to discuss the verdict.

After a few minutes noisy consultation a portion of the jury turned round and said they were divided, as 'one or two old men wouldn't fall in with the others', whereupon the 'one or two old men' nodded their heads sagaciously, and in a manner to indicate that they had 'a reason for it'.[79]

Jurors served for an entire session of the court and were often drawn from men who had served before, even quite recently; jurors were thus often old hands who well understood the procedures and the tasks expected of them. The evidence of the *Old Bailey Sessions Papers* suggests, moreover, that while jurors were in harmony with, and deferential towards, the judge, they were not simply passive auditors but asked questions and, on occasions, stated their reasons for a verdict. In January 1766, for example, an Old Bailey jury acquitted Brian Swinney on a charge of highway robbery and 'declared that they had a very bad opinion of the prosecutor'.[80] Sometimes, during the supremacy of the Bloody Code, juries brought in verdicts reducing the value of property stolen to bring the accused out of range of a capital statute; such behaviour was connived at, or often directed, by the judge. There could be an exchange of views with the judge if he queried a jury's verdict, and it was not unknown for judges to reinstruct juries and request them to deliberate again should they have returned a verdict that the judge believed to be incorrect. Some judges exerted much greater influence over juries than others. Lord Mansfield drew the fire of John Wilkes's supporters for brow beating and bullying juries; and this may further have disadvantaged the accused since it appears that when Mansfield was on the bench there were marginally more convictions than usual.[81] Interplay between the magistrates and the jurors at quarter sessions was probably much the same, but the paucity of evidence remaining for such proceedings probably makes any detailed analysis impossible.

The right to a trial by a jury of his peers was, indeed still is, lionised as one of the key rights of the free-born Englishman. Yet it is probably the case that, even during the eighteenth century, the most common experience of the law and of courts, for the bulk of the people, was the magistrate sitting alone, or with one or two colleagues more formally in petty sessions. Justice in these instances was administered summarily and while, during the eighteenth and nineteenth centuries, juries gradually became less and less active participants in the higher courts, so did new legislation bring more and more cases within the remit of the magistrates acting without a jury. Considerable concern was expressed about this development. Sir William Blackstone condemned summary jurisdiction as 'fundamentally opposed to the spirit of our constitution'. In 1772 the *London Chronicle* condemned the new Game Act, which established summary jurisdiction in certain poaching offences and thus undermined 'the great Bulwark of an Englishman's Rights, the Trial by Jury'. Over half a century later *The Times* expressed similar regrets in a wide ranging review of the activities of magistrates.[82] But requirements that justice be speedy, and that it put the minimum burden on the prosecutor's time and pocket, were paramount.

Technically, summary jurisdiction in the eighteenth and early nine-teenth centuries only covered misdemeanours; felonies had to be tried on indictment before a jury. The spread of summary jurisdiction, however, increasingly blurred the distinction as legislation gave the prosecutor greater discretion in how he wanted to proceed against an offender and also what kind of punishment he wanted; punishments under summary jurisdiction were limited to either a fine, a whipping, or, at most, a few months' imprisonment. An employer wanting to prosecute the organisers or perpetrators of industrial action could use summary jurisdiction; a variety of trades were covered by individual acts of parliament before the notorious Combination Acts, which were in force between 1799 and 1824. But if he wanted to inflict a terrible example he could opt for a prosecution on indictment at a higher court on a charge of larceny, if the offence was the appropriation of materials, or on a charge of conspiracy, if the offence involved some kind of strike activity; in both instances punishment could amount to transportation. Similarly the increase of summary jurisdiction in poaching offences gave the prosecutor a wide choice: he could choose between the new summary jurisdiction, the more serious prosecution on indictment, and even a civil suit by which the plaintiff sued for half of the fine to be imposed and, if he won, he also collected twice the cost of the prosecution.[83]

As the examples of summary jurisdiction noted here suggest, certain of the increasing summary categories were delicate ones for the relation-ships between social groups. Of all others, from the late seventeenth until well into the nineteenth century, it was the Game Laws that pro-voked the greatest anxiety and outcry. These laws manifestly preserved the privileges of sporting gentlemen possessed of wealth and property. Many magistrates were such gentlemen, or were closely involved with such, and concern developed about the partiality of Game Law cases before summary tribunals. This concern culminated in the petition of John Deller, which was presented to parliament in 1823 in the midst of the early nineteenth-century debates on law reform. Deller was a Hampshire farmer whose farm was bounded in part by land belonging to the Duke of Buckingham. He had been brought before the Duke on a complaint from two of the Duke's gamekeepers for coursing hares on his own farm. Deller protested that the hares had done between £30 and £60 damage, but this did not prevent the Duke from fining him £5 and warning him that any impertinence would lead to the stocks or to gaol. Subsequently Deller had brought a complaint against one of the Duke's servants for entering upon his land with three dogs, but two clerical justices had continually postponed the hearing while binding Deller over for assault:

> [Y]our humble petitioner has heard much talk about the liberty and
> property of Englishmen; but . . . to his plain understanding, a state
> of slavery so complete as that in which he has the misfortune to live,
> cannot be found in any other country in the world.[84]

Yet, whatever the mythology and the occasional instance of cases like Deller's, Game Law offences do not seem to have dominated eighteenth-century summary tribunals; furthermore, the most sober recent study of the workings of these laws concludes that, especially after the 1750s, 'openly biased tribunals were less common than the game laws' critics have assumed'.[85]

The Combination Acts have a similar notoriety to the Game Laws, yet there has never been a detailed analysis of their use; indeed, given the paucity of evidence surviving from summary tribunals, probably there cannot be. Similarly the trade-specific predecessors of the Combination Acts have received little serious attention and, again, the lack of evidence militates against detailed statistical assessments.[86] The poor man and the employee probably did have the cards stacked against them in eighteenth- and early nineteenth-century summary tribunals, but there were magistrates who sympathised with them and who were especially critical of the employers who used illegal truck payments.[87] Furthermore, partly through public pressure, but also no doubt because the ruling class believed the rhetoric of the law's impartiality, magistrates were keen to demonstrate their own impartiality. In 1824 the *Kent and Essex Mercury* condemned an Essex magistrate who prosecuted a waggoner for obstruction and inflicted an on-the-spot fine of ten shillings.[88] Ten years later, West Country newspapers were highly critical of a Devon magistrate who, after having been fined £5 for violently assaulting his children's nurse, went into an adjacent room to try another assault case.[89] But such incidents appear exceptional and the outcry that they provoked reinforces this assumption. There was a tradition, clearly apparent in the eighteenth century, that magistrates should not try cases in which they had a personal concern;[90] and when they stepped down from the bench they could not be sure that colleagues and friends would find in their favour.[91] The problem is, of course, assessing the extent to which economic and social and/or class prejudice displaced the desire of most magistrates to demonstrate the impartiality allowed within the framework of the law. In those instances where the partiality seems blatant the problem disappears. During the eighteenth century many magistrates enforcing labour legislation were employers in the industries concerned. This was especially true in big manufacturing boroughs, like Norwich, but could also be true in mid-eighteenth-century rural manufacturing areas, like Wiltshire. In early nineteenth-century Wigan, magistrates linked with local industry appear to have administered justice with relative impartiality, except in cases of industrial theft; after the Municipal Corporations Act this partiality took on party political and sectarian hues.[92] Across the Pennines in West Yorkshire, however, some manufacturers in the woollen and worsted trades held summary hearings in their homes or factories, and they showed no qualms about judging their own employees here on charges of embezzlement.[93] In the second quarter of the nineteenth century, as noted earlier, there was a change in the composition of the magistracy in the various jurisdictions of the Black Country as industrial entrepreneurs began to dominate over landowners; this change was accompanied by increasing activity in prosecuting for industrial theft and in seeking to control the workforce by means of the Master and Servant Act. It has been suggested that while, in comparison with the size of the labour force, prosecutions under the Master and Servant Act in the third quarter of the century were small in number, they were not confined to exceptional cases. In fact the Act appears to have been regarded as an essential weapon for controlling labour.[94] Changes in the magistracy were quite different in neighbouring Warwickshire, however, where landed gentry displaced clergy on the bench to become the dominant group and where, during industrial troubles, notably those in the mines during the 1840s, most magistrates had no direct interest.[95] Finally, it is also probable that the increasing appointment of professional lawyers as stipendiaries and as recorders to supervise the part-time magistrates, particularly at borough sessions, checked the most blatant abuses.

The relaxed, relatively informal magistrates' tribunals of the eighteenth century had little place in the increasingly urbanised England of the nineteenth century with its emphasis on decorum and bureaucratic formality. The system of magistrates sitting singly or in petty sessions was not spread uniformly throughout eighteenth-century England; while petty sessions met in Hampshire and Dorset, for example, none appears to have met in Berkshire.[96] Populous urban districts had difficulty in finding gentlemen of the first rank to act as magistrates and 'trading justices' had begun to appear in and around the metropolis during the seventeenth century. These were gentlemen, generally of modest property, who could be relied upon to act in these urban districts for the sake of the fees that they could collect for resolving petty disputes and for granting and signing particular documents. The 'trading justices' of the Kent parishes bordering London were far busier than the justices of rural Kent from the very beginning of the eighteenth century; they were looked down upon by their country cousins because they took fees, and some of them became justifiably notorious, but manifestly they were fulfilling a need.[97] The Bow Street magistrates' office grew out of the trading justice system, though from the mid-eighteenth century the magistrates here, notably Henry and later Sir John Fielding, received money from the Treasury rather than relying on fees. The system of stipendiary magistrates established for London in 1792, primarily as a police measure, created a more general, and more formal precedent for the way in which magistrates adjudicated lesser offences. In 1839, ten years after the creation of the Metropolitan Police, the stipendiary magistrates of London lost their police role and their offices were transformed into the Metropolitan Police Courts, vividly described for the *Illustrated London News* by Angus Reach:

In Bagnigge Wells road . . . that glaring and dusty summer thoroughfare, stands a large pile of buildings, generally ornamented by numerous lounging policemen, and further diversified and adorned by crowds of shabby-looking people, a vast proportion whereof may be observed to have their personal appearance improved by such additional attractions as are contributed by blackened eyes, plastered-up foreheads, and noses with broken bridges.

The buildings form the Clerkenwell Police Court and its appurtenances; the lounging constables are the guardians of last night's peace, waiting to prefer charges against its disturbers; the maltreated gentry about are the sufferers – some of them, perhaps, the active, as well as passive partakers in the constant drunken rows which such districts as Clerkenwell – a favoured abode of those unfortunate helots of the hod, generally complimented as the 'low Irish' – naturally furnish, from day to day, for police adjudication.

We enter – we traverse a long, dirty passage: the passages leading to Police Courts are always dirty – the walls are always greasy – glazed, so to speak, by the constant friction of frowsy rags. A turn to the left – a push at a swinging door – and we stand in the midst of a similar crowd to that which we left outside, to that which we passed in the lobby – the disreputable public of a Police Court.

The room is a larger one than most of the 'Worthy Magistrates' are blessed with – in fact, a handsome, airy, wainscoted apartment. You glance at once towards the judicial armchair, and see it faced and flanked

*by the usual Police Court arrangements – a square, open box in the
centre, bounded, so to speak, on one side by the bench, on the others by
the particular boxes occupied by Clerks, Police Inspectors, Reporters,
Barristers, and last, not least, Culprits. The part of the room not taken
up by these pens and boxes, forms the* locus standi *for that portion of
the enlightened public who come to improve their tempers by the
contemplation of the placid equanimity of a Greenwood – or to see how
perfectly even the balance of justice, as between a private individual and
a policeman, can be held by a Combe.*[98]

By the middle of the century there were thirteen such courts in London
with twenty-three magistrates like Messrs Combe and Greenwood, dispensing justice in cases of misdemeanours such as common assault, drunk
and disorderly, gambling, suspicious behaviour, unlawful possession and
vagrancy. Justice in these courts was speedy with little time available for
deliberation; at the beginning of the twentieth century Edward Carpenter
reckoned that cases took 'on an average say three minutes to dispose of'.[99]
At the same time, and in keeping with the notion that the law was impartial, these magistrates were also charged with providing 'a system of poor
man's justice' that could 'encourage in the common people a habit of looking to the law for protection'. There is no question but that many of them
took this charge seriously, and that they sometimes used their power and
authority to conform to popular conceptions of justice rather than the
strict letter of the law.[100]

A few fast-growing provincial urban districts began contemplating the
appointment of stipendiary magistrates from the moment they appeared
in London; but the first such appointments were not made until the
early nineteenth century and it was not until 1835 that legislation made it
possible for any borough that so wished to appoint a stipendiary. The
arguments in favour of stipendiaries were manifold. Many of the fastest-
growing urban–industrial sprawls had no resident magistrate since they
were not incorporated boroughs, and county magistrates, even with property in the town, were often reluctant to commit themselves to the time
necessary for dispensing justice in such areas.[101] Concerns were raised by
some individuals about the capabilities of the part-time gentleman magistrate and about the need for stricter regulation of the administration of justice. There was also a lobby calling for some kind of more professional
tribunal to try cases not serious enough for quarter sessions or assizes, but
too serious for the amateur magistrate sitting alone or in petty sessions.
Lord Brougham, for example, expressed his concerns to parliament about

both the constitution of the different tribunals of magistrates and the way in which they exercised their powers. *The Times*, in contrast, believed that while the system of unpaid magistrates had its faults:

the interference of lawyers in the magisterial business of a county is often more mischievous than useful, and . . . the love of justice, and the household common sense of country gentlemen, are more efficacious in the accomplishment of the ends of justice than the labours of professional magistrates.

Nevertheless, the increase in summary jurisdiction was undesirable and there were cases that required 'a more skilful and practised tribunal'.[102] A Juvenile Offenders Bill discussed in parliament in 1840 contained a clause that would have done away with the 'evil' of petty sessions being held in public houses. The proposer wanted:

to erect an intermediate tribunal between the magistrates and the superior courts, in order to prevent young persons of 12, 11, and 10 years of age, and perhaps even younger children, from being sent to prison for first and trivial offences.[103]

Three years later, following an enquiry from the Buckinghamshire quarter sessions for clarification on the use of the magistrate's own home for the transaction of judicial business, the Home Office urged:

that in any district in which there is a regular and fixed place for holding the petty sessions, to which the public have access, the most desirable course to adopt is that the cases which are to be brought before magistrates should be there heard and adjudicated, though, certainly, it is not illegal for the magistrates to hear cases at the office of their clerk.

The *Morning Herald* put a gloss on this, emphasising that privacy was not a good thing; justice should be seen to be done in public.[104]

The middle years of the nineteenth century witnessed legislation that gave much greater organisation and formality to the summary courts and brought more cases within their remit. A series of measures, known collectively as Jervis's Acts, were passed in 1848. These dealt generally with the judicial work of the magistrates, established stricter procedures for preliminary hearings, granted greater protection to magistrates for any innocent breach of the law that they might accidentally commit, and, perhaps most importantly, amended and consolidated existing legislation on summary jurisdiction. In February 1847 Sir John Packington, M.P. for Droitwich, requested leave to introduce a bill to permit the summary trial of juvenile offenders. Packington's intention was to ensure that such offenders did not spend days or weeks in prison awaiting assizes or quarter sessions; he feared that such a period could only expose them to the corrupting influence of hardened criminals. Furthermore, he urged 'that good would result from young offenders being taught to feel that their crimes would be followed by immediate punishment'. Concern was initially expressed that such trials would be in secret; once again the requirement was that justice be seen to be done. There was also anxiety in some quarters about 'upsetting the great principle of trial by jury'.[105] Nevertheless Packington's Bill was eventually accepted. The Juvenile Offenders Act of 1847 empowered magistrates assembled in petty sessions to try juveniles under the age of fourteen years who were charged with simple larceny. A second Juvenile Offenders Act, passed in 1850, raised the age limit to sixteen.

During the second reading of Packington's Bill Robert Palmer, the member for Berkshire and a former chairman of quarter sessions, had suggested that the value of articles stolen would be a better criterion for deciding which offences should be subject to summary justice since 'not three-fourths of the criminal cases were, if they looked to the value of the articles stolen, worth the trouble of being brought into court'.[106] Palmer's suggestion was ignored in 1847 but eight years later the Lord Chancellor, Lord Cranworth, introduced a bill on this principle. The problem, as Cranworth saw it, was that the law was being dragged into disrepute by the spectacle of men, held in prison for a long time before assizes or quarter sessions came round, being prosecuted for trifling thefts; furthermore, both the accused's time in prison before trial, and the trial itself, cost a great deal of money. Again concerns were expressed about the impact that an increase in summary jurisdiction would have on 'that great safeguard of our liberties – trial by jury'. There was also worry that the proposed legislation would give new 'tyrannical' power to the police; and William Henry Watson, M.P. for Hull, a Q.C. and Bencher of Lincoln's Inn expressed the anxieties of his profession:

although we were much indebted to the magistracy for the zealous and conscientious manner in which they discharged their duties, the country could scarcely have confidence in them as competent persons to be intrusted with summary jurisdiction in criminal cases.[107]

The Criminal Justice Act nevertheless passed into law much to the consternation of those barristers who specialised in criminal cases and who feared for their fees.[108] The Act empowered two magistrates meeting in petty sessions to try cases of theft or embezzlement of goods to the value of less than five shillings when the accused was agreeable to a summary trial; they were empowered also to hear cases where the value of expropriated goods exceeded five shillings, but only when the accused entered a plea of guilty. The results of all such proceedings had to be recorded at quarter sessions.

The extension of cheap and speedy summary justice, while it did nothing to check the growing dominance of the police as prosecutors, appears to have led to an increase in the actual number of larcenies prosecuted and, at the same time, to a marked decline in the number of cases brought before quarter sessions.[109] In 1879 summary justice was extended further, but the fear for English liberties with the removal of trial by jury from yet more cases was no longer an issue. Opposition in 1879 centred on the fear that magistrates might be able to throw out cases on the grounds that, regardless of what the law said, they personally did not regard a particular offence as a crime; and once again the perquisites of the legal profession were brought up. Two Liberal Q.C.s feared that the extension of summary trial would lead to a dramatic reduction in the emoluments of clerks of the peace, by perhaps as much as £500 or £600 a year. In the Lords, however, Lord Aberdare praised the magistracy:

on the whole, considering that Justices of the Peace were qualified for their office more by social status than by legal knowledge, it was creditable to them that so few complaints were heard of their administration of the law.[110]

The 1879 Act raised from 5s. to £2 the value of goods, for the theft or embezzlement of which, offenders might be brought before the summary courts.

In 1857 the justices in petty sessions were estimated to be handling twenty times the number of cases dealt with by all the other criminal courts combined, and by the end of the century eighty per cent of indictable offences were being dealt with summarily.[111] The rise of the summary courts led to questions being posed about assizes and quarter sessions. Many of the county towns where these courts were held were fast being superseded in size and importance by the newer commercial and industrial centres. More important, however, the speed of summary jurisdiction highlighted the long waits often forced upon those whose cases were to come before assizes or quarter sessions; this waiting could mean many weeks in prison before trial for the accused. Various means were proposed and tried in order to remedy the problem. Some old assize towns had their court abolished, and a few new assizes were established. During the 1820s

Peel experimented with a third assize held in the winter in Essex, Kent, Hertfordshire, Surrey and Sussex.[112] The number of assizes was increased from two to three a year in the middle years of the century; then, in 1876–77, some counties were given a fourth assize. There was, however, insufficient business on either the criminal or the civil side of the assize courts to justify the increase and, in 1888, most counties had their assizes reduced to three a year. Some proposed that the problems of too little work for the assizes might be solved by handing over the bulk of the criminal work to quarter sessions; in 1857 quarter sessions were handling four times the criminal work of the assizes. The stumbling block to this proposal, at least as far as the legal profession was concerned, was that few magistrates were qualified in the law. They had the advice of their clerks, who were solicitors, in some instances they were bolstered by stipendiaries, who had legal training, or they might receive guidance from a recorder, who was a barrister, but there was no requirement that a magistrate, even the chairman of the bench at quarter sessions, should have any legal qualification. In the event no nineteenth-century government was prepared either to extend the powers of quarter sessions or to require legal qualifications for magistrates.[113]

The English system of criminal prosecutions and trials entered the twentieth century shot through with paradoxes that, interestingly, few contemporaries appear to have been aware of, or, at least, much concerned about. There was no formal system of state prosecution run by state officials; the prosecution of a criminal offender was still perceived as the right of any individual, although such prosecutions were increasingly being dominated by the professional police. Trial by jury continued to be trumpeted as one of the central pillars of English liberty and constitutionalism; yet, increasingly and overwhelmingly, criminal prosecutions were being brought before summary courts, which conducted their business without juries. Finally, while the legal profession was advancing and consolidating its monopoly in civil law and in the higher criminal courts, most criminal business was being handled before tribunals composed of lay magistrates.

Notes and references

1 **Douglas Hay**, 'Controlling the English prosecutor', *Osgoode Hall Law Journal*, **21** (1983), pp. 165–86 (at p. 167); **Clive Emsley**, 'An aspect of Pitt's "Terror": Prosecutions for sedition during the 1790s', *Social History*, **6** (1981), pp. 155–84; *idem*, 'Repression, "terror" and the rule of law in

England during the decade of the French Revolution,' *E.H.R.*, C (1985), pp. 801–25.

2 *Northampton Mercury*, 6 and 13 August 1753.

3 **George Rudé**, *Criminal and Victim: Crime and society in early nineteenth-century England*, Clarendon Press, Oxford, 1985, pp. 59–60. Rudé cites four examples; the first three (from *O.B.S.P. 1810, 1820* and *1830*) were instances of the victim being impeded in his pursuit of the offender; in the fourth instance (from 1840) the victim was helped.

   Rudé asks: 'does this denote a change in popular attitudes towards criminal and victim?' Obviously it will take far more than four examples to prove anything like this, and it should also be remembered that hue and cry had a long pedigree.

4 **Raphael Samuel** (ed.), *East End Underworld: Chapters in the life of Arthur Harding*, RKP, London, 1981, pp. 43–5.

5 **Peter Linebaugh**, 'The Tyburn riot against the surgeons', in **Douglas Hay, Peter Linebaugh** *et al.*, *Albion's Fatal Tree: Crime and society in eighteenth-century England*, Allen Lane, 1975, pp. 107–8.

6 *Huntingdon, Bedford and Cambridge Gazette*, 2 and 16 August 1817; Beds. R.O. QSR 23/1817/230–31.

7 *Huntingdon, Bedford and Cambridge Gazette*, 15 and 22 July 1815, 22 March 1817; Beds. R.O. QSR 23/1817/508.

8 H.O. 45.7323. My thanks to Professor John Bohstedt for this reference.

9 **David Jones**, *Crime in Nineteenth-Century Wales*, University of Wales Press, Cardiff, 1992, pp. 11–12; for an example of charivari or rough music in mid-nineteenth-century Liverpool see *Liverpool Mercury*, 12 November 1855, though the cause appears to have been sexual transgression rather than crime.

10 In June 1847, for example, Ann Wood, a widow of Edingley, Nottinghamshire, left her house in the care of one of her daughters. In the mother's absence a second daughter stole several articles of clothing together with some money and then ran off. She was eventually arrested in Derbyshire by a police constable. Notts. R.O. QSD/1847. See also **Jennifer Davis**, 'Prosecutions and their context. The use of the criminal law in late nineteenth-century London'. in **Douglas Hay** and **Francis Snyder** (eds), *Policing and Prosecution in Britain 1750–1850*, Oxford U.P., Oxford, 1989, pp. 415–16.

   This issue has been rarely noted with reference to England; research in France has shown that the law, the police and the infamous *lettre de cachet* were regularly used to discipline unruly children. See, *inter alia*, **Claude Quétel**, *De Par Le Roy: Essai sur les lettres de cachet*, Privat, Toulouse,

1981, pp. 137–40 and 146–8; **Arlette Farge** and **Michel Foucault,** *Le Désordre des Familles: Lettres de cachet des archives de la Bastille,* Gallimard Julliard, Paris, 1982, ch. 3.

11 Notts. R.O. QSM 1788–96; East Retford 10 October 1794 and 16 January 1795.

12 *O.B.S.P. 1796–97,* no. 43, p. 65.

13 Beds. R.O. PM 2629, Notebook of Francis Pym (1832–4); see also Beds. RO. QSR 1830/34.

14 **Jennifer Davis,** 'Law breaking and law enforcement: The creation of a criminal class in mid-Victorian London', unpublished Ph.D., Boston College, 1984, ch. 5 especially.

15 Notts. R.O. QSM 1761–67; Nottingham 13 January 1766.

16 Beds. R.O. PM 2629, Notebook of Pym.

17 Davis, 'Law breaking and law enforcement', pp. 307–10.

18 See below, pp. 225 and 229.

19 **John Styles,** 'Sir John Fielding and the problem of criminal investigation in eighteenth-century England', *T.R.H.S.,* 5th series, 33 (1983), pp. 127–50; *idem,* 'Print and policing: Crime advertising in eighteenth-century provincial England', in Hay and Snyder (eds), *Policing and Prosecution;* **Gwenda Morgan** and **Peter Rushton,** *Rogues, Thieves and the Rule of Law: The problem of law enforcement in north-east England, 1718–1800,* U.C.L. Press, London, 1998, p. 38.

In 1827 John Pilstow, a shopkeeper of Northampton, stopped at a Woburn Inn on his way to London. During the night he was robbed. He promptly had some handbills printed offering a £1 reward for the arrest of a suspect; the handbills led directly to an arrest two days after the robbery, in Leicester. Beds. R.O. 1827/295.

20 **Elizabeth Silverthorne** (ed.), *Deposition Book of Richard Wyatt J.P. 1767–76,* Surrey Records Society, vol. xxx (1978), nos 64–7; Beds. R.O. QSR 1830/495.

21 Wilts. R.O. Stourhead Archive, 383/955, Justice Book of R. C. Hoare 1785–1815, has several examples of warrants issued on suspicion, for example: '21 Feby [1795] Granted a Warrant on Information of Giles Jupe of Mere to search the houses of Edmund Williams, Thomas Herridge, Hugh Deverill, Edward Mills, John Miles and Edward Avery, for wood stolen from the coppice of Deverill Longwood.' Wood was found in the possession of Herridge and Mills, and acting summarily Hoare fined them both 10s.

For an example leading to a more serious charge see *O.B.S.P. 1800–01,* no. 99, for a warrant issued to Richard Jones, a soap and perfume manufacturer of Shoreditch, to search the lodgings of his former foreman whom he rightly suspected of pilfering large quantities of goods to set up in the trade on his own account.

22 Beds. R.O. 25/1822/610 contains a letter from a magistrate, the Reverend Orlebar Smith, suggesting that a certain Sinfield be indicted for felony. Sinfield had gone to Smith for a warrant accusing William Pilgrim of stealing his watch. He had then used the warrant to frighten Pilgrim into returning the watch and to paying Sinfield 30s. in compensation; the business completed to his satisfaction, Sinfield had then, illegally, destroyed the warrant.

23 Beds. R.O. QSR 17/1792/119.

24 Silverthorne (ed.), *Deposition Book of Richard Wyatt*, no. 207.

25 **Elizabeth Crittal** (ed.), *The Justicing Notebook of William Hunt 1744–49*, Wiltshire Record Society, xxxvii (1982), pp. 13–14.

26 **Alan F. Cirket** (ed.), *Samuel Whitbread's Notebooks, 1810–11, 1813–14,* Bedfordshire Historical Records Society, vol. 50 (1971), nos 210, 215, 224.

27 **P. B. Munsche,** *Gentlemen and Poachers: The English Game Laws 1671–1831,* Cambridge U.P., New York, 1981, p. 92. The apology inserted in the newspaper could be used in assault cases (e.g. Beds. R.O. QSR 16/1789/284), in seditious libel cases during the 1790s (Emsley, 'An aspect of Pitt's "Terror" ', pp. 159–60), and even in poaching cases (e.g. *Sussex Weekly Advertiser*, 11 June 1796).

28 **P. J. R. King,** *Crime, Justice and Discretion in England 1740–1820,* Oxford U.P., Oxford, 2000, p. 91.

29 Hay, 'Controlling the English prosecutor', p. 168; *idem*, 'Manufacturers and the criminal law in the later eighteenth century: Crime and "police" in South Staffordshire', *Past and Present Society Colloquium: Police and policing,* 1983, pp. 39–41.

30 Leeds City Archives, LC/QS 1/12, f. 132; and for similar examples see ibid. f. 126 (William Hartley), f. 175 (Thomas Brumfutt), and f. 176 (Jesse Holmes).
    This kind of downgrading the value of stolen property could also occur in the higher courts during trials. Catherine Hart was tried at the Old Bailey in December 1784 for stealing clothing from John Norfolk valued in total at £2.17s. according to the indictment. The judge asked the prosecutor what was their value noting that 'if they are above forty shillings . . . it will be a capital offence'. Norfolk then valued the goods at 30s., 'in order to save her life, because the wretch's life is no value to me'. *O.B.S.P. 1784–85,* no. 124, p. 174.

31 Hay, 'Controlling the English prosecutor', pp. 168–9; Emsley, 'An aspect of Pitt's "terror" ', p. 168; *idem*, 'Repression, "terror" and the rule of law', p. 819.

32 *P.P.* 1828 (533) vi, *Select Committee on Police of the Metropolis*, p. 83.

33 **Henry Fielding,** *An Enquiry into the Causes of the Late Increase of Robbers, with some Proposals for Remedying this Growing Evil*, 2nd edn, London, 1751, pp. 168–71.

34 **Peter King,** 'Prosecution associations and their impact in eighteenth-century Essex', and **David Philips,** 'Good men to associate and bad men to conspire: Associations for the prosecution of felons in England 1770–1860', both in Hay and Snyder (eds), *Policing and Prosecution*. See also **Adrian Shubert,** 'Private initiative in law enforcement: Associations for the prosecution of felons, 1744–1856', in **Victor Bailey** (ed.), *Policing and Punishment in Nineteenth-Century Britain*, Croom Helm, London, 1981.

35 Notts. R.O. WSM 1782–88; Nottingham 3 October 1785.

36 Leeds City Archives, LC/QS 1/12 f. 36 and see also ff. 82 and 88; King, *Crime, Justice and Discretion*, p. 49; **Janet Gyford,** ' "Men of bad character": Property crime in Essex in the 1820s', unpublished M.A., University of Essex, 1982, p. 22.

37 **Peter King,** 'Decision-makers and decision-making in the English criminal law, 1750–1800', *H.J.*, **27** (1984), pp. 26–58 (at p. 28). My own study of prosecutors at the Bedfordshire quarter sessions, based on the indictments and recognisances every five years 1750 to 1810 gives a similar breakdown:

Gentry (esquires, yeomen)	34
Professionals (clergy, schoolmasters etc.)	4
Farmers	10
Tradesmen and artisans	45
Husbandmen and gardeners	11
Labourers and servants	10
Total	114

38 *Hansard*, new series, xiv (1826), col. 1230.

39 Fielding, *Enquiry*, p. 164.

40 *P.P.* 1819 viii, *Select Committee on Criminal Laws*, p. 8.

41 Hay, 'Controlling the English prosecutor', p. 170.

42 H.O. 42/114/182–84, reply from Shadwell, 27 February 1811; H.O. 42/114/168–70, reply from Hatton Garden, 26 February 1811; H.O. 42/114/172–73, reply from Mr Fielding, Queen's Square, 26 February 1811. (The reply from the other two magistrates of Queen's Square is in H.O. 42/114/186–87, 27 February 1811; it is shorter, but not significantly different.)

43 U.C.L. Chadwick MSS 11 f. 35: T Division response to q. 14.

44 H.O. 42/114/151–56, reply from Worships St. 25 February 1811; *The Times*, 26 July 1847, for the case of the Reverend Ridley Bray.

45 See above, pp. 105–6.

46 Gyford, ' "Men of Bad Character" ', p. 15; U.C.L. Chadwick MSS 11 f. 38: D division response to q. 16.

   Committed 'evangelical' atheists during the Victorian period refused to swear oaths and therefore could not commence proceedings. G. J. Holyoake was prevented in this way from swearing a writ against the cab driver who, while drunk, ran over and mortally injured his son. (**F. B. Smith**, 'The atheist mission, 1840–1900', in **Robert Robinson** (ed.), *Ideas and Institutions of Victorian Britain*, Bell, London 1967, p. 233.)

47 U.C.L. Chadwick MSS 11 f. 36: responses of E and M divisions to q. 15; f. 38: responses of B and H divisions.

48 Fielding, *Enquiry*, p. 164; U.C.L. Chadwick MSS 11 f. 42: H division response to q. 18.

49 **John E. Archer**, *'By a flash and a scare.' Arson, Animal Maiming and Poaching in East Anglia, 1815–1870*, Clarendon Press, Oxford, 1990, pp. 145–7.

50 U.C.L. Chadwick MSS 11 ff. 50–1: G division response to q. 22, and see also ff. 47–8: responses to q. 21.

51 U.C.L. Chadwick MSS 11 f. 41: C division response to q. 17; there were similar responses from other divisions.

52 U.C.L. Chadwick MSS 11 f. 39: L division response to q. 16.

53 U.C.L. Chadwick MSS 11 f. 44: V division response to q. 19. As late as the 1880s, many of the same reasons were being given as deterring prosecutions in Wales, even in cases of arson. (Jones, 'Welsh and crime', p. 88 and note 22.)

54 *Hansard*, new series, xiv (1826), col. 1232.

55 Quoted in Hay, 'Controlling the English prosecutor', p. 176.

56 Hay, 'Controlling the English prosecutor', pp. 178–9, lists fourteen acts, excluding the Vexatious Indictments Act, passed between 1791 and 1888 that infringed the discretion of the private prosecutor.

57 Emsley, 'Aspect of Pitt's "terror" ', pp. 161–2; Gyford, ' "Men of Bad Character" ', pp. 18–19.

58 **Clive Emsley** and **Robert D. Storch**, 'Prosecution and the police in England since 1700', *Bulletin of the International Association for the History of Crime and Criminal Justice*, **18** (1993), pp. 45–57. See also **David Philips**, *Crime and Authority in Victorian England*, Croom Helm, London, 1977, pp. 101 and 123–4.

59 Charles Dickens, 'The ruffian', *The Uncommercial Traveller*, xx (1868), pp. 421–4; also *idem*, footnote to 'Stories for the first of April', *Household Words*, xv (1957), pp. 217–22.

60 *P.P. 1854–55 (481) xii, Select Committee on Public Prosecutors*, q. 2929.

61 See below, p. 238.

62 U.C.L. Chadwick MSS 11 f. 36.

63 H.O. 45.2742, Yarker to Grey, 6 September 1849; H.O. 48.41, Law Officers' Opinion, 7 November 1849.

64 In 1859, for example, of the ninety-two indictments brought before the Nottinghamshire quarter sessions, the police preferred only fourteen and a parish constable one. For the limited number of prosecutions by the police in London see Davis, 'Law breaking and law enforcement', p. 195.

65 *The Times*, 11 September 1856, for a letter from a Cornish attorney (following similar complaints from Devon and Yorkshire), critical of the paucity of costs allowed by Cornish magistrates and instancing a respectable tradesman who, in order to prosecute a serious case of felony, had to travel 50 miles and spend three nights in a hotel, for all of which he was allowed one guinea in expenses.

66 *Bedford Mercury*, 30 March 1844, quoting *The Globe*.

67 Emsley and Storch, 'Prosecution and the police', pp. 51–6.

68 In six of the twelve cases brought before the Bedfordshire Epiphany Sessions for 1832 the Chairman of the bench noted 'Defence says nothing'. Beds. R.O. PM 2629, Notebook of Pym.

69 For a general description of the plight of the accused in court see V. A. C. Gatrell, *The Hanging Tree: Execution and the English People, 1780–1868*, Clarendon Press, Oxford, 1994, pp. 537–8.

70 *O.B.S.P. 1796–97*, no. 302, p. 291; *C.C.C.S.P. 1856–57*, no. 600, pp. 58–9; see also Rudé, *Criminal and Victim*, pp. 58–9.

71 For the development of the legal profession see Brian Abel-Smith and Robert Stevens, *Lawyers and the Courts: A sociological study of the English legal system 1750–1965*, Heinemann, London, 1967, pp. 19–27.

72 *Bedford Mercury*, 23 March 1844.

73 *Hansard*, 3rd series, xvi (1833), cols 1202–3.

74 J. J. Tobias, *Crime and Industrial Society in the Nineteenth Century*, Penguin, Harmondsworth, 1972, p. 267.

75 Philips, *Crime and Authority*, pp. 104–5.

76 Graham Parker, 'The prisoner in the box – The making of the Criminal Evidence Act', in J. A. Guy and H. G. Beale (eds), *Law and Social Change in British History*, Royal Historical Society, London, 1984.

77 **A. H. Manchester**, *A Modern Legal History of England and Wales 1750–1950*, Butterworths, London, 1980, p. 100; Abel-Smith and Stevens, *Lawyers and the Courts*, pp. 32 and 135–6.

It is worth noting that a form of legal aid had existed for the accused in Scotland since the late Middle Ages.

78 **John H. Langbein**, *The Origins of Adversary Criminal Trial*, Oxford University Press, 2003, pp. 342–3.

79 **Martin Madan**, *Thoughts on Executive Justice*, London 1785, pp. 143–4; *Bedford Mercury*, 23 March 1844. See also Gatrell, *The Hanging Tree*, pp. 529–41.

80 *O.B.S.P. 1765–66*, no. 73, p. 55.

81 King, *Crime, Justice and Discretion*, p. 224.

82 For Blackstone and the eighteenth-century debate on summary jurisdiction see **Norma Landau**, *The Justices of the Peace 1679–1760*, University of California Press, Berkeley and Los Angeles, 1984, pp. 343–5; *London Chronicle*, 12 March 1772; *The Times*, 4 May 1829.

83 Munsche, *Gentlemen and Poachers*, chs 1 and 4 *passim*.

84 *Hansard*, new series, viii (1823), cols 1292–8.

85 Munsche, *Gentlemen and Poachers*, p. 162; while noting that game offenders were probably punished more severely, King found a far greater incidence of wood, fruit and vegetable theft brought before summary jurisdiction in eighteenth-century Essex (*Crime, Justice and Discretion*, pp. 99–103).

86 **John Styles**, 'Embezzlement, industry and the law in England 1500–1800', in **Maxine Berg, Pat Hudson** and **Michael Sonenscher** (eds), *Manufacture in Town and Country before the Factory*, Cambridge U.P., Cambridge, 1983, pp. 200–4.

87 **R. E. Swift**, 'Crime, law and order in two English towns during the early nineteenth century: The experience of Exeter and Wolverhampton 1815–56', unpublished Ph.D., University of Birmingham, 1981, pp. 329–30.

88 *Kent and Essex Mercury*, 27 January 1824, quoted in Gyford, ' "Men of Bad Character" ', p. 24.

89 Swift, 'Crime, law and order', pp. 125–6.

90 Landau, *Justices of the Peace*, pp. 356–8; Silverthorne (ed.), *Deposition Book of Richard Wyatt*, p. x and nos 108–10.

91 Francis Pym recorded stepping down from chairmanship of the Bedfordshire bench at the Midsummer Sessions in 1833 when Samuel Barnes was tried for a larceny in stealing wood from Pym's land. He also recorded 'verdict of *acquitted* on the ground that it was trespass and not a felony'. Beds. R.O. PM2629.

92 **P. C. Barrett**, 'Crime and punishment in a Lancashire industrial town: Law and social change in the borough of Wigan, 1800–50', unpublished M.Phil., Liverpool Polytechnic, 1980, pp. 84–6 and 88–98.

93 **Barry Godfrey**, 'Judicial impartiality and the use of criminal law against labour: The sentencing of workplace appropriators in Northern England, 1840–1880', *Crime, histoire et sociétés/Crime, history and societies*, 3 (1999) pp. 57–72 (at p. 66).

94 **D. C. Woods**, 'The operation of the Master and Servants Act in the Black Country 1858–75', *Midland History*, vii (1982), pp. 93–115.

95 **R. Quinault**, 'The Warwickshire country magistracy and public order, c. 1830–70', in **John Stevenson** and **Roland Quinault** (eds), *Popular Protest and Public Order: Six studies in British history, 1790–1820*, Allen and Unwin, London, 1974, pp. 189, 207.

96 **Olwen Hufton**, 'Crime in pre-industrial Europe', *Newsletter of the International Association for the History of Crime and Criminal Justice*, **4** (1981), p. 15.

97 Landau, *Justices of the Peace*, ch. 6.

98 *Illustrated London News*, 22 May 1847, p. 322. Charles Dickens gave a far less attractive picture with his portrayal of Mr Fang (based on the notorious Mr Laing of Hatton Garden) in *Oliver Twist*, ch. xi.

99 **Edward Carpenter**, *Prisons, Police and Punishment*, London, 1905, p. 70.

100 **Jennifer Davis**, ' "A poor man's system of justice": The London police courts in the second half of the nineteenth century', *H.J.*, **27** (1984), pp. 309–35: quotations at p. 315. See also *idem*, 'Law breaking and law enforcement', pp. 297–8.

101 **Clive Emsley**, *Policing and its Context 1750–1870*, Macmillan, London, 1983, pp. 22 and 47–8; Tobias, *Crime and Industrial Society*, p. 265.

102 *Hansard*, new series, xviii (1828), cols 166–7; *The Times*, 4 May 1829.

103 *Hansard*, 3rd series, lii (1840), col. 652.

104 *Bedford Mercury*, 11 February 1843.

105 *Hansard*, 3rd series, xc (1847), cols 430–8; and xcii (1847), col. 38.

106 *Hansard*, 3rd series, xcii (1847), col. 46.

107 *Hansard*, 3rd series, cxxxvi (1855), col. 1871; cxxxvii (1855), col. 1168; and cxxxix (1855), cols 1867, 2018.

108 Abel-Smith and Stevens, *Lawyers and the Courts*, p. 31.

109 Philips, *Crime and Authority*, pp. 132–4.
    Reference to the quarter sessions minute books of both Beds. and Notts. shows the dramatic decline in cases brought before these courts in the second half of the century. At the Epiphany Sessions in the middle years of the

century, for example, the counties were hearing, on average about twenty and between thirty and forty cases respectively; by the late 1890s these numbers had fallen, generally, to less than half a dozen in both instances. At the same time the number of cases heard summarily was soaring; at the Epiphany Sessions by the mid-1860s Beds. was recording around fifty and Notts. around 100 cases under the Criminal Justice Act, with another half dozen or so under the Juvenile Offenders Act. In addition they were also filing, respectively, around 150 and around 300 other summary convictions for assault, drink offences, malicious damage, game offences, highway offences, vagrancy, etc.

110 *Hansard*, 3rd series, ccxliii (1879), cols 1099 and 110–13; and ccxlvii (1879), col. 1703.

111 Abel-Smith and Stevens, *Lawyers and the Courts*, pp. 31–2; **David Bentley**, *English Criminal Justice in the Nineteenth Century*, London, Hambledon Press, 1998, p. 20.

112 *Hansard*, new series, vi (1822), col. 1320.

113 Abel-Smith and Stevens, *Lawyers and the Courts*, pp. 31–2.

CHAPTER 9

Detection and prevention: the old police and the new

The period 1750–1900 witnessed a marked increase in the number of professionals employed in England and Wales to combat crime. The old police system, generally dependent on part-time constables and watchmen, was being condemned as inadequate in the metropolis well before the close of the eighteenth century. The first manifestation of the new police was the 3,000 uniformed constables of the Metropolitan Police who began their beat patrols in London between September 1829 and May 1830. The Municipal Corporations Act 1835, in theory, spread the new police into provincial boroughs. The Rural Constabulary Act 1839 enabled counties, or parts of counties, to establish police forces. The County and Borough Police Act 1856 capped this legislation, making the new police obligatory for all local authorities. The arguments and assessments of the late eighteenth- and nineteenth-century police reformers were, generally speaking, accepted by historians of the English police well into the second half of the twentieth century. They insisted that the old system of policing was inefficient, that offenders tended to be caught more as a result of luck than anything else. The new system of uniformed beat policemen, in contrast, helped to prevent crime and made the arrest of offenders much more certain. Many of the Whig historians of the new police have tended to look back from an idealised contemporary model, to assume that there was no alternative and that this was the model the far-sighted reformers and politicians of the late eighteenth and nineteenth centuries had in mind. The new system of police thus fitted precisely with the requirements of society. Many of the recent critics of this 'Whig' view have also perceived a fit. They have emphasised the public order role of the new police development and the control requirements of capitalism.[1]

For most of the eighteenth century in England, as elsewhere in Europe, the word 'police' had the general meaning of the management and government of a particular piece of territory, particularly a town or city. In England the idea of a uniformed body of policemen patrolling the streets to prevent crime and disorder was anathema. Such a force smacked of the absolutism of continental states. The models for such police forces were to be found in the organisation commanded by the *lieutenant général de police* in Paris, and in the military police, the *maréchaussée*, which patrolled the main roads of provincial France. The fact that these models were French, in itself, was sufficient to make most eighteenth-century English gentlemen conceive of a police force as something inimical to English liberty. Policing in eighteenth-century England was perceived as a local government task, and like other areas of local government it depended upon local men being selected, or voluntarily coming forward, to serve in an official capacity, but generally for a limited period, part-time, and usually unpaid.[2]

The constables of eighteenth-century England were neither a preventive nor a detective police. The high constables of counties were often men of some social standing. These were selected in a variety of ways, depending on traditional local practice. They had a variety of tasks; the most important of which was supervision of the collection of the county rates. In respect of crime, they had an obligation to pursue any felonies reported to them, and this might involve primitive detective work as when, in 1818, John Shaw, high constable of the hundred of Redbornstoke in Bedfordshire found a footprint near the hiding place of some stolen wine and was subsequently able to fit a shoe to it.[3] The high constables had supervision of the petty constables. The latter were men of less social significance; again they were selected in a variety of ways depending upon local custom. Their tasks were many and varied, and they were allowed expenses and fees. The pursuit of offenders was often undertaken by victims, as described in the preceding chapter; but the constable was charged with making arrests. They were also required to serve warrants, to move offenders from place to place – either transporting a vagrant out of the parish, or taking an accused party to court; they might even have to accommodate offenders, temporarily, in their homes. Such tasks were burdensome; if a man had a trade, any time spent on constable's duties could cost him business. Occasionally the tasks brought threats of violence; Edward Wright, constable of the parish of Egham, Surrey, deposed:

When he served a summons on Samuel Smith younger of Chertsey who stands charged with getting a bastard child on the body of Ann Jacob,

Samuel Smith the elder swore that if ever he came to his house after his son he would do for him. Informant now has a warrant to apprehend Samuel Smith the younger which he is afraid to execute, Samuel Smith the elder having sworn that he would do him some bodily harm.

Hostility to constables in the execution of their duty did not always stop at verbal threats and abuse, as a glance at any eighteenth- or early nineteenth-century newspaper or run of quarter sessions indictments will show. In 1817 Constable Henry Thompson of Ruardean in Gloucestershire was shot dead by William Turner after he had arrested the latter's wife in possession of stolen wheat. A more typical example of violence towards constables occurred one Saturday evening in the late summer of 1827. Thomas Franklin, the constable of Leighton Buzzard, was called to a public house where a quarrel was leading to blows. William Smith, a butcher, who was to go to Franklin's aid, described what happened as he was walking past the pub:

I saw Thomas Franklin . . . coming out . . . backwards. John Brandon . . . was opposite and close to the constable. I saw the said John Brandon strike the said constable twice 'bang full in the face' the blows knocked the constable down on his back John Brandon fell down with him. Sarah Adams . . . got on top of the constable and jostled his head against the ground . . . The constable appeared very much hurt and his face was all over blood.[4]

Brandon and Adams were both indicted for assault. Yet some men were prepared to take on the post of constable full time; in return for an initial payment they agreed to act in place of the man selected and then sought to earn their living through the fees. There was nothing especially new in this; Elbow, the simple constable in Shakespeare's *Measure for Measure*, was described as acting in this way. Of course the fact that some men were prepared to take on the tasks of constable full time does not mean that they were, necessarily, any good at the job. Many parish constables probably were as bad and as uncommitted to their tasks as the police reformers made out. But others were competent and were relied upon;[5] a serious analysis of the men who fulfilled this role during the eighteenth and early nineteenth centuries is long overdue and it may well prompt a major revision of the traditional picture.

Preventive policing in eighteenth-century England was largely confined to urban areas where watches patrolled the streets after dark. Again for the Tudor period Shakespeare provided a comic example with the watchmen who act under the bumbling Dogberry and Verges in *Much Ado About Nothing*. The problem is that too often these fictional, comic characters have been taken as representatives of a reality spanning the period from the Tudors to the late Hanoverians because they fit so well with the police reformers' condemnations of the old system of policing.[6] In fact eighteenth- and early nineteenth-century watchmen have been subject to even less serious study than constables. It is, however, clear that at least in some metropolitan parishes there were determined attempts to ensure that the night watch was competent and capable a hundred years before the Metropolitan Police took to the streets.[7] Some watchmen were fully prepared to stop men on suspicion, and their suspicions could prove valid: one night towards the end of 1796 John Wilson was picked up on suspicion by two London watchmen; he was taken to the Hanover Square parish watch-house where he was searched by a constable and found to have five pewter pots concealed about his person; the pots had been taken from a pub in Carnaby Street and Wilson was subsequently tried and convicted at the Old Bailey. The evidence given in an Old Bailey burglary trial twenty years later suggests a watch system functioning in some parts of the metropolis which possessed men behaving in the active and observant way that, according to the Whig historians, was introduced only with the new Metropolitan Police:

On the night of the 12th December, I was calling four o'clock in the morning; I came by Mr. Levy's house, in Wentworth-street; I saw the prisoner standing in the court there; I did not know him before, I thought he might live in the court; I went up the court, and took particular notice of his dress, as I passed him; I went on, and returned again; I missed him; I went up the court, and saw Levy's side door was open, it is in the court; I returned to my box, and in a few minutes, the prisoner came by my box; I stepped out, and called to him, he stopped, and I crossed over to him, and asked him what he did at the house round the corner – he said 'what house', and seemed strange. I asked him, what he had got upon him, his pockets appeared full, and bulky – he said, 'nothing at all', and that he was a different character to what I took him to be . . . Levy's house is considered a receiving house. I have been on that beat fifteen months . . .

The watchman found stolen lace hidden in the prisoner's hat, and took him into custody.[8] The Select Committee enquiring into the police of the metropolis in 1828 heard largely complimentary comments on the watches in Marylebone, St James's, and St George's Hanover Square; the majority of these watchmen appear to have been ex-soldiers – 'stout tall fellows', according to the inspector in St James's, 'not exceeding forty years of age'.[9] This is not to argue that the watch was not in need of reform, but simply that the traditional image of the 'Charlie' as old, decrepit and, like as not, drunk or asleep when needed, is a generalisation not always borne out by the evidence.

Occasionally a provincial magistrate might be found who was interested in solving a crime and detecting offenders, and he could go to considerable trouble and expense in so doing.[10] But if a victim could not follow up an offence in person, with friends, or by advertisement, the only other recourse – apart from a visit in rural areas to the cunning man – was to a thief-taker. Until the establishment of a special group of thief-takers in the office of the Bow Street magistrates in the middle of the eighteenth century, the thief-takers were private individuals. They lived off the rewards from the courts for bringing offenders to justice,[11] and the rewards from victims who paid to get property returned. Both kinds of reward were liable to abuse. The reputation of the thief-takers is low primarily because of the notorious career of Jonathan Wild, the self-appointed 'Thief-taker General of Great Britain and Ireland', who was exposed, in 1725, as a leading receiver of stolen goods who kept himself in the thief-taking business by the occasional sacrifice of a thief on the gallows. The Stephen McDaniel affair, which blew up some thirty years later, was less far reaching, but re-emphasised the dangers of rewarding thief-takers by results when the result, as like as not, was an innocent body swinging from the gallows.[12] Not all pre-police thief-takers were like Wild and McDaniel, especially the semi-official detectives like Richard Green who combined his detective work with being keeper of the lock-up at Knott Hill, Manchester, and John and Daniel Forrester who worked in the City of London from 1817 to 1857.[13]

It was the metropolis that witnessed the major developments and the major proposals for police reform during the eighteenth century; both the square mile of the City of London proper, which had its own police system organised under the Lord Mayor and the City Marshals, and the sprawls of the City of Westminster, urban Middlesex and, south of the Thames, urban Surrey.[14] The best-known architects of these developments and proposals were the Fieldings, who established the group of paid thief-takers – the celebrated Runners – in the 1750s and who, after some abortive starts, organised paid patrols of part-time constables circulating the central thoroughfares and the main roads into the metropolis from evening until midnight. By the end of the century the Bow Street Patrol consisted of sixty-eight men divided into thirteen parties. Sir John Fielding drew up plans for a centralised police for London with five or six separate police offices under the overall supervision of Bow Street. This central office, he argued, could act as a clearing house for information about different crimes and different offenders; detailed information and descriptions, readily available to different peace officers, were regarded by the Fieldings as central in the 'war' against crime. Sir John's proposals for a systematised and centralised police in London came to nothing during his lifetime, but they influenced the abortive legislation of the 1780s and the Middlesex Justice Act 1792.

In 1772 and 1773 Sir John circulated the clerks of the peace of all the English and Welsh counties with his General Preventative Plan. His idea was to make the Bow Street Office a central clearing house for information about serious crimes and offenders encompassing the whole country; he wanted provincial magistrates to supply Bow Street with details of offenders and offences, gaolers to supply descriptions of those committed to their custody via the assizes calendars already received in his office, and both officials and members of the public to give descriptions of stolen horses. The proposal was well received and, from the autumn of 1773, with government backing to the tune of £400 per annum, this information was collected in Bow Street, collated, and circulated in the form of a newspaper, *The Hue and Cry*. The extent to which the circulation of information in this way improved the clear-up rate cannot be ascertained, for one thing there is no data on which to base a measurement of the situation beforehand, yet it does appear to have contributed to several arrests. But Fielding's subsequent proposals, circulated in February 1775, were scarcely responded to. These were far more radical, recommending what would have amounted to a system of paid professional policemen. Fielding wanted high constables to be resident on the main roads for at least one hundred miles' distance from London; they were to display a board announcing their office outside their home, they were to undertake the pursuit of offenders, and to be paid a salary for keeping a horse for these pursuits. In addition the numbers of petty constables were to be increased. The cool reaction to these proposals probably stemmed partly from a reluctance on the part of the county benches to reorganise the tasks of their constables, especially when high constables were men of some standing who would have baulked at being simply the pursuers of common felons. Probably also the magistrates could see little value in the proposals for their own localities; provincial England was not London with its urban sprawl and its apparently disproportionate amount of serious crime. Local constables could handle the vagrants on the roads; there were few highway robberies in the provinces and seemingly few fugitives moving along the roads from one district to another. What appeared of value from the centre of London to suppress the city's unique crime problem, had little value outside.[15]

Yet whatever the concerns of men like Fielding about crime in eighteenth-century London, the fear of a French system of police was greater. A bill brought before parliament in 1785 proposed dividing the entire metropolis into nine police divisions each with three stipendiary magistrates and twenty-five constables; it foundered partly on the fear that a system of regular police was alien to England, and partly because of the hostility of the City of London, which brought its powerful parliamentary lobby into play to protect its independent jurisdiction. When, seven years later, the Middlesex Justice Bill was introduced, the territory of the Lord Mayor and his Marshals was studiously omitted from the proposal. The legislation of 1792 established seven police offices, six north of the Thames – Queen's Square, Westminster; Great Marlborough Street; Hatton Garden, Shoreditch; Whitechapel; Shadwell – and one south of the river in Southwark. Each office had three stipendiary magistrates and six constables. Among the first of the magistrates was Colquhoun, who poured a steady stream of voluminous letters in miniscule writing in the direction of different offices of state; many of these letters urged various reforms and improvements.[16] Attempts to spread the system failed, probably because of expense, but in 1798 Colquhoun was instrumental in the creation of the Thames Police Office at Wapping with, ultimately, three stipendiaries and 100 constables to police the river. The system of stipendiary magistrates and their constables working alongside the Bow Street Patrol, and the various parish constables and watches (Table 9.1), with the City jealously guarding its separate jurisdiction, saw London into the new century. The stipendiary magistrates and some of their constables rapidly assumed the role of experts on crime to be consulted when ministers or parliament, pressurised by reformers like Romilly and Mackintosh or by events like the Ratcliffe Highway murders, mounted enquiries into aspects of crime and policing in London. In February 1811 a circular was sent to the police offices requesting the magistrates' opinions on whether the recent abolition of the death penalty for picking pockets had led to any change in the incidence of the crime, of prosecutions for the crime, or convictions.[17] Magistrates and constables became regular witnesses before parliamentary committees. Some of the constables, like George Ruthven and John Townsend of Bow Street, acquired formidable reputations as detectives and the apprehenders of offenders; the assistance of such Bow Street officers was

TABLE 9.1 *Watchmen, patrols, superintendents and beadles acting in the jurisdiction of the Police Magistrates, Union Hall, Southwark, 1 January 1812*

Parish or district	Population	Number of beadles/ superintendents	Number of watchmen	Number of 'patrols'	Total police
Christchurch, Southwark	11,050	1	23	—	24
St George, Southwark	27,967	1	17	2	20
St John, Southwark	8,370	1	14	—	15
St Olave, Southwark	7,917	1	16	—	17
St Thomas, Southwark	1,466†	—	2 (private watch)	—	2
St Saviour's Southwark	15,349	1	11	—	12
St Saviour's Clink Libery		2	—	14	16
Manor of Hatcham				Patrolled by Bow Street Patrol	
Bermondsey	19,530	1	13	—	14
Camberwell		1	16	3	20
Dulwich	11,309‡	—	2	1 (horseman paid by subscription)	3
Peckham		1	7	2	10
Clapham Town	5,083§	1	14	2	17
Clapham Road		—	10	2	12
Lambeth	41,644		Patrolled by Surrey Watch, some private watchmen, numbers unknown.		—
Newington	23,853	1	24	2	27
Rotherhithe	12,114	1	14	6	21
Streatham	2,729	1	2	6	9
Surrey Watch	—	1	42	2 (horsemen)	45

Source: Based on information in H.O. 42.114.29, and population statistics drawn from the 1811 census

The area of urban Surrey covered by the magistrates at Union Hall was the largest jurisdiction of the seven police offices established in 1792; from the centre in the borough of Southwark it ran about five miles south-west up the Thames to Clapham, four miles east downstream to Rotherhithe, and six miles due south to Streatham † Includes the 'population' of St Thomas's and Guy's Hospitals

‡ Population of the Parish of Camberwell, which included Dulwich and Peckham

§ Population of Clapham Parish

often sought by provincial authorities faced with a spate of robberies, a gang of poachers or a difficult murder. Yet the concerns about 'blood money' continued. Most of the constables had underworld informants known as 'noses',[18] and on occasions links with the underworld became rather too friendly. Even Bow Street officers were suspended and occasionally prosecuted for compounding, or conspiring, with offenders whom they subsequently brought before the courts on capital charges so as to claim the reward.[19]

The revelations of corruption, the scare created by the Ratcliffe Highway murders, the publication of statistics giving a public picture of crime, the reports of crowd behaviour in revolutionary Paris aggravating fearful recollections of the Gordon Riots, combined with the writings of men like Colquhoun to make gentlemen of property concerned about the policing of London. Yet parliamentary committee after parliamentary committee was reluctant to recommend a completely new police system; a centralised system still appeared inimical to English liberty, it was something peculiarly French, and under Napoleon the police system of the old enemy had achieved an authoritarian model of even more alarming proportions.

Early in 1822 Robert Peel took over as Home Secretary. He was determined to reform and revise the criminal code and he considered the establishment of a preventive police as integral to this. His involvement in the creation of the Police Preservation Force when Chief Secretary for Ireland during the preceding decade had convinced him of the utility of police reform, and he was assured that police were no threat to liberty as he and other liberal, reforming Tories perceived it. Peel's police reforms were centred on London and, initially, on the expanding Bow Street establishment; in 1805 a horse patrol had been established and in 1821 a dismounted night patrol. In the summer of 1822 Peel set up a force of twenty-four men as the Bow Street day patrol. Wearing a uniform of blue coat and red waistcoat – hence their nickname of 'redbreasts' – these men, mainly ex-soldiers, patrolled the main streets of the centre of the metropolis between 9 a.m. and 7 p.m. In 1828 Peel was successful in getting a new parliamentary enquiry into the police of London; he was equally successful in getting men appointed to the committee who shared some of his ideas. The committee recommended the creation of a centralised, uniformed, preventive police for London, and in the following year Peel skilfully guided the legislation establishing the Metropolitan Police through parliament; he carefully avoided a confrontation with the City by omitting the Lord Mayor's square mile from the jurisdiction of the new force.

The view of the Whig historians of the English police is that 1829 was the turning point: the new Metropolitan Police, by its example of checking crime and disorder, provided a model for the rest of the country, indeed, for the rest of the world. The reformers, from the Fieldings to Colquhoun, and on to Peel and the first two commissioners of the Metropolitan Police, Colonel Charles Rowan and Richard Mayne, thus became far-sighted men; those who opposed the reforms as un-English or who criticised the police as a military body, as 'gendarmes', thus became myopic, foolish, or worse. The creation of a police force of 3,000 uniformed men answerable directly to a minister of state was, indeed, something new and something possibly deserving the adjective 'revolutionary' in the English context. But the new police force, with its uniformed men and hierarchical structure, was not a logical extension of the developments originating with the Fieldings. Moreover, whether this police force provided, overnight, a new level of efficiency in the struggle against crime is debatable, and the point noted above with reference to provincial magistrates' reluctance to adopt Fielding's proposal in 1775, might also be raised in explanation of the opposition to police reform in the provinces over the next few decades: what relevance did this metropolitan model have for the rest of the country?

The police reform clauses of the Municipal Corporations Act 1835 appear to have been included, not so much from any recognised success of the metropolitan model, but because municipal policing had always been the preserve of local government, and if the entire system of municipal government was to be reformed and rationalised, then it was logical, indeed necessary, to include municipal policing. Some boroughs appear to have had disciplined and fairly efficient police systems at their disposal before the act,[20] what was singularly absent was any degree of uniformity. The act required boroughs to establish Watch Committees, which, in turn, were to appoint police forces. Yet while Watch Committees generally appear to have been set up fairly quickly, many boroughs were dilatory in fulfilling the statutory obligations relating to police forces; of the 178 boroughs mentioned in the 1835 act, only 100 could claim to have police forces by the beginning of 1838, and fifteen years later at least six still had no force.[21] In some boroughs the creation of police merely meant that various town functionaries like the sword bearer, the beadle, and the watch simply donned uniforms and began to be called policemen. The nine policemen of the borough of Bedford appointed in January 1836 included the mayor's sergeant, the bellman and the beadle; and the old system of one group of men to patrol by day and another by night was maintained

into the 1850s. The division of day and night police was similarly maintained in Exeter and Nottingham where the new police were also largely
recruited from the old.[22] In towns without charters local worthies had long
been developing police systems to their own needs. Some had their own
lighting and watching committees established through private acts of parliament. The Lighting and Watching Act passed by parliament in 1833
provided an umbrella under which urban districts could set up such committees without any special legislation. A private town act had enabled
Wolverhampton to establish a watch in 1814; a police force was established in the town in 1837, eleven years before incorporation. The
worthies of Wolverhampton recruited Richard Castle, a sergeant of the
Metropolitan Police, to command their new force; but half of the twelve-
man force were veterans of the watch.[23] In 1838 the leading residents of
Horncastle in Lincolnshire, with a population of just under 4,500, determined to establish a police force under the terms provided by the Lighting
and Watching Act 1833. They approached the commissioners of the
Metropolitan Police for a possible chief policeman, but were informed that
no member of that force would go to Horncastle for less than 30s. a week.
In the event they were lucky enough to find a local man who had served
in London and who was willing to act for 16s. a week. The new police of
Horncastle consisted of two men.[24]

This desire for men from the Metropolitan Police to command the new
borough forces has been interpreted as a desire to follow the London
model. Up to a point this may be true: the municipal authorities of early
nineteenth-century England wanted value for money; the Metropolitan
Police had acquired a reputation for efficiency and consequently a chief
policeman with experience of London policing was to be valued precisely
because of this experience. But the actual practices of policing did not
always owe much to a metropolitan model; the division between day
police and night police, which continued well into the 1850s in some areas,
was a legacy of traditional policing. The relationship between policemen
and the municipal authorities was also different. The Metropolitan Police
were responsible directly to the Home Secretary. This was a matter of concern and annoyance to metropolitan parishes during the early years of the
police, and the issue was raised again towards the end of the century; after
all, local ratepayers contributed directly, and significantly, to the force.[25]
Municipal ratepayers financed municipal police forces in nineteenth-
century England, and they had no intention of letting anybody give them
orders or instructions other than the municipality. Municipal governments,
through their watch committees, kept firm control of their policemen, and

the relationship was very much that of master and servant with the police-men occasionally required to perform tasks that would never have been required of any metropolitan police constable.[26] Again this reflected the continuation of 'pre-police' traditions and by no means the triumph of any new model.

Lord Grey's Whig government contemplated a bill for the creation of a national police system between October 1831 and June 1832. The discussions were prompted by the extraordinary tumults and fears created by the Reform Bill crisis and a succession of industrial disorders. The proposal lapsed as the unrest subsided; the government apparently concluded that the need was no longer as pressing, and that without obvious need it would be difficult to get such legislation through parliament because of possible constitutional fears and, above all perhaps, because of the cost of such a measure.[27] Four years later, however, in 1836, the Whigs turned their mind specifically to the policing of the counties, appointing the Royal Commission on a Rural Constabulary. Three men served as commissioners: Edwin Chadwick, Colonel Charles Rowan of the Metropolitan Police, and Charles Shaw Lefevre, an M.P. who had only recently served on the Royal Commission on County Rates. Chadwick was largely responsible for writing the report, but his Benthamite notions of centralisation and his desire for close links between rural police and the new poor law organisation were not shared by his fellow commissioners. Nevertheless, such aspects of centralisation as were recommended in the report, published in March 1839, provoked hostility and disquiet. Rowan was amazed and suggested to Chadwick that one way of avoiding the supposed:

danger to the liberties of the country would be to give the power absolutely *of dismissal to the magistrates. Thus if the Secretary of State should take it into his head to endeavour to enslave a whole country (which is not at all [illegible] likely, after paying 20 million to enfranchise the* niggers) *by sending six or seven additional Police Constables 'armed with a bare bodkin' into that county, the magistrates might, seeing the immency [sic] of the danger, immediately dismiss the said six dangerous individuals and thus frustrate the base attempt. It is impossible to maintain gravity on the subject.*

He concluded with a sentence prefiguring the thinking of Whig historians of the police 'What a pity it is that all men who are not Rogues should be fools'.[28]

Melbourne's government was too weak to push through parliament such a contentious reform as a national constabulary even if it had so wished. Moreover, it seems that the Home Secretary, Lord John Russell, and interested cabinet colleagues never contemplated anything other than permissive legislation with the new county forces firmly under local control. The Royal Commission's recommendation that the Treasury pay one-quarter of the cost of rural constabularies and that the Metropolitan Police train and appoint their members was not included in the Rural Constabulary Bill, which swept through parliament in the summer of 1839 alongside bills to establish police forces in Birmingham, Bolton and Manchester. Chartist activity provided the government with the opportunity for legislation, particularly in the case of the three urban police acts. The Rural Constabulary Act enabled any county that so wished to authorise the appropriate rate and to establish its own police force. Two crucial points in the origins and early workings of this legislation have been too little emphasised. First, the Royal Commission's investigations revealed that provincial England during the 1830s was not unpoliced, and that such policing as there was did not always depend upon the old constable system. In 1829 parliament had authorised the creation of a county police system in Cheshire. The Cheshire Police were not centralised under a single chief constable but were based on the hundred or petty sessional division; each hundred was supervised by a paid high constable who maintained close communication with the local magistrates. The system was amended slightly by act of parliament in 1852. Edwin Corbett, the vice-chairman of the Cheshire quarter sessions, informed the 1853 Select Committee on Police that he did 'not think it possible for any police force to work better than it does' and that the London Metropolitan Police was 'more completely organised than we should be able to establish in the rural districts'.[29] Elsewhere, sometimes established under the Lighting and Watching Act 1833, there were a variety of small, professional police forces functioning under local magistrates and/or local gentlemen. In some places they were financed out of a local rate, elsewhere by subscription. Second, the quarter sessions' debates over whether or not to implement the legislation in 1839 and 1840 did not divide simply into those who wanted a county force similar to that recommended by the Royal Commission but under the county bench, and those who wanted to maintain the old system. Some conservative backwoodsmen could be found to demand the preservation of the old parish system, but these were a minority. Some could also be found who condemned the idea of a uniformed constabulary as un-English. More concern, however, was expressed about cost. Some magistrates were uneasy about the power to raise new rates that the legislation gave them; unlike the borough magistrates, those in the counties were unelected and unrepresentative. There were others who felt that police reform was desirable, but they preferred smaller forces under immediate local control, rather than constabularies covering whole counties.[30] There is discrepancy in the figures, but of the fifty-four provincial counties in England and Wales (that is excluding Middlesex and dividing Yorkshire into its three constituent ridings) only two-thirds had established constabularies under the 1839 act by the mid-1850s, and in nine instances these 'county' forces were confined to one or two divisions or hundreds within the county.[31]

The forces established under the 1839 act were not based on any one simple model drawn from the London experience. Men who had served in new police forces were recruited by the counties, particularly for the more senior positions. But men were also recruited from the old police: Henry Goddard, the first chief constable of Northamptonshire, was a former Bow Street officer; two long-serving constables from the old police, William Craig from Stowbridge and James Kings from Bromsgrove, were appointed superintendents in the new Worcestershire Force.[32] Gloucestershire magistrates had employed Metropolitan Police officers for temporary emergencies during the 1830s, but when it came to establishing a county force in 1839, they turned to the Irish model; the first chief constable, Anthony Lefroy brought thirteen men with him from Ireland as a cadre for the 250-man Gloucestershire force. Other counties also looked to Ireland.[33] Like the borough police, the new county constabularies remained firmly under local control; but the relationship between the magistrates on the police committees and their police forces was not so obviously the master–servant relationship of most boroughs. The chief constables of the counties were, generally speaking, of more genteel origin than their borough counterparts. There was, in addition, a significant presence of military officers among them, and this presence increased as the century wore on: seven out of the twenty-three chief constables appointed to English counties before 1856 had army or naval experience; twenty-two out of the twenty-four appointed between 1856 and 1880 had such experience.[34] The perception of the police as a kind of soldiery informed much of the thinking behind the County and Borough Police Act 1856 and, both before and after this legislation, several chief constables were eager for their men to receive military training so that they might act as auxiliaries to the army in case of invasion. Many magistrates perceived their county constabularies as the first line of defence against an internal enemy, which, in cases of popular disorder, led to their being deployed in a military fashion.[35]

Those counties that did not take advantage of the 1839 act did not always leave their police systems unchanged. Some districts organised patrols under the Lighting and Watching Act 1833, some utilised the enabling legislation of the Parish Constables Act 1842. The latter reaffirmed the old system of local policing and selection of parish constables; it also authorised the recruitment of paid, superintending constables to oversee the parish constables of a petty sessional division. For many, including persons in those counties where rural constabularies had been established, the act was a godsend. It offered a policing system that was both cheaper and better suited to the needs of a rural society. In Nottinghamshire, for example, the quarter sessions received 224 petitions from different groups of ratepayers urging that the new constabulary be disbanded. Among these petitions was one from the parish of Harworth, which expresses clearly and fully the sentiments of the dissatisfied ratepayers:

The parish of Harworth has paid during the last year upwards of 21 .. 9 .. 2 pounds [sic] as their quota of the expenses incurred by the maintenance of [the County Constabulary], without discovering they have received any benefit whatever. And legislation has provided for a considerable increase of parish constables (men who know all the suspicious characters in the neighbourhood and who are specially interested in keeping a good lookout and in whom their neighbours can place implicit confidence) the Ratepayers and other Inhabitants of the Parish of Harworth respectfully request the Magistrates will take their case into their most serious consideration.[36]

In the event, none of the new constabularies was disbanded, though many were reduced in size, and the old parish constable system continued to be developed and refined. In 1850 amending legislation extended the provisions of the 1842 act and eventually the provisions were adopted by fourteen counties. The new lease of life injected into the old system was popular not only because it was cheaper than a full-blown county constabulary but also because it kept control of the police within the smaller, traditional units of parishes and petty sessional divisions.

Even the most thoughtful of the Whig historians of the police have written off the superintending constables as a failure, yet the evidence given to the 1853 Select Committee on Police suggests that in counties where they were established some were quite satisfied with the system. Lieutenant Colonel Henry Morgan Clifford M.P., chairman of the Herefordshire quarter sessions, insisted that they were 'quite sufficient; the diminution of crime is very great'. Sir Robert Sheffield, Bart., chairman of the quarter sessions for the parts of Lindsey, Lincolnshire, believed that the new system was working well; he was not sure what the long-term impact was going to be on crime, but 'certainly the county looks to the superintendents very much as protectors', and they had reduced the number of vagrants. Richard Healey, the Chief Constable of the Hundred of Aveland in the parts of Kesteven, Lincolnshire, was of the opinion that the creation of a rural constabulary would be very unpopular in his district: 'the farmers . . . and the ratepayers are exceedingly well satisfied with things as they are'. Maurice Sawbey, a former police magistrate, and a county magistrate for Buckinghamshire, Middlesex and Surrey, urged that a rural constabulary be established in Buckinghamshire, but he had to admit that the ratepayers did not complain about any threat to their property and seemed satisfied with the protection they received from the superintending constable system. William Hamilton, one of the superintending constables in Buckinghamshire and a veteran of sixteen years' service in the Royal Irish Constabulary and the Lancashire and the Essex constabularies, was highly critical of the superintending constable system, and particularly of the parish constables who served under him; David Smith, another veteran of the Essex force and a superintending constable in Oxfordshire was similarly critical. But George Carrington, a Buckinghamshire magistrate, was not surprised:

I think those men naturally wish for the discipline of a regular force; but that is their opinion, and I am only giving mine. The man who was examined from our county gave me a general idea, before he came to the Committee, what he was going to say; he came to me afterwards, and told me that he was asked whether he could say it was efficient; he said, he thought he could not say so. He has told me that some of the [parish] constables are efficient men, and ready to act with him; of course not so ready to act as men whom he might dismiss at a moment's notice. What he said was, 'I can lead them, but I cannot drive them'.

Carrington wished to see how the system developed in Buckinghamshire, but he felt that it would be perfectly adequate for the preservation of the peace and the protection of property.[37] The superintending constables, however, were swept away by the County and Borough Police Act 1856, which made the new, uniformed police obligatory.

The County and Borough Police Act stemmed from a variety of beliefs and concerns. Palmerston, briefly Home Secretary in 1852 and 1853, was convinced of the necessity for reform; he was apparently moved by the criticisms of the patchwork system of policing in the early 1850s, which prompted logical demands for uniformity and rationalisation. The Select Committee that he established, which met in 1853, lacked the reforming fervour of a Chadwick at the helm, but, nevertheless, stacked the evidence in favour of consolidation and a uniform system across the country. The desire for new legislation was also fostered by the belief that a reformed police would assume some kind of auxiliary military role; in addition there were fears brought about, first, by the virtual end of transportation, which threatened persons of property with having more 'habitual criminals' discharged from prison on to the highways and byways, and second, by the prospective demobilisation of brutalised soldiery from the Crimean campaign. Yet the legislation eventually steered through parliament by Palmerston's successor at the Home Office, Sir George Grey, was a compromise. The initial plans to amalgamate the smaller borough forces and five small county forces with their larger neighbours provoked an outcry and were dropped. The police forces of provincial England and Wales remained under local control, but the new legislation imposed some basic standards and uniformity, notably with the creation of a national system of supervision by the three Inspectors of Constabulary; there was also a greater degree of central government involvement with the different forces thanks to the Treasury's agreement to pay one-quarter the cost of pay and clothing for forces declared 'efficient' by the inspectors. Twenty years later the grant was increased to one-half and greater pressure was put on the smaller boroughs to amalgamate with their surrounding county force.

In spite of the urgings of reformers and chief constables, notably Admiral MacHardy, the Chief Constable of Essex, the police were not trained as military auxiliaries. Their tasks, however, were many and varied. The continuing 'servant' role of many borough policemen led to them acting as collectors of market tolls, poor law relieving officers, and the local fire brigade. Emergencies stretched manpower; following disorders and an alleged spate of pickpocketing in the summer of 1867, the Home Secretary lamented to the Commons that some 300–400 members of the Metropolitan Police were having to be employed to keep cattle plague out of the city.[38] The Metropolitan Police, county forces and the largest urban forces were often called upon as riot squads to assist outside their districts; the smaller borough forces were too small to cope with large crowds. But the maintenance of public order did not just mean riot control; from their creation the new police were employed to clamp down on those working-class leisure activities that offended middle-class sensibility.[39] Order, in its broadest sense, also meant keeping the traffic moving and keeping the streets tidy and safe: in October 1841 the Bedford Watch Committee expressed its concern to the Chief Constable about harrows, ploughs and other articles exposed for sale on Market Hill, and left there after dark when they became a danger to pedestrians. In Manchester during the 1890s the Watch Committee and Chief Constable were vexed by the traffic problems ranging from ice-cream stalls to 'scorching' cyclists, and to schoolchildren throwing fireworks near horses on the run-up to Guy Fawkes' Day.[40]

Yet in spite of this variety of tasks, crime was perceived as the key *raison d'être* for the new police. The Fieldings, Colquhoun and Peel had all argued that a preventive police was essential in the struggle to combat crime in the metropolis. The *New Police Instructions* published in September 1829 announced: 'It should be understood at the outset, that the object to be attained is "the prevention of crime".'[41] It was crime – its amount and its seriousness – rather than any of the other tasks that subsequently fell to policemen, which dominated the debates in quarter sessions over whether or not to establish a constabulary during 1839 and 1840. Once formed, the county forces had their preventive role emphasised in the instructions drafted by chief constables: Lefroy in Gloucestershire used, word for word, the London formulation quoted above; Gilbert Hogg, in Staffordshire, informed his men that: 'It should be understood that the principal object to be attained is the *prevention of crime*.'[42] The reformers had great hopes of prevention; the regular patrols of the police constable, the impersonal agent of the law, would, it was hoped, deter potential malefactors. So confident of success was Sir Richard Mayne, Rowan's fellow commissioner, that in 1834 he suggested to a parliamentary committee the possibility of reducing the number of police in London in one or two years when 'the present race of thieves, who may be called the schoolmasters, are sent abroad, as we hope they soon will be, and the rising generation will become better'. Almost forty years later the Chief Constable of Chester boasted that, in just under a decade, he had successfully removed from his district the forty-seven known thieves and depredators:

There is, I am afraid, a widely spread feeling that, as there always have been criminals in society, so there always must be. I am not entirely of that opinion. Given the power, I really see no great difficulty, if not in stamping out professional criminals, at least in reducing their numbers very materially, especially in a comparatively small place such as Chester.[43]

It is difficult to measure the effectiveness of prevention. Whig historians of the police, like the police reformers, lauded the new system and asserted its success. But contemporary newspapers often carried complaints that the police were not around when they were needed either to prevent crime or to help victims seize offenders. One night in April 1844 William Radley Mott had his pocket picked in Brighton and the *Brighton Gazette* reported that 'he searched the town from Steyne to Ship Street without being able to find a single policeman to take the rascal into custody'. Twenty-four years later, worthies of the East End of London were protesting that metropolitan policemen were spending too much time warning children not to play with their hoops in the street and protecting the wealthy of the West End. According to the *East London Observer*: 'In the leading thoroughfares outrages of all kinds are perpetrated – frequently in broad daylight – and to look for a policeman is out of the question.' 'Where are the Police?' demanded *The Times* after a warehouse robbery in High Holborn in 1875 that must have taken the perpetrators two or three hours. On the other hand, some petty offenders were foolish enough to attempt crimes under the eyes of watchful, uniformed policemen – like John Mason and Richard Kidd who, in November 1836, tried to pick a pocket in Blackfriars in full view of P.C. Charles Goff; and some street robberies were committed within calling distance of the beat policeman who was able to assist the victim and catch an offender – as when P.C. William Cottle caught James Adams running away after the attack on a merchant seaman in Shadwell in April 1857.[44] The more critical and thoughtful among the historians of crime and policing have suggested that the new police contributed to the statistical decline of theft and violence in the second half of the nineteenth century.[45] It seems reasonable to acknowledge that the physical presence of the uniformed policeman on the streets did deter some petty theft from shops, stalls or individuals. But empirical evidence of the situation with and without police is impossible to come by. The proposal of a Bedfordshire magistrate in 1844 to remove the county force from two divisions of the county and to measure the result, was rejected by his fellows on the county bench; contemporary experiments and research suggests that the removal of police patrols makes little difference to the level of reported crime yet it is probably equally true to say that policing does have some impact in keeping crime to a certain baseline level.[46]

A police constable could not report to his superiors and, at the top of the hierarchy, a chief constable could not report to his Watch Committee or County Police Committee, that their activities had prevented a particular number of crimes over a given period. The new police could demonstrate their worth, however, by publishing the statistics of arrests. The easiest arrests to make, except where there was a positive identification of a thief or of a violent offender, were those for petty public order offences. Such offences as begging, drunk and disorderly, drunk and incapable, illegal street selling, and soliciting, were generally committed in the street and were often readily observable by the beat policeman. Moreover, the removal of the drunk, the nomadic street seller, the prostitute or the vagrant was popular with respectable Victorians, who perceived these individuals as members of the dangerous or criminal classes. The creation of new police forces saw an increase in the statistics for these offences.

Yet if success could be claimed for the new police in dealing with some of the behaviour of the criminal class, there were crimes about which a uniformed constable patrolling an urban or a rural beat could do little. After all, individual beats could be large: in London, in 1870, the average daytime beat was seven-and-a-half miles, the average night-time beat was about two miles;[47] in rural districts beats could be very much larger and villages without a resident constable might rarely see one. Major crimes in urban areas often, if not generally, took place behind closed doors and closed windows. If, for example, burglars could observe a police constable pass on his beat and then enter a property, especially when the householder or factory owner was away, then there was little that the police could do other than record the offence when reported, and then seek to detect the offenders. Following the conviction of several burglars in London early in 1865, the Commissioner of the City of London Force urged businessmen and property owners not to leave external fastenings unsecured, to replace those that were defective and not to leave 'shops and warehouses stored with goods of great value entirely unattended at night, and throughout the whole of Sunday'. *The Times* quoted him as emphasising that a policeman's beat:

was on the street. They were bound to see that no house was broken into, but they could not guard equally against operations conducted by thieves left snugly locked up in houses by their occupiers, and indulged with six-and-thirty hours of licence.[48]

Other senior policemen were sometimes quite candid about the difficulties of catching determined thieves while patrolling in uniform on the beat. A year before one select committee heard Mayne look forward to a reduction in police numbers, another committee heard one of his superintendents report that '[a] man in uniform will hardly ever take a thief'. Indeed Rowan and Mayne confessed to the committee that they were informed that most felons were arrested by men in plain clothes; and according to the Earl of Chichester, Rowan was later to suggest that the beat system could not really work in the countryside: 'a rural police was rather to prevent crime by detecting offenders rather than to prevent it by their actual presence in every village'. Edwin Corbett, lauding the Cheshire system of police before the 1853 Select Committee stated:

There is one objection, I think, to the Rural Police Act, namely, that the policemen should be in uniform. It may be very useful in towns, where there a great number of police always parading about [sic], but in the country where they are only moving about the country, and particularly when they have an object in view, they should pass unobserved, which at other times they would not. I know several instances in which constables have gone to watch at night, when a burglary has been suspected, and where they have been successful in apprehending the burglars; if two or three policemen had been found coming to a given point, there would have been an alarm raised, but a man in coloured clothes could come without exciting any observation.[49]

Both Rowan and Mayne were reluctant to employ their men in plain clothes, and not simply because of their faith in uniformed, preventive patrols. There was concern that the new police should not be reminiscent of a 'Continental Spy system', and the recollection of the spies and secret agents employed against English Jacobins and Regency Radicals remained painful. For the first decade of their existence the Metropolitan Police functioned side by side with the old London Police Offices, each with its complement of plain-clothes constables; indeed, some men left the Metropolitan Police to take up the better paid position of constable under the stipendiary magistrates.[50] The policing tasks of the stipendiaries' offices, together with their constables, were abolished in 1839. Three years later, with some reluctance, Rowan and Mayne were forced to admit the need for, and to appoint, a small group of full-time detectives. Concerns about European spy systems, together with fears that men in plain clothes were much more susceptible to corruption, meant that this body was increased only slowly over the next twenty-five years – from eight men to fifteen. Even those who praised the old police office constables to the detriment of the new police could unwittingly indicate dangers inherent in the detective system. W. H. Watts, for example, argued during the 1860s that the new police had been singularly unsuccessful against burglars and robbers, and while the developing detective system was an improvement on uniformed constables periodically adopting disguises, it remained inferior:

One reason is, that the old officers were generally of a better class, had more general experience, possessed larger funds, and were permitted a wider field of action, being sure to have the protection of their own magistrates if, in the capturing or ferreting out of offenders, they over-stepped those strict limits which it might be conceived were proper for a police officer to observe.[51]

Following hard on the failure of the Metropolitan Police in intelligence gathering during the Fenian outrages of 1867, full-time divisional detectives were established in 1869. Nine years later, after the exposure of four detective inspectors for involvement in an international swindling racket, the divisional detectives were centralised into the Criminal Investigation Department under a young former army officer and barrister, Howard Vincent, who brought himself to government notice with a report on the detectives of the Paris Police. By the mid-1880s Vincent's department had grown from 250 to 800 men.[52]

The *modus operandi* of the new detectives, indeed of the new police in general, when it came to investigating offences and pursuing offenders, does not appear to have been greatly different from the more conscientious and determined of their predecessors. Policemen in plain clothes watched and followed suspicious characters, sometimes with reward as when constables George Legge and Samuel Evans followed two young men who were gazing into jewellers' shops in Cheapside; the suspects 'watched the [uniformed] policeman on the beat away', and then attempted a smash-and-grab raid.[53] Policemen in uniform on their beats stopped suspicious characters, as the best of the old watchmen had done, again sometimes with success;[54] and until the developments of fingerprinting and forensic science, detection still often simply involved matching a suspect's shoes to footprints at the scene of the crime, perhaps with the occasional refinement of digging such footprints up, preserving them between boards and presenting them in court as evidence.[55] The telegraphic communications, photographic records of offenders and centralised record keeping, all of which were utilised and developed by the new police, can be seen as technical aids to the kind of information gathering, circulation and storage urged by Sir John Fielding. Finally, the occasional revelations of both uniformed and detective policemen profiting from links with a criminal underworld demonstrate that the new police did not sweep away all the abuses of the old.[56]

The uniformed police constable received only a modicum of training – much of it military-style drill – before being put on his beat. Few of the early recruits seem to have conceived of the police as a career; many appear to have volunteered to tide themselves over a period of unemployment. Of course some stayed in the police, sometimes transferring to different forces to gain promotion, and some prospered. But while the pay may have been regular, unlike the pay in many working-class occupations, it was not high. Moreover, there were niggling restrictions on the constables' ability to make money on the side. A constable in Northamptonshire protested to a local M.P. in 1880 that his pay was less than that of a farm labourer; in addition there was:

the ban on police keeping dogs, fowls, or more than two pigs, neither of which must be a brood sow. To supplement the family income I am not permitted to take in a lodger; nor can I sell the produce from my garden . . .

Others protested that, unlike the wife of a rural worker, the country policeman's wife was forbidden to keep a cow, and unlike the wife of an urban worker, the urban policeman's wife could not run a small shop.[57] Even if a man were eligible, before 1887 policemen were denied the vote for fear of political partiality.[58] The constables worked long hours in all weathers; chest and rheumatic complaints accounted for more than one-quarter of the men pensioned for disability from the Metropolitan Police between 1840 and 1860.[59] Discipline was harsh and enforced by fine, demotion or dismissal. These conditions and regulations led to an enormous turnover of manpower. They also provoked dissatisfaction leading to petitions and strikes within some forces.[60] The complaints found a national focus in the *Police Service Advertiser*, first published in February 1866, which urged improvements in pay, conditions and pensions. 'Probably', it lamented, 'no public servant is so ill-used by his employer as the policeman'.[61]

The *Police Service Advertiser* helped to develop the idea of the ordinary policeman as a professional, yet the idea of police as professionals and, consequently, as experts in the war against crime was fostered early on by the demands of the government and the legislature. Like the magistrates and constables from the London Police Offices, senior officers, first from the Metropolitan Police and then from other forces, were called upon to give evidence to committees and commissions. As noted earlier, the Royal Commission on a Rural Constabulary received and published lists of known criminals prepared by local forces, and from 1857 all forces were required to prepare such details for the annual Judicial Statistics; the definition of known criminals was left to the discretion of the individual police forces. This requirement fed upon itself to reinforce the perception among policemen, their political masters and commentators on criminality, that a criminal class existed. At the same time the labelling of individuals as criminals, and of the districts in which they lived as criminal, could become self-fulfilling by propelling first-time offenders into further crime since they were now stigmatised, and by urging any 'respectable' families to do their best to move out of a stigmatised neighbourhood. Labelling as a 'criminal' might not even have occurred as the result of an initial offence. Gilbert Hogg advised his men that arrest on suspicion was one means of ensuring the principal object – prevention; the constable could, therefore, arrest an individual:

whom, from his situation and character, the law judges to be likely to commit some felony, and whom [the constable] has just cause to suspect is about to do so . . . Though no charge be made, yet if the constable suspect a person to have committed a felony, he should arrest him; and if he have reasonable grounds, founded on fact, for his suspicion, he will be justified, even though it should afterwards appear that no felony was committed.[62]

Woolly directives of this sort were open to abuse, and not always deliberately, given that the constable on the beat had so little training. Occasionally constables were criticised by magistrates and the objects of their suspicion were promptly released, but this was not always the case. Two men were arrested and charged with the garrotte robbery of James Pilkington M.P. The police had no direct evidence against them other than information that they claim to have received, but the accused, both ex-ticket-of-leave holders, were sentenced to three months' imprisonment each as suspicious characters.[63] Perhaps the labelling process only affected a minority of offenders in the nineteenth century, turning but a few into recidivists or 'professional' criminals, but it gradually enhanced the professionalism of the police by giving them an identifiable enemy to observe, catalogue and, when appropriate, to arrest for the good of society.

Rowan put it to a select committee that 'we look upon it that we are watching St James's and other places while we are watching St Giles and bad places in general'.[64] It was in these 'bad places' among the poorer working class that persons were to be found indulging in the boisterous popular culture that so offended Victorian sensibilities and which the police were directed to control. In the same places, and from the same groups, were to be found the street traders who were 'moved on', the men on the tramp and the seasonal workers suspected of being criminals simply because they were on the roads; Chadwick, and several other witnesses to the Select Committee of 1853 urged the value of a centralised, uniformed constabulary for bringing about a significant decline in vagrancy – 'a great source of crime . . . they begin by being vagrants, and they end by becoming thieves'.[65] It was from among these groups in general that, it appears, the police found 'suspicious persons'; and in garrison towns from the mid-1860s to the mid-1880s it was young women from the working class who were stopped and questioned on suspicion of being prostitutes under the Contagious Diseases Acts. The new police might also be felt as a pressure by members of the working class who broke their contracts and thus, under the provision of the master and servant legislation, were subject to criminal prosecution, as well as by workers taking strike action who sought to dissuade police-protected 'blacklegs' from working. Yet the new police were not simply a pressure on the working class. Police constables knocked men up in the morning to enable them to get to work on time or to be first in the queue for the distribution of casual work. They could be called in or used as a potential threat against an obstreperous neighbour, even in a notoriously 'criminal' quarter like Jennings Buildings in Kensington. When all else had failed a distraught parent might summon a constable to deal with a difficult child; thus in March 1871 P.C. Alexander Hennessy of the Metropolitan Police was called upon to arrest Catherine Driscol, aged 14$\frac{1}{2}$, charged by her mother with stealing clothing.[66] Lost children were also reported to, and found by, the new police; indeed some children from the poorer districts may deliberately have got themselves lost, or been encouraged so to do by their parents, since they enjoyed a period of play with a few toys and bread and jam supplied in the police station.[67] Moreover, the working class were as much, if not more, the victims of theft and they could, and did, use the police in precisely the same way that middle-class victims did. Assisting in the domestication and disciplining of the working class may have been one role imposed upon the police – both old and new – but it must not be forgotten, first, that many radical working-class activists were sympathetic to such domestication and discipline, and second, that the system of beat policing, which was central to the new police, was designed for the prevention of crime – and what men understood by crime was essentially theft and, to a lesser extent, assault.

Notes and references

1 Among the most significant of the Whig police histories are **Charles Reith,** *The Police Idea*, Oxford U.P., Oxford, 1938; *British Police and the Democratic Ideal*, Oxford U.P., Oxford, 1943; **Sir Leon Radzinowicz,** *A History of English Criminal Law*, 5 vols, Stevens, London, 1948–69; **T. A. Critchley,** *A History of Police in England and Wales*, 2nd edn, Constable, London, 1978.

Critics of the Whig interpretation include most notably **Allan Silver,**
'The demand for order in civil society', in **D. J. Bordua** (ed.), *The Police:*
Six sociological essays, Wiley, New York, 1967; **Robert D. Storch,** 'The
policeman as domestic missionary: Urban discipline and popular culture
in Northern England, 1850–80', *Journal of Social History* (summer 1976),
pp. 481–509; 'The plague of blue locusts: Police reform and popular resistance
in Northern England, 1840–57', *International Review of Social History*, xx
(1975), pp. 61–90.

The most recent interpretations that address the Whig/revisionist debate
are **Clive Emsley,** *The English Police: A political and social history*, 2nd edn,
Longman, London, 1996, and **David Taylor,** *The New Police in Nineteenth-*
Century England. Crime, conflict and control, Manchester U.P., Manchester,
1997.

2 For the contrast with France see **Clive Emsley,** *Policing and its Context*
1750–1870, Macmillan, London, 1983, ch. 2 *passim*.

3 Beds. R.O. QSR 23/299; for a similar 'detection' by the Constable of Ampthill
see ibid, QSR 1827/316.

4 **Elizabeth Silverthorne** (ed.), *The Deposition Book of Richard Wyatt J. P.*
1767–76, Surrey Records Society, vol. xxx, 1978, no. 154, 10 March 1772;
Bryan Jerrard, 'Early policing methods in Gloucestershire', *Transactions of*
the Bristol and Gloucestershire Archaeological Society, c (1982), pp. 221–40
(at p. 227): Beds. R.O. QSR 1827/338.

5 In August 1838, for example, when Henry Towlson a cordwainer of
Mansfield was robbed of a silk handkerchief he went to Thomas Meltham the
local constable. Meltham set off in pursuit of two suspects: 'I traced (them)
on the Worksop Road and at last found them in a house at Mansfield
Woodhouse. I immediately charged them with the robbery and on searching
them I found the handkerchief . . . in the prisoner Dennington's hat'. Notts.
R.O. QSD 1838, deposition of Meltham, 8 August 1838.

6 Emsley, *English Police*, pp. 10–13. The point generally ignored in Whig police
history about Dogberry, Verges and their watchmen is that they do catch the
villains.

7 **Elaine A. Reynolds,** *Before the Bobbies: The night watch and police reform in*
Metropolitan London, 1720–1830, Macmillan, London, 1998.

8 *O.B.S.P. 1796–97*, no. 43, p. 65. Patrick McCarty (apparently a watchman,
though this is not stated) was less fortunate than the men who detained
Wilson when, a few months after their success, he stopped William Gore who
had 37 lbs of lead in his possession. Gore was indicted but was acquitted at
the Old Bailey as no-one knew to whom the lead belonged. Ibid, no. 166,
p. 244. *O.B.S.P. 1816–17*, no. 224, pp. 94–5.

9 *P.P. 1828 (533), vi, Police of the Metropolis*, pp. 25–6, 60, 92–3, 123–4, 126.

10 One of the best examples is John Hewitt, a magistrate based in Coventry who corresponded with officials as far apart as London and Newcastle in his pursuit of a criminal gang. See **Gwenda Morgan** and **Peter Rushton**, *Rogues, Thieves and the Rule of Law. The problem of law enforcement in north-east England 1718–1800*, U.C.L. Press, London, 1998, pp. 43–4 and 89–90.

11 An act of 1692 was the first significant reward statute promising £40 to anyone apprehending and successfully prosecuting a highwayman. This was followed over the next half-century by a series of statutes promising similar financial reward or, sometimes, 'Tyburn Tickets', which exempted their holders from parish or ward office. See **John H. Langbein**, 'Shaping the eighteenth-century criminal trial: A view from the Ryder sources', *University of Chicago Law Review*, 50 (1983), pp. 1–136; (at pp. 106–10); Radzinowicz, *Criminal Law*, ii, 155–61 especially.

12 **Gerald Howson**, *Thief-Taker General: The rise and fall of Jonathan Wild*, Hutchinson, London, 1970; **Ruth Paley**, 'Thief-takers in London in the age of the McDaniel gang, c. 1745–1754,' in **Douglas Hay** and **Francis Snyder** (eds), *Policing and Prosecution in Britain, 1750–1850*, Oxford U.P., Oxford, 1989.

13 **J. J. Tobias**, *Crime and Police in England 1700–1900*, Gill and Macmillan, Dublin, 1979, pp. 54–6; *idem, Prince of Fences: The life and times of Ikey Solomons*, Valentine Mitchell, London, 1974, p. 31.

14 Reynolds, *Before the Bobbies*; **J. M. Beattie**, *Policing and Punishment in London, 1660–1750: Urban crime and the limits of terror*, Oxford U.P., Oxford, 2001; **Andrew T. Harris**, *Crime and Legal Authority in London c.1780–1840*, Ohio State U.P., Columbus, Ohio, 2004.

15 **John Styles**, 'Sir John Fielding and the problem of criminal investigation in eighteenth-century England', *T.R.H.S.*, 5th series, **33** (1983), pp. 127–49.

16 Radzinowicz, *Criminal Law*, has references to Colquhoun's letters in the Home Office files. The abortive London Police Bill 1786 was taken over and modified by the Irish Law Officers and, as a result, professional magistrates and police were established in Dublin in 1786. Six years later, as the new London stipendiaries were being appointed, a campaign against the Dublin Police was gaining momentum. The Dublin Police system was condemned as expensive and inefficient, and the policemen themselves were criticised as brutal and oppressive. In 1795 the system was dismantled and magistrates elected by the Lord Mayor and the Corporation replaced the stipendiaries. See **Stanley H. Palmer**, *Police and Protest in England and Ireland, 1780–1850*, Cambridge U.P. Cambridge, 1988, chs 3ii and 4ii *passim*. Policing in Edinburgh developed under a series of acts of parliament establishing lighting and watching commissioners. By the early nineteenth century the Edinburgh Police – one superintendent, or captain-lieutenant, three lieutenants, a sergeant-major, two dozen sergeants and about two hundred watchmen – seem closer to a Parisian-style police than anything English. The lieutenants,

for example, took turns at supervising night duty and had strict instructions on daytime tasks, which began before breakfast with the supervision of scavengers, and involved checking streets and lanes, inspecting pavements, removing 'nuisances', ordering repairs to unsafe structures, and visiting lodging houses on the look-out for suspicious characters. (See Edinburgh R.O., Minute Book of Watching Committee, March 1820 to February 1827, ff. 25–32.) When the force was reorganised in 1843, however, William Haining, the Superintendent, applied to the Commissioners of the Metropolitan Police for a man to serve as one of the Lieutenants and to assist in the reorganisation. W. F. N. Smith, from the Greenwich Division, subsequently moved to Edinburgh (Edinburgh R.O., Minute Book of Watching Committee, April 1839 to June 1844, ff. 172–3). There is no detailed modern study of how what appears by 1900 to be a largely English model of police came to predominate in Scotland.

17 H.O. 42. 114.

18 **W. H. Watts**, 'Records of an old police court', *St James's Magazine*, x (1864), pp. 353–60 and 458–65 (at p. 463); xi (1864), pp. 444–52; xii (1865), pp. 232–41 and 499–506.

19 See e.g. *The Times*, 23 and 25 September 1816 for the affair of Constable George Vaughan; *The Times*, 24, 27 February and 30 March 1818 for the affair of Constable Thomas Limbrick; Tobias, *Prince of Fences*, pp. 53–4, for the affair of Bow Street Constable Bishop who, in 1828, agreed, for a reward, to get back property stolen from a jeweller and, eventually, returned the property less £50-worth of jewels.

20 Newcastle-upon-Tyne, for example, had a system of town sergeants, constables and watchmen. Extracts from the *Tyne Mercury* for the years 1829–30 reveal Mayor George Shadforth instructing his sergeants on the enforcement of street regulations and requiring them (in French style) to collect weekly lists of the lodgers and inmates of both the lodging houses and the 'houses of ill fame' in their districts. Shadforth weeded out constables who were infirm or who did not live within their district and issued them with detailed instructions on their duties. Lax and corrupt watchmen were removed and this may, in turn, have prompted others to an excess of zeal. On 30 October 1829 Watchman Whittingham brought Mary Bateman before Alderman Reed in the Mayor's court charged with being disorderly. 'It appeared that when taken she was doing nothing, but the watchman said she used bad language, and *she had been* just before quarrelling in the street.' Reed released Bateman and advised Whittingham: 'You are not to take people into custody for using bad language. Persons are not to be imprisoned for nothing.' **H. A. Mitchell** (ed.), *A Report of the Proceedings in the Mayor's chamber, Newcastle-upon-Tyne, during the Mayoralty of Geo. Shadforth, Esq. 1829–30*, Newcastle, no date.

21 **Jenifer Hart,** 'Reform of the borough police, 1835–56', *E.H.R.,* lxx (1955), pp. 411–27 (at pp. 414–16).

22 Beds. R.O. Bedford Borough Records: Watch Committee Minutes B 3/1 f. 3; **R. E. Swift,** 'Crime, law and order in two English towns during the early nineteenth century: The experience of Exeter and Wolverhampton 1815–56', unpublished Ph.D., University of Birmingham, 1981, p. 142; **Geoffry G. Everitt,** 'The development of law and order in Nottingham', unpublished M.A., University of Sussex, 1971, copy in Notts. R.O. at M24,550; see also **John Field,** 'Police, power and community, in a provincial English town: Portsmouth, 1815–75', in **Victor Bailey** (ed.), *Policing and Punishment in Nineteenth-Century Britain,* Croom Helm, London, 1981, pp. 48–9; **B. C. Jerrard,** 'The Gloucestershire constabulary in the nineteenth century', unpublished M.Litt., University of Bristol, 1977, pp. 40–2.

23 Swift, 'Crime, law and order', pp. 358, 368, 381.

24 **B. J. Davey,** *Lawless and Immoral: Policing a country town 1838–57,* Leicester U.P., London, 1983, p. 55.

25 Emsley, *English Police,* pp. 26–7 and 85–6; U.C.L. Chadwick MSS 16, Police Memoranda etc. (1880–90), for a draft 'Bill for Placing the Police of the Metropolis under the Control of the Ratepayers, February 1889'.

26 **Carolyn Steedman,** *Policing and the Victorian Community: The formation of English provincial police forces 1856–80,* RKP, London, 1984, pp. 15–16, 39, 53–5; Emsley, *English Police,* pp. 82–4.

27 **David Philips** and **Robert D. Storch,** 'Whigs and Coppers: the Grey Ministry's National Police Scheme, 1832', *Historical Research,* lxvii (1994), pp. 75–90.

28 U.C.L. Chadwick MSS 1722/70–1, Rowan to Chadwick, 26 May 1839. The government had emancipated slaves in the British Empire, with £20 million paid in compensation to slave owners, in 1833. For a detailed analysis of the 1839 legislation see **David Philips** and **Robert D. Storch,** *Policing Provincial England 1829–1856: The politics of reform,* Leicester U.P., London, 1999.

29 *P.P.* 1852–53 (71) XXXVI, *Select Committee on Police,* qq. 2235 and 2257.

30 Philips and Storch, *Policing Provincial England,* ch. 8.

31 Emsley, *English Police,* p. 44.

32 **Henry Goddard,** *Memoirs of a Bow Street Runner,* London, 1956. I am grateful to Elizabeth Lally, the former curator and archivist of the West Mercia Constabulary, for information on Craig and Kings.

33 Jerrard, 'Gloucestershire Constabulary', pp. 61–2; **David Philips,** *Crime and Authority in Victorian England,* Croom Helm, London, 1977, p. 65.
    Of the forty-seven chief constables appointed to English county forces between 1839 and 1880, fourteen had experience in the Royal Irish

Constabulary as opposed to three with the Metropolitan Police and one with a borough force. Steedman, *Policing the Victorian Community*, p. 48.

34 Ibid.

35 *P.P.* 1852–53 (71) xxxvi, *Select Committee on Police*, qq. 166–8, 212–27, 231–2 and appendix 1, no. 7; Steedman, *Policing the Victorian Community*, pp. 21–5 and 32–8; **Clive Emsley**, ' "The thump of wood on a swede turnip": Police violence in nineteenth-century England', *C.J.H.*, **6** (1985), pp. 125–49, (at pp. 135, 136).

36 Notts. R.O. QAC 2/1, Petition from Harworth, 26 June 1843. The petitions are to be found in QAC 2/1–6 and appear to have been prompted initially by a proposal at the Michaelmas Sessions 1842 to increase the new county force.

37 *P.P.* 1852–53 (71) xxxvi, *Select Committee on Police*, quotations respectively, at qq. 3833, 610, 641, 3444, 855–6, and 3228.

38 *Hansard*, 3rd series, clxxxvii, 6 June 1867, cols 1664–6.

39 Storch, 'The policeman as domestic missionary'; *idem*, 'The plague of blue locusts'; Emsley, *English Police*, pp. 74–8.

40 Beds. R.O. Bedford Borough Records: Watch Committee Minutes B 3/1 13 October 1841; Manchester Police Museum, Manchester Watch Committee Minutes 1895 onwards, vol. 2, ff. 113–16 and 152, vol. 3, f. 97; *Manchester Police Instruction Book* (1908 edn), p. 113.

41 *The Times*, 25 September 1829.

42 Gloucs. R.O. Q.Y2.1.1, Chief Constable's General Order Book, 1840; Staffs. R.O.C. PC Box VI, *Rules and Regulations for the Government and Guidance of the Staffordshire Constabulary*, 1859, p. 3.

43 *P.P.* 1834 (600) xvi, *Select Committee on the Police of the Metropolis*, q. 433; U.C.L. Chadwick MSS 16, Police Memoranda etc. (1880–90), MS extract from the *Guardian*, 17 December 1873.
    Not everyone was as sanguine, see e.g. U.C.L. Chadwick MSS 1017/3–13, M.D. Hill to Chadwick, 12 January 1868; and Rowan, in an undated memorandum to Chadwick, lamented: 'We have used out best exertions and we find that crime and depredation are reduced to a certain extent, but there is still a good deal which we appear to be unable to reach, as our monthly returns for a year past both of the number of crimes and the value of property [stolen?] is wonderfully near one month to the other.' (Chadwick MSS 1722/130.)

44 *Brighton Gazette*, 25 April 1844; *East London Observer*, 5 December 1868; *The Times*, 24 March 1875; *C.C.C.S.P. 1836–37*, no. 71, p. 83; *C.C.C.S.P. 1856–57*, no. 560, p. 30; for a similar example to the arrest of Adams see *C.C.C.S.P. 1865–66*, no. 157, pp. 212–13 when, again, the victim was a merchant seaman.

45 **V. A. C. Gatrell**, 'The decline of theft and violence in Victorian and Edwardian England', in **V. A. C. Gatrell, Bruce Lenman** and **Geoffrey Parker** (eds), *Crime and the Law: The social history of crime in Western Europe since 1500*, Europa, London, 1980, pp. 277–8; **D. J. V. Jones**, 'The new police, crime and people in England and Wales, 1829–88, *T.R.H.S.*, 5th series, **33** (1983), pp. 151–68 (at pp. 162–3).

46 **Clive Emsley**, 'The Bedfordshire Police 1840–1856: A case study in the working of the Rural Constabulary Act', *Midland History*, vii (1982), pp. 73–92 (at pp. 87–8).

47 **[Samuel Smiles]** 'The Police of London', *Quarterly Review*, cxxxix (1870), pp. 87–129 (at p. 100); U.C.L. Chadwick MSS 16, Police Memoranda etc. (1855–69), contains a printed report on the Metropolitan Police Superannuation Fund by William Farr M.D., F.R.S. (April 1862), which gives the average day beat as 376 acres or 0.542 square miles, and the average night beat as 160 acres or 0.2495 square miles.

48 *The Times*, 1 and 25 March 1865.

49 *P.P.* 1833 (627) xiii, *Report from the Select Committee on the Petition of Frederick Young, and others . . . complaining that Policemen are employed as Spies*, q. 1127; *The Times*, 15 October 1850; *P.P.* 1852–53 (71) xxxvi, *Select Committee on Police*, q. 2276.

50 *P.P.* 1834 (600) xvi, *Select Committee on the Police of the Metropolis*, qq. 2156, 2165 and 1446–8.

51 Watts, 'Records of an old police court', xii, 505.

52 For the development of the detective police in London see **Phillip Thurmond Smith**, *Policing Victorian London: Political policing, public order, and the London Metropolitan Police*, Greenwood Press, Westport, Conn., 1985, ch. 3 *passim*; **Wilbur R. Miller**, *Cops and Bobbies: Police authority in New York and London, 1830–70*, University of Chicago Press, Chicago, 1977, pp. 33–4.

53 *C.C.C.S.P.* 1856–57, no. 6, p. 13; for a similar example see *C.C.C.S.P.* 1898–99, no. 114, p. 128, when P.C.s Stainton and Longridge, in plain clothes, foiled an attempted street robbery in Shoreditch.

54 *C.C.C.S.P.* 1836–37, no. 4, p. 11 and no. 68, p. 82.

55 *Bedford Mercury*, 23 March 1844; for other examples see Notts. R.O. QSD 1847. Statement of Police Superintendent Frederick Willis about checking the blood- and fat-stained boots of a suspect with footprints in a field where sheep had been feloniously killed (10 May 1847); see also *C.C.C.S.P.* 1856–57, no. 79, p. 54.

56 See above, p. 251. For police negotiating with offenders for the return of stolen property see *P.P.* 1844 (549) xvi, *Select Committee on Dog Stealing (Metropolis)*, q. 196.

57 'Life on a Labourer's Wage', *Police Review*, 29 March 1985, pp. 651–2; see also *Police Service Advertiser*, 27 April 1867 and, for the counter-case, 11 May 1867.

58 The constables of some boroughs do appear to have had the vote, and to have used it before 1856. *P.P.* 1852–53 (71) xxxvi, *Select Committee on Police*, qq. 2028–30 and 2127. For discussions among policemen over whether or not they should be enfranchised during debate on the Second Reform Bill see *Police Service Advertiser*, 30 March and 6 April 1867.

59 U.C.L. Chadwick MSS 16. Police Memoranda, etc. (1855–69), Report to the Secretary of State on the Metropolitan Police Superannuation Fund by William Farr M.D., F.R.S., April 1862.

60 Emsley, *English Police*, pp. 95–9.

61 *Police Service Advertiser*, 26 January 1867.

62 Staffs. R.O. C.PC Box VI, *Rules and Regulations*, pp. 39–41.

63 **Jennifer Davis**, 'The London garrotting panic of 1862', in Gatrell, Lenman and Parker (eds), *Crime and the Law*, p. 204.

64 *P.P.* 1834 (600) xvi, *Select Committee on the Police of the Metropolis*, q. 166.

65 *P.P.* 1852–53 (71) xxxvi, *Select Committee on Police*, q. 844; see also qq. 3575–79 and 3653.

66 P.C. Hennessy's notebook is in the Metropolitan Police Museum. For Jennings Buildings, five courts of narrow, slum tenements in the middle of fashionable Kensington, and how they were policed, see **Jennifer Davis**, 'Law breaking and law enforcement: The creation of a criminal class in mid-Victorian London', unpublished Ph.D., Boston College, 1984, ch. 6.

67 **Raphael Samuel** (ed.), *East End Underworld: Chapters in the life of Arthur Harding*, RKP, London, 1981, p. 36. For an assessment of the role of U.S. police forces in the care of lost children, and the impact on police/public relations see **Eric H. Monkkonen**, *Police in Urban America, 1860–1920*, Cambridge U.P., Cambridge, 1981, pp. 109–28.

CHAPTER 10

Punishment and reformation

The treatment of convicted offenders during the years 1750 to 1900 saw a shift from death or transportation being considered as the predominant punishments for felony to incarceration. At the same time there was a shift, admittedly less marked, from the personnel of the courts making all the key decisions about the offender to the experts in the new prison system making some of these decisions. Finally, once it was generally accepted that most offenders should be sent to prison, the crucial arguments centred on to what extent the prison was a place for punishment or for reformation.

The histories concerned with these changes in the treatment of the offender divide in a similar way to histories of the police. The traditional Whig interpretation largely accepts the case argued by eighteenth- and nineteenth-century reformers that the 'Bloody Code' was arbitrary and savage, and that the reformers' stance was morally and rationally unassailable. Penal reform thus begins with the abolition of capital statutes urged by Romilly and Mackintosh and largely carried out by Peel and Russell; it develops and gathers pace as the government takes an increasing role in the organisation and supervision of prisons with the opening of Millbank in 1816 and Pentonville in 1842, with the creation of a prison inspectorate in 1835 and, ultimately, with the centralisation of the entire system under the Home Office in 1877. Revisionist historians have accepted the savagery of the 'Bloody Code', although they have been more subtle in assessing its 'arbitrariness'. Furthermore, in relating penal reforms to changing economic and social structures they have emphasised the parallels between the new prisons and other developing institutions in the late eighteenth and nineteenth centuries, most notably the workhouse established under the New Poor Law; the new prison thus becomes another institution concerned with discipline and social control.[1] In many respects the arguments of traditionalists and revisionists are the mirror image of each other. In the Whig interpretation the humanitarian and progressive nature of penal reform fits with the humanitarian and progressive requirements of the liberal-democratic society that emerged in the early nineteenth century. In the revisionist account there is a fit between the new system of prison and punishment and the control requirements of the developing capitalist system.

There was a range of punishments available to judges and magistrates when they passed sentence during the eighteenth century. The most serious offences against persons and property tried at assizes or at the Old Bailey were punishable by death; the legacy of the Middle Ages left one or two borough sessions with the authority to impose a capital sentence[2] but county quarter sessions had no such power. Execution was usually by hanging; the more grisly punishments inflicted on the offender's body were rarely used in the mid-eighteenth century, though traitors could still be sentenced to death by beheading, drawing and quartering, and, until 1790, women found guilty of high or petty treason (which included coining) could be burned at the stake. The lesser forms of mutilation, which were not part of a capital sentence, such as burning in the hand, were also declining. Whipping remained a common punishment for petty offences. The offender, male or female, was stripped to the waist and flogged along a public street or at a fixed whipping post. The judiciary introduced private whipping from the middle of the eighteenth century, and this was given statutory approval in 1779. The public whipping of women was abolished in 1817, but for men the punishment continued until the mid-1830s.

Individuals convicted of some capital offences could escape the death penalty by pleading benefit of clergy; this was a left-over from the right of clerics to be tried before ecclesiastical courts alone, which, by the mid-seventeenth century, had been extended to men and women who were not clerics but who could demonstrate basic literacy. The courts had begun to clamp down on benefit of clergy in the early eighteenth century and many of the capital statutes passed during the century were specifically declared to be non-clergiable; however, the right to plead benefit of clergy in some offences remained until Peel's rationalisation of the criminal law in the 1820s. Conviction on a capital charge did not automatically lead to a death sentence, or, at least, did not automatically lead to an execution. Even though in the century following the Glorious Revolution of 1688 many more capital statutes found their way on the statute book, there was considerable debate about, and interest in, secondary punishments. Two alternatives dominated this debate: prison and transportation.

Custodial confinement in some form of institution went back at least to the Middle Ages and was always available as an option for eighteenth-century judges and magistrates. Eighteenth-century gaols held the accused before trial; some petty offenders were sentenced to short periods in gaol, in particular those who were perceived to be on the slippery slope to perdition and therefore in need of correction – the disorderly, the idle, the vagrant, and even some described simply as 'pilfering persons'. The more well-to-do among the lesser offenders might be punished with a fine, the less well-to-do with a whipping sometimes, to give maximum emphasis to the punishment, at the scene of the offence.[3] Both the pillory and the stocks also remained available: the pillory for serious public crimes such as fraud, cheating, some sexual offences, sedition and libel; the stocks for petty local offences – indeed the use of the stocks continued at least until the middle of the nineteenth century.[4] No-one seriously suggested extending the use of the pillory or the stocks, but perceived crimewaves did prompt suggestions for the more severe physical punishment of offenders. More importantly in the late seventeenth and early eighteenth centuries the various merits of prison and transportation were rehearsed and experiments were made in the desire to find a satisfactory secondary punishment. The Transportation Act 1718 more or less resolved the matter for roughly fifty years. Transportation provided for the removal out of the Kingdom of those offenders who, for a variety of reasons – their youth, the actual nature of their offence, the fact that it was a first-time offence – were not considered to be deserving of the death penalty but to be deserving of something more than a whipping and a discharge. The sentence was generally for periods of seven or fourteen years; sometimes it was for life. Transportation across the Atlantic began to lose favour in the middle years of the century and was effectively ended by the outbreak of the American War of Independence. The courts, however, continued to pass sentences of transportation, so some expedient had to be found to cope with the offenders thus sentenced. In 1751 a committee of the House of Commons had proposed hard labour in the Royal Dockyards as a suitable alternative to transportation, but the proposal had not been taken up. The difficulties created by the American war led parliament to adopt a temporary solution along these lines, however. In the years between the Declaration of Independence and the departure, in 1787, of the first 778 convicts for the new penal colony of Botany Bay, the government took over itself the management and organisation of a large number of convicted felons within the kingdom as those sentenced to transportation were incarcerated in old, rotting ships – the hulks – and set to work dredging rivers or labouring in the naval dockyards.

The appalling state of the hulks gave the reformers yet more ammunition in their campaign to establish well-regulated prisons, designed to reform offenders, as the principal, and much-expanded secondary, punishment in the criminal justice system.[5]

One of the key errors of many historians, both Whig and revisionist, has been to take the eighteenth-century 'Bloody Code' at a face value based on modern perceptions of the law; thus they have assumed that the increase in capital statutes during the eighteenth century was a meaningful one. In reality the new capital legislation of the eighteenth century generally defined offences in a very narrow way and often made reference to a specific institution or piece of property only; as a consequence the number of prosecutions likely to follow the passing of a capital statute was tiny. Destroying Westminster Bridge was the same kind of offence as destroying Fulham Bridge, but each offence had its own capital statute. Peel made much of such legislation when, in 1826, he proposed his rationalisation of the law relating to felony. There were, he explained, twenty statutes concerning the protection of trees from theft and wilful damage; for example, the legislation for the prevention of stealing or destroying madder roots and for the preservation of hollies, thorns and quicksets in forests was tacked on, respectively, to acts relating first, primarily to sugar brought from the Americas and second, to customs duties. 'If an offence were committed in some corner of the land,' protested Peel:

a law sprang up to prevent the repetition, not of the species of crime to which it belonged, but of the single and specific act of which there had been reason to complain.[6]

As was noted in the introduction with reference to Henry Banke's bill to prevent the invasion of mines, matters were rarely that simple. Nevertheless, Peel was right in drawing attention to the fact that eighteenth-century parliaments did not legislate for species of crime; while there were efforts to consolidate the vagrancy laws and the game laws, eighteenth-century legislators never attempted to codify capital legislation, indeed they did not think in terms of general codification or going back to first principles.

More important, perhaps, in any assessment of the 'Bloody Code' is to recognise that the majority of those executed during the eighteenth century were prosecuted under legislation that went back to the Tudors and Stuarts. Furthermore, there were far more executions during the late sixteenth and early seventeenth centuries than during the eighteenth; and one or two offences ceased to be capital: at least two Jacobite pamphleteers were executed for sedition, but at the end of the eighteenth century,

FIGURE 10.1 *The pattern of capital convictions and actual executions on Assize Circuits, 1749–1819*

Jacobin pamphleteers, if convicted, even at worst were rarely sentenced to more than two years in gaol.[7] Figure 10.1 shows the pattern of capital convictions and actual executions based on figures in the appendices of the *Report from the Select Committee on Criminal Laws 1819*. Convictions and executions follow roughly the same pattern with marked increases in the aftermath of the American War of Independence, when gentlemen were expressing concern about a crimewave, and in the famine year of 1801 'though, interestingly, London and Middlesex saw no marked increase on this occasion'. Equally noticeable is the widening gap between capital convictions and actual executions in the aftermath of the Napoleonic Wars. Possibly this was because the promptings of reformers critical of the Bloody Code were having an effect on the courts and because the alternatives of transportation and the penitentiary were perceived as readily available. At the same time, however, there may have been a recognition that it would simply not be acceptable to execute so many individuals. V. A. C. Gatrell has argued that the Bloody Code collapsed, not simply because of an increase in humanitarianism and sensibility, but rather more because of the increasing numbers of successful prosecutions. If larger numbers

FIGURE 10.1 *(cont.)*

were not to be executed – and realistically this was neither acceptable nor possible – then increasing numbers convicted of capital crimes had to be pardoned. As many as ninety per cent of those convicted in the post-Napoleonic War period were pardoned, as opposed to between fifty and sixty per cent in earlier years. This was making the judicial system appear an unsustainable lottery.[8]

Within the pattern of convictions and pardons it is instructive to see what were the principal offences for which persons were executed (Table 10.1) and what percentage of capital convictions were carried out for the major offences (Table 10.2). It is clear from these figures that the

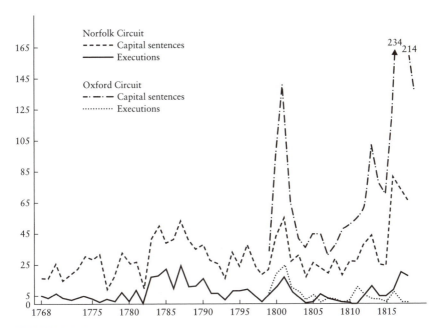

FIGURE 10.1 *(cont.)*

TABLE 10.1 *Principal offences for which persons were executed, 1755–1814*

	London and Middlesex* (a)	(b)	Home Circuit	Western Circuit	Norfolk Circuit
1755–1764					
Total executed	162	191	96		
Burglary	18 (11.1%)	23 (12.0%)	17 (17.7%)		
Forgery	24 (14.8%)	28 (14.6%)	4 (4.1%)		
Highway robbery	58 (35.8%)	65 (34.0%)	28 (29.1%)		
Murder	17 (10.4%)	26 (13.6%)	23 (23.9%)		
Horse stealing	6 (3.7%)		6 (6.2%)		
Housebreaking			1 (1.0%)		
Sheep stealing			3 (3.1%)		
1765–1774					
Total executed	278	303	139	43[†]	33[‡]
Burglary	86 (30.9%)	53 (17.4%)	24 (17.2%)	8 (18.6%)	14 (42.4%)
Forgery	20 (7.1%)	19 (6.2%)	3 (2.1%)	1 (2.3%)	1 (3.0%)
Highway robbery	79 (28.4%)	57 (18.8%)	63 (45.3%)	11 (25.5%)	7 (21.2%)
Murder	29 (10.4%)	30 (9.9%)	14 (10.0%)	14 (32.5%)	
Horse stealing	2 (1.0%)		7 (5.0%)	1 (2.3%)	1 (3.0%)
Housebreaking	3 (1.0%)		6 (4.3%)		1 (3.0%)
Sheep stealing			1 (0.7%)	2 (4.6%)	1 (3.0%)
1775–1784					
Total executed	414		197	85	67
Burglary	108 (26.0%)		56 (28.4%)	18 (21.1%)	30 (44.7%)
Forgery	21 (5.0%)		3 (1.5%)		4 (5.9%)
Highway robbery	124 (29.9%)		87 (44.1%)	29 (34.1%)	12 (17.9%)
Murder	17 (4.1%)		20 (10.1%)	23 (27.0%)	4 (5.9%)
Horse stealing	1 (0.2%)		9 (4.5%)	3 (3.5%)	3 (4.4%)
Housebreaking	6 (1.4%)		5 (2.5%)	2 (2.3%)	2 (2.9%)
Sheep stealing			2 (1.0%)	5 (5.8%)	5 (7.4%)

1785–1794

Total executed	375		404		234		180		126
Burglary	103	(27.4%)	154	(38.1%)	54	(23.0%)	30	(23.8%)	3	(2.3%)
Forgery	27	(7.2%)	24	(5.9%)	1	(0.4%)	3	(1.6%)	36	(20.0%)
Highway robbery	121	(32.2%)	122	(30.1%)			96	(41.0%)	23	(18.2%)
Murder	18	(4.8%)	22	(5.4%)	9	(3.8%)	24	(13.3%)	14	(11.1%)
Horse stealing	12	(3.2%)			23	(9.8%)	27	(15.0%)	4	(3.1%)
Housebreaking	12	(3.2%)			12	(5.1%)	10	(5.5%)	6	(4.7%)
Sheep stealing	2	(0.5%)			6	(2.5%)	12	(6.6%)		

1795–1804

Total executed	142		166		217		160		78
Burglary	23	(16.1%)	29	(17.4%)	48	(22.1%)	34	(21.2%)	16	(20.5%)
Forgery	40	(28.1%)	46	(27.7%)	4	(1.8%)	11	(6.8%)	2	(2.5%)
Highway robbery	22	(15.4%)	29	(17.4%)	58	(26.7%)	25	(15.6%)	15	(19.2%)
Murder	18	(12.6%)	23	(13.8%)	14	(6.4%)	25	(15.6%)	4	(5.1%)
Horse stealing	3	(2.1%)			17	(7.8%)	15	(9.3%)	15	(19.2%)
Housebreaking	2	(1.4%)			8	(3.6%)	4	(2.5%)	1	(1.2%)
Sheep stealing					10	(4.6%)	19	(11.8%)	9	(11.5%)

1805–1814

Total executed	137				142		82		39
Burglary	24	(17.5%)			30	(21.1%)	13	(15.8%)	6	(15.3%)
Forgery	44	(32.1%)			13	(9.1%)	22	(26.8%)	3	(7.6%)
Highway robbery	13	(9.4%)			12	(8.4%)	7	(8.5%)	1	(2.5%)
Murder	21	(15.3%)			21	(14.7%)	20	(24.3%)	9	(23.0%)
Horse stealing					11	(7.7%)	4	(4.8%)	6	(15.3%)
Housebreaking					8	(5.6%)				
Sheep stealing					13	(9.1%)	5	(6.0%)	2	(5.1%)

* There are two separate returns for London and Middlesex in the appendices for the 1819 Report from the Select Committee on Criminal Laws. Column (a) is based on the more detailed figures in Appendix No. 5; column (b) is based upon Appendix No. 2

† Figures for 1770 to 1774 only
‡ Figures for 1768 to 1774 only

TABLE 10.2 Capital convictions and executions for principal offences, 1775–1815

	London and Middlesex			Home Circuit			Western Circuit			Norfolk Circuit		
	Convicted	Executed	Executed as percentage convicted	Convicted	Executed	Executed as percentage convicted	Convicted	Executed	Executed as percentage convicted	Convicted	Executed	Executed as percentage convicted
1775–1784												
Burglary	185	108	58.3%	115	56	48.6%	99	18	18.0%	73	30	41.0%
Forgery	37	21	57.7%	4	3	75.0%	14	—	—	4	4	100.0%
Highway robbery	318	124	38.9%	227	87	38.3%	158	29	18.3%	35	12	34.2%
Murder	18	17	94.4%	25	20	80.0%	30	23	76.6%	4	4	100.0%
1785–1794												
Burglary	220	103	44.2%	120	54	45.0%	139	51	36.6%	79	30	37.9%
Forgery	38	27	71.0%	2	1	50.0%	32	3	9.3%	3	3	100.0%
Highway robbery	309	121	39.1%	224	96	42.8%	111	36	32.4%	50	31	62.0%
Murder	19	18	94.7%	11	9	81.8%	25	24	96.0%	23	23	100.0%
1795–1804												
Burglary	168	23	13.6%	176	48	27.2%	130	34	26.1%	56	16	28.5%
Forgery	61	40	65.5%	9	4	44.4%	20	11	55.0%	2	2	100.0%
Highway robbery	127	22	17.3%	134	58	43.2%	84	25	29.7%	42	15	35.7%
Murder	20	18	90.0%	17	14	82.3%	26	25	96.1%	4	4	100.0%
1804–1815*												
Burglary	226	18	7.9%	158	30	18.9%	118	13	11.0%	53	6	11.3%
Forgery	84	47	55.9%	17	13	76.4%	30	22	73.3%	9	3	33.3%
Highway robbery	196	17	8.6%	62	12	19.3%	39	7	17.9%	16	1	6.2%
Murder	26	26	100.0%	26	21	80.7%	28	20	71.4%	9	9	100.0%

* London and Middlesex figures, 1812–18

TABLE 10.3 *Capital convictions for animal theft*

	Convictions	Executions	Executions as a percentage of convictions
Home Circuit, 1755–1814			
Cattle theft	42	7	16.6%
Horse theft	549	73	13.2%
Sheep theft	381	35	9.1%
Norfolk Circuit, 1768–1818			
Cattle theft	37	4	10.8%
Horse theft	267	36	13.4%
Sheep theft	278	25	8.9%
Western Circuit, 1770–1818			
Cattle theft	98	15	15.3%
Horse theft	355	50	14.0%
Sheep theft	457	48	10.5%

It is probably significant that the peak year for convictions for sheep stealing on all three circuits was the famine year of 1801: 44 convicted, of whom 3 were executed on the Home Circuit; 24 convicted, of whom 4 were executed on the Norfolk Circuit; and 40 convicted, of whom 16 were executed on the Western Circuit

largest number of capital sentences were passed on those convicted of the more serious kinds of theft, namely burglary and highway robbery. The theft of various animals – cattle, horses and sheep – could bring a capital sentence, but it was also more likely to bring a reprieve (Table 10.3). It is equally noticeable that, while the numbers capitally convicted on charges of burglary and, to a lesser extent, highway robbery remained high into the early years of the nineteenth century, the percentage of executions that were actually carried out fell. The capital offences for which reprieves were most rarely given were, first and foremost, violent offences against the person, notably murder but also sexual offences (Table 10.4). If, as has been argued, the threat of the gallows was employed during the eighteenth century to enforce an unequal division of property, it must, nevertheless, be recognised that the offenders least likely to escape the gallows were those guilty of offences against the persons of others. There is one significant exception to this: to modern eyes the most startling figures are probably those of the percentage executed out of those convicted for forgery. The offence was made capital in 1729 (2 Geo. II c. 25) following disquiet aroused by the South Sea Bubble affair and a succession of subsequent frauds. The new legislation swept up members of the lower classes who forged documents to obtain the prize money or the earnings of seamen, but it was aimed principally at forgers from the respectable classes, people who rarely appeared as defendants in the courts and especially not on capital

TABLE 10.4 *Capital convictions for sexual offences*

	Convictions	Executions	Executions as a percentage of convictions
London and Middlesex			
1756–1804			
Rape	19	11	57.8%
Sodomy	9	5	55.5%
1812–1818			
Rape	3	2	66.6%
Sodomy	4	4	100.0%
Home Circuit			
1755–1814			
Rape	38	18	47.3%
Buggery	14	12	85.7%
Norfolk Circuit			
1768–1818			
Rape*	15	11	73.3%
Buggery and sodomy	4	3	75.0%
Western Circuit			
1770–1818			
Rape[†]	29	20	68.9%
Carnally knowing an infant under 10 years	4	3	75.0%
Sodomy	7	4	57.0%

* Includes two cases of rape committed on infants
† There is a discrepancy in the figures between the annual totals for the Western Circuit and the overall figures for particular offences given in Appendix 9 and Appendix 10 of the 1819 Report The figures given here are for the offence totals in Appendix 10; the annual figures, given in Appendix 9 when totalled come to 26 convictions and 17 executions. The discrepancy appears to be for the period 1810–18

charges. The old punishment had been the local humiliation of the pillory. The use of the gallows to punish this offence, as Randall McGowen has forcefully argued, addressed the whole community and made a significant public statement about behaviour that threatened to destroy commerce and the production of wealth by undermining a system in which paper credit was becoming more and more important. The offence was not seen in purely economic terms, rather it was a question of morality and upholding norms that made economic and social life possible. The judiciary, as well as the parliament that passed the new legislation, thought in this way. Judges sustained prosecutions in spite of procedural difficulties that could have brought them to a halt, and rejected appeals for pardon that, in the normal course of events, they probably would have forwarded given the social origins of the defendant.[9]

Crowds massed around pillories and gallows in both London and the assizes towns. Public punishment was theatre. In as much as the ruling class or the state had devised such punishment it was didactic theatre: the gallows and the pillory were to provide lessons and warnings for other would-be transgressors of the law. But for the crowds, drawn from all social groups, the proceedings appear to have been melodrama of the rudest sort: at one extreme there could be villains to jeer and abuse, at the other there were unfortunates to be cheered and cherished. The crowd had a positive role to play at the pillory; under the watchful eye of a sheriff or other law officer, it was authorised to pelt the offender with fruit, vegetables, eggs, dung and so forth. But increasingly the manner in which the crowd played its role did not fit the prepared text of the authorities. Pilloried offenders, to whom the crowd had taken a dislike, were cruelly treated; some lost eyes, some died as a result of their treatment. But others became popular heroes, and their time in the pillory became a moment of triumph. John Williams, for example, a bookseller, fell foul of authority for selling both prints which ridiculed the Earl of Bute and a reprint of John Wilkes's *North Briton*. His hour in the pillory in February 1765 only aggravated the government's discomfiture, however, since, rather than pelting him with anything that came to hand, the crowd cheered him and raised a collection for him amounting to £200. The situation became such that, from roughly the middle of the eighteenth century, the pillory was used less and less to punish cases of sedition in which the crowd's sympathy might be with the person pilloried. But, as a result, a greater proportion of those sentenced to the pillory were unpopular with the crowd and were savagely pelted and ill-treated. This, in turn, aggravated concerns about crowd behaviour in the public space around the pillory.[10]

The crowd did not have such a defined, participatory role at public executions. Here it was very much the audience, yet it still made its views felt. It generally execrated the hangman when the offender was not a murderer or when it felt that he or she was being executed unjustly. Members of the crowd appear to have sympathised most with those with whom they could readily identify; thus respectable people recorded being particularly shaken by the execution of someone from their own social class, a forger, for example, like the Reverend William Dodd in 1777. But the majority in the crowd was plebeian, and it appears to have been particularly approving when the victim came from a higher social class. Until executions were established immediately outside prisons – as they were from 1783 in London with the erection of the new drop at Newgate – the journey to the scaffold could begin the tumult and reveal the crowd's attitude. In August

1754 Mary Smith was executed at Tyburn for robbing a three-year old girl. The *General Evening Post* reported that:

instead of Pity and Prayers, generally used on these Occasions [the crowd] especially the Females, vented bitter Execrations as the Cart went along; particularly a poor Woman in Oxford Road, who, to show her Indignation to the Criminal, held up a Child in her Arms, which this Wretch had stripped, rejoiced in her Punishment, and seemed pleased to exhibit a remarkable Proof of her offence.[11]

On occasions the condemned behaved with the kind of penitential decorum suited to the authorities' requirements for the didactic theatre of punishment; they ascribed their ruin to drink or 'to the Association of lewd Women, who drove them to unlawful Courses, in order to escape the Extravagances of these Daughters of Plunder'.[12] Even if the condemned was not penitent, enterprising printers provided cheap handbills with appropriate 'last dying words' or doggerels illustrating his or her moral decline. Some of the capitally convicted refused to play the game and insisted that they did not deserve death:

James Holt, the Smuggler, behaved very penitently, but did not seem convinced that his Sentence was just, or that Smuggling merited Death. Amongst his last words were, 'It is very hard to be hanged for Smuggling'.[13]

Others struggled with the executioner or, probably fortified with strong drink, affected an air of heroic nonchalance. Penitence, protest or nonchalance might further help to shape the responses of the crowd. So too might a botched execution, or the decision to convey the body of an executed felon to a surgeon for dissection; crowds strongly objected to the latter, particularly when the condemned had made 'a good end' or when the popular feeling was that he or she did not deserve to be executed.

If, for most of the eighteenth century, the Bloody Code was not actually increasing the numbers of those being executed, nevertheless there does appear to have been an increase in judicial violence. The Murder Act of 1752 extended gibbeting and dissection as the judiciary began to introduce private whipping. It seems probable that this was regarded by the plebeian crowds as a violation of accepted norms, as the law failing to reflect popular ideas of culpability and justice, and as evidence of a contempt for popular culture. At the same time, the growth of the press meant greater publicity for executions, which, in all probability, led to greater crowds. Larger crowds, and plebeian frustration, provoked greater turmoil around the scaffold; well before the end of the century the authorities had lost control of the pillory.[14] At the same time they began to feel that they were losing control of 'the hanging tree'. There was disquiet that the crowds were not taking the appropriate message and that they were not behaving as they should; this was linked to an increasing distrust of crowds, and also to the almost wilful misapprehension that the crowds who assembled to watch executions were uniformly plebeian. Concerns about the behaviour at executions, together with demands for a better regulated system of intermediary punishment were being voiced by men like the Fieldings in the mid-eighteenth century. These concerns received a boost with the publication of two books: in 1767 came the first English translation of Cesare Beccaria's *Dei Delitti e delle Pene*; and in 1777 John Howard published *The State of the Prisons in England and Wales*.

Beccaria's treatise, originally appearing in Italy in 1764, was seized upon by progressive thinkers throughout Europe as proposing, in the most succinct way, the kind of system of punishment best in keeping with the ideas of the Enlightenment. Existing punishments, he insisted, were arbitrary and barbaric, and they did not diminish crime. Punishment should have aims that were explicable and rational; it should be the certain outcome of any lawbreaking; it should suit the offence; it should prevent the culprit from offending again; it should deter potential offenders. Rather than relying upon the death penalty for many offences it would be more salutary, Beccaria believed, to deprive offenders of their liberty, and to compel them to recompense society for their transgressions with a period of hard labour visible to the public. In November 1770 Sir William Meredith, the Rockinghamite M.P. for Liverpool, urged the Commons to mount an enquiry into the criminal law; his speech was suffused with Beccarian ideas. He was concerned:

that a man, who has privately picked a pocket of a handkerchief worth thirteen pence, is punished with the same severity, as if he had murdered a whole family of benefactors.

Such punishment, Meredith maintained, only served to make the petty thief worse and more dangerous and, he went on:

none should be punished with death, but those who could not be made safely useful, except in cases of murder, where a capital punishment, as it would be less common, would operate more forcibly in terrorem, *and consequently more effectually answer its end.*[15]

The following year William Eden published the influential *Principles of Penal Law* rejecting the existing system centred on capital punishment, querying the value of transportation and, on Beccarian lines, recommending some kind of continuing public display of useful punishment. Eden was also doubtful about the value of prison sentences; he believed that confinement often made offenders worse. Within a decade, however, he was helping to draft new penitentiary legislation. Eden's conversion to the idea of putting offenders into regulated, orderly prisons, like the similar conversion of other reformers, was largely through the work of John Howard.

Howard, a philanthropic, nonconformist gentleman with an estate at Cardington in Bedfordshire, had become county sheriff in 1773. He was appalled by the squalor of the county gaol, which his new post led him to visit; he was also shocked by the plight of the prisoners, notably those who, although acquitted by the courts, were compelled to remain incarcerated because they could not pay the discharge fee required by the gaoler. These problems and abuses were not unique to Bedfordshire nor were they unknown before Howard's publications. The office of gaoler was typical of other petty offices during the eighteenth century: the holder was expected to be an entrepreneur who augmented such wage as he might receive with fees and the sale or rent of goods to those in his charge. What impressed the public about *The State of the Prisons* was certainly Howard's moral fervour but, perhaps more important, the systematic way in which he had gone about categorising every imaginable detail from diet to size of cell in every prison in England and Wales; more than this, he had contrasted the squalor of these gaols with, in particular, the Rasp Houses of Amsterdam and Rotterdam and the Maison de Force in Ghent. The book was an indictment of the administration of those local justices who rarely took seriously their responsibilities in supervising their local gaols and gaolers; yet, as Michael Ignatieff emphasises, the book was not couched as an indictment but rather as 'a confrontation with Evil in the abstract'. Magistrates could therefore accept the conclusion without feeling that they themselves were being condemned.[16] Further editions of the book were brought out in 1780 and 1783, and Howard expanded his empirical research in Europe publishing, in 1789, *An Account of the Principal Lazarettos in Europe*, which was itself reprinted in 1791, the year after his death.

Yet in spite of the enthusiastic reception given to the work of Beccaria and Howard and the boost which they gave to reformers, change remained slow and continued to depend on the zeal and initiative of private individuals rather than on any government direction. In 1779 parliament passed the Penitentiary Act; drafted by Blackstone, Eden and Howard, this

provided for the construction of two penitentiaries in the metropolis, one
for 600 men, the other for 300 women. Here offenders, otherwise liable
for transportation, could be imprisoned for up to two years. They were to
be uniformed, kept to hard labour in association with each other by day
and shut in solitary confinement by night. Section 5 of the act emphasised
the reforming intention of the penitentiaries: inmates were to be inured
'to Habits of Industry'. But conscious of complaints that some of the poor
might prefer the clothing, diet and lodging of the penitentiaries to their
hard life outside, the legislators were determined to make confinement
sufficiently hard, rigorous and disagreeable to deter any such preference. In
the event, these penitentiaries were never built. Death and resignation
broke up the original board of commissioners established to oversee implementation of the act. There were problems over the purchase of land. But,
probably most important, none of the ministries between 1779 and 1785,
when plans finally lapsed, had the building of the penitentiaries among
their prime concerns even though the end of the American War initially
threatened, and then statistically showed, an increase in prosecutions.
Ministers had to busy themselves with concluding the war and struggling
for the continuance of their shaky administrations.[17] The hulks were
accepted as 'temporary expedients' and for the government to take on the
expense of permanent structures would not have been popular in years
when economic reform and retrenchment were watchwords. Such a
reform, even though it had passed through parliament, might also have
been condemned as enlarging the patronage of the Crown and encroaching
on the rights of local boroughs and counties to administer gaols.
Furthermore, the belief continued that prisons, and the hulks, by throwing
first offenders together with recidivists, only served to make all offenders
worse. Jonas Hanway, an advocate of solitary confinement from the early
1770s, branded the London Bridewell as 'a nursery for thieves and prostitutes'.[18] The House of Commons Committee on Transportation argued
similarly in 1784 and went on to explain that, while prisoners released
from the gaols and the hulks could get neither work nor parish relief and
consequently returned to crime, transportation to America had 'tended
directly to reclaim the Objects on which it was inflicted, and to render
them good Citizens'.[19] The Transportation Act 1784 signalled a continuing
preference in central government circles for removing offenders overseas,
even though the site for a new penal colony was still to be found. Nor was
it only among government circles that such sentiments existed. In March
1786 the Lord Mayor and Aldermen of the City of London petitioned
George III about 'the rapid and alarming increase of crimes and depredations

in this city and its neighbourhood, especially within the last three years'. The petitioners asserted that the end of transportation and the release of offenders back into English society were 'alone sufficient to account for all the evils that are so heavily felt and so justly complained of'. The only punishments mentioned in the petition were death and transportation, 'without which all other regulations must prove nugatory and abortive'.[20] In the closing decades of the eighteenth century it was influential figures in county administrations who organised the building of new gaols or the refurbishing of old ones, and who introduced new regimes of regular work, solitary confinement, and the separation of different classes of offender – men from women, first-time offenders from recidivists, those convicted from those awaiting trial. Notable among these reformers were the Duke of Richmond in Sussex, Sir George Onesiphorus Paul in Gloucestershire, and Thomas Butterworth Bayley in Salford.

By the decade of the French Revolution the exertions of local reformers together with the steady stream of printed propaganda were beginning to make the penitentiary a viable alternative punishment. Furthermore, it was a punishment with the added advantage, according to its advocates, of reforming the prisoner for the benefit of English, as opposed to a colonial, society. Those released from the rigours of the penitentiary would be accustomed to hard work, instead of idleness, while religious teaching and periods of solitary confinement would have helped the offender to contemplate the evils of wrong-doing, thus inculcating morality and virtue. But there was no steady triumph of a single penitentiary idea. Reformers themselves were divided about the kind of work and about the role and effect of solitary confinement. In 1791 Jeremy Bentham threw his intellectual weight behind prison reform with his own plan, *Panopticon*. The panopticon structure was to enable the constant supervision of convicts working, and thus reforming, for perhaps as many as sixteen hours a day; it also provided for the supervision of the prison guards, for here Bentham parted company with other reformers in suggesting that the custodians themselves might need watching. Bentham's principal gaoler – Bentham himself – was to be the entrepreneurial gaoler *par excellence* running the panopticon as a profitable commercial enterprise and selling the products of the convicts' labour; the need to have a fit and healthy workforce would, according to Bentham, ensure that the convicts were looked after. In 1794 legislation provided for the construction of the panopticon and Bentham acquired a site at Millbank, but the Treasury never released the money for construction. In addition to their differences over the best system, the prison reformers received setbacks from the criticisms levied at the realities even of new gaols by political radicals. The English Jacobins who spent time in prison for sedition or under the suspension of the Habeas Corpus Act were few in number, but they were articulate and able publicists. Paul's Gloucester Penitentiary and, more especially, the House of Correction in Coldbath Fields were the focus of this criticism. Coldbath Fields had been opened in 1794, designed with Howard's principles in mind, but it was unfortunate in acquiring as its first governor a former baker, Thomas Aris, who turned out to be precisely the kind of grasping gaoler of whom Howard was critical; the problem was compounded by the Middlesex justices giving Aris a free hand in the administration of the gaol.[21]

The wars against Revolutionary and Napoleonic France again involved government departments in the organisation and administration of large numbers of prisoners on British soil. The wars created problems in transportation, not the least of which was the higher cost of freight; this led to more and more convicts being incarcerated on the hulks, and while contemporaries did not really do the sums, those lodged in this way were less costly than those shipped to Botany Bay, and their labour on public works, notably for military purposes, proved valuable.[22] But prisoners in the government's charge during these years were not simply convicts; there were also prisoners of war in unprecedented numbers who, because of the duration and new style of war, had to be kept over a longer period than in previous conflicts. It is impossible to measure the precise impact on penal policy of keeping large numbers of convicts on the hulks and enemy servicemen in prisoner of war camps, but in 1816, the year following the battle of Waterloo, the first national penitentiary was opened at Millbank. The go-ahead for the penitentiary was the result of the report of a parliamentary committee appointed in 1810 under the chairmanship of George Holford. This committee, packed with keen advocates of the penitentiary idea, was primarily concerned with choosing between different forms of penal discipline: that exemplified by the Gloucester Penitentiary where solitary confinement was given a key role in an attempt to change the offender's character by bringing him, through religion, to an awareness of his wrong-doing; and that which gave offenders incentives to work in association with each other in the belief that instilling the habit of work would drive out the bad habit of idleness, which led to crime. Holford's committee came up with an amalgam of the two: the first part of a convict's sentence was to be spent in separation, the second part in association. It rejected Bentham's plans for running the prison like a factory as well as his elaborate panopticon structure, though elements of Bentham's structural ideas for supervision were incorporated into Millbank's seven massive pentagons. Bentham himself was compensated financially for his efforts spread over the preceding two decades. The construction of Millbank was begun in 1812 and eventually cost the enormous and quite unexpected sum of £450,000. It was the largest prison in Europe when it opened and marked a significant step in the state taking on the management of convicts in an institution on native soil.

But while the government was sucked more deeply into penal adminis- tration and reform, the running for the changes in penal policy continued to be made by a small group of M.P.s passionate in their philanthropy and politically tending towards the opposition Whigs. The Gaol Fees Abolition Act 1815 which signalled the beginning of the end for the entrepreneurial gaoler was introduced into parliament by one of these reformers, Henry Grey Bennet. But most notable among this group was Sir Samuel Romilly. Prison improvement was just one element of Romilly's campaign to mitigate and rationalise the Bloody Code. From the early years of the new century he campaigned vigorously for a reduction in the number of capital statutes. He protested that there was a 'lottery of justice' in that there was uncertainty about the punishment for different offences; even when a capital sentence was passed it was far from certain that it would be carried out and consequently there was no lesson for the public. Judges, he feared, had too much potentially tyrannical discretion; furthermore they responded to different offences in their own individual ways.

Romilly and reformers like him have been lionised by the Whig histor- ians of criminal justice; they have been portrayed as far-sighted humanitar- ians beset on all sides by die-hard reaction. Humanitarians they certainly were, yet whether their achievements were as great and whether the issues were as clear cut as Whig history would suggest, is a moot point. It was emphasised earlier that there were never 200 or so separate and completely different offences that were liable to a capital sentence, while the graphs and tables at the beginning of this chapter reveal a proportional decline in the numbers executed for property crime. '[T]he legal massacres . . . when "the prisons of the metropolis are emptied into the grave" '[23] were being queried long before Romilly began his campaign. Put in the context of a growing unease about the Bloody Code and its ritual paraphernalia the role of Romilly as a courageous initiator of reform is less pronounced. Rather he, and other early nineteenth-century law reformers, were able to get things done because parliamentary opinion, across the political spectrum, was already beginning to accept some of the arguments that they were employing. In his *Memoirs*, Romilly protested that the French Revolution had made it exceedingly difficult to get 'legislative reform on humane and liberal principles' and he cited the abuse that his 1808 bill to abolish the death penalty for pickpockets had prompted from the younger brother of a peer. What he does not mention is the fact that his bill went through parliament without a division and received the royal assent less than six weeks after its introduction.[24] Admittedly other bills were less successful: in 1810, 1811, 1813, 1816 and 1818 the Commons passed bills to abolish capital punishment for stealing from a shop to the value of five shillings; on each occasion the Lords rejected the bill. But the statistics collected by the government revealed that between 1805 and 1820, when the Stealing in Shops Act was passed, no-one was executed for the offence.[25]

As with the opponents of police reform, the early nineteenth-century opponents of reform of the criminal law had a coherent and logical case, though few historians have given them credit for such. Anti-reformers insisted that justice was not a lottery and that judicial discretion was sensibly and conscientiously practised; as the reformers could point to cases of injustice so their opponents could point to examples that showed the system working with mercy and moderation – no-one was executed for stealing from a shop goods worth under five shillings, but the potential was there if a sufficiently evil character did face such a charge and if an example was required *pour décourager les autres*. Probably the strongest plank in the platform of the traditionalists was their doubt that there could ever be a significant measure of certainty in the way that a punishment was meted out to fit a particular crime. The Criminal Law Commissioners who were appointed in 1833 ran into major difficulties when they sought to establish a rational system of punishment: in their second report, in 1836, they specified four overall classes of crime each with two alternative penalties; in their fourth report, three years later, there were fifteen overall classes of crime, each with a far greater range of penalties; by 1843, and their seventh report, the scale of penalties had reached forty-five, more than double the number of twenty that they had initially specified as the absolute maximum. The attempts of the commission to establish precise penalties for precise offences eventually foundered.[26] Randall McGowan has argued, persuasively, that the issue in dispute between traditionalists and legal reformers in the early nineteenth century:

was not how to secure the greater efficiency of the criminal justice system, but how to present a more pleasing image of justice. The desire was not just to reduce crime but to secure wider support for the legal order.[27]

The traditionalists were defending an aristocratic and paternalistic image of justice and focused on the practice of the courts and the use of mercy;

the reformers focused on existing severity and proposed an image of impersonal justice in which the law was above the suspicion of dependence on any personal discretion. The problem for the opponents of reform was that influential Tories like Peel were also pressing for change. It remains a matter of debate whether this was a result of humanitarianism and rationalist ideas rooted in the Enlightenment and larded with evangelicalism and Benthamite utilitarianism, whether beneath this, as McGowen argues, there were in addition the deeper structures of developing class alliances in a fast-changing society, or whether, as Gatrell maintains, Peel and his colleagues were seeking primarily to shore up and revitalise a system in danger of collapsing under the weight of increasing convictions and the corresponding necessity for more pardons. What has to be recognised is the logic of the traditionalists' case; what has to be rejected is the notion that the reformers had a far-sighted vision of nineteenth-century progress that would culminate in the modern legal system.[28]

It was under Peel's reformist regime at the Home Office during the 1820s that the first significant moves were made by a government to rationalise the criminal justice system. Urged on by the energetic philanthropists of the Prison Discipline Society, Peel sponsored a Gaol Act in 1823, and amending legislation in the following year, which sought to establish a measure of uniformity throughout the prisons of England and Wales. The legislation was informed by the idea of the penitentiary: it spelled out health regulations and religious regulations; it required the separation of different categories of prisoner and facilities for hard labour; it directed magistrates to inspect their local gaols three times a quarter, and demanded that annual reports be sent from each gaol to the Secretary of State. Many local gaols ignored at least some of these regulations, including the requirement for an annual report. Peel was reluctant to antagonise local sensibilities about independence and consequently made no attempt to impose sanctions in the legislation or a national system of inspection. It was not until 1835 that the reforming Whig government of Melbourne, with Lord John Russell at the Home Office, established a prison inspectorate of five. Yet from Peel's time onward, home secretaries were interventionist and every government had to develop some sort of policy on the punishment of criminal offenders.

The death penalty began to lose its central role in the criminal justice system with Peel's rationalisation of the law, even though the numbers capitally convicted continued to rise roughly in line with the rise in criminal statistics during the 1820s and early 1830s. Nevertheless, following on from Peel's reforms, the number of capital offences continued to be

TABLE 10.5 *Capital sentences, number executed and number executed for murder, 1805–54*

Ten-year period	Average number capitally convicted per annum	Average number executed per annum	Average number executed for murder per annum
1805–14	443	66	13
1815–24	1073	89	16
1825–34	1218	53	12
1835–44	199	13	10
1845–54	57	9	9

Source: Based on figures given in Parliamentary Reports

reduced throughout the 1830s and early 1840s.[29] By the late 1830s it was rare for anyone to be executed for any offence other than murder (Table 10.5), and by the mid-1840s a significant movement had developed for the total abolition of the death penalty.[30] With the decline in the use of the death penalty, prisons of different varieties had more of a central role to play in the criminal justice system, but until the middle of the century transportation also remained an option for the courts when dealing with those deemed serious offenders.

The numbers transported began to increase from about 1,000 to about 2,500 a year with the perceived crimewave at the end of the Napoleonic Wars. They increased further during the 1820s and reached a peak in the early 1830s with about 5,000 convicts being shipped to Australia each year from Great Britain and Ireland; the numbers transported from England and Wales constituted roughly two-thirds of the total. From the beginning of the second decade of the nineteenth century until the mid-1830s, about one-third of all those convicted at assizes or quarter sessions were either sentenced, or had a death sentence commuted, to transportation. This fraction began to fall rapidly over the subsequent decade to about one-seventh. Except for the early years and the very last years of the system, between two-thirds and three-quarters of those sentenced to transportation were actually shipped to Australia.[31]

During the eighteenth century doubts had been expressed about the extent to which transportation was a punishment; one penal reformer, writing in the aftermath of the loss of the American colonies, suggested that those who had been transported had actually been given the opportunity to become 'profitable members of another state'.[32] Similar doubts were raised about conditions in Australia. The relatively liberal and reforming regime of Governor Lachlan Macquarie in New South Wales was criticised in J. T. Bigge's official enquiry into the conduct of the colony published in 1822. As a result of Bigge's report, restrictions were put on the governors of the colonies and policies of greater severity were applied towards convicts. Even so in 1826 the Reverend Sydney Smith could write to Peel satirising a sentence of transportation as follows:

translated into common sense [it] is this: 'Because you have committed this offence, the sentence of the Court is that you shall no longer be burdened with the support of your wife and family. You shall be immediately removed from a very bad climate and a country over burdened with people to one of the finest regions of the earth, where the demand for human labour is every hour increasing, and where it is highly probable you may ultimately gain your character and improve your future. The Court have been induced to pass this sentence upon you in consequence of the many aggravating circumstances of your case, and they hope your fate will be a warning to others.'[33]

Stories circulated of men committing crimes simply to get transported.[34] Yet the treatment of many convicts in Australia was appalling, and some of this was brought out in evidence to the Select Committee on Transportation, which met between 1837 and 1838 under the chairmanship of Sir William Molesworth. The problem, as the committee rightly pointed out, was that the penal colonies were so far away that people in England were unaware of the severity of the life and, consequently, there was no deterrence.[35] The committee condemned the existing system of transportation and favoured the building of penitentiaries; the majority proposed penitentiaries in both Britain and the colonies but Molesworth himself opposed their establishment in the colonies on the grounds that this simply perpetuated transportation under another name. The report did ultimately lead to changes in the system of convict labour and to experiments aimed particularly at the reformation of convicts, but the practice of shipping abroad the more serious offenders was not abolished as a judicial sentence until 1857 and for ten years after that a few offenders continued to be sent to Western Australia. It was as much pressure from the colonists, increasingly proud of their new land, as any growing faith in prisons as the best means of punishment that finally brought about the demise of transportation in the British penal system.[36]

As the wave of colonial opposition to transportation built up during the 1830s and 1840s so a particular concept of prison discipline began to dominate from Westminster. The Select Committee of the House of Lords whose report, in 1835, recommended the appointment of a Government

Inspectorate of Prisons, also advocated a common system of discipline for all prisons based on silence. Wakefield Gaol and Coldbath Fields had adopted the silent system the preceding year; overnight, recalled the governor of the latter institution, 'all intercommunication by word, gesture or sign was prohibited'.[37] But a different group of experts advocated the separate system in preference to silence; notable among these were William Crawford, a leading figure in the Prison Discipline Society, and the Reverend Whitworth Russell, a former chaplain at Millbank; both men were among the first five appointees to the prison inspectorate. Separation, or solitary confinement, had been central to the thought of many early advocates of the penitentiary. A visit to the United States by Crawford convinced him of the superiority of the separate over the silent system and on his return he published a massive study of American prisons explaining his conclusions. More importantly, while there was no unanimity among the prison inspectorate, both Crawford and Whitworth Russell took every opportunity to urge their preference in their inspectors' reports. Somewhat hesitantly Lord John Russell authorised the construction of a new national penitentiary in London and Captain Joshua Jebb of the Royal Engineers was entrusted with the design. Jebb, subsequently appointed Surveyor-General of Prisons, was favourable towards the separate system himself, but his evidence to a parliamentary committee in 1850 suggests that the leading advocates of the system were not averse to a bit of blackmail:

I was requested by . . . Mr Crawford and Mr Russell . . . to allow them to be associated with me in the consideration of the plans, and they urged this reason: they said, 'We do not wish to control your professional opinion; but if you erect a prison which we do not consider to be adapted for the enforcement of the system which we advocate, we will not certify the cells, and the prison will be useless.[38]

Pentonville, the end-product of Jebb's designs and Crawford's and Whitworth Russell's urgings, was opened in 1842.

The inmates of Pentonville were kept in solitary cells. They wore a mask, the 'beak', when they were moved around the building so that anonymity was preserved. At the required church parades each convict was confined to a separate box so that communication with his fellows was all but impossible. The plan was for the solitary confinement and anonymity of Pentonville to last for eighteen months before a man was transported. It was believed that, thrown in upon themselves, in the quiet, contemplative state of the solitary cell, convicts, assisted by their bibles and the exhortations of the chaplain, would come to a realisation and repentance of their wrong-doing. The Reverend John Clay, another ardent supporter of the separate system recorded how:

a few months in the solitary cell renders a prisoner strangely impressible. The chaplain can then make the brawny navvy cry like a child; he can work on his feelings in almost any way he pleases; he can, so to speak, photograph his thoughts, wishes and opinions on his patient's mind, and fill his mouth with his own phrases and language.[39]

The problem was that not every convict was quite as malleable; some abused and assaulted warders, others developed serious psychological disorders or attempted suicide. Before the end of the 1840s even the annual reports of the prison's commissioners were compelled to admit that there were difficulties with the system.[40]

The initial, optimistic logic of the separate system, together with increasing pressure from the Home Office for national uniformity, led to some county and borough authorities establishing a cellular system in existing or in purpose-built prisons. But, as with policing, developments in provincial gaols were limited by cost. The Bedfordshire justices ruled out the construction of a miniature Pentonville for their county on the grounds that it could not be done for less than £25,000. When, in 1848, they did embark on a rebuilding programme on a tender of just over £17,000 they faced a vociferous protest from ratepayers. Northernhay Gaol in Exeter was completed in 1819; by the 1830s it was insufficient for the number of prisoners sent to it but, primarily because of the expense, there was no new gaol and no provision for the separate system. The Lancashire magistrates, partly at the prompting of Clay, were committed to the separate system by the middle of the century, but a ratepayers' revolt helped to put the brakes on any successful implementation.[41]

Religion was central to the convict's reformation in the eyes of the experts who advocated the separate system. This led to the eclipse of the idea that useful and profitable labour could be an element in reformation. Preston Gaol had provided the model for the industrial prison with its inmates sub-contracted by three local textile firms and being allowed a proportion of the monetary value of their work. The practice was vehemently condemned by Sydney Smith in a celebrated article for the *Edinburgh Review*. In Preston itself the practice received little support from Clay, while Crawford objected that prisons were not intended as training schools for artisans. Work had a place, but only as a privilege, and to prevent the convict from dwelling too much on his previous evil way of life.[42] As a consequence, labour in prisons from the 1820s tended to be increasingly pointless marching on the treadmill, turning a handcrank or picking oakum in the solitude of a cell, or shifting cannonballs along a line of men from point A to point B and back.[43] But, again, whatever the theories of the influential experts some local gaols continued to go their own way. During the 1840s the inmates of Durham Gaol were producing cloth, mats, nets and rugs for sale in nearby markets; indeed one of the prison inspectors even suggested employing a tailor to teach his trade to the prisoners and replacing a treadmill with a smithy and a workshop.[44]

To a lesser extent the arguments over work in prisons were replicated in arguments over education. Moral reformation did not necessarily require the development of basic skills in literacy and numeracy; and, it was argued, prison should punish offenders not reward them with educational advancement. Nevertheless, some prisons did offer such opportunities to their inmates,[45] and few seriously questioned the necessity of educating, and thus reforming and rescuing, juvenile offenders. Here again institutional developments began primarily through the efforts of enthusiastic philanthropists.

The need to separate young offenders and thus prevent their total corruption by hardened recidivists had been urged for generations. As early as 1818 magistrates in Birmingham were sentencing some juveniles to short periods in a local reformatory financed by private subscription.[46] Melbourne's government took a positive step towards separating the juvenile offender in 1838 when a former military hospital on the Isle of Wight, Parkhurst, was opened with a reformatory regime for convicts under the age of eighteen prior to their transportation. The experiment was short lived. During the 1850s a band of indefatigable reformers including Mary Carpenter and Matthew Davenport Hill proselytised in favour of reformatories and industrial schools while private organisations, like the Philanthropic Society, established such institutions on an independent basis to reform and educate juvenile delinquents. In 1853 a Select Committee on Criminal and Destitute Children recommended a degree of state assistance for reformatory schools and the Youthful Offenders Act 1854 provided for persons under sixteen years to be sent to such schools for from two to five years following a prison sentence. Three years later legislation sanctioned the sending to industrial schools of children between the ages of seven and fourteen who had been committed for vagrancy. A perceived decline in juvenile crime during the second half of the nineteenth century was often attributed by the reformers to the reformatory and industrial schools; though they also insisted that a lack of trained staff and a reluctance on the part of magistrates to use the provisions were unnecessarily limiting the success of the schools.[47] It is, of course, unlikely that a decline in juvenile crime can be put down to one single element and, taking the country as a whole, it is clear that there was no common sentencing policy with reference to juveniles, the number of places available in these schools varied from locality to locality,[48] and the majority of convicted juveniles continued to be sent to ordinary gaols. Furthermore, locality and gender both appear to have influenced sentencing decisions: more urban than rural offenders were sent to prison, more boys than girls; also disproportionately more Irish children were incarcerated. All of which suggests sentencing practices in keeping with perceptions of crime and offenders.[49]

The deaths of both Crawford and Whitworth Russell in 1847 removed the two most ardent advocates of the separate system at the centre of national prison administration. The system had never been implemented across the nation with the uniformity and rigour that they had wished for; and within a decade of their deaths the debates about the penal system had shifted from whether that system should be separate or silent to other questions: how to handle convicts who, because of the end of transportation, were now released into the home community; and was the whole penal system sufficiently severe? Furthermore the deaths of Crawford and Whitworth Russell contributed to the balance of the system swinging away from the idea of religion as a central and significant aspect in the convict's reformation and towards a more rigorous application of the idea of prison as punishment.

The ticket-of-leave, introduced by the Penal Servitude Act 1853, was not entirely new.[50] Releasing convicts on licence following good behaviour had become a feature of the system in the penal colonies; moreover, large numbers of persons sentenced to transportation were, for a variety of reasons, never shipped abroad and were released in Britain after a term in gaol. The virtual end of transportation in the early 1850s required that something be done for those convicts in the national penitentiaries who were expecting a release on licence at some stage after they reached Australia. Jebb warned the Home Office of a build-up of tension among frustrated convicts and while there were considerable qualms expressed by both the Home Secretary, Lord Palmerston, and his civil servants, the ticket-of-leave seemed to offer an answer. The ticket-of-leave was a conditional pardon with remission granted towards the end of a sentence to any convict not guilty of idleness or misconduct. Initially the press and members of parliament appear to have been sympathetic to convicts released on licence in this way, particularly when they seemed unable to get work or seemed to be the objects of police harassment.[51] But there was the major problem of a lack of an administrative bureaucracy organised and primed to cope with the ticket-of-leave system. Furthermore, by the mid-1850s both sections of the press and some members of parliament had become vociferously hostile, linking a perceived rise in violent crime with ticket-of-leave men now prowling the English streets rather than those of the antipodes. Probably also the suspicions about ticket-of-leave men were linked with the perceptions of criminals as a group. While Mayhew himself was sympathetic to the plight of ticket-of-leave men, the picture that he, and others, sketched of criminals as a class apart brought up to their own, skilled criminal trades, was not conducive to the ex-convict being accepted and re-assimilated as an unfortunate, *former* offender who had paid his debt to society. Amending legislation in 1857 tightened up the system and extended prison sentences so that seven, rather than four years' penal servitude in England, became the equivalent of seven years' transportation to Australia. Momentarily, the concerns subsided, but they erupted again with the garrotting panic of 1862. Garrotting was seen in many quarters as the work of ticket-of-leave men; it was defined as a 'science' along with housebreaking.[52] Parliament responded with the 'Garrotters' Act', which authorised up to fifty strokes of corporal punishment in addition to any other punishment inflicted on those guilty of armed or violent robbery, and a Royal Commission was appointed to investigate the legislation relating to transportation and penal servitude. The report of the Royal Commission resulted in a new Penal Servitude Act 1864, which required police supervision of ticket-of-leave men and specified minimum sentences of penal servitude: five years for a first offence, seven years for any subsequent.

There was doubt about the precise meaning of the term 'penal servitude' when it was first enshrined in law in 1853; the doubt continued. Even though the Home Office was increasingly responsible for, and issuing directions about, prison administration, no government was prepared to commit itself as to whether the penal system as a whole, and penal servitude in particular, was designed to deter, to punish, or to reform. The Penal Servitude Acts were *ad hoc* legislation rather than the product of any consistent, reasoned policy. The initial legislation established 'penal servitude' (whatever it was) to balance the declining use of transportation, with those sentences that were served at home to be marginally less than those in the colonies. The amending legislation ironed out the problems that emerged, but also generally made penal servitude sentences longer in response to concerns about the end of transportation, the ticket-of-leave system and the garrotting scares of 1856 and 1862.[53]

The year 1863 can be singled out as a key one for the increasing severity of the penal system, though primarily through coincidence. In addition to the Garrotters' Act it was in that year that Joshua Jebb died. Knighted and promoted to a major-general, Jebb nevertheless died with the regime that he had administered as Director of Convict Prisons coming increasingly under attack for being too soft on dangerous men. That same year Edmund Du Cane, another officer of the Royal Engineers and a strict disciplinarian who was ultimately to take over the directorship, was appointed an Assistant Director of Convict Prisons. Finally, but by no means least, a Select Committee of the House of Lords, chaired by the Earl of Carnarvon, presented its report on Gaol Discipline. The Carnarvon Committee disputed the suggestion that moral reformation was more important than punishment and urged greater severity with the prisons extolling the virtues of the crank, the treadmill and shot drill. The Committee also urged the closure of small prisons and the withdrawal of Treasury support from any local gaol that did not conform to Home Office regulations. Many of the recommendations, particularly those advocating greater severity, were incorporated in the third Penal Servitude Act. The results were not always what was intended. While the crank and the treadmill were recommended for those sentenced to penal servitude, they seem to have been more likely the lot of the short-term prisoner confined to a local gaol for a petty offence, and often a first-time offence. After nine months of solitary confinement in Millbank or Pentonville, where they generally picked oakum or sewed, long-term penal servitude convicts were removed to the public works prisons of Chatham, Dartmoor, Portland or Portsmouth where, often at great risk to life and limb, they generally quarried stone or constructed fortifications and dockyard facilities.[54] Some of the smaller local prisons also continued to go their own way and it was not until 1877 that all prisons were brought under central control, which in practice then meant the strict supervision of Du Cane.

The hardening attitude towards prison discipline drew on the changing perception of the offender. There was little point in attempting the reformation and education of those who the social Darwinian and positivist thinkers were describing as innately criminal and inferior.[55] Yet these attitudes also coincided with further limitations on capital punishment, the final shift of physical punishment away from public view, and an increasing tendency to have decisions made by experts regarding the fate or treatment of offenders. While in practice since the 1840s no-one had been executed for any crime other than murder, it was not until the Offences Against the Person Act of 1861 that parliament finally abolished the death penalty for all crimes except murder and high treason. In 1856 a select committee recommended the ending of public executions. A Royal Commission made the same recommendation ten years later. The deterrent effect of a public execution was perceived as negligible and far outweighed by the problems and dangers created by the large crowds that such executions attracted. The last public execution took place outside Newgate on 26 May 1868. Except for the occasional glimpse of a convict gang in the vicinity of a public works prison or the possible sight of a convict being escorted by guards by rail, the penal system was now completely private. After sentencing in court – justice as personified by the courts still had to be *seen* to be done – the convict was not seen again by the public until release; the capitally convicted convict was never seen again in public, unless subsequently reprieved and released. In the eighteenth and early nineteenth centuries the decision as to whether or not a felon should go to the gallows had been a royal prerogative; the decision was actually made in the King's Council. But by the mid-nineteenth century the prerogative of mercy was administered by the home secretary and his bureaucrats.[56]

The removal of the convict and of punishment from public gaze robbed the felon of any moment of glory or martyrdom. It was also in keeping with notions of dignity and decorum so important to Victorian sensibility, but which certainly pre-dated Victoria's reign.[57] Whether the mystery of punishment increased its deterrence is a moot point.[58] Whether the dramatic reduction of the number of capital offences together with the bringing down of the curtain on the theatre of public executions produced a qualitatively more humanitarian penal system is also open to debate. Of course convicted criminals were no longer executed, or at least sentenced to be executed, in large numbers. The early reformers like Howard and then the gaol inspectorate led to prisons being better regulated and cleaner; the chance of death from that variety of typhus known as gaol fever was all but removed. The replacement of the entrepreneurial gaoler with an increasingly centralised and regulated system also meant a common diet for all prisoners whatever their financial situation. Yet whatever the boasts of the experts the diet was not particularly nourishing and regularly brought on the most unpleasant and painful stomach complaints. If public spectacle had gone, brutal punishment still remained with the added variant of electric shock treatment – 'galvanising' – for convicts suspected of malingering. In addition to the official brutality of the birch, the crank, the electric shock and the treadmill, there was the psychological suffering brought about by solitary confinement and enforced silence. Warders, like policemen, had discretion and were not always under the eyes of upright superiors; some showed kindness and generosity towards those in their charge; others were noted for lashing out unofficially with boot, club and fist. Convicts responded in kind.[59]

Entrepreneurial gaolers and the officials responsible for penal colonies could coerce their charges, but once the notion of reformation came in sanctions became necessary to make the recalcitrant conform even if they did not intend to reform; if one or two convicts were allowed to set bad examples the system would be undermined. By the same token rewards were gradually introduced to encourage compliance and to reward the well behaved. Ferocious abuse from a warder, a bread and water diet, solitary confinement, or a flogging provided the stick; gratuities for good conduct and industry among long-term prisoners, and the ability to work time off the end of a long sentence by collecting high 'marks', provided the carrot. The 'marks' system was finalised to mechanical perfection under Du Cane and, at the same time, different uniforms were designed to denote what stage a convict had reached in his sentence, and whether his behaviour had been good or bad.[60]

The increasing role of prison staff in deciding the punishment or treat-ment of convicts in their charge developed as arguments and unease con-tinued about sentencing policy in the courts. While some late eighteenth- and early nineteenth-century reformers had sought particular punishments to fit particular crimes, the improved bureaucracy and record keeping at both national and local level meant that previous convictions could more easily be brought to a court's attention before sentence was passed.[61] For some offenders a criminal record became a veritable millstone around their necks; being 'known to the police' and being found in suspicious circum-stances could lead in itself to magistrates inflicting a short sentence as a suspicious person. As noted in the previous chapter there was insufficient evidence to convict the two ex-ticket-of-leave men charged with garrotting James Pilkington M.P., but the police magistrate nevertheless sentenced them to three months' imprisonment as suspicious persons.[62] Liberal public concern centred on the discretion and veracity of the police. In 1866, following proven corrupt evidence by police in a burglary trial and a mag-istrate's initial refusal to hear evidence for the defence, *Fun* ridiculed the Metropolitan Police Courts with a cartoon of a magistrate rejecting a ragged boy while a smug policeman looked on:

Learned Magistrate: – *Hear the evidence for the defence? Nonsense! I won't hear a word of it! What's the use? I could not think of doubting a policeman's word.*[63]

The sentence of penal servitude gave magistrates and judges the opportunity to inflict ferocious sentences on persons who, while undoubtedly pests in that they were continually being brought before different courts, never carried out any particularly serious offence. The prosecution and sentences of Crowsley, Hudson and Taverner offer examples of this (Table 10.6); it is worth noting, in passing, the three-month sentence imposed on Taverner in March 1861 for being a suspicious person. But again it must be stressed that the use of this legislation varied from place to place. The magistrates in the industrial districts of the north west used the legislation more than those in London or in rural counties; and Gloucestershire and Hampshire stand out among the rural counties for their use of the Penal Servitude Acts, almost certainly because of the influence of T. B. Lloyd Baker and the Earl of Carnarvon on their respective county benches.[64]

Sentences of this sort on relatively minor, if persistent and infuriating offenders, brought forth criticism from liberal-minded reformers.[65] Concern was also expressed that sentences for property offences often seemed excessive in comparison to those meted out to violent offenders. But, as in the case of prison policy, no consensus could be reached on how to improve the sentencing system. There was a basic conservatism in the legal profession and especially among the judiciary that worked against proposals for a codification of the law. Codification was a foreign route; and while it was a last resort, Francophobia could always be enlisted to bolster arguments that, whatever the merits of the Code Napoleon, the reasons for its creation were not relevant to England, and the means by which it was established were alien to the English constitution. When even Du Cane criticised the system of sentencing, his comments served, not to foster change, but to reveal a division within the Home Office over whether government should appear to give directives to judges and magistrates. Throughout the century judges and magistrates continued to use their discretion and to be swayed by influences external to the case before them when they came to pass sentence; and while reformers and codifiers might lament it, others boasted, in contrast, that herein lay one of the strengths of the system. 'It seems to me', remarked Baron Alderson in 1854:

a very unwise thing to abolish the common law principles of decision, which can accommodate themselves to the varying circumstances of the times, and thus, as it were, to stereotype them by Act of Parliament in verbal definitions, many of them inaccurate. *This will leave the courts only to construe precise words, instead of adapting old principles to new cases as they arise.*[66]

TABLE 10.6 *'Penal servitude' for petty recidivists*

(a) Prosecutions and convictions of William Henry Crosley, born c.1849, labourer

Offence	Court	Date	Sentence
Stealing provisions	†	7 July 1862	1 calendar month
Stealing bread	Bedford Borough	Easter 1863	Acquitted
Stealing tares		1 June 1863	1 calendar month
Assault		4 July 1864	1 calendar month
Wilful damage		5 Sept. 1865	1 calendar month
Stealing potatoes	Bedford Borough	Midsummer 1866	12 calendar months
Stealing growing crops		4 May 1868	2 calendar months
Using insulting words		7 Jan. 1870	7 days
Riot	Bedford Borough	Epiphany 1871	acquitted
Stealing 2½ pecks potatoes	Bedford Borough	Easter 1872	7 years' penal servitude and 7 years' police supervision

(b) Prosecutions and convictions of William Hudson, born c.1808, labourer

Offence	Court	Date	Sentence
Sheep stealing	Beds Quarter Sessions	Midsummer 1838	Acquitted
Stealing a spade	Beds Quarter Sessions	Midsummer 1838	6 weeks
Stealing a fowl	Beds Assizes	Lent 1839	1 year
Game Laws		Feb. 1844	6 weeks
Stealing hen and chickens	Beds Quarter Sessions	Epiphany 1845	acquitted
Sheep stealing	Beds Quarter Sessions	Epiphany 1845	Transported 15 years
Stealing potatoes		Aug. 1854	1 calendar month
Stealing hay	Beds Quarter Sessions	Midsummer 1860	7 days
Stealing meat	Beds Assizes	Lent 1867	3 calendar months
Stealing sickles, basket and other articles	Beds Quarter Sessions	Michaelmas 1868	7 years' penal servitude

(c) Prosecutions and Convictions of Samuel Taverner, born c.1839, labourer

Offence	Court	Date	Sentence
Stealing fowls	Beds Quarter Sessions	Michaelmas 1855	3 calendar months
Stealing iron		25 Mar. 1856	3 calendar months
Wilful damage		17 Nov. 1857	6 weeks
Stealing barley	Beds Quarter Sessions	Epiphany 1858	No true bill
Assault		8 June 1858	1 calendar month
Wilful damage		14 Sep. 1858	21 days
Stealing barley		14 Sep. 1858	21 days
Stealing a rat trap		31 Jan. 1860	1 calendar month
Suspicious person		5 Mar. 1861	3 calendar months
Drunk and riotous		21 Oct. 1861	21 days

TABLE 10.6 *(cont.)*

Offence	Court	Date	Sentence
Stealing manure bags	Beds Quarter Sessions	Epiphany 1862	3 years' penal servitude
Drunk and riotous		27 Sep. 1864	7 days
Stealing cabbages		10 June 1865	1 calendar month
Game Laws		19 Dec. 1865	2 calendar months or £3 8s. fine
Game Laws		18 Sep. 1866	1 calendar month or £2 14s. fine
Stealing barrow wheel and some iron (value 3s.)	Beds Quarter Sessions	Michaelmas 1867	7 years' penal servitude
Stealing 5 pieces of lindsey (value £1)	Beds Quarter Sessions	Epiphany 1874	10 years' penal servitude and 7 years police supervision

Source: Based on details in Beds. R.O. QGV 10/4[†]
[†] Where the court is unspecified in the records it was almost certainly petty sessions

Yet if controversy continued to remain about sentencing policy a significant change had taken place. In the space of 100 years a custodial sentence had become virtually the only punishment that the courts could award; fines continued to be imposed for many petty offences, but with the proviso that failure to pay would lead to imprisonment. These changes in the system of punishment have been related to the great changes taking place in society, implicitly by the Whig historians who thought in terms of progress with the past developing towards a more enlightened future, and explicitly by Marxists, and others, who have explained the development of the prison in terms of the control needs of bourgeois capitalism. The old notion of the 'truth' lying somewhere between the extremes will not do; why should the 'truth' necessarily be found between just two world views?

Humanitarianism counted in the reform of punishment. Whatever the psychological make-up of late eighteenth- and early nineteenth-century reformers which fostered their ideas of prison discipline,[67] they drew considerable inspiration from the humanitarian and rational elements within the Enlightenment. Brutal punishments, suffering in unregulated gaols, the apparent lottery of who was executed and who was not, all mattered to these reformers; they also convinced others that these things mattered, and notably they convinced men at the centre of government. The state played an important role in the changes in punishment. It was a capitalist state and, arguably, increasingly a bourgeois state. Anglo-Saxon historians have, perhaps, been too timid in acknowledging the role of the state in pushing ahead with many reforms in the nineteenth century. Albeit piecemeal and, at times, reluctantly, governments sponsored legislation that reduced capital punishment and were prepared to become involved in the administration of convicts and prisons; once involved it was probably impossible for the state to extricate itself as bureaucratic machinery spawned and renewed itself. But, at the same time, it is difficult to detect a simple 'state' or a 'class' line on punishment developing consistently during these years.[68] Serious divisions remained and at the beginning of the twentieth century Sir Robert Anderson lamented the way that punishment continued to swing between extremes:

Let anyone propose, for example, that a 'hooligan' shall receive the sort of punishment which at a public school would be meted out to the son of a duke for gross misconduct, and they will raise such an outcry as will stifle legislation to that end. Another minority, equally small in numbers, will always protest against any amelioration of the prisoner's lot. And thus the pendulum is kept swinging, while an easy going public remains perplexed and passive.[69]

Much of the legislation – the Penal Servitude Acts for example – was *ad hoc*; and when parliament legislated, or when the Home Office issued directives, many localities were reluctant to act promptly and thoroughly in accordance with the new law or the new directive, partly because of local pride but more often perhaps because of the expense. If the bourgeois capitalist state wanted a new system of punishment to help control the new and growing proletariat, the provincial bourgeois capitalists – even in the heartlands of the industrial revolution – may have been notably keen to see the Penal Servitude and Habitual Criminals legislation enforced, but they were most reluctant to pay increased rates to finance changes in policing and prisons. 'Prisons', according to one author,

like the workhouse under the New Poor Law, were not primarily for locking people up, but about disciplining those who were not in prison. So, although convicts might resist and obstruct prison discipline, their role in social control was assured simply by their existence.[70]

The fact that the new prison was developed at roughly the same time as the workhouse under the New Poor Law makes this equation appealing; the parallel with the control system of the new factory can also be drawn.[71] Clearly there are similarities: closed institutions are going to resemble each other from the very fact of being closed institutions, though this does not necessarily prove similar motives for their creation. Vagrancy and idleness were faults that reformers like Chadwick perceived as rampant in sections of the working class; these faults had to be eradicated and the threat of the workhouse was a means to this end. In this perception of the world vagrancy and idleness also led to crime, which gives further underpinning to the equation. But the equation requires some qualification; there were also considerable differences in intention between the two institutions, as well as considerable differences in perception, and it would be difficult to put these down simply to bourgeois hegemony. Provision for the very old, the very young, and the infirm was also supposed to be a part of the new workhouse; and the debate over whether prisons were meant to reform and inculcate good habits, or simply to punish, was never resolved. But perhaps most important is to look at the two institutions from the bottom up. There was no working-class sanction for the workhouse, as demonstrated by the disorders of the 1830s and 1840s and the continuing hostility throughout the nineteenth century. The workhouse hung over sections of the poorer working class like a sword of Damocles in a way that the prison never did. The workhouse was more visible; several of the great convict prisons were constructed well away from centres of population and what went on inside them was increasingly private – one reason perhaps for the apparent popularity of prison biographies that revealed this secret world for the vicarious pleasure of the nineteenth-century reader.[72] Groups of workers who profited from illegal fiddles and perks did not regard as 'criminals' those of their workmates who were caught, convicted and imprisoned for such offences. Yet other former convicts from the working class did find it hard to get accepted, not simply by employers, but also by some working-class communities after a prison sentence.[73] Since the working class were often the victims of crimes it is scarcely surprising if they had little time for many former offenders. The popular abuse heaped on certain unpopular offenders as they were conveyed to Tyburn Tree in the eighteenth century should warn against any notion of the working class automatically siding with convicted criminals against a common class enemy. There is no reason to suppose anything other than that, in the popular mind, the prison was accepted as being designed not as an encouragement to them to behave, but as a place where genuine offenders were to be punished.

Notes and references

1 The most detailed and subtle of the Whig studies is **Leon Radzinowicz**, *A History of English Criminal Law*, vol. 1, Stevens, London, 1948 and (with **Roger Hood**) vol. 5, 1986; the latter volume has been re-published as *The Emergence of Penal Policy in Victorian and Edwardian England*, Clarendon Press, Oxford, 1990. For a Whig view of the abolition of the death penalty see **David D. Cooper**, *The Lesson of the Scaffold*, Allen Lane, London, 1974. **Michael Ignatieff**, *A Just Measure of Pain: The Penitentiary in the Industrial Revolution 1750–1850*, Macmillan, London, 1978, constitutes one of the most stimulating works of revision, though Ignatieff has backtracked to some degree, see his autocritique 'State, civil society and total institutions: A critique of recent social histories of punishment', in **S. Cohen** and **A. Scull** (eds), *Social Control and the State*, Oxford U.P., Oxford, 1983. There is a passionate study of the reality of the public execution, its cultural meanings, and the role of these meanings in the gradual repeal of the Bloody Code, in **V. A. C. Gatrell**, *The Hanging Tree: Execution and the English people, 1770–1868*, Clarendon Press, Oxford, 1994. **David Garland**, *Punishment and Modern Society: A study in social theory*, Clarendon Press, Oxford, 1991, is a subtle and very readable analysis of the theoretical literature with a thoughtful and stimulating approach to assessing punishment as a cultural phenomenon that embodies and expresses the cultural forms of a society.

2 *P.P.* 1833 (344) xiii, *Select Committee on Municipal Corporations*, qq. 2730, 3088–9 and 6388–90; **R. E. Swift**, 'Crime, law and order in two English towns during the early nineteenth century: The experience of Exeter and Wolverhampton 1815–56', unpublished Ph.D., University of Birmingham, 1981, pp. 82–3.

3 For example, at the Old Bailey Sessions in January 1801 George Mell was convicted of stealing indigo from an East India Company warehouse in Billiter Lane; he was sentenced to six months in Newgate and a public whipping to be conducted for a distance of 100 yards in Billiter Lane. At the same sessions Richard Cain was convicted of stealing coal from a barge at Queenhithe; he was sentenced to twelve months in Newgate and a public whipping from Queenhithe to Queen Street. *O.B.S.P. 1800–1*, nos 111 and 112.

4 For the use of the stocks in the mid-nineteenth century see **Clive Emsley**, 'The Bedfordshire Police 1840–56: A case study in the working of the Rural Constabulary Act', *Midland History*, vii (1982), pp. 73–92 (at pp. 84–5); **B. J. Davey**, *Lawless and Immoral: Policing a country town 1838–57*, Leicester U.P., London, 1983, pp. 44, 143, 147, 162 and 164.

5 For the best survey of eighteenth-century punishment and the contemporary debate see **J. M. Beattie**, *Crime and the Courts in England 1660–1800*,

Oxford U.P., Oxford, 1986, chs 9 and 10. Beattie argues, convincingly, that the 1718 Transportation Act constituted a fundamental break with the practices and intentions of the penal policy of the past, and that it was, in consequence, as significant as the establishment of prisons in the last decades of the eighteenth century. See also, **A. Roger Ekirch**, *Bound for America: The transportation of British convicts to the colonies, 1718–1775*, Clarendon Press, Oxford, 1987.

6 *Hansard*, new series, xiv, col. 1220.

7 **J. A. Sharpe**, *Crime in Early Modern England 1550–1750*, 2nd edn, Longman, London, 1999, pp. 90–9; **Clive Emsley**, 'Repression, "terror" and the rule of law in England during the decade of the French Revolution', *E.H.R.*, c (1985), pp. 801–25 (at pp. 822–3).

8 Gatrell, *The Hanging Tree, passim*.

9 **Randall McGowen**, 'From pillory to gallows: The punishment of forgery in the age of the financial revolution', *P and P*, **165** (1999), pp. 107–40; see also, *idem*, 'Forgery discovered: Or the perils of circulation in eighteenth-century England', *Angelaki*, **1** (1994), pp. 113–29.

10 **Robert Shoemaker**, 'Streets of shame? The crowd and public punishments in London 1700–1820', in **Simon Devereaux** and **Paul Griffiths** (eds), *Penal Practice and Culture 1500–1900: Punishing the English*, Palgrave, London, 2004.

11 *Northampton Mercury*, 12 August 1754.

12 Ibid., 20 July 1752, quoting the *London Evening Post*.

13 Ibid. See also *Sussex Weekly Advertiser*, 30 August 1819, for the following: 'Upon arrival of the cart under the fatal tree the Rev Mr Noyce, the clergyman in attendance, ascended it and began to pray . . . requesting the unhappy man to join him, but this Piper refused to do, saying that he was a murdered man and that Pearce was perjured and that he never snapped a pistol at him . . . he went on to observe that there was no law for a poor man, and referred to a case last Assize wherein one prisoner was condemned to death and another, charged with a similar crime, was sentenced to two months imprisonment, and called down heavy vengeance on the heads of his prosecutors.'

   Martin Madan reported 'the understanding and policy of a low thief to say to *Judge Burnett*, once, at *Hertford* Assizes – "My lord, it is very hard to hang me for *only* stealing a horse". It was worthy the good sense and wisdom of the learned Judge, to answer – "Man, thou art not to be hanged *only* for stealing a horse, but that horses might not be stolen".' **Martin Madan**, *Thoughts on Executive Justice*, London, 1785, p. 105.

14 **J. S. Cockburn**, 'Punishment and brutalization in the English Enlightenment', *Law and History Review*, **12** (1994), pp. 155–79.

15 *Gentleman's Magazine*, xli (1771), p. 147.

16 Ignatieff, *Just Measure of Pain*, p. 57.

17 Lord North's government finally collapsed in March 1782; the second
    Rockingham administration lasted only till July 1782 and Lord Shelburne's
    administration, which followed it, fell in April 1783. The Fox–North
    coalition lasted from April to December 1783, and while the younger Pitt
    ultimately brought stability, he had to fight a general election in December
    1784.

18 **Jonas Hanway**, *The Defects of Police, the Cause of Immorality and the
    Continual Robberies committed, particularly in the Metropolis*, London,
    1775, p. 72; for similar criticism of the hulks see Madan, *Thoughts on
    Executive Justice*, pp. 74–6.

19 *Journals of the House of Commons*, xl, pp. 1161–4.

20 *Gentleman's Magazine*, lvi (1786), pp. 263–4.

21 Ignatieff, *Just Measure of Pain*, pp. 128–42.

22 **A. G. L. Shaw**, *Convicts and the Colonies: A study of penal transportation
    from Great Britain and Ireland to Australia and other parts of the British
    Empire*, Faber and Faber, London, 1966, p. 59.

23 *Gentleman's Magazine*, lvi (1786), p. 102.

24 **John Cannon**, *Parliamentary Reform 1640–1832*, Cambridge U.P.,
    Cambridge, 1973, p. 140, note 3.

25 Cooper, *The Lesson of the Scaffold*, p. 33, states that the 1820 legislation
    failed, but see **K. K. Macnab**, 'Aspects of the history of crime in England and
    Wales between 1850–60', unpublished Ph.D., University of Sussex 1965,
    appendices, pp. 22 and 24.

26 **Sir Leon Radzinowicz** and **Roger Hood**, 'Judicial discretion and
    sentencing standards: Victorian attempts to solve a perennial problem',
    University of Pennsylvania Law Review, **127** (1779), pp. 1288–349
    (at pp. 1290–9).

27 **Randall McGowan**, 'The image of justice and reform of the criminal law
    in early nineteenth-century England', *Buffalo Law Review*, **32** (1983),
    pp. 89–125 (at p. 96).

28 Of course no sensible historian has argued simply and explicitly that Romilly,
    Mackintosh and other reformers had a contemporary legal system in mind as
    the model toward which they aspired; yet this view often implicitly informs
    the work of the Whig historians. McGowan highlights this in his excellent
    critique of Radzinowicz: 'His volume on the death penalty is informed by
    one idea – that the gallows represented an inefficient and inhumane form of
    punishment. This observation is so obvious to him that he pauses to wonder

before thinkers and politicians who for so long resisted the "truth". The opponents of change are portrayed as simple reactionaries, blinded by self-interest or prejudice from seeing the value of new institutional forms.' Ibid., p. 94. Simon Devereaux recently has come to the defence of Peel against Gatrell by stressing that the real increase in executions came under Peel's predecessor at the Home Office, Lord Sidmouth. Peel, Devereaux argues, was more conscientious in his decisions over pardons and more sensitive to growing concerns about the number of executions. **Simon Devereaux**, 'Peel, pardon and punishment: The Recorder's report revisited', in Devereaux and Griffiths (eds), *Penal Practice and Culture 1500–1900.*

29 Macnab, 'Aspects of . . . crime', appendix 3, pp. 13–14, lists twenty-six acts of parliament removing capital punishment from particular offences between 1808 and 1835; subsequent legislation, in 1837, removed the death penalty from such offences as assembling with arms to assist smugglers, abortion, forging wills and power of attorney for the transfer of stock, attempted murder, burglary, piracy, arson of buildings or ships; and legislation of 1841 abolished the death penalty for rape, carnally abusing girls aged under ten, riot, and embezzlement by Bank of England servants. Following the Offences Against the Person Act 1861 the death penalty remained only for murder and high treason.

30 Cooper, *Lesson of the Scaffold*, pp. 45–53 and ch. 3 *passim.*

31 Shaw, *Convicts and the Colonies*, pp. 147–50; **L. L. Robson**, *The Convict Settlers of Australia*, Melbourne U.P., Melbourne, 1965, p. 9. Unless otherwise stated the discussion of transportation is based on the work of Robson and Shaw.

32 *Gentleman's Magazine*, lvi (1786), p. 103.

33 **Charles Stuart Parker** (ed.), *Sir Robert Peel: From his private papers*, 3 vols, London, 1891, i, 400–1.

34 **J. J. Tobias**, *Crime and Industrial Society in the Nineteenth Century*, Penguin, Harmondsworth, 1972, p. 246.

35 *P.P. 1837–38 (669) xxii, Select Committee on Transportation*, p. 20.

36 The end of transportation as a sentence in the British courts coincided with its increased use by the French and, in spite of the fact that the British were questioning their system, French politicians continued to use it as a model. **Patricia O'Brien**, *The Promise of Punishment: Prisons in nineteenth-century France*, Princeton U.P., Princeton, N.J., 1982, pp. 259–87; **Gordon Wright**, *Between the Guillotine and Liberty: Two centuries of the crime problem in France*, Oxford U.P., 1983, pp. 105–8 and 132–5.

37 Quoted in **Philip Priestley**, *Victorian Prison Lives: English prison biography 1830–1914*, Methuen, London, 1985, pp. 35–6.

38 Quoted in **Christopher Harding** *et al.*, *Imprisonment in England and Wales: A concise history*, Croom Helm, London, 1985, p. 152. There was little love lost between Jebb and these two inspectors, see **Eric Stockdale**, 'The rise of Joshua Jebb, 1837–50', *British Journal of Criminology*, **16** (1976).

39 **W. L. Clay**, *The Prison Chaplain: A memoir of the Rev John Clay*, London, 1861, p. 386.

40 Ignatieff, *Just Measure of Pain*, pp. 9–10; Priestley, *Victorian Prison Lives*, p. 38.

41 **Eric Stockdale**, *A Study of Bedford Prison 1660–1877*, Phillimore, London, 1977, pp. 165 and 176; Swift, 'Crime, law and order', pp. 87–8; **Margaret E. DeLacy**, 'Grinding men good? Lancashire's prisons at mid century', in **Victor Bailey** (ed.), Policing and Punishment in Nineteenth-Century Britain, Croom Helm, London, 1981, pp. 209–11.

42 **Sydney Smith**, 'Prisons', *Edinburgh Review*, xxxvi (1822); DeLacy, 'Grinding men good?', pp. 200–2.

43 Priestley, *Victorian Prison Lives*, pp. 121–31; Harding *et al.*, *Imprisonment*, appendix 3.

44 **James C. Burke**, 'Crime and criminality in County Durham 1840–55', unpublished M.A., University of Durham, 1980, p. 91.

45 Priestley, *Victorian Prison Lives*, pp. 108–11; Burke, 'Crime and criminality', pp. 93–6.

46 **Barbara Weinberger**, 'Law breakers and law enforcers in the late Victorian city: Birmingham 1867–77', unpublished Ph.D., University of Birmingham, 1981, p. 116.

47 **Jelinger C. Symons**, *Special Report on Reformatories in Gloucs., Shropshire, Worcs., Herefordshire and Monmouthshire, and in Wales* (printed in *P.P.* 1857–58 [2315] xlvi, *Minutes of the Committee of the Council on Education*); **John Trevarthen**, 'Hooliganism', *Nineteenth Century*, xlix (1901), pp. 84–9.

48 Stockdale, *Bedford Prison*, p. 153.

49 **John A. Stack**, 'Children, urbanization and the chances of imprisonment in mid-Victorian Britain', *C.J.H*, **13** (1992), pp. 113–39.

50 Unless otherwise stated what follows is drawn largely from **Peter W. J. Bartrip**, 'Public opinion and law enforcement: The ticket-of-leave scares in mid-Victorian Britain', in Bailey (ed.), *Policing and Punishment*.

51 Of course police harassment could be, and was, used as a defence in court by former convicts who insisted that because of the police they were unable to get a steady job. For example, in November 1856 Charles Hunter, accused of robbery with violence at the Old Bailey, protested: 'When I came home from transportation, I obtained a situation at a beer house in the Waterloo Road,

where I was getting a comfortable living, and supporting my wife and aged mother; I had been there a few weeks when sergeant Broad came and told the landlord that I was a ticket-of-leave man, and if he allowed such characters in his house he should indict it; he told me to go; after that I drove a costermonger barrow, and he followed me about the streets, telling my customers to see that their change was good, for I was a ticket-of-leave man; I was compelled to give that up; I went to live with my parents, and worked at tailoring, and every time I came in or out of the court where I lived, he would stop and search me, if any of the neighbours or their children were about; so that at last I could get nobody to trust me with anything; what had I to do? I would work if they would let me, but they will not.' *C.C.C.S.P. 1856–57*, no. 87, pp. 102–3. See above, pp. 178–80.

52 **H. W. Holland,** 'The science of garrotting and housebreaking', *Cornhill Magazine*, vii (1863), pp. 79–92.

53 **M. Heather Tomlinson,** 'Penal servitude 1846–65: A system in evolution', in Bailey (ed.), *Policing and Punishment.*; see also Bartrip, 'Public opinion and law enforcement'.

54 Priestley, *Victorian Prison Lives*, pp. 131–4. An exhaustive account of Carnarvon's ideas, and how these fed into Du Cane's practice, is to be found in **Sean McConville,** *English Local Prisons 1860–1900: Next only to death*, Routledge, London, 1995.

55 **W. J. Forsythe,** *The Reform of Prisoners, 1830–1900*, Croom Helm, London, 1987, ch. 8.

56 **Roger Chadwick,** *Bureaucratic Mercy: The Home Office and the treatment of capital cases in Victorian Britain*, Garland Publishing, New York, 1992.

57 In March 1825, for example, during discussions on a bill dealing with the punishment for sending threatening letters and a Felonies Pardon Bill, Ralph Bernal condemned the 'most unbecoming' practice employed at some of the London Police Offices 'of passing the prisoners, many of whom stood charged with common assaults, manacled through the streets from the offices to the prison'. Peel agreed about the 'indecency', though he considered that it would be too expensive to provide transport; he had advised the magistrates to use hackney carriages. *Hansard*, new series, xii (1825), col. 1167.

58 **Henry Fielding,** *An Enquiry into the Causes of the Late Increase of Robbers*, 2nd edn, London, 1751, was critical of the Tyburn executions and urged privacy drawing a theatrical parallel. 'Foreigners have found fault with the Cruelty of the English Drama, in representing frequent Murders upon the Stage. In fact, this is not only cruel, but highly injudicious: A Murder behind the Scenes, if the Poet knows how to manage it, will affect the Audience with greater Terror than if it was acted before their eyes.' He instanced Macbeth's murder of Duncan as performed by David Garrick (p. 193).

59 Priestley, *Victorian Prison Lives*, especially chs 7 and 9.

60 Harding *et al.*, *Imprisonment in England and Wales*, p. 229.

61 During the 1830s local gaolers kept the Bedfordshire Clerk of the Peace informed of men awaiting trial who had faced previous prosecutions. See, for example, Beds. R.O. 1834/634–5, 640 and 644–5.

62 See above, p. 244.

63 *Fun*, 13 October 1866, p. 51; the case that prompted the cartoon is reported on p. 49.

64 **S. J. Stevenson**, 'The "Criminal Class" in the mid-Victorian city: A study of policy conducted with special reference to the provision of 34 and 35 Vict., c. 112 (1871) in Birmingham and East London in the early years of registration and supervision', unpublished D. Phil., Oxford University, 1983.

65 Radzinowicz and Hood, 'Judicial discretion and sentencing standards', pp. 1310–11; *Sir James Fitzjames Stephen* argued in his *A History of the Criminal Law of England* (vol. 1, p. 479) that there could be some justification for bringing back the death penalty not only for brutal violence, but also for someone who, it was proved, was totally irredeemable. See the discussion in **Robert Anderson**, 'Our absurd system of punishing crime', *Nineteenth Century*, xlix (1901), pp. 268–84.

66 Quoted in ibid., pp. 1302–3 (emphasis in original).

67 Ignatieff, *Just Measure of Pain*, is excellent on the psychology of reformers like John Howard.

68 Simon Stevenson suggests, persuasively, a pendulum effect in the final third of the nineteenth century with the authoritarian side of Benthamite liberalism dominant among legislators from the mid-1860s to the mid-1870s, a swing to a more liberal intellectual outlook during the 1880s, with a swing back towards coercive solutions in the 1890s. Stevenson, 'The "criminal class" ' in the mid-Victorian city', pp. 389–422.

69 Anderson, 'Our absurd system of punishing crime', p. 278.

70 **Philip Rawlings** in Harding *et al.*, *Imprisonment in England and Wales*, p. 179.

71 See, for example, **D. Melossi** and **M. Pavarini**, *The Prison and the Factory: Origins of the penitentiary system*, Macmillan, London, 1980.

72 See the bibliography in Priestley, *Victorian Prison Lives*.

73 Weinberger, 'Law breakers and law enforcers', p. 156.

CHAPTER 11

Concluding remarks

Different contexts foster different areas for historical study. Many of the social historians who began the current wave of research into crime had been nurtured in the heady political enthusiasm of universities during the 1960s. Their inspiration came from studying 'history from below' and particularly the work of Eric Hobsbawm, George Rudé and E. P. Thompson. Much of their interest was directed to the enormous economic and social changes of the eighteenth and nineteenth centuries. In particular they concentrated on property crime and addressed what was perceived of as the criminalisation of customary practice. The criminal law and the courts were seen as one way into a deeper exploration of class relationships. A generation on, and now much more gender sensitive, there has been something of a shift towards studying crimes of violence – offences that might have been inter-class, but were rather more likely to be inter-gender. Increasingly the criminal law and the courts have been seen as a way into the exploration of gender norms and relationships.

All of the recent work has served to underline the fact that it is the law that defines crime, that it was, and remains, legislators who criminalised or decriminalised specific activities though sometimes pushed by the behaviour of the judiciary, of juries or of the population in general. The collective noun 'crime' encompasses a variety of activities from murder and rape to petty theft. Some of these activities are the result of careful planning and premeditation, and some are perpetrated largely because the opportunity presents itself. During the eighteenth and nineteenth centuries it was the small opportunist theft that was statistically the most common. Yet the petty nature of most criminality was, and still is, often obscured by the vicarious appetite for violence fed by sections of the newspaper press as well as by much popular literature, which implied that violence was part of crime *per se*. Violent crime was what worried people; it was central to the moral panics and crime waves; it provided good copy. But the incidence of serious inter-personal violence committed by thieves in the process of robbery was rare within the statistics of crime. Crimewaves did not centre on the fear of being murdered or assaulted by spouse, parent, child, other relation or acquaintance; statistically, except possibly for policemen, perhaps they should have done.

Monocausal explanations for property crime and for inter-personal violence both present difficulties. John Waldon's decision to sell his master's stool and the calm removal of 'over a million in sterling' from the strong room of Matheson and Jardine by a nephew of Matheson, were both thefts. Opportunity may provide part of an explanation, but whatever prompted the nephew's activities it can hardly have been real economic necessity. In contrast, there is some justification for accepting Waldon's plea of poverty. The murders of Jack the Ripper and Thomas Neill Cream, and the drunken return home of Patrick Barry, which resulted in his wife being kicked to death, all may help to illuminate gender relations in Victorian London, but it is something rather different to suggest that they had a common cause rooted in those gender relations. Murder, and especially serial murder, was not a common offence. Wife beating was, though it was not always brought before the authorities. The scale of such beating can only be guessed at, but there is no reason to suppose that it was necessarily any greater than the percentage of relationships that never witnessed physical violence. Assaults on the police – for which prosecution rates were running at roughly sixty-six per thousand of the population in the mid-1860s and 40 per thousand at the end of the century – illuminate some aspects of police–public relations, but do not tell the whole story. Furthermore, while assaults on policemen and assaults on women and wives were alike in being defined as assaults by the law, the term itself is of little value in understanding either motive or context.

Economic development during the eighteenth and nineteenth centuries brought increasing wealth, more goods in shops and warehouses, more moveable property in people's homes and at the workplace. All of these provided greater opportunities and greater temptations for property crime. The extension of the business and commercial worlds provided greater opportunities for embezzlement, fraud and corruption, offences that, generally, were far more difficult to uncover and prosecute than the straightforward theft of small, moveable property. All of these offences can be linked with the workplace, and they tend to make workplace crime too complex and varied to be explained solely in terms of an employer's determination to maximise his profits and an employee's desire to hang on to customary practices and perks; indeed it would seem that in some instances the employees preferred regular wage payments to old customary practices.

The increase in property crime recorded by the admittedly imperfect statistics during the serious economic slumps of the first period of industrialisation appears significant. But the equation of poverty leading to theft is too simple. Most offenders were young. There was, perhaps, a degree of alienation among them. Some suffered a marginal existence, they had no responsibilities, and no way of making their voice heard in society. In addition, there were the pressures of the peer group to enjoy communal leisure activities, activities that generally cost money. Any or all of these elements could combine, perhaps also with the thrill of breaking the law, to encourage criminal behaviour when an opportunity arose or was perceived. Economic hardship brought about by a slump exacerbated the situation and spread temptation further. But if there is a correlation between the peaks of property crime and the troughs of the business cycle, it is also apparent that the steepest overall increase in the criminal statistics during the period 1750 to 1900 coincides with fear for the social order, fear of 'the mob', fear of revolution and, during the 'hungry forties', the identification of, and anxiety about, 'the dangerous classes'. J. A. Sharpe has identified a similar statistical peak in crime coinciding with fears for the social order two centuries before.[1] The problem is explaining why these issues should coincide. Was it that, in times of social tension, people were more aware of their vulnerability to thieves and therefore more inclined to report offences and to prosecute if an offender could be identified? Was it also that an apparently shaky social order encouraged more people to reject accepted morality and to steal when the opportunity presented itself?

In his lively study of the 'respectable fears' about street crime and disorder during the nineteenth and twentieth centuries, Geoffrey Pearson suggested that such fears seem 'to serve a specific ideological function within British public life, as a convenient metaphor for wider social tensions which attend the advance of democratisation'.[2] The difficulty here is that some of the short-term panics that he identifies are not well synchronised with concerns about the social order and democratisation. The mid-nineteenth-century garrotting panic offers a good example. Chartism was scarcely perceived as a threat after 1848 and three years later the Great Exhibition ushered in a period of relative social peace and satisfaction. Yet it was precisely the ten years following the Great Exhibition that were punctuated by the 'garrotting' outbreaks.

Crime is rarely something that people experience regularly as victims, and perceptions of crime therefore depend largely on what they are told about it. When they are informed, authoritatively, that crime is a serious problem, and when this is reiterated and backed up with statistics and graphic instances, they will probably believe it. It seems that 'crime waves' and 'moral panics' could be accelerated, perhaps even generated, during the eighteenth and nineteenth centuries by newspapers eager to boost their sales or crusading for changes in the penal system.[3] The publication of national crime statistics, together with faith in the new science of statistics, the fearful example of European revolutions together with reports of riots and disorders at home, and the repetition of notions like the concept of the 'dangerous classes', possibly served to foster the perception of a longer term crime wave in the first half of the nineteenth century. As people's concern about crime was heightened so, arguably, more crime was reported and prosecuted. This is not to deny that necessity and need prompted some people to steal simply to exist in the early nineteenth century, but rather to re-emphasise that the increase in statistics was not just the result of more crime. By the same token, the general stability of the Victorian social order in the second half of the nineteenth century, the faith in progress, and the belief that, in spite of one or two spectacular failures, the police and the courts were improving and winning the war against crime, may have contributed to a decline in the reporting and prosecution of very minor offences. The greater regularity of employment in the second half of the nineteenth century may, similarly, have eased some of the pressures on those tempted to property crime.

Conceivably the belief in progress and civilisation might have contributed to the domestication of individuals prone to violence. Towards the end of the eighteenth century there appears to have been an increasing intolerance of violent behaviour; this is manifested in a greater conviction rate and a preference to punish with imprisonment rather than just a fine. Such intolerance may itself have worked upon the incidence of such offending, though, as ever, the mechanism would be hard to prove. The statistics of crime only show a decline in violent offences during the second half of the nineteenth century; and there could be another element at work here. As the century progressed it became a mark of respectability for the working-class man to be the sole breadwinner and for his wife to supervise the domestic sphere. This put much of the onus of establishing a family's respectability on the wife. It may be that a very positive side of the separate spheres came in the form of the exhortation and the moral influence of women on their menfolk to be 'respectable' and, as part and parcel of this, to eschew different forms of aggression.

It is probably true that the state has yet to be established in which the law treats those lacking power and influence in precisely the same way as those possessing power and influence. The law, the police, and the courts tend to reinforce divisions and inequalities. Yet often they seek also to overcome divisions and inequalities. Both the courts and legislators in the late eighteenth and early nineteenth centuries, recognising that poor victims were disadvantaged in prosecuting offenders, sought to remedy the situation. Possibly some of this was done out of self-interest and to bolster the notion of equality before the law. At the same time it would be arrogant to deny that, among members of the elite, there were sincerely held liberal beliefs in the value and existence of such equality as well as a determination to help the less well-to-do. Similarly legislators and the courts began very gradually to modify their attitude towards, and their treatment of female victims. Feminist activism had a role in this, but so too did Victorian notions of progress and decency, and also the Victorian understanding of gender differences. Again it is impossible to quantify the impacts of these shifting attitudes.

The main argument put forward for establishing the new police was that they could contribute significantly to the prevention of crime. From the moment that they took to the streets and country lanes, most of the new police forces were also deployed to enforce new concepts of order on the working class. But police aid was demanded by, and rendered to working-class communities and individuals. There were serious gaps. Policemen were not encouraged by their superiors to become involved in domestic disputes. They were a public force who were not expected to invade the private sphere of the family – after all, the Victorian image of the family was of a haven of safety and accord. Nevertheless the social welfare role of the police in working-class districts has been ignored too often by historians.

If the arguments for establishing the police were firmly rooted in the problem of how to prevent crime, the arguments for a new system of punishment were rooted in the Enlightenment's humanitarianism and rationalism. Of course, hidden agendas can be identified; and it is possible often to detect public arguments becoming more influential when change is already happening. But sometimes the identification of the hidden agenda can serve to obscure the significance of the public one. There was heightened concern about order in late eighteenth- and early nineteenth-century England, which contributed to the creation of the new police and led to their deployment in enforcing particular concepts of decorum and respectability. Allowing the hidden agenda 'order' role to mask the public agenda 'crime' role results in a distorted picture of police development. The gospel of work was central to Victorian ideology. Instilling habits of work and morality in the convict who was perceived, very often, to have taken the short step from idleness to crime, was regarded as being beneficial both to society and to the offender. Yet to conclude from this that the prison system that developed in the late eighteenth and nineteenth centuries, together with the new police, stemmed essentially from the control requirements of a new bourgeois capitalism is to shortcut a variety of processes and to obliterate many nuances in, and impediments to these new systems.

Changes in fashion and changes in technology lead to changes in the forms of offending: the cutpurse had to metamorphose into a pickpocket; the development of the internal combustion engine and the decline in horse-drawn transport made 'van dragging', by which goods were lifted from a moving vehicle, an extremely hazardous occupation.[4] The growth of the economy in the period 1750 to 1900 fostered new opportunities for criminal behaviour. As in other periods the statistical pattern of crime appears to follow concerns about social order, though the coincidence between the troughs of the business cycle and the peaks of crime in the first half of the nineteenth century also suggests some links between economic necessity and petty theft. The reorganisation and rationalisation of the criminal law, the changes in punishment, and the creation of new organs of containment and control reflect, in a variety of ways, the changing economic and social order. These developments also needed, and benefited from, a state that was increasingly prepared to be interventionist. The rhetoric of English rights and liberties contributed to the shape and extent of change in the criminal justice system. Finally, the extensive range of people who participated in this system, often with considerable discretion, militates against any simple equation of either a ruling class making and administering the law for its own benefit, or a system steadily ironing out problems and abuses and developing towards a modern system somehow legitimated by the concept of the rational march of progress.

Notes and references

1   J. A. Sharpe, *Crime in Early Modern England 1550–1750*, 2nd edn, Longman, London, 1999, pp. 263–8.

2   Geoffrey Pearson, *Hooligan. A history of respectable fears*, Macmillan, London, 1983, p. 230.

3 **Peter King**, 'Newspaper reporting, prosecution practice and perceptions of urban crime: the Colchester crime wave of 1765', *Continuity and Change*, **2** (1987), pp. 423–54; **Rob Sindall**, *Street Violence in the Nineteenth Century: Media panic or real danger?* Leicester U.P., London, 1990, especially ch. 3.

4 For 'van dragging' see **Raphael Samuel** (ed.), *East End Underworld: Chapters in the life of Arthur Harding*, RKP, London, 1981, pp. 70–1 and 284. There is an example in *C.C.C.S.P. 1898–99*, no. 106, the case of Michael William Hickey, aged 21, who was sentenced to nine months' hard labour for endeavouring to pull a post packet and seventeen postal orders off the back of a mail van. He was apprehended by the driver of the following van.

Further reading: further research

I have endeavoured to make the notes to each chapter as detailed as possible, not to obviate the need for a bibliography, but rather to supply a guide to further reading and to current debates and controversies under the relevant headings. What follows here is simply an attempt to point, first, to the most significant and useful texts and, second, to topics where new research might be undertaken.

Douglas Hay, Peter Linebaugh, E. P. Thompson *et al.*, *Albion's Fatal Tree: Crime and society in eighteenth-century England* (Allen Lane, London, 1975) was the first significant text by social historians interested in the history of crime. It remains a valuable starting point for eighteenth-century crime, and is usefully supplemented by the rather different angle of vision of the essays in **John Brewer** and **John Styles** (eds), *An Ungovernable People: The English and their law in the seventeenth and eighteenth centuries* (Hutchinson, London, 1980). The outstanding monographs on eighteenth-century crime and the courts are **J. M. Beattie**, *Crime and the Courts in England 1660–1800* (Oxford U.P., Oxford, 1986), which is based largely on material relating to Surrey, and **Peter King**, *Crime, Justice and Discretion in England 1740–1820* (Oxford U.P., Oxford, 2000), which works out from a detailed study of Essex. For a useful northern study that balances Beattie and King see **Gwenda Morgan** and **Peter Rushton**, *Rogues, Thieves and the Rule of law: The problem of law enforcement in north-east England, 1718–1800* (U.C.L. Press, London, 1998).

The pioneering academic study of nineteenth-century crime is **J. J. Tobias**, *Crime and Industrial Society in the Nineteenth Century* (Batsford, London, 1967; Penguin, Harmondsworth, 1972). The book remains useful for its survey of the contemporary literature, but subsequent research has challenged many of its basic assumptions and conclusions. **V. A. C. Gatrell** has produced a cogent case for the use of nineteenth-century criminal statistics in 'The decline of theft and violence in Victorian and Edwardian England', in **V. A. C. Gatrell, Bruce Lenman** and **Geoffrey Parker** (eds), *Crime and the Law: The social history of crime in Western*

Europe since 1500 (Europa, London, 1980), although this now needs to be set alongside **Howard Taylor**, 'Rationing crime: The political economy of criminal statistics since the 1850s', *Economic History Review*, **51** (1998), pp. 569–90. There are several nineteenth-century regional studies in thesis form, most of which show the influence of **David Philips**'s excellent study of the Black Country, *Crime and Authority in Victorian England: The Black Country 1835–60* (Croom Helm, London, 1977). More recent, valuable regional studies are **Carolyn A. Conley**, *The Unwritten Law: Criminal justice in Victorian Kent* (Oxford U.P., New York, 1991) and **David J. V. Jones**, *Crime in Nineteenth-Century Wales* (University of Wales Press, Cardiff, 1992). Both of these touch significantly on questions of gender, but the outstanding monograph on women before the law is **Lucia Zedner**, *Women, Crime and Custody in Victorian England* (Clarendon Press, Oxford, 1991). On rural crime, **John E. Archer**, '*By a flash and a scare*'. *Arson, Animal Maiming and Poaching in East Anglia 1815–1879* (Clarendon Press, Oxford, 1990) provides a valuable, level-headed account of what appears to have been peculiarly extreme violence in Norfolk and Suffolk. **Timothy Shakesheff**, *Rural Conflict, Crime and Protest: Herefordshire, 1800–1860* (Boydell, Woodbridge, 2003) addresses similar problems on the opposite side of England and drawing significantly on the concept of social crime.

No-one interested in the legal, penal and police reforms of the eighteenth and early nineteenth centuries can afford to ignore **Michel Foucault**, *Discipline and Punish: The birth of the prison* (Allen Lane, London, 1977). While the bulk of the illustrative material here is French, the arguments range much wider. These reforms, as they occurred in England, provide the focus for **Sir Leon Radzinowicz**'s exhaustive *A History of English Criminal Law* (Stevens, London, 5 vols, 1948–86). Alternative interpretations to Radzinowicz's fundamentally 'Whiggish' approach can be found in **Michael Ignatieff**, *A Just Measure of Pain: The penitentiary in the Industrial Revolution 1750–1950* (Macmillan, London, 1978) and **V. A. C. Gatrell**, *The Hanging Tree: Execution and the English people, 1770–1868* (Clarendon Press, Oxford, 1994). The intellectual underpinning of penal policy is expertly described by **Martin J. Wiener**, *Reconstructing the Criminal: Culture, law and policy in England, 1830–1914* (Cambridge U.P., Cambridge, 1990). For broad surveys of developments in police see **Clive Emsley**, *The English Police: A political and social history* (2nd edn, Longman, London, 1996) and **David Taylor**, *The New Police in Nineteenth-Century England: Crime conflict and control* (Manchester U.P., Manchester, 1997); but for a detailed focus on the crucial developments in provincial policing in the early nineteenth century see **David Philips** and **Robert D. Storch**, *Policing Provincial England 1829–1856: The politics of reform* (Leicester U.P., London, 1999). There is also a stimulating introduction to police and the use of the law in **Douglas Hay** and **Francis Snyder**, 'Using the criminal law, 1750–1850', in Douglas Hay and Francis Snyder (eds), *Policing and Prosecution in Britain 1750–1850* (Clarendon Press, Oxford, 1989).

Violence and sexual offending have become significant areas for research over the last decade. Important here are **Louise A. Jackson**, *Child Sexual Abuse in Victorian England* (Routledge, London, 2000) and **Shani D'Cruz**, *Crimes of Outrage: Sex, violence and Victorian working women* (U.C.L. Press, London, 1998). The latter has also edited a useful set of introductory essays, *Everyday Violence in Britain, 1850–1950: Gender and class* (Longman, London, 2000). **Martin J. Wiener**, *Men of Blood: Violence, manliness, and criminal justice in Victorian England* (Cambridge U.P., Cambridge, 2004) provides an important and stimulating argument about the use of the law to curb violence and reformulate notions of masculinity during the nineteenth century.

Most journals concerned with social history now regularly carry articles on crime and criminal justice. There is also a specialist, bi-lingual (English/French) journal *Crime, histoire et sociétés/Crime, history and societies* that anyone interested in the subject should consult.

The opportunities for archival research remain plentiful, especially now that there has been a shift away from property crime to gender differences in criminal behaviour and to inter-personal violence. Eighteenth- and nineteenth-century quarter sessions provide a rich mine; the county material is probably more detailed than that for the boroughs. Assize records in the Public Records Office and petty sessions records in local archives are rather more fragmentary, but the latter should prove particularly useful for the new direction of research. Perhaps the next generation of historians of crime should be less interested in counting and attempt more detailed studies based on depositions, which are, as yet, a greatly under-used source. There also remain a range of issues about which it would be useful to know much more: first, the workings of the old system of police, especially in rural areas, and the extent to which it survived during the nineteenth century; second, the way in which police prosecution and the courts developed during the nineteenth century; third, the way in which the law was interpreted and acted upon by different individuals, and in different contexts, not least in the summary courts; and fourth, the extent to which the civil courts may have heard cases involving criminal behaviour, particularly instances of assault.

Index

Aberdare, Lord 210
abortion 101
Acton, Dr William 79–80, 90n., 180
Ainsworth, William Harrison 83, 91n., 107
Alderson, Baron 285
Alison, Sir Archibald 68
Anderson, Sir Robert 54n., 288
animal maiming 118
Aris, Thomas 271
arson 116–18, 137n., 193
assault 29, 32, 39, 41, 44–9, 71, 98–9, 102–4, 134, 146, 186–7, 298
assizes 13–14, 105, 124, 159, 189, 190, 197, 207, 209–11, 254, 265, 271
  in Bedfordshire 131, 177, 184–85, 199
  in Norfolk 3
  in Nottinghamshire 118

Balfour, J. S. 163
Bankes, Henry 10, 19n., 256
Baring Brothers 163, 173
Barnett, Canon Samuel 115
Barry, Patrick 48, 298
Bartlett, Adelaide 99
Bath 64
Bayley, Thomas Butterworth 270
Beames, Revd Thomas 127
Beattie, J. M. 30, 33, 291n.
Beccaria, Cesare 267–8
Bedford see Bedfordshire
Bedfordshire 26, 35, 38, 44–6, 161, 175, 196, 219–20n., 222, 239, 268, 278
  Bedford in 148, 187, 230, 238
  Biggleswade in 118, 161, 177, 188
  Cardington in 38, 268

Dunstable in 39
Harrold in 154
Houghton Conquest in 130–2, 177
Leighton Buzzard in 223
Potton in 146
benefit of clergy 254
Bennet, Henry Grey 272
Bentham, Jeremy 270–2
Berkshire 205
Bidwell, Austin 173–4
Bidwell, George 173–4
Bigge, J. T. 276
Biggleswade see Bedfordshire
Binney, John 154
Birmingham 23, 68, 125, 129, 233, 279
Birnie, Sir Richard 63
Black Country 38, 105, 152, 157, 178, 205
Blackburn see Lancashire
Blackstone, Sir William 94, 202, 268
Bloody Code 1–11, 19n., 22, 33, 192, 202, 253, 256–8, 266, 272
Bolton see Lancashire
Booth, Charles 75–6, 156
Botany Bay 255, 271
Boulton, Matthew 190
Bow Street Police 225–9
Bradford see Yorkshire
Brereton, Revd Charles 115
Bright, John 161
Brighton see Sussex
Bristol see Gloucestershire
Brougham, Lord 88n., 207
Bravo, Florence 99
Buckingham, Duke of 203
Buckinghamshire 231

burglars/burglary 26–8, 32, 44, 72, 96, 126, 129, 175–7, 240–1, 263, 284
Burgon, Revd J. W. 131–2
Bushaway, Bob 121–2
Bute, Earl of 265

Cambridge 34, 132, 187
Cannock Chase see Staffordshire
Cardiff 47
Cardington see Bedfordshire
Carnarvon, Earl of 179, 282, 285
Carpenter, Edward 207
Carpenter, Mary 66, 279
Cass, Elizabeth 108
Central Criminal Court see Old Bailey
Chadwick, Edwin 24, 64–5, 174, 232, 237, 244, 250n., 289
Chartism/Chartists 37, 66, 68, 82, 233, 299
Chatham Prison 282
Chesney, Kellow 173, 177
Cheshire 233, 241
    Chester in 238
Chevalier, Louis 68
Chichester, Earl of 240–1
'chips' 149–50, 159
Clay, Revd John 68, 278
Clouston, T. S. 93
Cobb, Richard 123
Cobbett, William 120
coining 5, 72, 183, 254
Colchester see Essex
Coldbath Fields 271, 277
Collins, Wilkie 99
Colquhoun, Patrick 24, 61–3, 86n., 114, 126, 154, 176, 179, 227, 229–30, 238
Conley, Carolyn 106
constables (pre-police) 44, 187–8, 222–3, 225–6, 235, 241
Cooper, James Fenimore 68
Corbett, Edwin 233, 241
cornermen 122–3, 127
Cornwall 135, 153–5
courts 13–15
    adversarial practice in 198–201
    gender ratio in 93–4
    judges in 199, 201
    jurors in 201–2

lawyers in 198–200
    magistrates in 202
    see also assizes, petty sessions, quarter sessions
Cranworth, Lord 209
Crawford, William 277–8, 280
Cream, Thomas Neill 97, 298
crime,
    corporate 6–9, 18n., 57
    definition problem 2, 143–4, 297–8
    drink and 48, 63, 65–6, 71
    economic hardship and 25, 33–41, 63, 65, 67–8, 82, 299
    fear of disorder and 36–7, 41, 299–300
    heredity and 75–8
    idleness/immorality as cause of 58–68, 70–1, 289
    media and 26, 34, 66, 71, 82–4, 88n., 91n.
    pattern of property 32–41, 56, 299
    pattern of violence 32, 41–8
    predominance of petty theft 32, 56
    rural 116–22
    social 2–6, 10, 81
    urban 114–15, 123–30
    vagrancy and 26, 33, 41, 117, 121, 178, 244–5, 289
    village, open/closed 132–4
    war and 33–4, 52n., 64, 94
    white collar 57, 116, 144, 162–5
criminal class 23–4, 28, 49, 68–77, 96–7, 173–80, 240
criminal gangs 130–1, 148, 175, 177–8
Criminal Law Commissioners 273
criminal statistics,
    difficulties with 23–32
    gender ratios 93–5
    suggested value 30–1
    varieties 21–3
Cromer see Norfolk
Cumberland 14, 135
    Greystoke in 5

dangerous classes 37, 41–2, 48, 68, 240, 300
dark figure 24, 30, 95–6
Dartmoor Prison 282
Davidson, R. N. 125, 127
Davis, Jennifer 178

Derbyshire 118
Devon 121, 204
    Exeter in 124, 231, 278
Dickens, Charles 70, 83, 97, 107, 124, 195
Director of Public Prosecutions 195
Discharged Prisoners' Aid Society 180
Disraeli, Benjamin 82
Dorset 205
Du Cane, Sir Edmund 282, 284–5
Dublin 247n.
Dunstable *see* Bedfordshire
Durham 14, 125, 134–5, 279
Durkheim, Emile 116

East India Company 4, 189
Eden, William 267–8
Edinburgh 247n.
Edwards, George 147
Ellenborough, Lord 100
Ellis, Havelock 77–8, 80, 116
embezzlement 6, 9, 57, 152–3, 158–9, 164, 166, 188
Engels, Friedrich 68, 173
Essex 26, 31, 46, 146, 151, 189, 195, 204, 236–7
    Colchester in 34, 151
Estcourt, T. G. B. 105
executions 256–67, 272, 282–3
Exeter *see* Devon

Feeley, Malcolm 93–4
feme covert 94–5
Fenians 242
Ferri, Enrico 78
Field, Jonathan 174, 181n.
Fielding, Henry 58–62, 64–5, 70, 87n., 91n., 114, 120, 126, 128, 176, 187, 190–1, 206, 225, 230, 238, 267, 295n.
Fielding, Sir John 59–60, 63, 176, 187, 206, 225–7, 230, 238, 242, 267
Fletcher, Joseph 66
Foote, William 196
forgery 263–4
Fortescue, London 121, 123
Foucault, Michel 11–12, 19n.
Fraser, Col. James 126, 240

Frégier, H. A. 37, 68
French Revolution 25, 57, 272

game laws 4, 22, 81, 148, 203–4, 256
garrotting 26, 41, 164, 244, 281, 299
Gatrell, V. A. C. 31–2, 40–1, 48, 257, 274
Gay, John 59, 83, 91n.
George III 9, 34, 164, 269
George IV 36
gleaning 144–7, 156
Gloucester Penitentiary 270–1
Gloucestershire 223, 234, 238, 285
    Bristol in 64
Glyde, John 66, 132
Gordon Riots 36, 229
grand jury 105, 189–91
Greenwood, James 73–4, 152, 156, 160–1, 179
Grey, Sir George 111n., 237
Grey, Lord 232
Greystoke *see* Cumberland
Grummet, James 130–2

habitual criminals 23, 73, 95, 178–9, 237
Hammerton, James 104
Hammick, James T. 24, 115
Hampshire 121, 203, 205, 285
Hanway, Jonas 60–1, 87n., 269
Harding, Arthur 126–7, 154–5, 174–5, 178, 184
Harworth *see* Nottinghamshire
Hay, Douglas 10, 30–1, 82
Headington Quarry 132–3
highway robbery *see* robbery
Hill, Matthew Davenport 68, 279
Hoare, Sir Richard Colt 161
Hobsbawm, E. J. 297
Hogg, Gilbert 238, 244
Holford, George 271
Holland, Revd H. W. 68–9, 73, 79
homicide 5–6, 41–4, 47, 99–102, 267, 275
Horncastle *see* Lincolnshire
Hosler, John 131–2
Houghton Conquest *see* Bedfordshire
Howard, John 11, 268, 271, 283
Howells, Francis 133
Hoyle, William 48, 55n.

hulks 255, 269, 271
Hull *see* Yorkshire
Hunt, William 188
Huntington 183, 187

Ignatieff, Michael 12, 268, 290n.
income tax 28
infanticide 42, 100–1
Ipswich *see* Suffolk
Ireland 1, 229, 234

Jack the Ripper 41, 54n., 97, 298
Jacobins/Jacobinism 25, 36, 62, 241,
    257, 271
Jebb, Sir Joshua 277, 280, 282
Jennings Buildings 48, 245, 252n.
Jones, David 127
Jordan, Furneaux 103
judges 14–15, 96, 100, 104, 106, 108,
    189, 198–9, 201, 254, 264, 272, 285
jury/juries 40, 100–1, 104–5, 150, 164,
    189, 201–2, 209, 211
juvenile offenders 25, 63, 66–7, 75, 77,
    87n., 125, 174–5, 184, 208, 279–80

Kay-Shuttleworth, James 66
Kent 206
King, Fielder 121, 123
King, Peter 10, 31, 33, 87n., 93–4
Kirchheimer, Otto 11–14

Lancashire 196, 236
    Blackburn in 185
    Bolton in 233
    Oldham in 83
    Preston in 47
    Wigan in 157, 194, 205
Langbein, John 10, 16, 201
largesse 121–2
Lavater, Johann Kasper 74
law,
    codification proposed 285
    crime and 2, 28–9
    eighteenth-century 10–11, 256
    implementation of 13–16
    reform debates 273–4
    role in society 9–11
Laxton *see* Nottinghamshire
Leeds *see* Yorkshire

Lefevre, Charles Shaw 232
Lefroy, Anthony 234, 238
Leighton Buzzard *see* Bedfordshire
Lincolnshire 4, 236
    Horncastle in 130, 231
    Lincoln in 34
    Spilsby in 119
Linebaugh, Peter 158
Little, Deborah 93–4
Liverpool 23, 27, 48, 64, 121, 127, 163,
    173, 267
Lloyd Baker, T. B. 285
Lombroso, Cesare 78
London 41, 47, 60–4, 73, 95–7, 102,
    108, 116, 120, 122–3, 126–9, 153,
    156, 158, 162, 165, 178, 187, 191,
    197, 206, 221, 224–9, 238–44, 257,
    265, 269, 298
    centre of crime 24, 41, 114–15
    magistracy in 14, 24, 83, 180, 192–3,
        206–7, 224–6, 243, 284–5
Luddism 14

McDaniel, Stephen 225
McGowan, Randall 264, 273–4, 292n.
MacHardy, Admiral J. B. 237
Mackintosh, Sir James 11, 192, 227, 253,
    292n.
Macquarie, Lachlan 275
Madan, Martin 61, 201, 291n.
magistrates/magistracy 36, 103, 105,
    161, 197, 210, 226, 233–4, 276,
    284–5
    appointment and background 13–14,
        36, 210
    as police 225
    and prisons 268, 278
    problem of partiality 134, 157, 203–5
    see also courts, London, stipendiary
        magistrates, trading justices
Magniac, Charles 162
Malthus, Revd Thomas 37
Manchester 2, 26–7, 58, 69–70, 126,
    129, 166, 233, 238
Mansfield, Lord 202
Mars, Gerald 143
Marx, Karl 1
Matheson and Jardine 162, 298
Maudsley, Henry 75, 93, 95

Maybrick, Florence 99
Mayhew, Henry 70–3, 79, 120, 154, 173, 176, 179, 281
Mayne, Sir Richard 230, 238, 240–1
Melbourne, Lord 233, 274, 279
Meredith, Sir William 267
Merthyr Tydfil 127, 178
Methodism/Methodists 4, 135
Metropolitan Police 5, 27–8, 64, 115, 126, 154, 158, 174, 180, 193, 196, 206, 221, 224, 230–4, 237–8, 241–3
Millbank Prison 253, 270–2, 277, 282
Molesworth, Sir William 276
Monmouthshire 134
Morgan, Gwenda 177–8
Morrison, Revd William Douglas 29, 78, 115
mumming 122–3
murder see homicide

Napoleon 229, 285
Newcastle-upon-Tyne 64, 248n.
Newgate Prison 74, 265, 283
New Poor Law 38, 82, 166, 232, 253, 288
Norfolk 119, 147
    Cromer in 119
    Norwich in 34, 205
Northamptonshire 234, 243
    Bozeat in 154
    Northampton in 103
Northumberland 14, 125, 135
Nottinghamshire 105, 185, 187, 196–7, 217n., 219–20n.
    Harworth in 235
    Laxton in 133
    Nottingham in 231
    Worksop in 185
Nugent, Revd James 48

Obelkevich, James 147
offenders,
    contrasting gender of 32–3, 93–7
    Irish as 99, 123–4, 127, 280
    Jews as 123–4, 183
    miners among 134–5
    recruitment of 34, 189
    youth of 32–3
    see also juvenile offenders

Old Bailey 14, 38–9, 93, 98, 101, 108, 175, 186, 198–9, 202, 224, 254

Packington, Sir John 208–9
Palmer, Robert 209
Palmerston, Lord 236–7, 280
Parent-Duchâtelet, A. J. B. 90n., 180
Paris 68, 127, 222, 229, 242
Parkhurst Prison 279
Parry, Edward 7, 15
Parry, J. H. 101
Paul, Sir George Onesiphorus 270–1
pawnbrokers, pawning of stolen goods 38, 40, 58, 98, 129, 174, 177, 181n.
Pearson, Geoffrey 299
Peel, Sir Robert 13, 22, 56, 191–2, 194, 211, 229, 253–4, 256, 274, 276
Pentonville Prison 253, 277, 282
Perth Prison 75
petty sessions 13, 21–2, 161, 205
Philanthropic Society 279
Philips, David 29, 38, 178
pickpockets 60, 64, 70, 96, 125–6, 174–5, 227, 267, 302
Pike, L. O. 192–3
Pilkington, James 26, 244, 284
Plint, Thomas 67–8, 114–15
Plug Plot 37
poachers/poaching 3–4, 39, 72, 81, 92, 95, 116, 134, 174, 185, 229
police 62–3, 69–70, 96–7, 103, 117–18, 122, 126–7, 133–4, 161, 164, 174, 186
    assaults on 46, 99, 118, 134, 222–3, 298
    corruption and 165–6, 197, 229, 242
    crime statistics and 23, 26–8, 42, 239–40, 243–4
    detectives 179, 241–2
    discipline and restrictions 243
    discretion 2, 15–16, 177, 283–4
    established to prevent crime 238–41, 243, 245, 301–2
    historical interpretations of 15, 221, 224, 230, 235, 238–9
    impact on crime 41, 150, 238–41
    labelling criminal districts 129, 178, 243–4
    new system in boroughs 230–2

police (*continued*)
  new system in counties 232–5
  as prosecutors 195–7, 217n.
  supervision of suspect groups 23,
      178–80, 281, 294–5n.
  welfare role 245, 301
  see also Metropolitan Police
popular disosrder/rioting 3, 14, 133, 135,
      289, 299–300
  see also Gordon Riots
Portland Prison 282
Portsmouth Prison 282
Potton *see* Bedfordshire
Preston Gaol 68, 278
prison,
  discipline in 282–4
  early reformers 267–8
  education in 279
  government intervention in 253,
      271–2, 288
  historical interpretations of 253–4,
      272, 287–9
  inspectorate 274, 277
  need for separation in 63, 270, 274,
      279
  old system 255, 268
  religion in 271, 277–8
  staff in 283–4
  work in 278–9, 282
Prison Discipline Society 274, 277
Prisoner's Aid Society 180
prosecution system,
  deterrents in 28, 94, 96, 158, 190–4,
      197
  discretion in 157–8, 177, 185–90, 203
  expenses paid 28, 191–2, 197, 217n.
prosecution associations 191, 199
prostitution 15, 28, 79–80, 96–8, 104–5,
      108, 112n., 126, 180, 193
public prosecutor 194
punishment,
  capital 253–4, 256–67, 270, 272–5,
      282–3, 292–3n.
  corporal 158–9, 203, 254, 281, 284
  crank 279, 282–3
  fines 158–9, 203, 255, 287
  hard labour 255, 267
  increasingly private 283
  picking oakum 279, 282

pillory 255, 264–5, 267
prosecutor's discretion and 203
shot drill 279, 282
silent system 277, 283
solitary confinement 269–70, 277–8,
      283–4
stocks 255
treadmill 279, 282–3
see also prison, transportation

quarter sessions 13–14, 21, 124, 159,
      186, 189–90, 197, 207, 209–10,
      254, 275
  in Bedfordshire 130–1, 145, 166,
      186–8
  in Buckinghamshire 208
  in Cheshire 233
  in Hampshire 148
  in Leeds 190–1
  in Nottinghamshire 185, 187, 191,
      235

rape 105–7, 184–5, 193, 264, 293n.
  see also sexual offences
Ratcliffe Highway murders 41, 227, 229
Rawlinson, John 63–4, 126
Reach, Angus 2, 69–70, 128, 135, 136n.,
      206
receivers 150, 174, 181n., 225
  see also pawnbrokers
Redgrave, Alexander 7
Redgrave, Samuel 22
Redman, James 130–2, 178
Redman, Joseph 131–2, 178
Reynolds, G. W. M. 68
Richmond, Duke of 270
rioting *see* popular disorder
robbery 27, 41, 44, 63, 95, 116, 125
Roberts, Robert 124
'Rodneys' 178
Romilly, Sir Samuel 11, 192, 227, 253,
      272–3, 292n.
Routh, Charles 106
Rowan, Colonel Charles 230, 232, 238,
      240–1, 244, 250n.
Royal Commissions,
  on Rural Constabulary (1836–39)
      64–5, 155, 174, 193, 196, 232–3,
      243

Royal Commissions (*continued*)
  on Penal Servitude (1863) 281
  on Capital Punishment (1866) 101,
    283
  on Contagious Diseases Acts (1871)
    104–5, 112n.
  on Metropolitan Police (1908) 105
Rudé, George 39–40, 212n., 297
Rule, John 3
Rusche, Georg 11–12
Rushton, Peter 177–8
Russell, Lord John 233, 253, 274, 277
Russell, Revd Whitworth 277, 280
Ruthven, George 227
Rylands, L. Gordon 76–7

St Giles 70, 128–9, 244
Salford 124, 270
Sayer, John 63
Scotland 1, 194
sedition 25, 183, 190, 195, 255–6, 271
Select Committees,
  Crime in Metropolis (1772) 59
  Criminal Commitments and
    Convictions (1826–27) 3, 26
  Criminal and Destitute Children (1853)
    279
  Criminal Law (1819) 192
  Drunkenness (1834) 65–6
  Education in Wales (1847) 134
  Gaol Discipline (1863) 282
  Intemperance (1877) 48
  Payment of Wages (1842) 134
  Police (1852–53) 233, 235–6, 241,
    244
  Police of the Metropolis (1816) 63,
    (1828) 26, 63, 65, 126, 224, (1834)
    238
  Public Prosecutors (1855) 196–7
  Transportation (1784) 269, (1837–38)
    276
sentencing 254–5, 275, 280, 284–5
sexual offences 28, 51n., 105–7, 193,
  255
Shakespeare, William 223–4
Sharpe, J. A. 57, 120, 158, 299
Sheffield *see* Yorkshire
Sheppard, Jack 71, 83
Sindall, Rob 30

Smith, Adam 9
Smith, Revd Sydney 276, 278
smuggling 4, 72, 266
Solomons, Ikey 124, 174
Spencer, Herbert 6
Staffordshire 135, 153, 178, 238
  Cannock Chase in 81
  Wolverhampton in 127, 231
Statistical Society 23–4
statutes,
  Artificers and Apprentices, 1563
    (5 Eliz. c. 9) 37–8
  Abortion, 1624 (21 James c. 27)
    100
  Treason, 1696 (7 & 8 Will. c. 3)
    199
  Transportation, 1718 (4 Geo. I c. 9)
    255, 291n.
  Black Act, 1723 (9 Geo. I c. 22) 10, 13,
    19n.
  Embezzlement in manufactures, 1749
    (22 Geo. II c. 27) 158
  Expenses for prosecutions, 1752 (25
    Geo. II c. 36) 191
  Murder Act, 1752 (25 Geo. II c. 37)
    41–2, 266
  Short reeling, 1774 (14 Geo. III c. 44)
    159
  Embezzlement in manufactures, 1777
    (17 Geo. III c. 56) 158
  Expenses for prosecutions, 1778
    (18 Geo. III c. 19), 191
  Penitentiary, 1779 (19 Geo. III c. 74)
    268–9
  Transportation, 1784 (24 Geo. III
    c. 56) 269
  Middlesex Justices, 1792 (32 Geo. III
    c. 53) 61, 226–7
  Combinations in Restraint of Trade,
    1799 (39 Geo. III c. 81) 188,
    203–4
  (*idem*), 1800 (40 Geo. III c. 106) 188,
    203–4
  Abortion (section of Ellenborough's act
    dealing with Malicious Shooting or
    Stabbing) 1803 (43 Geo. III c. 58)
    100
  Larceny (pickpockets), 1808 (48 Geo.
    III c. 129) 192, 273

statutes (*continued*)
Gaol Fees Abolition, 1815 (55 Geo. III
  c. 50) 272
Repeal of Capital Punishment for
  stealing in shops, 1820 (1 Geo. IV
  c. 115) 273
Master and Servant, 1823 (4 Geo. IV
  c. 34) 157, 205, 245
Gaol, 1823 (4 Geo. IV c. 64) 274
Criminal Law, 1826 (7 Geo. IV c. 64)
  191
Metropolitan Police, 1829 (10 Geo. IV
  c. 44) 229
Cheshire Police, 1829 (10 Geo. IV
  c. 97) 233
Truck, 1831 (1 & 2 Will. IV c. 37) 7,
  134, 161
Lighting and Watching, 1833 (3 & 4
  Will. IV c. 90) 231–2, 235
Cruelty to Animals, 1835 (5 & 6 Will.
  IV c. 59) 119
Municipal Corporations, 1835 (5 & 6
  Will. IV c. 76) 14, 205, 221, 230
Prisoner's Counsel, 1836 (6 & 7 Will.
  IV c. 114) 200
Rural Constabulary, 1839 (2 & 3 Vict.
  c. 93) 221, 233–5, 241
Parish Constables, 1842 (5 & 6 Vict.
  c. 109) 235
Joint Stock companies, 1844 (7 & 8
  Vict. 110) 7
Juvenile Offenders, 1847 (10 & 11
  Vict. c. 82) 14, 29, 209
(*idem*), 1850 (13 & 14 Vict. c. 37) 14,
  29, 209, 220n.
Prevention of Aggravated Assault on
  Women and Children, 1853 (16 &
  17 Vict. c. 30) 102–3
Penal Servitude, 1853 (16 & 17 Vict.
  c. 99) 280, 285, 288
Youthful Offenders, 1854 (17 & 18
  Vict. c. 86) 279
Criminal Justice, 1855 (18 & 19 Vict.
  c. 126) 14, 27, 29, 157, 209, 220n.
County and Borough Police, 1856
  (19 & 20 Vict. c. 69) 23, 221, 234,
  236–7
Vexatious Indictments, 1859 (22 & 23
  Vict. c. 17) 195

Adulteration of Food and Drugs, 1860
  (23 & 24 Vict. c. 84) 161
Offences against the Person, 1861
  (24 & 25 Vict. c. 100) 101, 282,
  293n.
Poaching Prevention, 1862 (25 & 26
  Vict. c. 114) 81
'Garrotter's', 1863 (26 & 27 Vict.
  c. 44) 281–2
Penal Servitude, 1864 (27 & 28 Vict.
  c. 47) 281, 285, 288
Contagious Diseases, 1864 (27 & 28
  Vict. c. 85) 104, 245
(*idem*), 1866 (29 & 30 Vict. c. 35) 104,
  245
(*idem*), 1869 (32 & 33 Vict. c. 96) 104,
  245
Habitual Criminals, 1869 (32 & 33
  Vict. c. 99) 2, 23, 178–9
Elementary Education, 1870 (33 & 34
  Vict. c. 75) 28
Prevention of Crime, 1871 (34 & 35
  Vict. c. 94) 23, 178–9
Infant Life Protection, 1872 (35 & 36
  Vict. c. 38) 102
Licencing, 1872 (35 & 36 Vict. c. 94)
  166
Matrimonial Clauses, 1878 (41 & 42
  Vict. c. 19) 103–4
Prevention of Crime, 1879 (42 & 43
  Vict. c. 55) 14, 210
Ground Game, 1880 (43 & 44 Vict.
  c. 47) 81
Public Bodies Corrupt Practices,
  1889 (52 & 53 Vict. c. 69)
  165
Summary Jurisdiction (Married
  Women), 1895 (58 & 59 Vict. c. 39)
  103–4
Criminal Evidence, 1898 (61 & 62
  Vict. c. 36) 200
Poor Prisoner's Defence, 1903 (3 Edw.
  VII c. 38) 201
Stevenson, Simon 178, 296n.
street offences 15, 240, 244
stipendiary magistrates 13–14, 207
  see also London (magistracy in)
Styles, John 5
Sue, Eugène 68

Suffolk 66, 117–18, 132
  Ipswich in 125
summary jurisdiction 29, 147–8, 157–8, 188, 202–11
superintending constables 235–6
Surrey 32, 44, 236
  Egham in, 222
Sussex 4, 14, 33, 35, 81, 121, 270
  Brighton in 239
  Westfirle in 133
Swansea 47
Symons, Jelinger 66–7, 134

Tarde, Gabriel 78
Taylor, Howard 32
theft,
  of animals 40, 81, 116, 263
  gender difference in acts of 95–6
  of growing crops 40, 95, 147–8, 188
  of water 2–3
  of wood 95, 148, 188
Thompson, E. P. 6, 19n., 297
Thompson, Dr James 75
'thrums' 151–2, 159
ticket-of-leave 179, 244, 280–1, 294n.
Tobias, J. J. 29, 96, 116, 173, 177, 200
Tocqueville, Alexis de 9
Tönnies, Ferdinand 115
Townsend, John 227
trading justices 205–6
transportation 73, 203, 237, 254–5, 268–70, 275–6, 280, 290–1n., 293n.
treason 183, 199, 254
truck 7, 134, 157, 162, 204
Tuckniss, Revd William 73
Turpin, Dick 71, 83, 107
Tyburn 266, 289, 295n.
Tyburn Ticket 247n.

van dragging 302
vagrancy see crime
Vincent, C. E. Howard 242
violence/violent crime see assault, cornermen, homicide

Wade, John 66
Wakefield Prison 277

Waldon, John 38, 298
Walpole, Sir Robert 59
wars,
  American Independence 34, 61, 150, 255, 257, 269
  Boer 76
  Crimean 237
  French Revolutionary and Napoleonic 25, 28, 34, 36, 94, 100, 150–1, 257–8, 271, 275
  Seven Years 4, 150
Warwickshire 205
watchmen 223–5, 242
Watson, William Henry 209
Watts, W. H. 176, 241–2
Welch, Saunders 128
Westmoreland 14
Whitbread, Samuel 188–9
White, Arnold 76
Wiener, Martin J. 93
Wigan see Lancashire
Wild, Jonathan 59, 174, 181n., 225
Wilkes, John 202, 265
William IV 36
Wiltshire 42, 205
Winslow, Dr Forbes 75
witchcraft 119
'Wolds Rangers' 117, 178
Wolverhampton see Staffordshire
workplace crime,
  in agriculture 144–9
  in dockyards/docks 149–51, 154–5, 159
  by domestics 160
  in factory/industry 94, 156–9
  in metal trades 152–3, 158–9
  by milkmen 156
  in mining 153–4
  in out-work 151–3, 158–9
  by police 165–6
  by poor law officials 166
  in printing 153
  by retailers 160–2
  in transport work 154–5, 159
Worksop see Nottinghamshire
Worcestershire 234
wrecking 3–4
Wright, Gordon 12, 19n.
Wyatt, Richard 188

Yorkshire 94, 106, 152, 234
  Bradford in 122–3
  East Riding of 117–18, 178
  Hull in 64, 97, 99
  Leeds in 67, 154, 190–1
  North Riding of 117

Sheffield in 152
West Riding of 5, 125, 195, 205
York in 97, 124, 127
Young, Arthur 145

Zedner, Lucia 95